THE FIRST WORLD OIL WAR

The First World Oil War

TIMOTHY C. WINEGARD

With a foreword by Sir Hew Strachan

UNIVERSITY OF TORONTO PRESS
Toronto Buffalo London

© University of Toronto Press 2016
Toronto Buffalo London
www.utppublishing.com
Printed in Canada

ISBN 978-1-4875-0073-3

Printed on acid-free, 100% post-consumer recycled paper
with vegetable-based inks.

Library and Archives Canada Cataloguing in Publication

Winegard, Timothy C. (Timothy Charles), 1977–, author
The first world oil war / Timothy C. Winegard ; with a foreword by
Sir Hew Strachan.

Includes bibliographical references and index.
ISBN 978-1-4875-0073-3 (cloth)

1. Petroleum industry and trade – Government policy. 2. Petroleum
reserves – Government policy. 3. Imperialism. 4. National security.
5. World politics – 20th century. 6. World politics – 21st century.
7. War – Causes. 8. World War, 1914–1918 – Influence. I. Title.

HD9560.5.W55 2016   338.2'7282   C2016-904638-9

University of Toronto Press acknowledges the financial assistance to its
publishing program of the Canada Council for the Arts and the Ontario
Arts Council, an agency of the Government of Ontario.

Canada Council   Conseil des Arts
for the Arts   du Canada

ONTARIO ARTS COUNCIL
CONSEIL DES ARTS DE L'ONTARIO
an Ontario government agency
un organisme du gouvernement de l'Ontario

Funded by the   Financé par le
Government   gouvernement
of Canada   du Canada

Canada

To Becky and Jaxson for everything

Contents

List of Illustrations, Maps, and Tables   ix

Foreword by Sir Hew Strachan   xiii

Acknowledgments   xvii

Author's Note: On Words   xxi

Introduction   3

1 Oil and the Great Game   19

2 Petroleum and Pipeline Politics   43

3 The Last Crusade in the Middle East   69

4 The Black Blood of Victory   92

5 The Deployment of Dunsterforce   119

6 Basra to Baghdad to Baku   150

7 The Battle for Baku   178

8 Peace and Petroleum   214

9 Oil and the New Great Game   236

Conclusion   280

Epilogue   288

Contents

Appendix: Petroleum Situation in the British Empire,
Admiral Sir Edmond J.W. Slade, 29 July 1918   295

Notes   307

Bibliography   349

Index   367

Illustrations, Maps, and Tables

Illustrations

1.1 A Mesopotamian oil worker, Mosul, ca 1911   20
1.2 Enver Pasha and Djemal Pasha visiting the Dome of the Rock,
     1916   28
1.3 "The Harmless Necessary Cat." Cartoon from *Punch!*, 1907   34
2.1 "Next!" Cartoon from *Puck*, 7 September 1904   51
2.2 The Anglo-Persian Oil Company's Abadan Refinery, ca 1919   53
2.3 Winston Churchill with Kaiser Wilhelm II, 1906   60
2.4 The Anglo-Persian Oil Company fields at Karun, Persia,
     1912   67
3.1 Petrol depot on the Amiens-Albert Road, 1916   74
3.2 Lieutenant-General Frederick Maude enters Baghdad,
     12 March 1917   77
3.3 General Sir Edmund Allenby enters Jerusalem, 11 December
     1917   78
4.1 The kaiser with General August Mackensen in Romania,
     March 1917   94
4.2 Hand-dug oil pits near Mosul, ca 1911   101
4.3 Allied Petroleum stock position for all petroleum products,
     August 1918   105
4.4 Lord George Curzon, viceroy and governor general of India,
     1905   107
4.5 "Cannon-Fodder – And After." Cartoon from *Punch!*, 25 April
     1917   116
5.1 Armenian widows with children in Eastern Anatolia,
     September 1915   124

6.1 "Mesopotamia Day" poster raising funds, April 1916   152
6.2 Sergeant Crofford Campbell and fellow Canadians in Persia,
    1918   153
6.3 Dunsterforce Ford touring cars ready to depart Hamadan,
    June 1918   169
7.1 German officers consult with local leaders in Tiflis, Georgia,
    June 1918   187
7.2 A small portion of the oil installations at Baku, August 1918   192
7.3 Dunsterville's original map of the defences at Baku, 17
    August 1918   203
7.4 Dunsterville inspecting his Armenian defenders of Baku,
    August 1918   204
7.5 A British-Armenian signalling station above Baku, September
    1918   206
8.1 Lloyd George, Orlando, Clemenceau, and Wilson,
    May 1919   219
8.2 Crude oil average annual price per barrel, 1912–1925   227
9.1 The oilfields at Grozny in flames, March 1918   240
9.2 The Royal Air Force patrolling above Mosul, May 1932   249
10.1 Seven Sisters to the Big Four   283

Maps

1 The Greater Middle East, 1914   xxiii
2 Campaigns in the Middle East and the Caucasus, 1914–1918   xxiv
3 The Red Line Agreement, 1 July 1928   xxv

Tables

2.1 Foreign investment in Romanian oil, 1914   52
2.2 Foreign investment in Russian oil, 1914   56
2.3 Russian oil production by region, 1908–1916   57
2.4 British capital among Russian oil regions, 1914   58
2.5 Production of oil companies in Russia, 1910–1914   61
2.6 Anglo-Persian Oil Company Annual Production, 1912–1925   63
4.1 Sources of British oil, 1913   109
6.1 Baku election results, November 1917   164

9.1 Main sources of global oil production, 1913–1920   245
9.2 American and British percentage of global oil production, 1913–1920   246
9.3 Sources of British oil, 1937   271
11.1 Top twelve global oil producers, 2013   290
11.2 Break-even oil prices per barrel, 2015   293

Foreword

In his autobiographical account of the Chindit campaign in Burma in 1944, John Masters, the novelist and Gurkha officer, tells of his brigade's retreat after a bloody, close-quarter battle with the Japanese. A sergeant announces that "this campaign is a disgrace." Masters, exhausted and sodden, stiffens. The sergeant explains that he is attacking not the conduct of the battle but the reason for the war. Despite his shattered state, and fortified by the offer of a cigarette, Masters engages the sergeant in debate. A Communist party member before the war, the sergeant believes that "the oil companies insisted on the reconquest of Burma and bribed Churchill, Eden, and Attlee to commit troops to the job." For Masters, the war's causes are more numerous and more complex. For the sergeant, "he and I are lying under a wet blanket at map reference 227105, in the monsoon rain among our wounded," in order "to save the profits of the oil companies."

For those, like the sergeant, who believe in the conspiracy theory of history, oil has stood centre stage in explaining the causes of conflict in the twentieth century. In this narrative, war is fought to seize and control resources, just as it was by ancient and even more recent empires. Germany's demand for "living space" in 1939 or Japan's for a "greater East Asian co-prosperity sphere" (which was at least one reason why Masters and his sergeant were fighting) support the argument. So too do both the United States' Gulf Wars, in 1990 and in 2003. And yet, most Americans have opted to see their wars in more idealistic terms. Over the last hundred years the United States has, after all, enjoyed a plenitude of resources: in 1914, as once again in 2014, the U.S. was a leading producer of oil. Having no call to wage war for economic reasons, it preferred instead to internationalize America's "manifest destiny."

Its central role in the wars of the twentieth and early twenty-first century has tended both to support those who see war in political and ideological terms and to extend that interpretation of war's causation to its enemies, including Germany and Japan.

It is indeed hard to see the outbreak of the First World War in economic terms. None of the statesmen involved in the July crisis in 1914 pursued a policy that risked war in order to secure or control the supply of oil, or indeed any other commodity. Once war broke out, they rushed to define their public aims in terms of universal values rather than of territory and the riches that it might contain. And yet, as Tim Winegard makes clear in this book, oil was already transforming the world's economies. It was also of increasing importance to the exercise of maritime power. HMS *Queen Elizabeth*, the world's first oil-fired dreadnought, was completing her sea trials when the war broke out. Her needs and those of the next generation of warships were forcing the British Admiralty to look to ways of ensuring a secure supply of overseas oil with which to replace the south Wales coal that still powered the majority of Britain's capital ships. The fact that the First Lord of the Admiralty, Winston Churchill, was so determined to open hostilities with the Ottoman Empire, after it allied with Germany on 2 August 1914, is fuel (if the pun can be forgiven) for the conspiracy theorists. The dispatch of an Indian Expeditionary Force to the Persian Gulf seems to confirm their convictions. Its initial task was to secure the oilfields at Abadan managed by the Anglo-Persian Oil Company, in which the British government was the majority shareholder. But the Royal Navy's concerns about its supply of oil in wartime were not the only reason for the British campaign in Mesopotamia. Driven by the government of India in Delhi as much as, if not more than, by the British Cabinet in London, Indian Expeditionary Force D was diverted to Ottoman territory. The subsequent British advance from Basra to Baghdad reflected not just the importance of oil but long-term strategic concerns for the security of the empire. In 1914, fuel was only one consideration in a complex and multifaceted approach to policy.

The demands of protracted conflict, the shift in land transport from horse and railway to lorry and car, and the emergence of air power all changed the rank order of priorities. Now oil was a commodity vital for the waging of war in all its dimensions, not just an optional requirement for the conduct of war at sea. Oil may not have caused the First World War, but it certainly had an increasingly important role in shaping its strategy. Because it became so central to the conduct of the war, its control became a vital war aim, not least to enable the prosecution of any future conflict.

Tim Winegard's story is therefore a narrative that embraces many of the themes surrounding the use of power in modern times. It reaches its climax in 1917–18, with the race of four states to secure the oilfields of Baku – or at the very least to deny their use to others. This was not just a competition between enemies, it also generated tension between allies. Germans and Turks came to blows; Russians, French, and British jockeyed for position and territory in the wreckage of the Ottoman Empire. *The First World Oil War* accords pride of place to "Dunsterforce." Major General L.C. Dunsterville, an undistinguished officer whose principal claim to fame was his childhood friendship with Rudyard Kipling, was given command of a "hush-hush army" to cross Persia and reach the Caucasus. Diminutive, under-resourced, and ill-supplied, it was one of the more quixotic of late imperial ventures. However, it also pointed forward to later Western interventions in western and central Asia. Driven by the importance of oil, it ran afoul of local sensibilities and deep animosities, often with bloody consequences.

Tim Winegard's trenchant and readable, powerful book makes clear the importance of oil in shaping the First World War, especially its conclusion and aftermath. It sometimes trails its coat, but with a subject as inflammatory (metaphorically as well as literally) as this one, that is unsurprising. Here are the big themes of war in the twentieth century: resources, finance, hatred, atrocity, and greed. John Masters's sergeant would have had his preconceptions confirmed.

Sir Hew Strachan

Acknowledgments

As I get older and certainly no wiser, this section seems to expand with every book that I write. So for the sake of brevity I will now acknowledge everyone who has shared and helped.

The origins of this book lie in a series of questions. Having just submitted the final proofs for two books on indigenous peoples and warfare, my wife asked me, "What is your next book going to be on?" Wanting to return to my roots as a military historian, and having long ago written a journal article on the topic, I simply answered, "Oil and war." Bewildered, she ingenuously asked, "Isn't that a given?" She unknowingly answered her own question, and the premise of this book. And yes, it is *now* a given. But how, why, and when did this marriage between oil and war happen? During the First World War and its fraudulent peace. And, how, why, and when did the United States and the United Kingdom come to dominate global oil? During the First World War and its fraudulent peace. This book is, in essence, the answer to her question, and many more.

In a sense, my research trips for this book produced my own adventures. I was consumed by two tornadoes in the United States, was engulfed in a hotel fire in London, was subject to numerous cancelled flights, slept on countless airport floors and vinyl seats, and was forced to make an emergency landing at NORAD in Colorado Springs as the engine and baggage compartment of my plane were immersed in flames. During some of these mishaps, I wondered if General Dunsterville was mocking me from beyond, and if this book would ever get finished!

As usual, many friends, colleagues, and family members have had a hand in this project and deserve mention. A special thanks to Sir Hew

Strachan for writing the foreword, but also for his time, and keen eye and critiques, while traversing this manuscript – many years removed as my doctoral supervisor at Oxford.

I would also like to thank, in no particular order, Dr Sean Maloney, Dr David Murray, Dr Gregory Liedtke, Bruno and Katie Lamarre, Dr Alan Anderson, Jeff Obermeyer, Hoko-Shodee, Dr Scott Sheffield, and Dr Whitney and Jennifer Lackenbauer.

My colleagues and office podmates at Colorado Mesa University also deserve credit for their ideas, and for listening to me repeat the word "oil" during every seemingly casual conversation: Dr Susan Becker, Dr T. Timothy Casey, Dr Douglas O'Roark, Dr Sarah Swedberg, and Dr Bill Flanik. Thanks also to my players whom I coach on the Colorado Mesa University hockey team – you keep me young (and in shape).

I would also like to extend my gratitude to Jill Campbell and family, Debbie McGorm, and Pam Hendy (Gilmour) for providing me with the personal Dunsterforce collections and memoirs of their kin, and for their enthusiasm in this venture. I would also be remiss if I did not thank the wonderful staffs at the various archives and libraries visited during research. Thanks to Colorado Mesa University for financing the maps drawn by Natalie Smith, who also deserves mention. A big thank you to Len Husband and the staff at University of Toronto Press for your guidance and patience, and for making this possible.

As always, my dad and mom have been ever supportive and patiently read multiple manuscript versions, while offering invaluable comments and critiques. While mere words do not suffice – thank you and I love you both. You are my heroes. Love also to my sisters Casey and Kelly, and Tom and Whitter, and my niece and nephews: Madison, Mason, Tanner, Dawson, Calder, and Kessler. I miss you all, and my lake-front home in Canada. Fleeting visits pass, but still they have to satisfy.

To my son Jaxson, you are too young to understand why Dad had to leave for extended periods for research and be away from you. You often remarked, "I don't like it when Daddy has to leave," and trust me, I'd rather have been playing with you as well. Who else can save your Wayne Gretzky slapshot, catch your Matthew Stafford passes, or be Darius III to your Alexander the Great? Perhaps when you are older you might understand why I was away. At six years old you are already quite the historian and some day will no doubt surpass your old man! To my wife Becky, thank you for your patience and unconditional love, for putting up with my absences while away on research trips and speaking engagements, and for my seeming absence while at home writing. Oil doesn't light up my life, both of you do.

Lastly, while I have enjoyed the generosity of colleagues, friends, and family in writing and preparing this work, any errors remain mine alone. Nine years as an officer in the Canadian and British Forces taught me to seek and accept responsibility.

Thank you all,
Tim

Author's Note: On Words

Given the vast geographical and linguistic berth encompassed by this book, transliteration of names and places from numerous non-Latin-based alphabets is problematic and presents impracticable complications. In the Caucasus, for instance, each city has a number of different names ascribed to it, in various languages including English, Russian, Persian, and local tongues and dialects. More often than not, they are dissimilar. For example the city of Batumi, in modern-day Georgia, was known as Batum, and Tbilisi as Tiflis. Ganja, Azerbaijan's second-largest city, was also known in Russian as Elisavetpol or Kirovabad. The northern Iranian city of Enzeli (in English) was known as Bandar-e Anzali or Pahlevi (depending on the time period of Persia/Iran) in the Romanized-Persian translation. In addition, there are also disputes regarding spelling, even in the English Latin-based alphabet. For example, Grozny, the capital of the Russian province of Chechnya, can also be signified as Grozni, Groznyy, or Grosny, among other representations. The Caucasus will be used to represent its other forms: Transcaucasia, Trans-Caspian, and Caucasia. The spelling of personal names also varies. The surname of the Russian Cossack commander Lazar Bicherakov, who fought alongside Dunsterforce, and whom you will meet in the book, has numerous variations.

In general, as much as possible, place and personal names have been standardized to contemporary common imperial English usage during the First World War, and spelled accordingly: Batum, Tiflis, Enzeli, Constantinople rather than Batumi, Tbilisi, Bandar-e Anzali, Istanbul. The only deviation from this practice occurs within quotations, where the author's original spelling or naming remains, or in the proper names of government bodies and organizations such as the "Centro-Caspian

Dictatorship" or the "Transcaucasian Republic." Some common names are used interchangeably or switch to new forms as the evolving political situation dictates: Soviet/Bolshevik, Mesopotamia/Iraq, Persia/Iran, Rumania/Romania. At times, if clarity is required, a second designation will be placed in parentheses following the first usage of a place or personal name. Ottoman and Turkish will be used interchangeably, particularly in reference to the army, although various ethnicities such as Arabs, Kurds, Greeks, and Armenians had as much claim to portions of the empire as Turks did. The labels and lexis used, however, do not in the least signify any ethnic, political, or territorial loyalties or affiliations. Contemporary English standardization has been used simply to make the book more readable and accessible to the primary English-speaking audience.

Also to note, all translations from the French are my own, while those from the German, Turkish, and Russian were provided by bilingual colleagues, unless specifically stated otherwise. Non-English language, however, has been kept to a minimum, unless essential to explanation.

While I have done my utmost to standardize and to make the narrative more readable, it is impossible to be entirely consistent in all of these things; may common sense conquer and prevail.

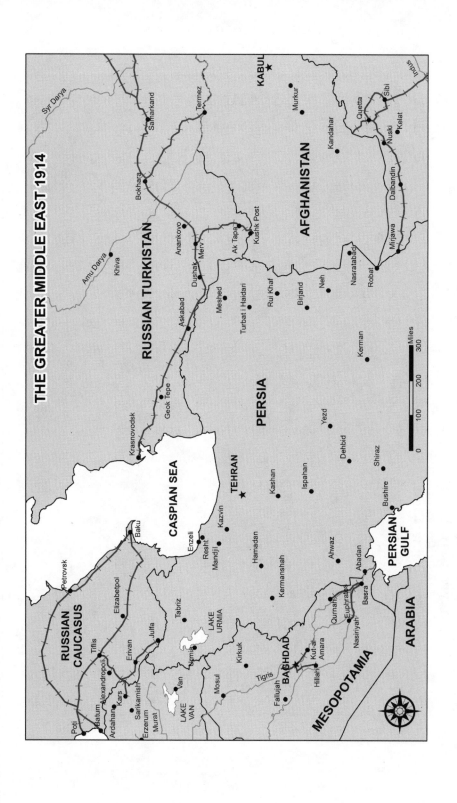

THE GREATER MIDDLE EAST 1914

RUSSIAN CAUCASUS

RUSSIAN TURKISTAN

AFGHANISTAN

PERSIA

CASPIAN SEA

MESOPOTAMIA

ARABIA

PERSIAN GULF

LAKE URMIA

LAKE VAN

KABUL

TEHRAN

BAGHDAD

Syr Darya

Samarkand

Termez

Murkur

Indus

Sibi

Quetta

Nuski

Kelat

Kandahar

Bokhara

Anankovo

Merv

Ak Tapa

Kushk Post

Dushak

Askabad

Dalbandin

Mirjawa

Robat

Nasratabad

Neh

Birjand

Rui Khaf

Turbat i Haidari

Meshed

Amu Darya

Khiva

Kerman

Geok Tepe

Krasnovodsk

Yezd

Dehbid

Shiraz

Ispahan

Kashan

Bushire

Kazvin

Hamadan

Enzeli

Resht

Mandjil

Baku

Ahwaz

Abadan

Basra

Kermanshah

Petrovsk

Elizabetpol

Tiflis

Erivan

Juffa

Tabriz

Alexandropol

Kars

Sarikamish

Ardahan

Batum

Poti

Erzerum

Murat

Van

Mosul

Kirkuk

Tigris

Fallujah

Hillah

Kut-al-Amara

Nasiriyah

Qurnah

Euphrates

Miles

0   100   200   300

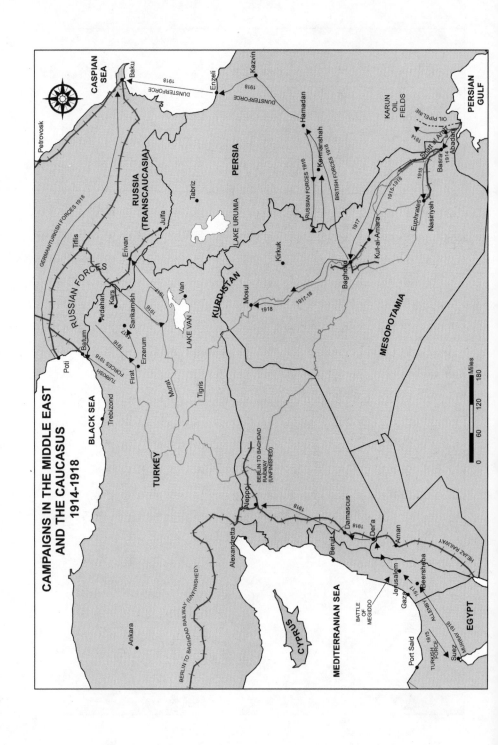

CAMPAIGNS IN THE MIDDLE EAST
AND THE CAUCASUS
1914–1918

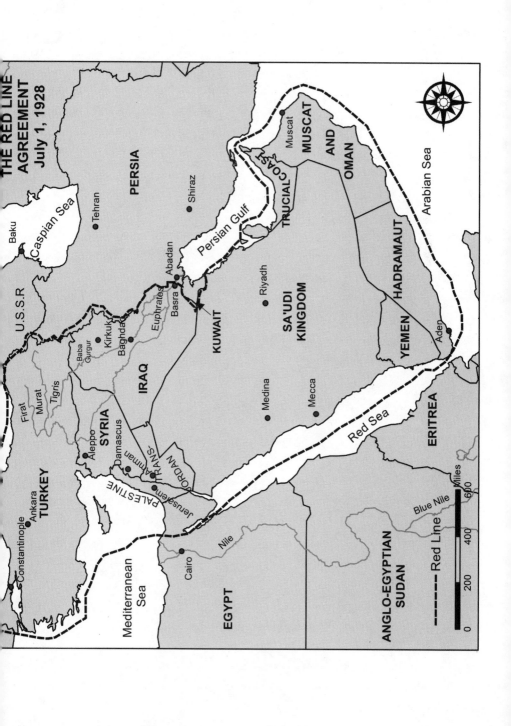

THE RED LINE AGREEMENT July 1, 1928

U.S.S.R

TURKEY

Constantinople

Ankara

Baku

Caspian Sea

Tehran

PERSIA

Shiraz

Firat

Murat

Tigris

Baba Gurgur

Kirkuk

Baghdad

Euphrates

Aleppo

SYRIA

Damascus

Amman

TRANS-JORDAN

Jerusalem

PALESTINE

Mediterranean Sea

Cairo

Nile

EGYPT

IRAQ

Basra

Abadan

KUWAIT

Persian Gulf

TRUCIAL COAST

Muscat

MUSCAT AND OMAN

Arabian Sea

Riyadh

SA'UDI KINGDOM

HADRAMAUT

YEMEN

Aden

Medina

Mecca

Red Sea

ERITREA

Blue Nile

ANGLO-EGYPTIAN SUDAN

------ Red Line

Miles

0   200   400   600

Oh ye Egyptians, they may say to you that I have not made an expedition hither for any other object than that of abolishing your religion ... but tell the slanderers that I have not come to you except for the purpose of restoring your rights from the hands of the oppressors.

Napoleon Bonaparte
Alexandria, 2 July 1798

Our armies do not come into your cities and lands as conquerors or enemies, but as liberators ... It is the hope and desire of the British people and the nations in alliance with them that the Arab race may rise once more to greatness and renown among the peoples of the earth.

Lieutenant-General Frederick Maude
Commander British Mesopotamian Expeditionary Force
Baghdad, 11 March 1917

Unlike many armies in the world, you came not to conquer, not to occupy, but to liberate, and the Iraqi people know this.

Donald Rumsfeld
U.S. Secretary of Defence
Baghdad, 29 April 2003

Introduction

In September 1916 as the Battle of the Somme was raging around him, a young second-lieutenant of the Lancashire Fusiliers huddled in the dugout of his trench scribbling brief notes and sketches in a field message pad. He would go on to publish his renowned novel *The Hobbit* in 1937 and his masterpiece follow-up *The Lord of the Rings* in 1954 after serving yet again in the Second World War. Samwise Gamgee was J.R.R. Tolkien's personified tribute to the archetypal British Tommy, with whom he served and whom he commanded during the Great War. In *The Lord of the Rings*, Sam stumbles into a bog while traversing the Dead Marshes with Frodo and Gollum, and exclaims,

> "There are dead things, dead faces in the water," he said with horror. "Dead faces!" ... "Who are they? What are they?" asked Sam shuddering, turning to Frodo who was now behind him.
> "I don't know," said Frodo in a dreamlike voice ... "They lie in all the pools, pale faces, deep deep under the dark water. I saw them, grim faces and evil, and noble faces and sad. Many faces proud and fair, and the weeds in their silver hair. But all foul, all rotting, all dead" ...
> "Yes, yes," said Gollum. "All dead, all rotten. Elves and Men and Orcs. The Dead Marshes. There was a great battle long ago ... They fought on the plain for days and months ... But the Marshes have grown since then, swallowed up the grave." "But that is an age and more ago," said Sam ... "Can't we get on and get away?"[1]

The great battle was the First World War. In this passage, Tolkien harkens back to many observations from his military service memory. He references the unknown soldiers, the forgotten names of those killed fighting for good or evil, and those left on the battlefields now covered over with grass, war having sequestered their bodies to an unknown grave. Almost three million soldiers are still listed as "missing" in the Dead Marshes of the Great War.[2]

And no, Sam, my naively innocent hobbit, we can't get on and get away, for the vestiges, legacy, and continuing reverberations of the First World War cling to contemporary civilization and march to the drumbeat cadence of current time. The so-called War to End All Wars and its peace created our reality. It was and continues to be our Great War for Civilization a century later. The war, fraught with illusion, marked the end of the old world and the beginning of the new in which we still live. Dreams of glory and chivalry perished in the trenches of Belgium and France with the advent of industrial war fuelled by blood and oil. The old world and priggish Victorian courtliness vanished over four and a half years amidst modern artillery, aircraft, machine guns, gas, and tanks. The Great War has often been referred to as an attempted "escape from modernity" amidst backlash against the social hierarchy and the perceived value of individual function subordinated to bourgeois material gain – under the umbrella of seething discontent for industrial society. Soldiers soon discovered, however, "that far from escaping industrialization, they were entirely dominated by it ... The war laid bare the material, technological, and mechanical reality that twentieth-century civilization concealed. 'Everything becomes machine-like,' one soldier wrote; 'one might almost term the war an industry of professionalized human slaughter.'"[3] The competing belligerents of the Great War embarked on a violent crusade for nation state, power, glory, and economic advantage. They also fought for scarce resources, none more important than oil.

The war (including the shattering influenza epidemic) and the negotiators of the peace redrew the demographic, geographic, religious, and economic map of the world. Underlying it all – was oil. The First World War transformed the art of war and ushered in an age of unprecedented slaughter fuelled by manpower, mechanization, industry, and oil, which supplanted coal as the world's industrial, economic, military, and political power source. Aptly dubbed the "First," it was truly the first war of its kind. It was the beginning of firsts, not the end. The Great War transformed humanity and our global village in every sense and made the world immeasurably smaller.

The opening year of the war brought the economic uncertainty and recalculations, and alliance systems, of Europe into a cataclysm with casualty rates surpassing anything in the historical record. As the war trudged on, seemingly taking on a life of its own, the belligerents tried innovative ways to break the stalemate of trench warfare. Gas was introduced (xylyl bromide) by the Germans as a weapon of war against the Russians at Bolimow in January 1915, and again, on a larger and more lethal scale (chlorine gas) in April 1915 against French–Colonial Moroccan and Canadian positions at the Second Battle of Ypres.[4] Antiquated cavalry charges gave way to the British "land ship" or tank at the Somme in 1916, and motorized vehicles replaced horse-drawn transportation (albeit not completely, especially in the case of Germany). By 1917, German submarines tormented Allied shipping in the middle passages of the Atlantic. Airplanes and artillery took on greater importance as the war progressed and were increasingly employed in combined-arms operations and set-piece battles. In fact, artillery accounted for 65 per cent of all casualties during the war. Toluol, a component of petroleum, was a key ingredient in munitions manufacturing. During the two-week artillery barrage preceding the 1917 Battle of Messines, Allied guns fired 3.75 million shells. Given the intense shelling, Major-General Charles Harington, chief of staff to General Herbert Plumer, remarked to the officers of the British Second Army on the eve of the battle, "Gentlemen, we may not make history tomorrow, but we shall certainly change the geography."[5] The industrial killing reached unprecedented levels at Verdun and the Somme in 1916, and Passchendaele in 1917. Mechanization dominated the battlefield, and industry required increasing quantities of oil to mass-produce these weapons of war.

During its initiation of combat on 23 August 1914 at Mons, Belgium, the British Expeditionary Force (BEF) had just 827 motor cars – of which 747 were requisitioned from civilian benefactors – and only fifteen motorcycles. On Armistice Day, 11 November 1918, the British transport vehicle field-fleet (excluding combat vehicles such as tanks and armoured cars), totalled more than 122,000. During the course of the war, British factories churned out 55,000 planes, 21,000 artillery pieces, 2,818 tanks of various design, 240,500 machine guns, and four million rifles.[6] France boasted 70,000 vehicles and 12,000 planes. These Anglo-French numbers exclude 50,000 vehicles and 15,000 planes imported from the United States, the 17,000 trucks purchased from the Italian Fiat Company, and the rapid industrialization and agrarian yields of India and the British dominions, most notably Canada. By 1917–18, Canada was responsible for one-third of the entire British imperial munitions supply and 42 per cent of its heavy artillery shells.[7]

Prior to the late 1700s, a lack of industry and institutionalized command resulted in severe limitations on the size of field forces, and armies greater than 100,000 men seem to exist mainly in lore and legend. "Napoleon was perhaps the ablest general who ever lived," contends Martin van Creveld. "Yet when he concentrated 180,000 men at Leipzig in 1813 even he lost control."[8] The American Civil War and Prussia's mobilization against Austria in 1866, and France in 1870, altered war by extensively employing railway transportation and telegraph communication, allowing for the mass mobilization, concentrated force, and speedy deployment of significantly expanded field armies. Creating war potential now meant not only the mobilization of millions of men, which was progressively possible, but also the synchronization of all available resources, including industry, agronomy, transport, communication, and fuel as a coherent whole. For example, a division during the Franco-Prussian War (1870–1) required roughly 50 tons of supplies per day. By 1916, this figure had increased to 150 tons, and to 650 tons by 1944 on the Western Fronts. As mobile, industrial war and the mechanization of the weapons of war advanced, so too did the necessity and prerequisite for petroleum.[9] This dyad began with the First World War.

This modernization, and the industry required to produce these weapons of war, was increasingly fuelled by oil. During the Allied offensives of the Last Hundred Days on the Western Front, British imperial forces consumed twelve thousand barrels of oil daily. In addition, by 1918, 40 per cent of the Royal Navy was oil-fired.[10] In August 1916, as the Battle of the Somme entered its second horrific month and would shortly witness the introduction of the tank to the battlefield, Lewis Vernon Harcourt impressed upon his superiors that "the war has made it clear that it is imperatively necessary ... to take immediate and effective action to safeguard the future oil supplies of the British Empire ... The problem of supply is no longer merely a commercial question; it is an Imperial question of the first magnitude."[11] Winston Churchill's strategic paradigm for control of petroleum resources, where and however they could be acquired, was being promulgated by other converts within the corridors of Whitehall. Churchill was instrumental in creating the modern petroleum, political, military-industrial complex with his 1914 pre-war governmental acquisition of 51 per cent of the Anglo-Persian Oil Company (BP) to feed the new destroyers and dreadnoughts of the Royal Navy being champagne-christened at British shipyards.

The First World War was the first conflict to be fuelled by oil. For the first time in warfare, petroleum possession became the lifeblood of armies, and it entered into the strategic machinations of military planners from all nations involved. "By 1914," concedes Valerie Marcel, "oil had become important enough for Britain to take measures to thwart regional ambitions toward its oil interests."[12] For the first time in history, territory was conquered specifically to possess oilfields and resources, which were vital cogs in the continuation of not only this industrialized war of attrition, but also for strategic advantage in future wars. Following the war, oil concessions were a contentious issue around the negotiating tables of the peace conferences, creating a diplomatic oil war between Britain and the United States (and France to a lesser degree). Oil imperialism was conceived during the First World War, ushering in a new framework for war and aggression. Consequently, during the Great War the oil front of the Ottoman Empire "was a veritable tower of Babel, an unprecedented conflict between international armies."[13] This precedent set by, and imitated from, the First World War shows no signs of ebbing and remains omnipresent. The Middle East and the Caucasus were (and remain) the petroleum targets for all belligerents. The quest to possess these petroleum prizes produced some of the most enigmatic and altogether strange sideshows of the war, most notably the 1918 British deployment of Dunsterforce – an undersized, elite secret unit made up of 450 choice soldiers from across the empire. Its seemingly simple mission was to seize the oil installations at Baku on the western shore of the Caspian Sea.

The geographical regions encompassed in these oil wars of 1917–20 witnessed events that altered the course of history. During the progression of the war and into its early peace, ethnic nationalism and sectarian divides spawned movements and conflict across the Middle East and the Caucasus, many of which remain sources of tension and violence. Arabs led by Sherif Hussein of Mecca were given a hollow promise of an Arab state by the British, if they agreed to shrug off the yoke of Ottoman rule with the aid of modern arms and leadership channelled through the alluring Thomas Edward (T.E.) Lawrence (of Arabia). Today, the 1915 Armenian genocide is still a controversial topic. The Sykes-Picot Agreement of 1916 divided up the Ottoman Empire into French and British (and Italian and Russian, to a much lesser extent) spheres of influence. While the Paris Peace Conference doled out League of Nation mandates, oil was the core issue in establishing the borders of the modern Middle East. Correspondingly, the 1917 Balfour Declaration established, on paper and in principle, a Jewish homeland and Zionist state in Palestine/Israel, in conflict with previous pledges made to the Arabs. The legacy of this event continues to haunt the Middle East and the global political order.

The formulation of British strategy in the greater Middle East has been branded a "hydra-headed political organism" operating under "unpleasing Machiavellism" and hollow promises.[14] These oil wars hastily thrust the Middle East and the Muslim world into contemporary geopolitics, for which they were unprepared and ideologically unaccustomed, and created the crevices in the East-West divide and the current clash of civilizations. In the aftermath of the Great War, the Western powers, specifically Britain, introduced "European-type notions of territorial sovereignty to an area where tribes were much more important than the state, where tribal borders were better understood than international ones, and where the law of the desert prevailed … Whatever their gains for British imperial ambitions, these arrangements planted seeds for long-term conflict in the Middle East."[15] Prior to the birth of these British and French protectorates or "nation states" within the crucible of colonialism, Islam itself was the organizing and cohesive foundation in Muslim lands. "The inherent contradictions of the nation-state," writes Karen Armstrong, "would be especially wrenching in the Muslim world, where there was no tradition of nationalism. The frontiers drawn up by the Europeans were so arbitrary that it was extremely difficult to create a national 'imaginary community.'"[16] These Middle Eastern borders drawn in 1922 by Sir Percy Cox remain the source of tension and dispute in our contemporary world.

Modern Islam, including but in no way typical of al-Qaeda (The Base) and other zealot religious factions, is the product of these shifts associated with the Great Oil War. While Islam (and jihad) existed in 1914, it was the war, more specifically the ruin of the Ottoman Empire and the caliphate, and the Western powers' thirst for oil in Islamic lands, that spawned the modern Islamic order. The tempestuous "Arc of Crisis," as American strategists now call it, was born in the blood and oil of the Great War. By the time of the peace talks in Paris, this arc stretched from northern Africa through the Middle East, penetrating central and southern Asia. This map has no doubt occupied a strategic location on the desk of every Western military planning operations centre and oil and gas prospector ever since. In 1906, Baron Max von Oppenheim, the famed German orientalist, archaeologist, diplomat, and head of the Intelligence Bureau for the East during the war, roused the kaiser to understand that "we must not forget that everything taking place in a Mohammedan country sends waves across the entire world of Islam."

He went on to predict, "In the future Islam will play a much greater role ... [T]he striking power and demographic strength of Islamic lands will one day have a great significance to European states."[17] With the insatiable Western thirst for petroleum in Islamic domains, Oppenheim's prophesy remains just as ominous today.

In 1917 the Russian revolution unfolded, escorting in the sweeping introduction of communism as a global political and economic entity with the advent of the Soviet Union. Its arrival sounded the beginnings of the Red Menace and the Cold War that consumed the world until 1991, followed by its wars of decolonization and the recent resurgence of Russian imperialism under Vladimir Putin. While America's entry into the war in April 1917 nurtured an atmosphere for Allied victory, it also announced its geopolitical arrival as an economic and military superpower within realpolitik and its unquenchable thirst for petroleum.

The 1919 Treaty of Versailles redrew the map of the world, most notably Eastern Europe, the Balkans, Africa, and the Middle East, and fostered the environment for future war, none more shattering than the successor to its fraudulent peace. As Geoffrey Wheatcroft mused, "The First World War changed everything; without it, there would have been no Russian Revolution, no Third Reich, almost certainly no Jewish State."[18] It might be added that oil would have had to wait to take its pre-eminent place in the geopolitical-military game. Oil, and the quest to control it, was in part responsible for the failed peace, which created the breeding ground for future hostilities.

The pivotal role of oil in the calculation of British strategy and war aims in Mesopotamia, Persia, and the Caucasus during the First World War has been overlooked. In fact, the protection of British oil interests was the catalyst for the deployment of imperial forces to the head of the Persian Gulf – a shallow waterway flowing some five hundred miles from the Strait of Hormuz to the Shat-al-Arab, at the confluence of the Euphrates and Tigris Rivers. This decision was made at the outbreak of war in 1914, before the actual declaration of war on the Ottoman Empire on 5 November. This initial deployment led to a swelling of British forces in the Middle East and the Caucasus throughout the war. Sarah Shields notes that historians continue to argue whether the British "were really most interested in oil, with some claiming that this was really the overriding issue."[19] Certainly politicians and historians have debated the influence of oil on British policy both during and after the "Great War for Civilization."

There were numerous economic, political, and military factors at
hand, but British oil interests played a role in the initiation of hostilities in the Middle East and became increasingly vital as the war progressed. In the official British history of the Mesopotamian campaign,
F.J. Moberly cites the importance of deploying British troops and
propaganda to support Arab independence from the Ottoman Empire,
and notes that "the Arabs were to be conciliated and to be shown that
we were prepared to support them against Turkey." Moberly adds,
however, "We [the British Empire] went to Mesopotamia primarily to
defend our essential interests [oil] at the head of the Persian Gulf and to
counter Turco-German designs to embarrass us in the Middle East. As
the operations progressed, however, it became increasingly apparent
that – owing to the Turco-German attempts to exploit the weakness of
Persia, the latent hostility to us in Afghanistan and the unreliability of
the tribes on the north-west frontier of India – the presence of our force
on the Tigris was of material assistance to the security of India."[20] The
term *Middle East* itself was coined in the British *National Review* in 1902
by the American naval strategist Alfred Thayer Mahan in reference
to "those regions of Asia ... bound up with the problems of Indian ...
defence," or "the neck of land which joins Africa to Asia ... Asiatic Turkey, Persia, Egypt, the basin of the Mediterranean Eastern."[21] Mahan's
The Influence of Sea Power upon History: 1660–1783, published in 1890, is
considered the single most influential account of naval strategy. It has
been argued that the adoption of the principles of this work by most
major powers led to the naval arms race preceding the First World War –
and by extension, to the abrupt shift from coal-burning to oil-burning
vessels in the one-upmanship of pre-war economic and naval programs
of Britain and Germany.

Another school of thought suggests that British intentions in the Middle East were purely imperialist, motivated by the goals of expropriating
territory from the crumbling Ottoman Empire – dubbed the "Sick Man
of Europe" by Tsar Nicholas I – within the resurrected "Great Game"
between European imperialist powers, while safeguarding India and
its vast wealth. Spies, intelligence agents, propagandists, and archaeologists from Germany and Britain had long littered the region to sway
the political and economic allegiance of Persia, Afghanistan, and the
Arab and Caucasus expanses. John Buchan's 1916 bestseller *Greenmantle*, full of German espionage and shadowy intrigues, simply fictionalized official British views and "contains characters who might easily
have escaped the pages ... for Buchan himself was closely involved in

intelligence work at this time, and had ready access to secret reports on what the Germans were up to in the East."[22] After reading his friend's book, T.E. Lawrence observed, "*Greenmantle* has more than a flavour of truth."[23] Although the Great Game, previously confined to British and Russian imperial spheres in Central Asia, had been quiescent in recent years, it was rejuvenated with new players shortly before the First World War. Germany's ambitious *Drang nach Osten* (thrust towards the east) hinged on completion of the Berlin to Baghdad railway. The "Young Turk" Ottoman leadership, specifically Enver Pasha, sought to incorporate the Muslim peoples of the Caucasus and Central Asia into a utopic pan-Turanian state. Russia looked south towards Persia and Eastern Anatolia with lusting eyes. For Britain, the scheming of these nations within the resurrected Great Game threatened its preeminent position in Egypt, Persia, and most importantly, India.

A blending of British national interests and shifting priorities during the war, allied to the capricious strategic situations on the Eastern Front and in the theatres of the Middle East and the Caucasus, influenced British war aims and their implementation in these regions. The importance of oil, however, should not be overlooked, and by 1918 it became the crux of British policy throughout the Middle East and the Caucasus. According to F. William Engdahl, "The role of oil in the events leading to war in 1914 is too little appreciated. When the historical process behind the war is examined from this light a quite different picture emerges."[24]

It must be remembered that economic advantage through foreign wealth and overseas markets for domestic and colonial goods was a central element of European imperial design. The First World War, at least in its closing year and into the peace talks, was the first war in which non-regional belligerents, or otherwise, sought to secure global petroleum interests (specifically in the Middle East and the Caucasus) through military might, and during the armistice negotiations at Paris. As noted by Brock Millman, "British operations in the Middle East ... were generally intended less to secure territories important in themselves, than to limit the damage the Central Powers could do to Britain's regional interests in this war or the next, while facilitating and preparing for more important operations elsewhere. Territories conquered here were important, because it was anticipated that they would provide some of the small change to be used in negotiating a peace. British war aims in the Middle East, therefore, were either instrumental or contingent. They were in no sense permanent."[25]

Artin H. Arslanian elaborates by contending, "If the documents of the British oil administration were studied outside of the larger context of concerns which triggered British involvement in Transcaucasia the temptation to discuss British postwar policy in terms of oil imperialism would be irresistible."[26] In October 1918, for example, the British government contemplated delaying the acceptance of the armistice entreaty by the Ottomans until British forces had captured the oilfields at Mosul, which was in the French sphere of influence under the 1916 Sykes-Picot(-Sazonov) Agreement, officially known as the Asia Minor Agreement. Despite the signing of the Armistice of Mudros on 30 October, Lieutenant-General William Marshall occupied Mosul on 2 November to ensure that Britain retained the oil by "right of conquest." The American administration told the British bluntly, and in hindsight quite ironically, "It is all bad ... They [the British] are making it [the Middle East] a breeding place for future war."[27]

During the interwar years, the governments of Britain and the United States gave political and economic support to their respective oil companies, as they sought concessions around the globe, chiefly those in the Middle East. The inherent oil wealth of Mesopotamia and Persia became the focus of both competing nations. Tensions grew between them in what has been dubbed the "Anglo-American oil war," which, after protracted negotiations and diplomatic hostility had run their course, created a worldwide Anglo-American oil monopoly.[28] As French economist Francis Delaisi wrote in 1920, "Oil had not yet entered the danger zone of diplomatic conflicts. For fifty years it was the most peaceful of industries; no one could have imagined that one day it would trouble the peace of the world ... Oil makes its bow upon the *diplomatic* stage where international rivalries are played."[29]

The quest for oil was not limited to the Middle East. When Romania joined the Allies in August 1916, the Germans quickly seized the oilfields at Ploieşti, although the wells and refineries had been severely sabotaged by British agents before they were abandoned. Once repaired, however, the Ploieşti installations produced one million tons of oil for Germany, which also expropriated two million tons of Romanian grain – resources that, according to German Quarter Master General Erich von Ludendorff, "made possible the ... continuation of the war into 1918."[30] Romania was the only significant source of oil west of the Black Sea. Oil shale production in Estonia began in 1918 but produced very low yields. Estonian oil did, however, become important during the Second World War.

In 1918, therefore, the British, Turks, Germans, and Bolshevik Russians all raced to secure Baku's precious Caucasus oil.

This pattern continued through the Second World War in both North Africa and the Caucasus: "The capture of the Caucasus would kill two birds with one stone: the Soviet armies would be deprived of the oil needed to fight, and Germany would capture the oil she required to combat Britain and the United States."[31] Hitler's drive for the Caucasus oil fields centred at Baku was foiled at the 1942–3 battles of Stalingrad and Kursk. When the Germans reached the northern Caucasus oilfields of Maikop, which produced two million tons annually, they found the wells, refineries, and stockpiles burning and destroyed. German forces were halted 100 miles west of Grozny and its invaluable oilfields, the annual production of which exceeded all German supplies. Farther east, the primary German target of Baku, and its twenty million tons of oil annually (three times Germany's yearly consumption) also remained out of reach.[32] Indeed, Hitler was right when he prophesied to his general staff in August 1942, "Unless we get the Baku oil, the war is lost." Hindered by inadequate fuel supplies during his North African campaign, General Erwin Rommel lamented to his wife, "Shortage of petrol. It's enough to make one weep." His Afrika Corps reached El Alamein in July 1942 with no fuel, a mere nineteen serviceable tanks, and an ammunition depot 1,100 miles to the rear in Tripoli, "though Axis forces drove back and forth across the undiscovered oilfields of Libya."[33]

During the world wars, Germany, like its allies, was hampered by a lack of oil to fuel its military machine. During the Second World War, roughly 90 per cent of global oil output was controlled by the Allies, while the Axis nations controlled a mere 3 per cent. The staple German source from Romania was not of sufficient quantity for protracted war and was threatened by its geographic location to the areas of operations themselves.[34] The bounty of oil and other natural resources, including rubber, also prompted Japanese aggression in the South Pacific before and during the Second World War. Contemporary aircraft carriers travelled twenty to thirty-five feet per gallon of fuel, or consumed upwards of 150,000 gallons of fuel per day. According to Richard Overy, "The Allies had long regarded oil as the German Achilles heel ... It would be wrong to argue that oil determined the outcome of the war on its own, though there could scarcely have been a resource more vital to waging modern combat."[35] During a dinner for Winston Churchill's birthday in the middle of the 1943 Tehran Conference, Joseph Stalin rose to propose one of his numerous toasts: "This is a war of engines and octanes. I drink to the American auto industry and the American oil industry." Of the seven billion barrels of oil used by the Allies in the Second World War, six billion was pumped from American wells.[36] As modern war advanced, oil became exponentially more important.

The 1956 Suez Crisis was primarily about oil. Oil was paramount to the violence in East Timor between 1974 and 2000, to the American-led coalition Gulf Wars, and to NATO actions in the Balkans during the 1990s. Oil is the root cause of the ongoing violence and ethnic clashes in the Caucasus, including the Nagorno-Karabakh War between Azerbaijan and Armenia, the Georgian-Abkhazian War, and the Russian forays into Chechnya, Georgia, South Ossetia, and its recent meddling in the Ukraine. This "new Great Game" refers to the competition for petroleum and profit in the Caucasus and Central Asia following the dissolution of the Soviet Union. Oil also feeds, fuels, and finances al-Qaeda, Islamic State of Iraq and the Levant (ISIL), other regional terror organizations, rebel movements, and also the opposing "War on Terror."[37] Upon the triumphant entrance of British imperial forces into Baghdad on 11 March 1917, General Frederick Maude, the thirteenth conqueror of the city, proudly declared, "Our armies do not come into your cities and lands as conquerors or enemies, but as liberators." Eighty-six years later, in 2003, President George W. Bush would eerily repeat this phrase after American-led coalition forces entered Baghdad in April and toppled the twenty-four-year dictatorship of Saddam Hussein.[38] In fact, Maude's Baghdad Proclamation was written by Mark Sykes, the very same Sykes who negotiated the Sykes-Picot Agreement in 1916 dividing the post-war Middle East between British and French spheres of influence. Arnold Wilson, the British civil commissioner for Mesopotamia, tartly remarked that Maude's proclamation "bears in every line the mark of [Sykes's] ebullient orientalism."[39] Accordingly, back in London, British politicians used Maude's victory as leverage for oil concessions, justifying their claims by saying, "Clearly it is our right and duty, if we sacrifice so much for the peace of the world, that we should see to it we have compensation."[40] This exoneration was again used in 2003.

Oil is the direct cause of the civil unrest following the recent partitioning of the Sudan, of the rebel movements in Nigeria, Somalia, and Yemen (not to mention the African conflicts of gold and diamonds). The squabbling among wealthy northern nations about oil rights is shrouded in a veil dubbed "arctic sovereignty."[41] These are but a few examples in a long list of twentieth- and twenty-first-century oil wars.

The oil battleground dominates all current political and economic discourse between the supplying nations of the Middle East and North Africa and their Western (and now Brazil, India, and China) importers. Oil continues to fuel petroleum proxy wars. Mesopotamia, Persia and the Caucasus (read the greater Middle East) were the epicentres of the First World Oil War. A century later, these oil wars, flowing directly from the Great War, still dominate the headlines of global newspapers, online media, and presumed coalition-excused military campaigns.

The First World Oil War, and its strategic parameters, was a harbinger of the interwoven geopolitical, economic, and military realities of things to come, and, in essence, helped produce and mirrored many of the embryonic conflicts mentioned above. In fact, *all* of the aforementioned conflicts can trace their roots to the aftermath of the "War to End All Wars," within the geographic and ethnic remodelling of Europe, Africa, and the Middle East during the Paris Peace Talks, and the mandates imposed by the League of Nations. In transit to these talks in 1919, U.S. President Woodrow Wilson prophetically declared to his entourage, "I am convinced that if this peace is not made on the highest principles of justice, it will be swept away by the peoples of the world in less than a generation. If it is any other sort of peace then I shall want to run away and hide ... for there will follow not mere conflict but cataclysm."[42]

The shear enormity of the global conflagration between 1939 and 1945 recast the "Great War" as the "First World War." Now, however, it is almost ahistorical convention to refer to the world wars as a single conflict interrupted by a period of fragile peace while a vanquished and vengeful Germany and two aggrieved former Western allies, Italy and Japan, regrouped and were reincarnated under tyrannical totalitarian and fascist regimes. The American novelist F. Scott Fitzgerald captured the carnage and foreshadowing futility of the war to end all wars in *Tender Is the Night* (1934). As the main character Dick Diver tours the Somme battlefield near Thiepval, he confides to his companion, "See that little stream, we could walk to it in two minutes. It took the British a whole month to walk to it – a whole empire walking very slowly, dying in front and pushing forward behind. And another empire walked very slowly backward a few inches a day, leaving the dead like a million bloody rugs. No Europeans will ever do that again in this generation."[43] Yet the butcher's bill of the First World War, trumped only by its sons in the Second, is still, a century later, beyond comprehension.

On 22 August 1914 alone, the French suffered 27,000 men *killed*, as they stubbornly weathered the onslaught of the German invasion at the outset of the war during the Battles of the Frontiers. In the months of August and September, 400,000 French soldiers perished, and by the close of 1914 the war had already taken over two million lives. This war would not be over by Christmas and, given its current connections to contemporary conflicts, has still not run its full course. To put these numbers into context, the French suffered more fatalities on that one day than the United States suffered over four months during the 1945 battles of Iwo Jima and Okinawa *combined*. This one single day accounts for half of the Americans killed in Vietnam *between 1956 and 1975*. By comparison, the single bloodiest day in American military history occurred at the Battle of Antietam on 17 September 1862 during the Civil War. The opposing forces suffered 23,000 total casualties, including *only* 3,654 killed. The Battle of Gettysburg between 1 and 3 July 1863 inflicted 46,000 casualties, including 7,863 fatalities. The Civil War claimed the lives of roughly 750,000 Americans, more than all other U.S. wars combined, and the equivalent of 8.5 million Americans today. The Civil War illustrated the devastating potential of modern warfare and was a harbinger of the industrial killing of the Great War.[44] For example, on 1 July 1916, the opening day of the Battle of the Somme, the British imperial forces suffered 60,000 casualties, including *20,000 dead*.

By the end of the war, 890,000 soldiers from across the British Empire had served in the Middle Eastern theatre, suffering roughly 93,000 casualties, with a financial cost of £350 million.[45] It was into this muddled, increasingly volcanic "secondary" theatre of war that Dunsterforce was deployed to secure the Caucasus oil. During the course of the war, oil would become progressively more important in British strategic thought and action, most notably in 1918, and into the peace negotiations. In addition, the industrial output of the belligerents rapidly accelerated during the war, which itself was becoming increasingly mechanized with innovations and introductions of various war machines from the aeroplane to the tank. Beginning with the mass industrialization and weapon developments of the American Civil War, "Modern industry and militarism have always been associated throughout ... their simultaneous flowering."[46]

Simply put, the slaughter in the trenches and no-man's-land of the Great War went far beyond the contemporary historical record. During the First World War, 10 million soldiers and 6 million civilians died (although the statistics for civilian deaths remain imprecise and disputed), and 28 million soldiers were wounded. Nor do the 10 million include those who perished in the 1918–19 influenza epidemic. Abetted by cramped trench conditions and repatriation centres harbouring soldiers returning home to all four corners of the globe, influenza killed upwards of 100 million people, roughly 5 per cent of the world's population. Also excluded are the wars of the peace, particularly the Russian Civil War, 1917–22 (9–14 million casualties), the Greco-Turkish War, 1919–22 (475,000 casualties), and the Arab revolts in the Middle East. If so inclined, one could also add the casualty figures from the wars, including the Second, that were a continuation of this Great War. But this work details the legacy and influence of the first of the enduring oil wars.

The intention of this book is not to retell the history of the Middle Eastern theatre of war. In recent years, due in part to the 2003 invasion of Iraq, a flurry of books have been published or re-released on this topic. Nor is the intention here to discuss the Russian Revolution or the resultant Allied interventions. This has also been previously accomplished. These works are cited in the bibliography for the reader's reference. The oil designs of all nations concerned, however, were invariably connected to the larger strategic issues of the war, the evolving campaigns of the Middle East, and the fortunes of the Russians in the Caucasus and northern Persia. When pertinent to the oil wars within the larger Great War, references to occurrences in these broader campaigns will be detailed. Generally, however, this book probes Anglo-American (and French to a lesser extent) oil imperialism.

Beginning with the First World War, oil became a reason for war and correspondingly led to the mechanization and industrialization of war itself, inviting warfare to occupy tiers never seen before, resulting in the horrific history of total war during the twentieth century. Oil initiated a complete transformation in the art of war, and oil wars became wars worth fighting. The First World War was the foundation upon which oil gained status as a pre-eminent strategic commodity, imperative to the national security of the so-called Great Powers. In James W. Blinn's novel, *The Aardvark Is Ready for War* (1995), mirroring Joseph Heller's satirical classic *Catch-22* (1961), a navy sailor bound for the Persian Gulf cynically explains to his fellow crewman the indivisible marriage between oil, economy, and nation states: "Oil Companies are nationalities. This plane oughta say EXXON on the side instead of U.S. Navy."[47]

Consequently, during the Paris Peace Conference and the decades that followed, the quest for oil concessions became the new Great Game played out by Western powers and was behind all international "oleaginous diplomacy." Only nuclear weapons (and nuclear propulsion) has challenged the domination of oil as a military-economic trump card. But the eight nuclear-weapons states are loath to give up this leverage, just as those without begrudge it, as evidenced by North Korean nuclear developments and the Iranian-Israeli (and U.S. and Syrian) posturing in confrontation over the Iranian nuclear program.[48] The First World War was the beginning of this oil supply-and-demand military-economic relationship.

The First World War created an imperial Anglo-American oil cartel known as the Seven Sisters – all majority-owned by Britain and/or the United States – five American, one British, one Anglo-Dutch – with enduring and current ramifications. The founders were Anglo-Persian Oil Company (APOC) now British Petroleum (BP); Royal Dutch Shell; Standard Oil of California (SOCAL), which became Chevron in 1984; Gulf Oil, which merged with SOCAL in 1984 shortly before it became Chevron; Texaco, which was incorporated by Chevron in 2001; and Standard Oil of New Jersey (SONJ), which became Esso and then Exxon, which merged with Standard Oil of New York (SONY), which became Mobil, to create ExxonMobil in 1999. This oil monopoly is more imposing and omnipresent a century later, as with mergers, takeovers, and name changes, by 2010 the seven became only four: British Petroleum (BP), Chevron, ExxonMobil, and Royal Dutch Shell. Since the collapse of the Soviet Union in 1991 and an increase in global drilling, especially in what had been untapped geographical terrain as the result of advances in technology, a new Seven Sisters, predominantly state-owned, is challenging the monopoly of the Big Four: Saudi Aramco, China National Petroleum Corporation (CNPC), Gazprom (Russia), National Iranian Oil Company (NIOC), Petrobras Brazil, PDVSA Venezuela, and Petronas Malaysia.

Prior to the 1973 OPEC (Organization of the Petroleum Exporting Countries) oil crisis, however, the Seven Sisters controlled 85 per cent of the world's petroleum. How did this happen? The origin of this oil monopoly was a direct result of the First World War. What follows is this story.

Chapter One

Oil and the Great Game

In August 1898, German geologists masquerading as anthropologists sent their kaiser an urgent message from Mosul in northern Mesopotamia. They had, at last, found oil. The Mosul *vilayet* (province), they enthusiastically reported, offered "even greater opportunities for profit than the rich oilfields of the Caucasus."[1] Shortly thereafter, on 18 October 1898, Kaiser Wilhelm II's grand tour of Sultan Abdul Hamid's Ottoman Empire, which included Mosul, began in Constantinople.

On 29 October, mounted on an ink-black charger, Wilhelm, in the white ceremonial uniform of a German field marshal and wearing a helmet crowned with a gold imperial eagle, triumphantly entered the holy city of Jerusalem through an expressly made breach in the wall. The occasion received global media attention, and to one reporter, "It seemed to me that Wilhelm imagined he had taken the city by sword, instead of arriving there as a tourist. His behavior was ludicrous beyond description."[2] Overwhelmed by his reception, he impulsively "placed himself, his army, and his Empire in the service of the Mother of Christ," and went so far as to telegraph Pope Leo XIII to officially offer his messianic protection to Christians in the Holy Land. Eleven days later, on 8 November in Damascus, the kaiser paradoxically addressed the crowd at a banquet thrown in his honour by Sheikh Abdullah Effendi: "May the Sultan, and his 300 million Muslim subjects scattered across the earth, who venerate him as their Caliph, be assured that the German Kaiser will be their friend for all time."[3]

Four days later Wilhelm impetuously wrote to his "dear friend Nicky" (Tsar Nicholas II), "Remember what you and I agreed upon at Peterhof never to forget that the Mahometans were a tremendous card in our game in case you or I were suddenly confronted by a war

1.1 A Mesopotamian oil worker beside an oil pit and drums,
Mosul, ca 1911 (Library of Congress).

with the certain meddlesome Power! ... Fetish adoration has created a supreme contempt for the Christians with the Moslems. My personal feeling in leaving the holy city was that I felt profoundly ashamed before the Moslems and that if I had come there without any Religion at all I certainly would have turned Mahommetan!"[4] The specious goal of this correspondence, however veiled, was to convince both Russia and the Ottomans that Britain was the true enemy, while also planting the seed of an organized Muslim revolt in India, and elsewhere, against British hegemony.

The "meddlesome Power" was Britain, whose empire contained over 100 million Muslims, making it, without contest, the largest "Muslim power" in the world. The kaiser seemed unaware or unconcerned that Russia, containing roughly 20 million Muslims, was equally vulnerable to Muslim unrest, specifically in her southern regions and the Caucasus. In fact, the kaiser's own upstart German Empire was home to 2.5 million Muslims. In 1914, of the 270 million Muslims in the world, only 35 million were actually governed by other Muslims, the vast majority within the Ottoman Empire, with the remainder in Persia and Afghanistan, which endured only as nominally "independent" under British and/or Russian patronage to maintain a balance of power in the region: "At this stage, moreover, none of these powers had anything like the economic might that would come from the later growth of oil wealth."[5] In contrast, the Christian population in 1914 represented 560 million (a Christian-Muslim ratio of 2.1 to 1) of varying denominations, with 68 per cent living in Europe, 14 per cent in the United States, Canada, and Mexico, and with ancient pockets sewn into the chequered religious fabric of the Middle East, North Africa, and Central Asia.

Rumours that the kaiser had converted to Islam, and that the Hohenzollern line descended from the Prophet Mohammed (or his sister), quickly disseminated through the bazaars of the Middle East, fostered by obscure passages from the Koran indicating that the kaiser had been ordained by Allah "to free Muslims from infidel rule." With the help of German bribes, his declaration was reported in Turkish and Arabic newspapers, and thousands of colour postcards bearing his words and photo were freely distributed in the hopes that they would be mailed, or disseminated through trade, to India and other parts of the Muslim world. *Hajji* Wilhelm Mohammed Guillaiano, as he was now said to call himself, would be the protector of Islam, fighting with his brothers to shrug off the yoke of European imperialism: "Like the Kaiser's conversion, it was a half-truth at best: Germany had her own Muslim colonies, principally in West Africa, which put the lie to the claim that her hands were clean. But contradictions have never bothered visionaries ... Inspired by their Kaiser's powerful vision, a new generation of intellectuals and adventurers would sketch in the contours of Germany's *Drang nach Osten*."[6]

Ten years prior to his awakening to Islam, in 1888 Wilhelm II succeeded his father as emperor of Germany at twenty-nine years of age. Like Wilhelm, Germany itself was a young nation pieced together in 1871 from the jigsaw of Teutonic kingdoms, principalities, and city states. Following successful wars against Denmark, Austria, and, finally, France during the brief Franco-Prussian War (1870–1), under the political vision of Otto von Bismarck and the military genius of Helmuth von Moltke (the Elder), a new nation in the heart of Europe was created primarily under Prussian leadership. On the surface, Germany was brimming with youthful ambition and energy, masking an adolescent insecurity shared by its future kaiser.

The young Wilhelm believed that Germany was destined to have its rightful place in the sun, with an empire to rival those of Britain and Russia. He was vain, impetuous, hypersensitive, and prone to bouts of rage and depression. He was determined above all else, however, to be respected and taken seriously, and to be accepted as an equal by his extended noble family, by throwing a naive Germany onto the world stage of his *Weltpolitik* – a decisive departure from Bismarck's platform of realpolitik.[7] This clash of ideologies led to Bismarck's resignation as chancellor in March 1890, whereupon the obstinate emperor declared to his nation, "The duties of officer of the watch on the ship of state have fallen to me ... The waves of opportunity are now beating against our shores. The course remains the same. Full steam ahead!"[8] Wilhelm was now free to steer his country into the vast, unchartered waters of the geopolitical Great Game, with disastrous global consequences.

The Great Game refers to the strategic rivalry and conflict between Britain and Russia for imperial hegemony in Central Asia in the years between the Russo-Persian Treaty (1813) and the Anglo-Russian Entente (1907). By 1885, however, Germany, Turkey, and to a lesser extent France and Italy, entered the competition. The final phase of the Great Game was played in tandem with the Russian Revolution between 1917 and 1920, which is the backdrop for this book. The origins of the term are attributed to Arthur Conolly, an intelligence officer with the Sixth Bengal Light Cavalry, who in 1839 expressed his views on British imperialism in Central Asia in a letter to Major-General

Sir Henry Rawlinson, the famed orientalist and father of Henry and Alfred, who will later play a part in this story. The phrase was also found in Conolly's private papers. The term gained widespread use and popularity with the publication of Rudyard Kipling's picaresque novel *Kim* (1901), the story of an Anglo-Indian boy and his Tibetan lama mentor thwarting Russian penetration of India in the wake of the Second Anglo-Afghan War (1878–80). Rising politician George Curzon clearly defined the stakes of the Great Game in his 1892 book *Persia and the Persian Question*: "Turkestan, Afghanistan, Transcaspia, Persia – to many these names breathe only a sense of utter remoteness ... To me, I confess, they are the pieces on a chessboard upon which is being played out a game for the domination of the world." To Queen Victoria it was simply "a question of Russian or British supremacy in the world." Prime Minster Lord Salisbury declared in 1899, "Were it not for our possessing India, we should trouble ourselves but little about Persia." He added that it was vital to "prevent Persia from becoming an outlying Russian dependency."[9]

While the British may not yet have seen the potential of Persian oil, S.G.W. Benjamin, the first American ambassador to Persia, did. In 1883, he compared the prospective rewards to that of Baku, "a large and rapidly growing European city, with a highly important commerce. What has done this? The answer is *petroleum*."[10] American economic interests in both the Middle East and the Caucasus, however, were relatively trivial. Its presence in the region was limited to cultural, anthropologic, and pious missionary endeavours, with a growing stream of tourists, albeit still small, wanting to catch a glimpse of the antiquities and holy places of biblical lore. American missionaries accounted for the largest, U.S. presence, and by 1914 they had established over four hundred schools, nine post-secondary institutions, over a dozen hospitals, and countless Christian hermitages across the region.[11] In contrast, American foreign policy at this time was isolationist and confined largely to projecting influence over the Western Hemisphere in accordance with the Monroe Doctrine of 1823. America adopted a zealous abstinence from absorption in Europe's historic meddlesome quarrels and imperial enterprises. The Middle East was viewed by American diplomats as an imperial extension of Europe; therefore, the traditional policy of non-intervention applied. In 1912, the Middle East represented only 1.2 per cent of American imports (mainly Turkish tobacco and liquorice), and was the recipient of a paltry 0.17 per cent of U.S. exports.[12] Both the Middle East and the Caucasus, however, would become hotly contested petroleum prizes among imperialist powers, and an increasingly aggressive United States, during the First World Oil War.

Imperialism in some form has existed in the Middle East, Central Asia, and the Caucasus since the dawn of agronomy in Mesopotamia circa 8,500 BCE in the cradle of civilization between the Tigris and Euphrates Rivers, followed by emergence of the first Sumerian city states around 4,000 BCE.[13] Great empires expanded through imperialism, conquest, and political or economic leverage. Each was defeated and replaced by another, continuing a cyclical rise and fall of ancient kingdoms. In the Middle East, the Sumerians and Akkadians were replaced by the Egyptians, Babylonians, and Hittites, who gave way to the Assyrians and finally to the Persian Achaemenian dynasty founded by Cyrus the Great in 550 BCE. This prolific empire was then incorporated into Alexander the Great's Hellenistic Empire, which gave way to the Romans, followed by the advent of modern Christianity. The ensuing Sassanid and Byzantine Empires collapsed or were weakened by the expansion of Islam during the mid-seventh century and the ensuing waves of mounted archers from the Asian steppes.[14]

Unlike the burgeoning German Empire, the Ottoman Empire was a decaying relic of this forlorn era. Its origins were initiated by the westward invasions of nomadic, marauding horseman from the steppes and plains of central and northeast Asia, which began around 1,000 CE. Commanded by driven leaders like Genghis Khan (d. 1227) and Tamerlane (d. 1405), they conquered vast territories, carving out mighty empires. By 1,300 CE, Turkish-speaking horseman who had converted to Islam united under the warrior-king Osman I (namesake of the Osmanli or Ottoman Empire) and began northern campaigns against the southern flanks of the Eastern Roman (or Byzantine) Empire. After their victory at Kosovo in 1389, Ottoman Turks quickly invaded the Balkans and proceeded north into Eastern Europe. Their capture of Constantinople in 1453 finalized the end of the Byzantine Empire, which had existed for over a thousand years. In 1517, the Ottomans established rule in Egypt, pressing west through North Africa. Under Suleiman the Magnificent (1520–66), the empire reached its zenith, with Ottoman forces penetrating into Serbia, Bulgaria, Romania, and southern Hungary, while gaining control of Mesopotamia from the Persians in 1535.[15]

The Ottomans remained an imperialist power until their historic defeat at the Battle of Vienna in 1683, marking the end of European expansion, at a time when the empire's population numbered some forty million people of over twenty different nationalities. By contrast,

Britain's population was roughly four million. The administration of the empire, however, was chaotic and incoherent. While Islam was a fusing factor for the majority Sunni Muslims, the seventy-one other sects of Islam, primarily the Shi'ites, were in opposition with Sunni doctrine and refused to recognize the sultan's claims to the caliphate.[16] In addition, 25 per cent of the population was composed of Christian-based faiths, paganism, and mystic spiritual beliefs. For these minorities, like the Shi'ites, religion was a discordant rather than unifying dynamic. Economic growth of the empire was measured in slaves and the spoils of war, not on a foundation of internal production or external trade. Following the setback at Vienna, over the next three centuries, "when the conquests turned into defeats and retreats, the dynamic of Ottoman existence was lost; the Turks had mastered the arts of war but not those of government ... Most of the reforms took place only on paper; and as an anachronism in the modern world, the ramshackle Ottoman regime seemed doomed to disappear."[17]

Between 1800 and 1914, revolts and wars slowly eroded the land base of the Ottoman Empire, which, although having instituted military, legal, and economic reforms, could not negate the potency or aspirations of imperialist European powers. During his now famous Albert Hall speech in 1898, British Prime Minister Lord Salisbury categorized the "nations of the world as the living and the dying. On the one side you have great countries of enormous power growing in power every year, growing in wealth, growing in dominion, growing in perfection of their organization." The other side was composed of failing or failed states sponsored by corruption and mismanagement of governance, shrinking empires, all decaying within the popular Victorian notion of the survival of the fittest among nations – an appendage of Social Darwinism applied to race, culture, and nation states. Today the international community views failing or failed states as a threat to global security, or as parasitic sanctuaries for international smuggling cartels (including narcotics, weapons, and humans), or as hosts for al-Qaeda or other fanatical narco-terror cells. During this era of the Great Game, however, imperialist powers viewed them as an opportunity for imminent annexation. "The living nations," Salisbury concluded, "will gradually encroach on the territory of the dying, and the seeds and causes of conflict among civilized nations will speedily appear." The decaying Ottoman Empire, the leper and sick man of Europe, along with the "dying nations" of China, Persia, and other parts of the Middle East, were ready to be portioned among the "living nations."[18]

The decisive Russian victory in the Russo-Turkish War (1877–8), the sixth since 1768, resulted in the annexations of Ottoman territory. Austria-Hungary occupied Bosnia-Herzegovina, Britain seized Cyprus, and Russia claimed the western Caucasus and the Anatolian provinces of Kars, Ardahan, and Batum (which will play a key role in the unfolding story). The Ottoman holdings of Romania, Bulgaria, Serbia, and Montenegro gained independence. In 1882, Britain occupied Egypt and the Sudan, safeguarding the sea lanes to India while bridging the British Empire between London and Calcutta and later New Delhi. Over three million Muslim refugees from these regions flooded back to the heartland of the empire, while an equal number were brutally killed. During the Russian advances in the Caucasus, between 500,000 and 800,000 Muslim Circassians were killed or relocated, and many of those in the Crimea and the Balkans drifted towards what remained of the Ottoman Empire.[19]

The crumbling Ottoman Empire was facing external and internal threats, and rebellions and strikes plagued Sultan Abdul Hamid II, who, citing social unrest, suspended parliament (the Sublime Porte or the Porte) in 1878. His precarious leadership was being questioned, and the fragile environment was ripe for revolution. In 1908, a union of modern, secularist Turkish nationalists, including many military officers, together with those who blamed the sultan for the recent political and military blunders, revolted in mid-April, gaining widespread support as they marched on Constantinople from Thessalonica. These Young Turks, as they were known, gathered support from other dissident groups under the umbrella Committee of Union and Progress (CUP). As rebellion spread, on 24 July the sultan reinstated parliament and the constitution, after failing to suppress the revolt led by Mehmed Talaat and army officer Ismail Enver. After a futile countercoup in April 1909, the sultan was deposed and replaced by his brother Mehmed V, who was little more than a figurehead.

The revolution did little to change the fortunes or delay the atrophy of the Ottoman Empire. Italy defeated the Ottomans during the Italo-Turkish War (1911–12), appropriating Libya and the Dodecanese Islands. These decisive victories encouraged the Balkan states to wage war against the Ottoman Empire and to seize its remaining European possessions during the First Balkan War (October 1912 to May 1913). The Balkan League (Serbia, Montenegro, Greece, and Bulgaria) achieved rapid success against inferior Ottoman forces. On 23 January 1913, in the midst of losing the war, the Young Turks initiated a coup d'état, storming the Porte, killing the minister of war, and forcing the resignation of the leader of the cabinet (grand vizier). The coup resulted in the ascent of the dictatorial triumvirate or "the three pashas," who ruled the Ottoman Empire until it final dissolution in the wake of the First World War. All three were members of the CUP and of the original 1908 revolution: Mehmed Talaat (minister of the interior), Ismail Enver (minister of war), and Ahmed Djemal (governor of Constantinople and minister of the navy). The three pashas rounded out their government with close allies and friends: Halil Bey (president of Chamber of Deputies), Mehmed Djavid (minister of finance), and Prince Said Halim (grand vizier and foreign minister). The new leaders decided to continue the Balkan War, which ended in a humiliating defeat. As a result, almost all of the Ottoman European possessions were partitioned among the victors, and Albania was given independence.[20]

Dissatisfied with its spoils of war, Bulgaria attacked its former allies of Serbia and Greece, as well as Romania, igniting the Second Balkan War (June–August 1913). The Ottoman Empire joined the coalition against Bulgaria, hoping to regain recently lost territory. It retained eastern Thrace, including Adrianople (Edirne), the vanguard fortress protecting the European invasion routes (by land) to Constantinople, Asia Minor, and the Middle East. As the result of its vital strategic location, it has been the site of sixteen decisive battles, leading military historian John Keegan to label Adrianople "the most contested spot on the globe."

By 1914, the Ottoman Empire was a shadow of its former self, with a population of roughly 24 million. This diverse ethnic and religious collective consisted of 20 million Muslims, including 12 million Turks, 6 million Arabs, and 2 million Kurds. The remainder included 1.8 million Greeks, predominantly in the western provinces and Aegean islands, 1.68 million Armenians, largely in the eastern provinces, and 187,000 Jews.[21] In a broad geographic appraisal, it encompassed most of what are now Turkey, Israel, Lebanon, Jordan, Syria, and Iraq – approximately six times the size of Texas.[22] Yet the Young Turks, now possessing complete control over policy, sought to restore the glory of the Ottoman Empire by uniting Turkish peoples under their pan-Turanian ideology. In a political age of coalitions, pacts, and treaties, however, they still required a European ally within the Great Game, which was being played out on their doorstep.

Despite inheriting a shrinking empire from the ousted regime, the CUP also took over military and economic ties with Germany, but by no means did this guarantee their eventual alliance during the Great

1.2 Enver Pasha visiting the Dome of the Rock in Jerusalem accompanied by Djemal Pasha to his left, 1916. The two leaders travelled across Syria, Palestine, and the Hijaz in early 1916 to assess the war in their Arab provinces (Library of Congress).

War. The origins of Germany's interests in the Ottoman Empire were primarily cultural. In 1845, the German Oriental Society was inaugurated. By the 1870s and 1880s, German archaeologists and academics, along with other European orientalists, flooded the Ottoman Empire, primarily in Syria, Palestine, and Mesopotamia. In 1882, Sultan Abdul Hamid secured German assistance to modernize and train the Ottoman military, after its defeat during the recent Russo-Turkish War. Following the kaiser's first Ottoman tour in 1889, and Bismarck's dismissal the following year, German military and economic relations with Turkey steadily increased under Wilhelm's new *Weltpolitik*. With the influx of German bankers, businessmen, engineers, and military advisors, also came German spies and intelligence agents.[23] Shortly before the outbreak of war, German newspapers decreed, "A free hand must be given to Germany for the development of her commercial and industrial relations with Turkey. This would mean a recognized sphere of German influence from the Persian Gulf to the Dardanelles."[24]

The cornerstone of the kaiser's ambitious drive to the east, and his desire to instigate a Muslim jihad in British colonial possessions, was the Berlin-Baghdad Railway, which would eventually run, or so it was planned, to the Persian Gulf and thence to British India. The existing line already extended from Hamburg through Berlin, Prague, Vienna, Budapest, Belgrade, and Sophia to Constantinople. This corridor was the setting for Agatha Christie's *Murder on the Orient Express* (1934) and Ian Fleming's *From Russia, with Love* (1957). Two more recent splinter lines connected Constantinople to Ankara in the eastern interior, and also to Konya in the south, towards Baghdad. In 1909, German engineers and craftsmen completed the lavish neo-classical Haydarpasa Terminal in Constantinople (Istanbul) – the crowning castle-like representation of the kaiser's ambitious project (which was severely damaged in a 1917 bomb attack).

Although the kaiser was stirred to Islam during his 1898 tour of the Ottoman Empire, the purpose of the trip was to secure the concession to extend the Konya line southeast to Baghdad and beyond. German oil rights would accompany the railway across the deserts of Mesopotamia and propel Germany into the oil-driven era. The British Foreign Office was adamant that if the Germans "also get the oil-concessions in Mesopotamia and Persia they cannot fail to acquire enormous political influence at British expense, in regions which are of supreme importance to India."[25] Bids for construction, however, had also been submitted by Britain, France, and Russia. Prior to 1914, there was only one British railway in Turkey, heading southeast from Smyrna (Izmir) to Aydin, some eighty miles along the interior coast of the Aegean Sea. The sultan was chary of making any immediate decision. After all, this was the same kaiser who, following the murder of two German missionaries in China in 1897, landed troops at the port city of Tsingtao, transforming it into a formidable German naval station, challenging British maritime might in the Far East. The kaiser gloated, "Hundreds of German traders will revel in the knowledge that the German Empire has at last secured a firm footing in Asia ... Hundreds of thousands of Chinese will quiver when they feel the iron fist of Germany heavy on their necks, while the whole German nation will be delighted that its government has done a manly act."[26] He reacted to the 1900 Boxer Rebellion in China by pledging to use such force that "for a thousand years ... no Chinaman, no matter whether his eyes be slit or not, will dare look a German in the face."[27]

While a preliminary deal was signed with Germany in 1899, it was not until 1903 that the contract was solidified, funding was secured, and construction began on the first relatively flat and unproblematic section from Konya to the outskirts of Adana. According to historian David Fromkin, "The British originally encouraged and supported the project, little aware at the outset of the dangers it might pose. Eventually the project became a source of discord between Britain and Germany, which, however, was resolved by an agreement reached between the two countries in 1914."[28] Prior to the war, the British were willing to accept construction so long as it did not continue past Baghdad, or at most, the port city of Basra at the confluence of the Tigris and Euphrates Rivers: "Britain not only kept a watchful eye on her interests in Mesopotamian navigation and irrigation, but also cultivated a growing interest in the oil-fields of the Mosul and Baghdad vilayets."[29] Behind the scenes, the British had secured pledges of allegiance from the Gulf sheikhs, including the emir of Kuwait, in exchange for protection, financial handouts, and dividends from the Anglo-Persian Oil Company (APOC). The March 1914 settlement referenced above will be detailed in chapter 2, but essentially Germany, via the Baghdad Railway Company, agreed to recognize the APOC's exclusive rights to southern Mesopotamia and southwestern Persia, while the oil, Basra, and other Gulf ports remained under British control. By this time, the railway had made little progress in the direction of Adana, hampered by political discord and financial and geographical constraints.[30] Barely two hundred kilometres had been laid down, less than one-tenth of the distance to Basra.[31] With the outbreak of war four months later, all arrangements were invalidated, and Britain sought to extend her oil empire into the northern Mesopotamian *vilayet* of Mosul. In May 1914, the *London Petroleum Review* published a map entitled "The Petroleum Deposits of Mesopotamia," dubbing the region "a second Baku in the making." When war came, Britain sought to control these resources.[32] The Berlin-Baghdad Railway was only one element of the kaiser's *Weltpolitik* within the Great Game being played by Europe's imperialist powers in the decades preceding the First World War.

The outbreak of the First World War shattered almost a hundred years of relative peace in Europe. Its nations had circumvented large-scale conflict since the defeat of Napoleon in 1815 through treaties, alliances, and an aspiration to maintain a balance of power in Europe and empire. One goal was to maintain the integrity of the Ottoman Empire, primarily its Asiatic holdings. This was a direct result of Napoleon's Egyptian-Syrian campaign (1798–1801), which threatened British India, and Russia, which feared a Franco-Ottoman alliance. In place of war, European armies were deployed to the fringes of empire to gain territorial acquisitions within the "imperial scramble," or to quell indigenous rebellions in existing colonies.[33] By 1914, the pan-European empire covered 84 per cent of the globe, compared with 35 per cent in 1800. Britain's empire, with an imperial population of 445 million, encompassed one-quarter of the world, with the Russian Empire occupying one-sixth.[34] America shrewdly guarded the Western Hemisphere, with British backing via Canada, through the 1823 Monroe Doctrine, essentially forbidding any further European colonization, while regarding any attempts to do so as an act of war. Germany, although arriving late to the game, was not without imperial ambitions, but the world was running out of space.

By 1890 through Bismarck's realpolitik diplomacy, the kaiser's gunboat *Weltpolitik* practices, or agreements such as the Treaties of Berlin in 1885 and 1899, Germany had acquired a fledgling empire. The 1885 Treaty of Berlin regulated the partitioning of Africa, and Germany came away with German East Africa, German South-West Africa, Cameroon, and Togoland. By 1896, the colonization of Africa was well on its way to completion.[35] As mentioned, Germany invaded Kiautschou Bay/Tsingtao in 1898 and quickly occupied the surrounding Shandong Peninsula. In the Pacific, partly as a result of the 1899 Treaty of Berlin, Germany retained or was granted Western Samoa, as well as smaller atolls including the Mariana, Marshall, and Caroline Island chains and the Bismarck Archipelago, all appendages of Kaiser-Wilhelmsland (northeast New

Guinea).[36] Few Germans, however, were willing to venture to these inhospitable colonies. While the United States and Canada witnessed a monumental influx of Germans between 1850 and 1910, no more than twenty thousand Germans ever lived in these imperial possessions.[37] By 1890, therefore, only the Middle East and Central Asia were vacant for colonial expansion and thus became the epicentre of the Great Game, which continued into the First World War, as oil entered into strategic imperial designs.

The starting point of the Great Game, as mentioned, is often cited as the Russo-Persian Treaty of 1813, officially known as the Treaty of Gulistan. In the aftermath of the Russo-Persian War (1804–13), the third since 1722, modern-day Azerbaijan, Dagestan, and eastern Georgia were absorbed into the Russian Empire, creating a buffer zone from further Ottoman or Persian penetration, while the Russian Grand Fleet secured exclusive rights to the Caspian Sea. In response, Britain and Persia negotiated a Treaty of Defensive Alliance in 1812, whereby Persia acted as a bulwark between Russia (and the Ottoman Empire) and India. Goaded by British agents to regain lost territory, the Persians initiated the Second Russo-Persian War (1826–8). Following another defeat, Persia relinquished the remaining portions of the southern Caucasus, with the Aras River acting as the boundary between the two empires.

Subsequently, British strategy was to use decaying Islamic regimes in Central Asia, such as Afghanistan, Persia, and the Ottoman Empire, as pawns in a broad buffer between Russia and British India, or a route to Egypt. British fears of Russian penetration in the east dominated its foreign policy. This diminished slightly after Russia's defeat during the Crimean War (1853–6), which was fought essentially by a French-British-Ottoman coalition to buttress an unstable Ottoman Empire and to thwart further Russian gains at Ottoman expense. The survival of the Ottoman Empire, even a severely debilitated one, was paramount to British interests, even if it meant a constant flow of capital from London. This changed in 1880 when Liberal leader William Gladstone, who zealously denounced the atrocities committed against Christian minorities by the Ottomans, replaced Conservative Prime Minister Benjamin Disraeli. Gladstone branded the Ottoman regime "a bottomless pit of fraud and falsehood" and withdrew British protection and financial stimulus from Constantinople.[38] Left isolated and vulnerable, the Turks eventually, and in actuality quite unwillingly, turned to Germany to fill the vacuum left by Britain's departure.

In 1873, Germany had entered into an alliance with Austria-Hungary and Russia with a desire to isolate France. Following the Russo-Turkish War, and with increasing tension in the Balkans and the exclusion of Russia from the German economic market, Russia left this League of Three Emperors in 1887. Alarmed by Germany's growing influence in Europe and the kaiser's rhetoric, France and Russia signed an alliance in 1894, bringing the two isolated countries together to counter Germany on both borders. The 1898 Fashoda Crisis in the Sudan brought France and Britain to the brink of war, but diplomacy prevailed, setting the stage for the Entente Cordiale between the two powers in 1904. This defensive military agreement also settled the majority of long-standing colonial issues between the two nations. The kaiser's attempts to rupture this friendship during the Moroccan Crises of 1905–6 and 1911 were embarrassing failures. The alliance, however beneficial, put Britain in a strategic dilemma on her position in the Middle East and Central Asia between the historic rivals of Russia and Turkey: "The Franco-Russian defence treaty, concluded in 1894, damaged France's position at the Porte no less dramatically than had the British occupation of Egypt a decade earlier. If there was a single unshakable law underlining the Eastern Question, it was that one could not be friends with both Turkey and her historic enemy at the same time."[39] The British foreign secretary, Sir Edward Grey, realized that "Russia was the ally of France ... we could not pursue at one and the same time a policy of agreement with France and a policy of counter alliances against Russia."[40]

More conclusive to the British, however, was the humiliating Russian defeat during the Russo-Japanese War (1904–5), marking a decline in Russian military might, and as a contender for British hegemony in Central Asia. As a result, Grey negotiated a treaty with Russia in 1907, cementing this fragile relationship. Accordingly, Britain was given paper-jurisdiction over Afghanistan (which was tenuous within Afghanistan itself); Tibet was considered neutral territory; and Persia was divided into three zones: a Russian zone in the north; a central nonaligned zone; and a British zone to the south, which formed a convenient cushion for India, while safeguarding oil interests in the region. Prior to the war, while the Russians sought to contain and neutralize eastern Anatolia, Persia was the primary target of Russian imperialism and influence. Soon after in 1908, however, the British discovered oil in the Persian "neutral zone." This area, including Basra and access to the Persian Gulf and the internal river systems, was quickly amalgamated into its own sphere to protect the burgeoning APOC. Persia's

THE HARMLESS NECESSARY CAT.

Bᴿɪᴛɪsʜ Lɪᴏɴ (*to Russian Bear*). "LOOK HERE! *YOU* CAN PLAY WITH HIS HEAD, AND *I* CAN PLAY WITH HIS TAIL, AND WE CAN
BOTH STROKE THE SMALL OF HIS BACK."
Pᴇʀsɪᴀɴ Cᴀᴛ. "I DON'T REMEMBER HAVING BEEN CONSULTED ABOUT THIS!"

1.3 "The Harmless Necessary Cat." Cartoon from *Punch!* depicting the
Anglo-Russian Entente of 1907, 2 October 1907.

nominal independence was never taken seriously by either power.[41] The
Anglo-Russian Entente of 1907 seemingly brought the Great Game to
its end.[42] As the War Office noted, Germany supplanted Russia as the
foremost threat to British interests by bringing "a militant possibility into
Arabia – on the flank of Egypt and the British route to the East."[43] Although
the Ottoman Empire was now isolated by three of the four great powers
of Europe, it still did not immediately fall into Germany's lap.

The alliances for marching as to war were now set, save for the
lonely Ottoman Empire: the Triple Entente (Allies) of Britain, France,
Russia, and their vast empires and dominions, opposite the Triple Alliance (Central Powers) of Germany, Austria-Hungary, and (a capricious
and suspicious) Italy.[44] According to Hew Strachan, "In the months
immediately before the war the Turks were more open to an alliance

with a member of the Entente than of the Triple Alliance," and both France and even Russia were tendered invitations. Britain was ignored, as Turkish overtures of alliance had been rebuffed in 1908, 1911, and, most recently, in 1913.[45] Winston Churchill had been the only advocate, recognizing in 1911 that Turkey "is the greatest land weapon wh the Germans cd use against us."[46] In May 1914, Talaat, Turkish minister of the interior, approached Sergey Sazonov, the Russian foreign minister, who was so dumbfounded by the offer that he did not know how to respond. This exemplifies just how desperate the Young Turks had become to find a suitable ally, as courting the Russians was the equivalent to handing a burglar the keys to your house, and then taking a long vacation. Two months later, Djemal, minister of the navy, sought out the French, who, attentive to Russian reservations, dismissed the offer. Finally, on 22 July, with the blessing of Talaat and Djemal, Enver, minister of war, formally requested an alliance with Germany, which was also rejected.[47] Thus, on the eve of war, the Ottoman Empire stood helplessly alone, an orphan of the Great Game. Djemal mused, "I should not hesitate to accept any alliance which rescued Turkey from her present position of isolation."[48] It was the kaiser who personally ordered alliance discussions to continue, in pursuit of his vision of a holy war against the British. Talks resumed on 24 July, with Turkey wiring Berlin an alliance proposal four days later.

On 1 August, however, Churchill commandeered for the Royal Navy two sea-ready British-made modern battleships destined for Turkey. The battleships *Reshadieh* and *Sultan Osman I* were both of the new Dreadnought class. David Fromkin provides a ground-breaking revisionist chapter on these events, and on the diplomacy between Turkey and Germany surrounding the seizure of these ships and Turkey's formal alliance with Germany.[49] As Turkey was desperately courting a European partner, on 2 August Enver promised Germany these two modern Dreadnoughts, in order to secure an ally. Enver, however, already knew as early as 29 July that the ships would be taken on strength by the Royal Navy when he made this agreement![50] In return, Germany demanded that Turkey take action against Russia. Enver had played Germany again! His primary goal had always been the recapture of territory lost to the Russians in 1878. On 2 August, an alliance was brokered, with Germany promising "by force of arms if need be, to defend Ottoman territory in case it should be threatened." Turkey, however, still remained neutral, as the actual wording of the treaty did not require Turkey to take up arms in defence of Germany, who was already at war with Russia. Enver had scored another brilliant diplomatic victory.

Although Britain and Russia would have preferred continued Ottoman neutrality, their actions did nothing to enhance this prospect. Moreover, the Young Turks now wanted war, as Turkey had been diplomatically craving the German guarantee to defend Ottoman territory for decades. With German backing, war provided the CUP with the opportunity to restore the glory of the Ottoman Empire, launch their pan-Turanian crusade, and regain forfeited territories. On 29 October, under secret orders from Enver, the Turkish fleet, including two German cruisers – the *Goeben* and *Breslau* which had earlier taken refuge in Turkish waters – bombarded the Russian Black Sea ports. The Ottoman Empire was now at war (for the tenth time against Russia in two hundred years). In keeping with his motivations, Enver initiated a winter campaign in 1914 against the Russians in the Caucasus to regain lost territory and unite Turkic peoples under his resurrected Ottoman Empire. The Great Game had been rekindled in the Caucasus and by 1918 would involve the main powers of Europe. This time territory was ancillary to the vital prize of oil.

The Caucasus straddles the strategic land route between Europe and Central Asia and has been at the crossroads of history and war for millennia. It was here that Prometheus was chained to a rock by Zeus as punishment for the creation of man from clay and his theft of fire for the benefit and progression of mortals. It was to Colchis in the Caucasus (Black Sea Georgian coast) that Jason and the Argonauts sailed in quest of the Golden Fleece. This same region was thought to be the homeland of the female-warrior Amazons of ancient Greek lore, and the site of the eternal fires worshipped by the Zoroastrians.[51] For over two thousand years, control of the Caucasus has been a strategic ambition for internal, external, and global forces, and while the region straddles two continents, it straddles time as well. It has been marked by regional conflict among local ethnicities, nations, and great empires jostling for geographical security, influence, and resources including oil. Steeped in war, the region is no less volatile today than it was a thousand years ago, or even during the First World War. In the fifth century, Herodotus wrote that the Caucasus comprised "the longest and loftiest of all mountain ranges, inhabited by many different tribes, most of whom live off wild scrub." The Romans required scores of interpreters when conducting business. The Arabs dubbed the region *djabal al-alsun* – "the mountain of languages" – commenting that the number of different people who lived there could be counted only by the one who made them. George Kennan, an American adventurer, recorded in 1870, "The Caucasian mountaineers as a whole are made up of fragments of almost every race and people in Europe and Western Asia, from the flat-faced Mongol to the regular-featured Greek ... How such a heterogeneous collection of the tatters, ends, and odd bits of humanity ever blended into one coherent and consistent whole I don't know; but there they are, offering problems ... which will be found very hard to resolve."[52] Indeed, the geography of the Caucasus consisting of mountains, valleys, deserts, jungle, and forests is as diverse as its inhabitants.

In 1914, the population of the greater Caucasus of roughly nine million was 60 per cent Christian and 35 per cent Muslim, with the remaining 5 per cent divided among Jews, Buddhists, and pagans. In fact, the region was home to no fewer than eighteen distinct races and forty-eight different languages and dialects.[53] Peter Hopkirk claims that the Caucasus was inhabited by "no fewer than forty-five different nationalities and ethnic groups ... In a region so riven by hatred, jealousy and mistrust – and no less so today – this might appear little better than suicidal."[54] The Caucasus, although completely absorbed by Russia in 1828, was not, as Hew Strachan notes, "ethnically Russian, but nor was it – if viewed as a whole – anybody else's."[55] Like the Roman god Janus who looked simultaneously to the past and the future, so does the Caucasus: "Burdened by territorial conflicts, radical religious movements ... and ethnic nationalism, the Caucasus ... must surely be a place of very long memories and very short tempers."[56]

The Caspian Sea is the world's largest inland body of water, five times the size of the runner-up, North America's Lake Superior. Although not connected to any ocean, the Caspian boasts 3,300 miles of coastline and is the centre of this tumultuous region (which is roughly half the size of the continental United States). Midway on the Caspian's western shore sits what Joseph Stalin dubbed the "Oil Kingdom" or the "Black City" of Baku (ancient Persian for "wind-pounded city"). On the modern-day map, Azerbaijan (inclusive of Baku) sits on the southwestern shore of the Caspian. Armenia and Georgia lie to the west, with the latter hugging the western shore of the Black Sea. Together these three now autonomous nations constitute the southern Caucasus. On the northwest side of the Caspian, above Azerbaijan and Georgia, are Russia and the turbulent northern Caucasus, including Chechnya, Ossetia, and Abkhazia. Kazakhstan is situated on the northeast side of the Caspian, with Turkmenistan to its south: "On the southern shore is Iran, with ambitions to be a dominant regional power and with interests going back to the dynasties of the Persian shahs."[57]

Geographically, some twenty-five million years ago two continental land masses collided to produce a mountain range running some seven hundred miles from the Black Sea in the northwest to the Caspian Sea in the southeast dividing the steppes and plains of Eurasia from the deserts of Anatolia and western Persia. This mountainous spine forms a natural border between the North and South Caucasus, and until recently there were few routes through the main range. The obvious bypasses were along the coasts either by sea or overland, hugging the narrow passage between mountains and water. While the eastern Caspian route, known as the Derbend Gap, was known in antiquity, the western land route shouldering the Black Sea was completed only in the 1890s when the Russians constructed a coastal road, followed by a rail line flanking the western slope of the mountains. The most hazardous route was to follow the natural rivers, contours, ravines, and passes through the heart of the range, while running the gantlet of raiders, kidnappers, slave traders, and brigands. By the 1790s, Russian army engineers had blasted this path into a modern "military highway" connecting Vladikavkaz in Russian North Ossetia to Tiflis (Tbilisi) in Georgia. While these options made north-south travel relatively accessible, it was not until the 1880s that Baku's oil boom necessitated construction of a modern east-west passage. Building of the Batum-Tiflis-Baku railway began in 1883 and was completed in 1900, finally joining the Black and Caspian Seas. In 1917, the construction of a modern east-west railway on the north side of the mountain range was finally realized.[58]

Prior to the Great War the political landscape of the Caucasus was fashioned by war and rivalry between the Russian, Persian, and Ottoman Empires. As discussed above, following the end of the Russo-Turkish War in 1878, Russia was the historical winner. However, the Russians were soon joined in the Great Game of the region by Britain, France, and Germany: "Imperial powers were seeking new clients. Old allegiances were being reworked. Religion and nationalism were being mobilized by rival claimants to legitimacy and by outside forces vying for influence. Soon Russians and Europeans would begin to see the Caucasus as a major arena in the strategic jockeying, underground intrigues, and business gambles that accompanied the quest for empire on the borderlands of Europe and Asia."[59] By design, the very nature of acquiring imperial possessions was invariably connected to the accumulation of wealth. They are not, and have never been, mutually exclusive.

Within the Russian, Ottoman, and Persian Empires, British officials often generously forwarded the interests of British financiers for political gains, with a view to creating an "informal empire" on the back of private economic enterprise. In fact, Turkey and Persia became so reliant on foreign capital and loans that they were forced to concede economic control of domestic resources to British business. After all, until the christening of the Suez Canal in 1869, the overland trade route from Britain to its imperial jewel of India traversed Ottoman domains. On the eve of the First World War, however, this foreign mammon now included oil (and corresponding railway concessions) mainly in the Middle East and the Caucasus. By 1917, the war became an instrument of Britain's oil empire.

When people think of the First World War, they automatically envision tired men caked in mud huddling in dank trenches waiting to go "over the top" to cross no-man's-land in the face of enemy machine-gun and artillery fire. They think of the sacrificial lion soldiers of the Western Front led by stubborn donkey generals, exemplified by Joan Littlewood's 1963 musical *Oh! What a Lovely War*.[60] They picture the horror of trench warfare accompanied by the casualties of Ypres, Verdun, the Somme, and Passchendaele. Our collective memory conjures images of frightened boys sent to slaughter in a futile conflict, the Great War for Civilization, and the war to end all wars. This interpretation of the conflict, however, is not complete.

While the war was won on the infamous battlefields of the Western (and to a far lesser extent, the Eastern) Front, in the final year of the war there were deviations from the typical mass armies that plagued both fronts. By 1918, the maturation of Allied strategy directly influenced the operational components of the overall British Expeditionary Force (BEF). This resulted in attempts to expedite victory by deploying missions that circumvented the Western Front. According to British Prime Minister David Lloyd George, "The events in those forgotten and despised theatres in the East brought the war to an end in 1918; but for them it might have dragged its bloody course into the spring and summer of 1919."[61] The most enigmatic of these operations was carried out by a secret force of "highly individualistic characters ... men of the do or die type" in Mesopotamia, Persia, and the Caucasus.[62] Dunsterforce exemplified the greater strategic thought that had evolved within Allied supreme command leading into the final year of the war. It was also a deviation from the typical trend to mass armies that plagued most European fronts throughout the war, and, in a sense, was a harbinger of modern special forces. According to war correspondent Edmund Candler, Dunsterville was "leading his band of adventurers into the unknown ... generally agreed that if anyone could form some sort of organism out of the Caucasus, or call into being a body with related front and flanks, capable of independent action, it was General Dunsterville."[63]

Major-General Dunsterville's first task was to organize a coherent body of resistance out of the miscellaneous, and often mutually hostile groups of anti-Bolshevik Russians, anti-Turkish Georgians, Armenians, and Assyrians spread across the Caucasus region.[64] Once they were established, the primary mission of his collective force was to guard the Transcaucasian Railway line from the Russian cities of Baku to Tiflis, in addition to protecting natural resources, including the oilfields at Baku, from the Turks (and the Germans), while defending the 51 per cent stake in the Anglo-Persian Oil Company owned by the British government. It was also hoped that Dunsterville could help establish and maintain an independent group of nations – Georgia, Armenia, and Azerbaijan – although this was a secondary objective, in order to facilitate the application of the primary concern – oil. Another reason for occupying Baku was to block the enemy route to India. The Berlin-Batum-Baku-Bokhara line was a more dangerous enemy route to the Indian frontier than was Kaiser Wilhelm's envisioned Berlin-Baghdad railway.[65] "We found it necessary to intervene in order to hold the Central Powers in check and prevent them from securing valuable supplies," wrote Lloyd George. "This was in the south, around the Caspian, where were the oil fields at Baku ... The expedition had served the purpose of keeping the oil wells of Baku out of reach of the Central Powers at a critical period of the War [and] played their part in maintaining opposition to what at one time appeared to be a very real and terrible danger of Prussian imperial expansion in Russia and across Asia ... and the oil of the Caspian."[66]

Most Allied planners expected the war to drag on well into 1919 and thus planned accordingly. The prospect of Germany or Turkey seizing the vital resources of the Caucasus and Central Asia, including Baku oil, altered Allied strategy. In 1914, out of Russia's total material output, the Ukraine and the Caucasus together supplied 87 per cent of its coal, 74 per cent of its pig iron, 63 per cent of its steel, 66 per cent of its sugar, 60 per cent of its wheat and flour, 65 per cent of its cotton, 95 per cent of its manganese, and 90 per cent of its oil.[67] These resources in the hands of an increasingly depleted and resource-exhausted Germany, brought to its knees by the Allied naval blockade, could reinvigorate its military and home front and prolong the war indefinitely. The British realized it was "very necessary to consider the future, and particularly possible enemy action in the East in 1919."[68]

With the advent of the Russian Revolution in 1917 and the Treaty of Brest-Litovsk in March 1918, the Germans, Ottomans, British, and Soviet Russians all set their sights on the Caucasus. The oilfields at Baku became the prize during the ensuing race among them. Lloyd George noted, "Russia had deserted the Entente and signed a separate peace with Germany ... We could not acquiesce in the vast accession of strength which Prussian Imperialism stood to gain from its treaty spoils, especially from its dominance over the Ukraine and ... the vast oil deposits of the Caspian. If Germany succeeded in provisioning itself freely from these sources, the whole effect of our blockade would be lost."[69] In addition, the collapse of the Eastern Front and the melting away of Russian forces on the Persian and Caucasus fronts created a vacant corridor whereby the Young Turk administration could realize its resuscitated imperialist pan-Turanian pursuit of uniting Turkic peoples and other Muslims throughout Central Asia and India, under a newly resurrected Ottoman Empire.

For the Germans, the precious resources, most importantly oil, of the Ukraine and the Caucasus were a windfall to the kaiser's ambitious Berlin to Baghdad scheme, his quest for imperial possessions, and his desire to ignite the Muslim world in jihad against British rule, primarily targeting India. On 30 July 1914, in one of his more colourful tirades, Kaiser Wilhelm, the self-declared protector of Islam, vowed that if war came, England "must be ruthlessly exposed and the mask of Christian peacefulness be publicly torn away ... Our Consuls in Turkey and India, our agents, etc. must rouse the whole Muslim world into wild rebellion against this hateful, mendacious, unprincipled nation of shopkeepers; if we are going to shed our blood, England must at least lose India."[70] Following the 2 August alliance with the Ottoman Empire, the German Foreign Office reiterated, "Revolution in India and Egypt, and in the Caucasus, is of the highest importance. The treaty with Turkey will make it possible ... to awaken the fanaticism of Islam."[71] The Ottoman entry into the war posed a direct threat to the security of British possessions in the Middle East and to India. German agents fanned out across the Middle East, North Africa, and India to stir up disaffection among Muslim populations in a not-so-secret attempt to ignite jihad against British rule.

John Buchan's 1916 bestseller *Greenmantle*, full of espionage and mysterious machinations, simply fictionalized official British views, warning of Germany's "Grand Design" of *Drang nach Osten*. According to Buchan's fictional head of British Intelligence, Sir Walter Bullivant, "The East is waiting for a revelation. It has been promised one. Some star-man, prophecy, or trinket – is coming out of the West. The Germans know, and that is the card with which they will astonish the world ... There is a dry wind blowing through the East, and the parched grasses wait a spark. And the wind is blowing towards the Indian border."[72] The memory of the 1857 Indian Mutiny and the Mahdist Rebellion in the Sudan/Egypt (1881–98) still haunted policymakers. The potential of similar occurrences could not be ignored, given a resurgence of Indian nationalism at the turn of the century, and the kaiser's spiteful bid to ignite revolution. Roughly 300 million Indian subjects were ruled by 1,200 British Indian Civil Service members and 77,000 British troops. In Egypt, the British garrison was a mere 5,000 presiding over 13 million Egyptians. The Indian Mutiny and the Mahdist Rebellion had exposed the British to the realization that the greatest threat to their eastern empire was the spread of pan-Islamic nationalism.[73]

The protection of India and the safeguarding of British oil interests formed the essence of British strategic policy in the Middle East and the Caucasus from the onset of war. These primary British war aims did not exist in isolation; rather, they formed a strategic couple. The fortunes of India rested on British dominance of these oil-bearing regions, and these geographical petroleum satellites secured, or buffered, the gates to India. To Arthur Balfour, former prime minister (1902–15), and foreign secretary from 1916 to 1919, "Every time I come to a discussion – at intervals of, say, five years – I find there is a new sphere which we have got to guard, which is supposed to protect the gateways of India. Those gateways are getting further and further from India, and I do not know how far west they are going to be brought by the General Staff."[74] The answer was all the way to the Mediterranean Sea ports on the west coast of the Middle East, and into the northern Caucasus, in order to secure oil and its transportation routes for the British Empire.

Chapter Two

Petroleum and Pipeline Politics

Shortly before the outbreak of war, Major Hubert Young of the 116th Mahratta Horse was being shuttled south along the Tigris River towards his destination of Baghdad. "Every now and then we tied up at some village, where I bought supplies while the raft-men mended and blew up any goatskin that had given way," he recalled. He also quickly realized that the British flag he had brought with him was a natural deterrent in frightening off the gangs of armed bandits who "ran alongside and threatened to shoot us." Roughly fifty miles below Mosul, he noticed the natural seepage of the oil springs of Quaiyara: "The entire river was coated with an iridescent film which looked like a contoured map on which the highest peaks were jet black and the lower levels were shown by concentric rings of every colour of the rainbow." Although for Young this oil simply provided curious scenery, it would soon become a contributing factor in plunging the Middle East and the Caucasus into four and a half years of appalling war.[1]

Oil, however, was a key objective for British policymakers before the outbreak of the Great War. At the declaration of war in August 1914, the British government had recently acquired 51 per cent of the Anglo-Persian Oil Company, and the future ships of the vaunted Royal Navy were to be propelled by oil, not by traditional coal.[2] While high-quality coal was abundant in the mines of Wales and northern England, oil was not a sizeable domestic commodity. After all, coal ensured Britain's hegemony in the industrial economy of the nineteenth century. This dichotomy compelled the secretary of state for India, Lord Crewe, to weigh in on what seemed to him an illogical conversion: "It is rather as though the owners of the *premier cru* vineyards in Gironde went about preaching the virtues of Scotch Whisky as a beverage."[3] Nevertheless, according to Winston Churchill, who became the First Lord of the Admiralty in October 1911, and was the prime proponent of the conversion from a coal to oil,

> To build any large additional number of oil burning ships meant basing our supremacy on oil. But oil was not found in appreciable quantities in our Islands. If we required it we must carry it by sea in peace or war from distant countries. We had, on the other hand, the finest supply of the best steam coal in the world, safe in our mines, under our own hand. To change the foundation of the Navy from British coal to foreign oil was a formidable decision in itself. If it were taken it must raise a whole series of intricate problems all requiring heavy initial expense ... To commit the Navy irrevocably to oil was indeed "to take arms against a sea of troubles." [Yet] we should be able to raise the whole power and efficiency of the Navy to a definitely higher level; better ships, better crews, higher economies, more intense forms of war-power – in a word, mastery itself was the prize of the venture.[4]

Not surprisingly, the debate and final resolution to convert the Royal Navy to oil occurred in tandem with the acquisition by the imperial government of a majority stake in the Anglo-Persian Oil Company. These decisions were not mutually exclusive. They were, however, hotly debated.

Since the turn of the century, Admiral John Fisher, the First Sea Lord from 1904 to 1909 and 1914 to 1915, pressed to modernize the Royal Navy, foremost by replacing coal with oil (an obsession that earned him the nicknames "the godfather of oil" and "oil maniac").[5] Fisher sought to hasten the transition to avoid a European war, or the chance that the emergent German navy "might join a Franco-Russian combination against Britain." At best, Fisher believed a powerful, modern Royal Navy could safeguard British maritime trade "for fear of German commerce raiding," while acting as deterrence for future aggression.[6] Oil-burning ships could negate the rising German naval power by increasing speed and duration at sea, and by reducing coal-stoking labour. The self-confident Fisher was the right man for the undertaking. He once replied to a question from an inquisitive King Edward VII with, "Why should I waste my time looking at all sides when I know my side is the right side?"[7]

The arms race with Germany was ongoing, and the burgeoning German navy, since the passing of the 1898 and 1900 Navy Laws, was a threat to British supremacy of the seas, the very might and embodiment of *Pax Britannica*. At the outbreak of war Britain possessed twenty Dreadnought and Super-Dreadnought battleships and four modern battle cruisers (thirteen more of various classes were under construction). On 1 August, as mentioned, Churchill commandeered two sea-ready British-made modern battleships destined for Turkey. The battleships *Reshadieh* and *Sultan Osman I* were both of the new Dreadnought class, and the *Osman* mounted more heavy guns than any battleship ever built. They were renamed the *Erin* and *Agincourt* upon seizure. The German Navy boasted thirteen Dreadnoughts and three battle cruisers (seven more variants were under construction).[8] Furthermore, the German merchant fleet was second only to Britain in size and was rapidly closing this gap. While Britain maintained an edge in the naval race, the German economy was far outpacing the industrial and capital output of the United Kingdom. As an indicator, total British defence expenditures rose from £33.4 million in 1894 to £72.5 in 1913 (117.1 per cent increase), while German military spending increased from £36.2 million to £93.4 (158 per cent increase).[9]

During the severe economic depression from 1873 to 1896, the British lost ground to Germany in most economic portfolios and in technological development. In fact, between 1870 and 1914, Germany amassed the most dynamic and all-encompassing economic and industrial growth seen in the past two hundred years. In the mid-nineteenth century, Britain accounted for 40 per cent of global trade, including two-thirds of the world's coal, half of its iron, and over 70 per cent of its steel. This overall output continued to decline to 32 per cent in 1870, and by 1914 to a mere 14 per cent. Between 1870 and 1912, British iron output fell from 50 per cent of the world's share to 12 per cent, and over the same period copper decreased from 32 to 13 per cent. German output in all fields, however, was increasing exponentially. By 1910, German coal output equalled that of Britain. German steel production increased tenfold between 1880 and 1900, leaving British steel fabrication lagging behind, as the cost of making German steel dropped to one-tenth the cost of that in the 1860s. At the outbreak of war, Germany was smelting twice the amount of pig iron as British foundries. By 1914, Germany produced nineteen million more tons of grain than Russia. Domestic German meat accounted for 95 per cent of its market share in 1913, despite the per capita meat consumption having doubled since 1870. In 1913, Britain imported 45 per cent of its meat, and 58 per cent of total daily per capita calories.[10]

Germany was also, albeit slowly, encroaching on British economic hegemony in the Persian Gulf and within the Ottoman Empire. In 1906, Britain (including India) accounted for 79 per cent of Gulf trade. In contrast, German trade was small at 4 per cent; however, this figure had doubled from 2 per cent over the previous decade, and Germany continued to make substantial gains in the region at the expense of the British.[11] More telling was the recent German arrival into the Ottoman market. In 1900, the British cut of Ottoman imports was 35 per cent, while the German share was a mere 2.5 per cent. By 1914, however, Germany's portion had risen to 12 per cent, while the British share tumbled to 21 per cent. Germany continued to make inroads into most Ottoman economic portfolios. In response, the British Board of Trade organized a working group in 1908 to analyse "steps which might be taken to strengthen the position of Great Britain in the Persian Gulf." Its memorandum concluded that it was essential to curtail "the evident efforts of Germany to create vested interests on which she may ultimately base a claim to be associated with the political as well as the commercial future of Southern Persia in the Gulf ... The whole history of the Persian Gulf has shown that commercial prosperity inevitably leads to political hegemony." Upon recommendation, in 1909 the Committee of Imperial Defence sanctioned an examination of all German threats to British interests in the Middle East. Another assignment was to ascertain pre-emptive measures necessary to ensure security of the strategic marine and land routes to India, including the Suez Canal, the rivers and trails of Mesopotamia, and the Persian Gulf to safeguard what Curzon dubbed the "maritime frontier of India."[12]

In addition to economic expansion, the German population, which grew from forty million in 1870 to sixty-seven million by 1914, was outpacing the British (and even more so, the French). During the same time period the population of the United Kingdom increased from thirty-two to forty-six million, while France saw a population growth of only two million from thirty-eight to forty million. Given the relative decline in British industrial output and trade, modernizing the Royal Navy was one way to reverse, or at least counter, the blossoming German economic and military threat. Published in 1903, civil servant Erskine Childers's bestselling fiction *The Riddle of the Sands* was a counsel to his fellow countrymen of the likely peril of a German invasion.[13] British defence policy, therefore, sprang from economic considerations as much as from perceived threats, and the "relative industrial decline obliged British policy makers to meet the growing rivalry of a hostile

Germany by recutting the strategic coat to fit the available imperial cloth."[14] Admiral Fisher warned Churchill in 1911 that if the adaptation to oil was not made, the Royal Navy would be rendered obsolete "when the new American Battleships are at sea burning oil alone and a German Motor battleship is cocking a snoot at our 'Tortoises.'"[15] Churchill was adamant that the British, under his tutelage, must confront this growing German menace, so much so that Lloyd George dubbed the Navy Churchill's "obsession." He playfully caricatured Churchill, teasing, "You have become a water creature. You forget that most of us live on land."[16]

Whether or not Churchill actually believed that the Navy was welded together by "rum, sodomy, and the lash," the thirty-six year-old had a more extensive and closer relationship with the navy within this position than any other politician of the twentieth century. Within his charge, nothing was off-limits, and he offered his opinion on matters that to many observers seemed trivial and beneath his station. Nevertheless, aside from creating a modern oil-driven navy, he prompted the Admiralty's first professional and functional naval staff, drastically improved environments for all ranks, opened up opportunities for the "Lower Decks" to attain an officer's commission, and sponsored the evolution of the embryonic naval air service. Although alienating a select portion of senior officers with "his inability to realize his own limitations as a civilian," with his typical Churchillian characteristics, he threw himself into upgrading and preparing the Royal Navy for a war that he was sure was just over the horizon. "The honour and security of the British Empire do not depend, and can never depend, on the British Army," argued Churchill during his first lengthy speech to the House of Commons in May 1901. Instead, the ex-army officer proclaimed, "It is the Navy which alone can secure the food and commerce on which the crowded population of England depends and which alone can keep this island itself free from the mighty hosts of Europe ... For more than 300 years we alone amongst the nations have wielded that mysterious and decisive force which is called sea-power." The might of the Royal Navy was, he declared, "the common treasure of mankind."[17]

Churchill was aware that sea-power was rapidly changing with the introduction of oil-fired ships. The first use of strictly oil fuel in a marine vessel was that of a Russian oil tanker in Baku in 1866, which proved unreliable and prone to mechanical malfunction. Developments, however, continued until in 1890 Italy incorporated new oil-burning technology into its naval fleet. Between 1903 and 1907, Western powers,

including Britain and the United States, had augmented their smaller
surface combatant fleets, mainly destroyers, with oil-burning vessels.[18]
While the navies of the leading powers were making the switch, merchant fleets, aside from the American merchant marine, were slower to
adopt the use of oil. In 1914, only 3 per cent of global shipping relied on
petroleum for power. Yet the use of oil fuel by the U.S. Navy rose from
360,000 barrels in 1912 to almost 6 million by 1919, while the merchant
marine consumed some 44 million barrels that same year.[19] While the
United States had vast quantities of secure domestic oil to fuel its sea-
borne vessels, Britain did not.

By the time Churchill entered office as the First Lord of the Admiralty
in 1911, the Royal Navy had built or was building fifty-six destroyers
and seventy-four submarines dependent on oil exclusively. The first
oil-fuelled modern Super-Dreadnought battleship, HMS *Queen Elizabeth*, was seaworthy in October 1912, quickly followed by her four sister
ships. The first corresponding American ship, USS *Nevada*, was seaworthy in July 1914.[20] Prior to the *Queen Elizabeth*, however, the capital
ships, the battleships that were the prize of the navy, still burned coal,
although coal was often soaked in oil before entering the ship's fur-
nace. After a series of tests conducted under Churchill, it was deduced
that coal-burning battleships could reach speeds of twenty-one knots.
Oil-propelled battleships could reach speeds upwards of twenty-five
knots (an increase of 16 per cent) and could be brought up to speed
much more quickly. Coal-fired ships took four to nine hours to reach
full power, while an oil-burning vessel took just thirty minutes. Fisher
barked at Churchill, "The first of all necessities is SPEED, so as to be
able to fight – *When* you like, *Where* you like, and *How* you like!" In
addition, oil also saved 78 per cent in fuel, 30 per cent in cargo space,
33 per cent in weight, and 25 per cent in manpower, and cut the required
number of stokers by more than half. Refuelling could be done at sea,
rather than at coaling stations, creating a radius of action four times
greater than that of coal-fired ships, and the tell-tale smoke emission
of coal, visible from up to ten kilometres away, was wholly negated.
As Fisher explained to Viscount Esher in September 1912, "Imagine a
silhouette presenting a target 33 per cent less than any living or projected battleship! No funnels – no masts – no smoke – she carries over
5,000 tons of oil, enough to take her round the world without refuelling!
Imagine what that means! ... The one sole vital point for the Navy about
the internal combustion engine is that you get rid of a mass of funnels.
I've seen a fleet 20 miles off and each ship spelling her name to me by

her funnels! And a single jet of black smoke has in my experience disclosed a fleet 40 miles off!"[21] Oil-fired ships could also mount additional and heavier guns and supplemental plated armour as a result of the buoyancy power provided by oil. Lastly, oil-fired ships were on average 12.4 per cent cheaper to build than those fuelled by coal.

Churchill listed these advantages in the parliamentary debates of 1912–14. He pleaded for a swift resolution, as did Admiral Fisher, because they had been confidentially informed by Marcus Samuel, chairman of Royal Dutch Shell, in late 1911 that a German shipping line had placed a ten-year contract for oil, in conjunction with secret experimentation by the German Navy.[22] After great deliberation and political bickering, Churchill and Fisher were mollified. The naval programs of 1912, 1913, and 1914 were the largest in expenditure and scope in the history of the Royal Navy, and all were based on the production of oil-burning vessels. Included in these overhauls was the April 1912 decision to manufacture five additional *Queen Elizabeth* and *Royal Sovereign* class oil-fired Dreadnoughts for a "Fast Division."[23] Churchill mused that "the supreme ships of the Navy, on which our life depended, were fed by oil and could only be fed by oil." The Royal Commission on Oil and the Oil Engine (also referred to as the Royal Commission on Fuel and Engines) was established in May 1912, headed by Fisher, to investigate the issues and potential problems raised by the oil conversion. Fisher, previously retired, proclaimed, "Though not intending to work again, yet my consuming passion for oil and the oil engine made me accept the chairmanship." His instructions from Churchill were blunt: "You have got to find the oil: to show how it can be stored cheaply: how it can be purchased regularly and cheaply in peace, and with absolute certainty in war. Then by all means develop the application in the best possible way to existing and prospective ships."[24]

The commission's initial report, *Memorandum on Oil and Oil Engines*, was released in 1912, followed by two more in 1913. The American naval attaché in London lauded the British advances in turbine technology, gun mountings, and in oil-fired "liquid fuel boilers."[25] Fisher increased the tempo of the committee after he received concrete intelligence that the German Navy had decided on the coal to oil exchange. "The one all-pervading, all absorbing thought," the fiery, temperamental Fisher proclaimed, "is to get in first with motor ships [diesel engines] before the Germans! Owing to our apathy during the last two years, they are ahead! *They have killed 15 men in experiments* [with oil engines] *and we have not killed one!* And a d–d fool of an English politician told me the other day that he thinks this creditable on us." The main impediment, according to Fisher, was that "oil don't grow in England."[26] Less than 2 per cent of global oil production in 1913 was within the British Empire.[27] Even the acclaimed *Economist* argued for national control of oil supplies. The transformation had been initiated before a tenable supply of oil had been secured. Although bids to supply the Royal Navy's liquid fuel were forwarded by twenty-five companies operating in remote corners of the British Empire, such as Newfoundland, Egypt, and Nigeria, the contract of enormous profit was destined to fall to one of the only two viable companies – Royal Dutch Shell Group (a merger of Royal Dutch and Shell in 1907) or the much smaller and teetering Anglo-Persian Oil Company. Fierce debate among the Foreign Office, the India Office, the Admiralty, and the companies themselves, accompanied a final verdict. At the outbreak of war, critics of Churchill and Fisher were forced to concede their errors, or as one naval adherent observed, "They have pissed on Churchill's plant for three years – now they expect blooms within a month!"[28]

Oil itself was a relative newcomer to the global economy. Indigenous peoples had used natural seepages for a variety of purposes for millennia – as far back as 4,000 BCE in Mesopotamia and China. Petroleum is mentioned on several occasions in the Old Testament, including "pitch" used in the construction of Noah's Ark. The Tower of Babel, Solomon's Temple, the Pyramids, the Sphinx, and the Hanging Gardens of Babylon were constructed in part by asphalt mortar or waterproofing pitch. Natural gas seepages burned at the temples of the Oracles at Delphi and Baku. Some evidence suggests that the Chinese used petroleum and gas for heat and light around 0–10 CE, fabricating bamboo "pipelines" to transport it from its source to its place of use. In the Americas, the Inca, Aztec, and the Iroquois used oil for a multitude of medicinal and ceremonial purposes, as recorded in the diaries of early European explorers. It was also used as a weapon in the form of a catapult predecessor to the Molotov cocktail, or "burning ship torpedoes" by the Persians, Seleucids, Parthians, Romans, and Byzantines. A Roman general doused a drift of pigs with oil, set them alight, and drove them through his enemy's ranks. The Greeks floated oil on the coast and set it ablaze as a defensive obstacle – a tactic the British contemplated during the Second World War in the event of Germany's 1940 Operation Sea Lion invasion.[29]

Commercial oil ventures, however, originated in the United States and Canada in the mid-1850s, coinciding with the dawn of the Industrial

2.1 "Next!" Cartoon from *Puck* depicting a Standard Oil storage tank as an octopus with many tentacles wrapped around the steel, copper, and shipping industries, as well as, a state house, the U.S. Capitol, and one tentacle reaching for the White House, 7 September 1904 (Library of Congress).

Revolution and the infancy of the internal combustion engine.[30] Edwin Drake is erroneously credited with pioneering the first commercial oil well at Titusville, Pennsylvania, in 1859, as similar technology had been used in Poland in 1854, Germany in 1857, and Canada in 1858. In 1870, the American self-made millionaire John D. Rockefeller founded Standard Oil, signalling the birth of the modern oil industry, and quickly monopolized American and foreign oil. His domination soon came to control all facets associated with oil production, including shipping and railway transportation. He constructed the first trunk line from the Pennsylvanian fields to Pittsburgh, a distance of some 60 miles. By 1900, eighteen thousand miles of pipeline were active in the United States. By the time Rockefeller's Standard Oil Company was controversially brought down in 1911 by the *Sherman Antitrust Act* (1890), it controlled 90 per cent of U.S. oil and nearly 80 per cent of global oil production.[31] While Standard was fragmented into thirty-four smaller companies, it quickly reverted to a monopoly as Standard Oil of

Table 2.1 Foreign investment in Romanian oil, 1914

Country	%	Quantity imported (tons)
Germany/Austria-Hungary	31	203,479
Great Britain	21	232,800
Netherlands	20	
France/Belgium	14	151,402
United States	7	
Romania	5	
Italy/Switzerland	2	118,643

Source: Pearton, *Oil and the Romanian State*, 68–9. By 1878 the Russian rouble had made the Romanian leu worthless; therefore, until 1914, most business was conducted in French, Turkish, Russian, or British currencies.

New Jersey (Exxon) and Standard Oil of New York (Mobil) became dominant by swallowing up smaller rivals and expanding their international portfolios. Global oil exploration quickly followed Rockefeller's Standard archetype. Wells across the globe were producing oil, albeit in varying quantities and qualities, by the 1880s, including Burma (1856), Galicia (1862), Romania (1863), Alsace (1870), and the Caucasus (1870), all of which adopted the pioneering Canadian system of drilling. Hundreds of expert Canadian drillers and engineers from the Oil Springs/Petrolia/Sarnia-Lambton region of southern Ontario were imported to these far-flung, upstart, oil-producing areas.[32]

By 1900, Romania's oil production was relatively small, 160,000 annual tons from 188 wells, in the absence of a Rockefeller or Nobel, who were blacklisted by the government. On a trip to Russia in the summer of 1912, the kaiser stressed to Russian diplomats the "importance of establishing a pan-European oil trust that would be able to compete with American Standard Oil."[33] Prime Minister Dimitrie Sturdza proclaimed to Romania's oil barons at its oil capital, Ploieşti, "Taking as a model the motto of Americans, 'America for Americans,' I have my motto 'Europe for Europeans' and especially 'Romania for Romanians' ... Guard yourself against the Standard Oil Trust and all who are in league with it." This changed in 1904, however, when Standard Oil purchased all Romanian petroleum holdings under its subordinate company Romano-Americana S.A., which quickly acquired more drilling lands and permits. One year later, profit margins had tripled. This led to an increase in oil exploration, and by 1914 companies from ten countries were represented in Romanian oil. As a result of this foreign

2.2 The Anglo-Persian Oil Company's Abadan Refinery, ca 1919
(Oil Museum of Canada).

capital and expertise, output increased from 160,000 tons in 1900 to
1,675,000 tons in 1914.[34]

At the onset of hostilities in 1914, the largest refinery was on the Persian island of Abadan at the mouth of the Shatt-al-Arab, constructed
in 1912–13 by the Anglo-Persian Oil Company, a subsidiary of the
Glasgow-based syndicate, Burmah Oil Company.[35] From the petroleum
fields, 135 miles of pipeline, the first oil artery in the Middle East, ran
south along the Karun River to the refinery at Abadan. Oil had first
been struck in Persia in 1908 by William D'Arcy, an eccentric Anglo-
Australian, who had, after cooperation and aid from the Crown, secured
oil rights in Persia and Mesopotamia in 1901. His oil expedition was the
first of its kind in the Middle East. D'Arcy's initial enterprise and oil
reconnaissance paid dividends. His experimental capitalist venture led
to the creation of the Anglo-Persian Oil Company, which was given a

sixty-year concession to oil rights across the Persian Empire, excluding the five northern provinces – Azerbaijan, Gilan, Mazandaran, Astarabad, and Khurasan – which by this time were subject to the Russian sphere of influence under the 1907 Anglo-Russo accord detailed in the previous chapter. In return, the Persian monarchy received a lump sum of forty thousand pounds, 16 per cent of the annual net profits, and four gold shillings for every exportable ton of oil. This Anglo-Persian agreement became the precedent for all future oil concessions in the Middle East for the next five decades.

In global production, however, Persia was an insignificant player. While there was potential for great oil wealth, it was still relatively dormant. Persia was an economic backwater boasting only eight miles of railway track, eight hundred miles of roads (two hundred paved), which were little more than mule tracks, and only three cities with a population larger than 100,000 in a country of roughly 10–12 million people. While a modern economy was slowly developing, Persia remained one of the most backward countries in the world. In 1913, the United States produced 140 times more oil than Persia and yielded 63 per cent of the world's petroleum. The tentacles of Rockefeller's oil imperialism were far reaching. Standard Oil began prospecting in Mesopotamia in 1910, two years after D'Arcy struck oil in Persia. In 1913, Standard had acquired rights to drill in modern-day Syria and Palestine. Although Britain (and America) sought alternative sources, 80 per cent of British oil burned during the First World War was still pumped from domestic American wells.[36]

While the oil industry in Mesopotamia and Persia was still in relative infancy at the outbreak of war, the production in the Caucasus had been booming since the early 1880s. On his travels during the winter of 1271–2, Marco Polo reported an oil spring near Baku that "spurts in voluptuous quantities, so much that one could fill a hundred shiploads at the same time with them. This oil is unfit for consumption, but it burns in an excellent way and moreover serves as a remedy against camels' scabies [mange]. Folk from remote areas come here to fetch this oil, since in none of the surrounding lands oil of this calibre can be found."[37] Baku was the site of the "eternal pillars of fire," the result of flammable gas escaping from porous limestone, and its oracle, worshipped by the Zoroastrians. The mountainous Caucasus, at the crossroads of the Ottoman, Russian, and Persian Empires, had traded hands, until the Persians relinquished their territorial claims in the 1820s. Aside from a short period spawned by the chaos of the 1917 Russian Revolution and ensuing paroxysm of civil wars, the Caucasus region remained within the Russian sphere until the collapse of the Soviet Union, and the 1991 creation of the nation states of Georgia, Azerbaijan, and Armenia (mirroring their short-lived independence in 1918). Baku was officially integrated into the Russian Empire with the 1813 Treaty of Gulistan.[38]

By 1829, there were eighty-two hand-dug oil pits at Baku, and the first commercial wells were drilled in 1871.[39] A British observer remarked, "The workmen who dig run a good deal of risk. There are many days on which they consider it most unlucky to work. It is no exaggeration to say that there are about two hundred such days in a year."[40] By 1873, after tsarist Russia relaxed private land ownership laws in Baku, the city boasted twenty small refineries, and it was at this time that the Nobel brothers and the Rothschild family entered the Baku oil scene. The Nobels paid their workers handsomely to avoid strikes, housed them in comfortable facilities, and constructed a "leisure park" for their use. They also introduced the first oil tanker *Zoroaster* in 1878, and the world's first oilfield-to-refinery pipeline in 1889, essentially creating a modern, fully integrated corporation (a business model later mirrored in 1908 by Henry Ford in Detroit). In 1879, Rothschild secured the licence to build a railway from Baku to the tiny fishing hamlet of Batum on the Black Sea, which was quickly followed by the Nobels' modern pipeline. By 1883 the line was operational, transforming Batum into a modern oil-exporting terminal almost overnight.[41] Although still smaller than Tiflis and Baku, by 1895 Batum was home to roughly twenty-eight thousand diverse inhabitants. As a 1913 Russian tourist guidebook described the blossoming urban city, "Georgians predominantly are salesmen, tavern-keepers, cooks, servants, bartenders, carriage drivers; the Armenians are traders and shopkeepers, porters, draymen; the Greeks are bakers, shoemakers, blanket-makers, traders; the Persians are gardeners, vegetable and fruit growers, keepers of eating houses and tea-houses; the Turks are fishermen, felucca sailors, port workers, keepers of coffee-houses; the Jews are traders; the Ajarians are immigrant peasants, farmers, and wardens. Apart from that, there are a lot of foreigners, thanks to the many different offices and steamship companies."[42] Like Baku, while this ethnic melting pot provided for an array of cultural shops, eateries, trade-specialties, and curios, it also fashioned economic and religious disparity and a seething racial divide.

In 1884, the Baku wells produced 10.8 million barrels, equivalent to one-third of total U.S. output, and a monumental increase from fewer

Table 2.2 Foreign investment in Russian oil, 1914 (thousands of 1914 gold dollars)

Foreign investor	Amount
United States	620
Belgium	3,800
Netherlands	5,600
Germany	7,300
France	26,400
Great Britain	86,000

Source: Hassmann, *Oil in the Soviet Union*, 28.

than 600,000 a decade earlier. By 1888, production reached 23 million barrels, more than four-fifths of American production, and at the turn of the century Baku produced nearly 52 per cent of the world's oil. By 1914, 320 companies were extracting Russian oil. Baku boasted 2,541 operational wells, owned by 198 different oil firms, including Standard and Royal Dutch Shell; however, British oil companies produced 43 per cent of Baku oil.[43]

The boomtown of Baku, an equivalent to the upstart gold- and silver-mining towns of San Francisco, Tombstone, or Dawson City in the United States and Canada, became a cosmopolitan mecca overnight. Opulent palaces and mansions, swank hotels, clubs, and casinos, fine-dining restaurants, theatres, and one of the world's finest opera houses littered the shoreline and grand promenade under the canopy of electric light, as foreigners and money poured into the city. The opera house built in 1883 by the Azeri oil baron and philanthropist Zeynalabdin Taghiyev staged the world's first Islamic opera, *Leyli and Majnun*, in 1908, written by Azerbaijani composer Uzeir Hajibeyov. The illiterate Taghiyev also constructed the world's first Islamic school for girls in Baku in 1901, followed by the Azerbaijan State University in 1919. These were among the first Muslim institutions to use the Latin alphabet instead of the Arabic script. He personally set up academic scholarships and sponsored young Azerbaijani students to study abroad in the universities of Europe in order to promote the international modernization of his country. He promoted universal suffrage, which was achieved in 1918, albeit briefly, when women in Azerbaijan gained the right to vote. He funded journals, newspapers, and a variety of creative endeavours, and the artistic and intellectual culture of Baku flourished.[44]

According to the British envoy Harry Luke, Baku combined "the opulence of a Riviera Casino, the vulgarity of some upstart town in

Table 2.3 Russian oil production by region, 1908–1916 (thousands of tons)

Year	Baku	Grozny	Maikop
1908	7,570	850	1
1910	8,230	1,210	21
1912	7,720	1,070	151
1914	6,950	1,610	66
1916	7,820	1,560	32

Source: Hassmann, *Oil in the Soviet Union*, 25.

the New World, the unrestrained lavishness of pre-War Russia and the colours and savours of the mediaeval East." The population rose from 14,000 in 1872 to over 240,000 on the eve of the war, made up of 35 per cent Azerbaijani Muslims, 25 per cent Russians, and 12 per cent Armenians. Baku rivalled Tiflis as the largest urban centre in the Caucasus, although at the turn of the century less than half of the population had actually been born in Baku.[45] This ethnic and religious diversity was, however, a powder keg.

The majority of the wealth and entrepreneurial positions belonged to Armenians, Russians, Jews, and foreign investors, while the Muslim population provided the labour. Strikes, fomented by socialist reformers, were frequent and violent, and devastated oil production. Between 1904 and 1913, Russian global oil exports fell from 31 to 9 per cent. Baku, however, still produced 80 per cent of Russia's total output and was the busiest port in the Russian Empire (Baku was also home to Russia's largest cotton and flour mills). The other Caucasus oil regions around Grozny and Maikop accounted for the majority of Russia's remaining 20 per cent, both of which by 1910 were primarily British owned. Oil extraction in Grozny began in 1833, with marketable production ensuing in 1890. Grozny developed into the second-largest oil centre in Russia, albeit far behind Baku. Although commercial drilling of the Maikop fields began in 1897, it took until 1908 for these wells to become productive. In addition to oil, by 1913, the region produced one-third of the world's manganese and had extensive enterprises in the mining and extraction of copper, silver, zinc, iron, gold, cobalt, salt, and borax.[46]

The Georgian-born Iosif Dzhugashvili, better known as Joseph Stalin, dubbed Baku "the Oil Kingdom" and remarked that he had honed his revolutionary skills as an agitator and strike organizer in the oilfields of Baku.[47] While the labour and ethnic unrest of the early 1900s – most

Table 2.4 British capital among Russian oil regions, 1914

Region	British capital (millions 1914 gold dollars)	British concentration (% of total concentration in region)
Baku	25.0	60
Grozny	13.2	50
Maikop	12.4	90
British total	50.6	
Others	35.4	
Total	86.0	

Source: Hassmann, *Oil in the Soviet Union*, 25.

notably the strikes associated with what Vladimir Lenin dubbed the "great rehearsal" of the 1905 Russian Revolution – stymied oil production, the oil potential and infrastructure remained. Baku became the prize for competing nations, during the pre-war Great Game and during the final year of the war. (Baku and its strategic importance will be further detailed in chapter 4).

Only two candidates met the criteria to supply oil to the refurbished Royal Navy – the Anglo-Persian Oil Company and Royal Dutch Shell. The latter was 60 per cent Dutch owned and 40 per cent British owned and had in 1912 purchased 25 per cent of the Turkish Petroleum Company (TPC). The German Deutsche Bank owned an equal 25 per cent of the TPC, and 50 per cent was maintained by the Turkish National Bank, which, ironically, was a British venture. Established in 1909 by wealthy British bankers at the request of King Edward VII to promote British interests, the bank sought "to act as an agent of Empire, and in doing so had tried quite genuinely to follow its government's wishes ... in so far as they helped strengthen the British position in an area of strategic importance. Mesopotamia, at the head of the Persian Gulf, guarding the major route to India, was such an area, and British interests in Mesopotamia were upheld."[48] In form and function, the Turkish Bank mirrored the Imperial Bank of Persia, which had been created as a financial agent of imperialism in 1889. These were strategic bids to annex colonies for the informal British economic empire and, in doing so, to wield multiple instruments of economic and political power in the Middle East. Thus far, British oil interests were limited to Russia and the United States, where, unlike Turkey and Persia, direct British diplomatic patronage was unnecessary or futile.

Also in 1912, Royal Dutch Shell purchased all of the Rothschild oil possessions in the Caucasus. In June 1913, Churchill tabled a memorandum, "Oil Fuel Supply for His Majesty's Navy," citing three main objectives:

(I) A wide geographical distribution to guard against local failure of supplies, to avoid undue reliance of any particular source, and to preserve as much expansive power or elasticity in regard to each source as possible;

(II) To frustrate as effectively as possible, by keeping alive independent competitive sources of supply, the formation of a universal oil monopoly and thus to safeguard the Admiralty from becoming dependent on any single combination; and,

(III) To draw oil supplies as far as possible from sources under British control or British influence and along those sea routes which the Navy can most easily and most surely protect.[49]

Discussion followed Churchill's report throughout the remainder of 1913 and into 1914, and it was generally agreed that,

in view of the vital necessity to the navy of a continuous and independent supply of oil in the future it was desirable that the Government should acquire a controlling interest in trustworthy sources of supply, both at home and abroad ... Our ultimate policy is that the Admiralty should become the independent owner and producer of its own supplies of liquid fuel, first by building up an oil reserve sufficient to make us safe in war and able to over-ride price fluctuations in peace; second, by acquiring the power to deal in crude oils as they come cheaply into the market ... third ... we must become the owners, or at any rate, the controllers at the source of a least a proportion of the supply of natural oil which we require.[50]

Given the aforementioned criteria, after much debate and lobbying by both firms, the Anglo-Persian Oil Company secured the contract. According to Churchill, Persia was "the only part of the world under British control from which they can rely, with any confidence, on sufficient supplies."[51] To this he added, "Look out upon the wide expanse of the oil regions of the world. Two gigantic corporations – one in either hemisphere – stand out predominantly."[52] Churchill was aware that Standard Oil and Royal Dutch Shell had a monopoly on global oil production. He intended to break their grip on petroleum resources by circumventing both.

It was deduced that Royal Dutch Shell, with its foreign majority ownership and its connection to the Turkish Petroleum Company, would be

2.3 Winston Churchill with Kaiser Wilhelm II at German Army Manoeuvres, 1906. Signed and inscribed by Wilhelm in English: "Herr Viscount Churchill, With Best Wishes for a Happy New Year, 1907. Wilhelm F.R." In private, the kaiser ranted to his inner circle that Churchill "was a man who could not be trusted" and had the unwelcome habit of showing up uninvited to German army manoeuvres (Library of Congress).

Table 2.5 Production of oil companies in Russia, 1910–1914 (thousands of tons)

Company	1910	1912	1914
Russian General Oil Corp. (U.K. holding and financed)	2,724	2,280	1,977
Royal Dutch Shell (40% U.K. owned)	1,260	1,262	1,513
Nobel	1,226	1,305	1,239
Other producers	4,470	4,514	4,493
Total	9,680	9,361	9,222

Source: Hassmann, *Oil in the Soviet Union*, 27.

subject to strong German influence. Furthermore, its sources of oil were scattered across the Dutch East Indies (53 per cent), the Russian Caucasus (29 per cent), and Romania (17 per cent), none of which were British imperial possessions, nor subject to British sway, and were deemed vulnerable in times of war. Conversely, supporting the bid of the Anglo-Persian company ensured that the always distressing vital interests of India were "sufficiently safe-guarded so long as the British sphere [in Persia] remains intact and British power is supreme at sea and controls the entrance to the Gulf."[53] In addition, the APOC relied on Shell tankers for transport. The tanker capacity of the Admiralty, however, was ever increasing. With this new contract, Shell could be completely relegated, and the Admiralty could transport its own oil when and where it desired, under escorting convoys of naval gunships.

According to Raymond Aron in his seminal study *The Century of Total War* (1954), "During the period between 1870 and 1914, there were instances in which diplomatic services of nations were mobilized on behalf of capitalists, and in which they vigorously defended certain private investments (as in Venezuela and Persia) ... they felt there were valid reasons for defending certain economic positions. The fact is that under the system of private ownership, the ambitions of certain corporations are genuinely identical with national interests."[54] Beginning with Churchill's 1914 Crown purchase of a majority stake in the APOC, oil has since occupied the pre-eminent place in this political-pecuniary partnership.

Before the deal was completed, however, the British executed a diplomatic and economic coup on the Turkish Petroleum Company, as outlined in the previous chapter. In April 1913, the foreign secretary, Sir Edward Grey, bluntly told the Ottoman ambassador in London that Britain was expecting "the Ottoman Government to make without delay arrangements in regard to the oil wells of Mesopotamia which will ensure British control and meet with their approval in matters of detail."[55] In both July 1913 and March 1914, Grey again protested against the Ottoman plans to raise an oil company in the *vilayets* of Mosul, Baghdad, and Basra. He sent strong political and economic ultimatums and bluntly stated that any company set up in these regions had to offer the APOC at least a 50 per cent stake. Shortly after Grey's March 1914 threats, and corresponding negotiations, the Turkish company was amalgamated into the Anglo-Persian, which received 50 per cent ownership. Essentially, the 50 per cent stake held by the Turkish National Bank was transferred to the APOC, with the Deutsche Bank and Royal Dutch Shell retaining their respective 25 per cent holdings.[56] "In the race to secure strategic control of the prized oil concessions in Mesopotamia," writes Christopher Clark, "British banks and investors, backed by London, easily manoeuvered the Germans into positions of disadvantage with a combination of hard bargaining and ruthless financial diplomacy."[57]

On 17 June 1914, Churchill's oil bill, the Anglo-Persian Oil Company Agreement, passed by a resounding vote of 254 to 18. Churchill's victory for the government acquisition of a private company was unprecedented, save for Prime Minster Benjamin Disraeli's 1875 procurement of stock in the Suez Canal, which was also a strategic and economic decision. With Churchill's bill, the British government acquired 51 per cent of the stock in return for an upfront investment of £2.2 million. The production target was six million tons of oil over a twenty-year contract, at a fixed price of 30s. a ton, excluding a rebate of up to 10s. per ton in proportion to profits. The Admiralty also reserved the power to sell surpluses. More importantly, the British government secured two positions on the board of directors that had veto power on any issues relating to Admiralty oil and in broader political matters. For the British Government it was an extremely lucrative deal. As an indicator, between January 1911 and June 1913 oil prices rose from 37s. to 77s. per ton. As mentioned, however, the Admiralty had secured a static price of 30s. per ton. On the day the agreement was ratified, the London market price was 65s. a ton, and at the outbreak of war in August, oil price quotations ceased altogether.[58]

Immediately following the assenting vote in Parliament, Churchill reorganized and repositioned the Mediterranean Fleet to add muscle to the Atlantic Fleet via Gibraltar. This strategic British Overseas Territory was the linchpin (or rock) between the Atlantic and Mediterranean waterways and protected the Suez Canal and the newly acquired

Table 2.6 Anglo-Persian Oil Company annual production, 1912–1925 (tons)

Year	Production	Year	Production	Year	Production
1912	43,000	1917	644,000	1922	2,327,221
1913	80,000	1918	897,000	1923	2,959,028
1914	274,000	1919	1,106,415	1924	3,714,216
1915	376,000	1920	1,385,301	1925	4,333,933
1916	459,000	1921	1,743,557		

Source: Ferrier, *The History of the British Petroleum Company*, 271, 370.

Persian oil fields via Malta, the eastern Mediterranean, the Red Sea, and the Gulf of Aden. The bill received royal assent on 10 August, six days after Britain's declaration of war on Germany. For the first time in history, Churchill had orchestrated and cemented the enduring strategic marriage of oil, national security, and global military and economic power, and "made the paradigm of the shift that occurred in the strategic perception of oil."[59] The Great War buttressed this perception. According to R.W. Ferrier, the official biographer of the APOC, it was "the obvious success of the operations in Persia in coping with the increasing war-time demands for fuel oil which principally effected the development of the company."[60] Britain's recently acquired oil, however, needed immediate protection at "the entrance to the Gulf."

During the first week of August, civil and military authorities in London and Delhi initiated contingency plans to safeguard British oil interests in Mesopotamia and Persia, as the India Office held the administrative mandate for the Persian Gulf region. While Churchill had misgivings about the mission, on 10 September, the Admiralty assigned the ships *Espiegle*, *Odin*, and *Lawrence* to protect the refinery at Abadan. His statement of 1 September that "there is little likelihood of any troops being available for this purpose ... we shall have to buy our oil from elsewhere" has been taken out of context. Although he supported the protection of the APOC, which he so recently acquired, Churchill was already lobbying for a campaign in the Dardanelles (Gallipoli) to deal "with the Turks at the centre" and to reopen this vital strait for Russian resources, including Baku oil.[61] By throwing full support behind the Abadan-Basra mission, he would have undermined his goal of securing resources for his push up the Dardanelles, which eventually occurred in 1915–16. The Gallipoli campaign ended in disaster and Churchill's dismissal/resignation from his naval post. By the third week of September 1914, however, concrete plans were initiated to send land forces from India to the head of the Persian Gulf. The 6th (Poona) Division, under the command of Lieutenant-General Sir Arthur Barrett, was selected for the task and was designated Indian Expeditionary Force D (IEF D). Its 16th Infantry Brigade, of roughly five thousand men, was ordered to deploy immediately. The 17th and 18th Brigades were designated as follow-on forces.[62]

According to A.J. Barker, protecting British oil supplies was "the original object of the expedition ... since oil interests were becoming the prime concern of Britain's economy." Oil was not, however, the only concern. By occupying the Basra-Abadan region, the British believed they could stymie Turkish-German aims in the region, secure the continued allegiance of the Gulf sheikhs (through a show of force and increased financial favours), and rally local populations to the British cause, ensuring that the Arabs and Persians did not join in the Turkish-German propagandist jihad.[63] In reality, the impetus for creating a secondary British theatre of war at the initiation of hostilities, far removed from the Western Front, was protection of British oil interests, chained to the protection of the approaches to India.

The 16th Brigade left Bombay (Mumbai) on 16 October with orders to occupy Abadan Island "with the object of protecting the oil refineries, tanks, and pipeline [and] Assuring the local Arabs of our support against Turkey," while initiating cordial relations with "Bin Saud, Shaik of Nejd, the Shaik of Muhammerah, [and] the Shaik of Kuwait."[64] On 6 November, one day after Britain's declaration of war on Turkey, the first landing parties of five hundred men, together with Royal Marines, occupied the fort at Fao against light Turkish resistance. Seemingly a minor engagement, Fao was the interface between the Turkish telegraph lines from upper Mesopotamia and the British lines to India and Persia, and was the logical first strike of the Mesopotamian campaign. The heaviest fighting to gain a foothold on the Persian Gulf occurred on 17 November on the outskirts of Basra during the Battle of Sahil. Following this intense engagement, the British advance on Basra, situated just south of the confluence of the Tigris and Euphrates Rivers, was unopposed, as "Basra itself was not so much captured by the British as abandoned by the Turks."[65] The British occupation of Basra was formalized with a ceremonial march and gunfire salute on 23 November. Once in Basra, it appeared, at least for the moment, that the British had "effectively achieved their objectives in Mesopotamia. They had driven the Ottomans from the head of the Persian Gulf and protected the strategic oil facilities in Abadan."[66] There was, however, a strong case being made, led by Sir Percy Sykes, to pursue the retreating Turks and to push north to Baghdad. These relatively easy gains in Mesopotamia at the outbreak of war gave the British a distorted sense of their own fighting abilities and led them to dangerously underestimate Turkish capabilities and resolve in the region.

From their headquarters at Basra, reinforced British forces slowly pushed north along the Tigris in December towards Qurna, the purported biblical site of the Garden of Eden, where the two great rivers of life meet. Baghdad was, and had to be, the goal. This advance would provide defence-in-depth to protect Basra and the oilfields, pipeline, and refinery against the inevitable Ottoman counter-attack. Qurna was also closer to the actual oil installations than was Basra. In early March 1915, IEF D was expanded and reconstituted as a corps, following complaints from the India Office about its weak strength. The orders that newly arrived commander Lieutenant-General Sir John Nixon received in April initiated what would be an ever-growing accretion of British forces in the Middle East for the remainder of the war:

> Your force is intended to retain complete control of the lower portion of Mesopotamia, comprising the Basra *Vilayet* and including all outlets to the sea and such portions of the neighbouring territories as may affect your operations. So far as you may find feasible with prejudicing your main operations you should endeavour to secure the safety of the oil-fields, pipeline and refineries of the Anglo-Persian Oil Company. After acquainting yourself on the spot with the present situation you will submit: (i) A plan for the effective occupation of the Basra *Vilayet*; (ii) A plan for a subsequent advance on Baghdad. In all operations you will respect the neutrality of Persia.[67]

When Nixon requested an additional brigade from India to undertake his implied offensive operations, the India Office retorted, "During the hot season Nixon must clearly understand that he is to confine himself to the defence of oil interests in Arabistan and of the Basra *Vilayet*."[68] This geographical area, however, also included Amara, some 90 miles north of Basra, and Nasiriya 135 miles northwest of Basra. Protecting the oil installations at Abadan, and its 4,300 employees, however important, was clearly "a formal justification for invasion rather than a final objective." Sir Percy Cox, the secretary to the government of India and the political officer to British Mesopotamian forces, raised the notion of "an advance to Bagdad ... difficult to see how we can well avoid taking over Bagdad," on 23 November, the same day the British formally entered Basra.[69] For the remainder of the war, Britain pushed on with Middle Eastern campaigns that were "relatively cheap in human life and valuable in terms of British power," and secured much-coveted oilfields.[70]

As British forces pushed north up the rivers towards Baghdad, engineers and geologists of the APOC were close behind conducting "extensive geological reconnaissance" and building numerous railways. Their final report of April 1918 confirmed large oilfields around Basra, Amarah, Qurnah, Rumaylah, Falluja, Nasiriyah, Karbala, Tikrit, Baghdad, and Mosul – names that became commonplace on the nightly news during the 2003 invasion of Iraq by the U.S.-led coalition. On the basis of early reports of 1914–15, the Admiralty and the Foreign Office concluded that the APOC should "be given complete oil rights over any portion of the Turkish Empire which may come under British influence … The oil question has an important bearing upon considerations of foreign policy."[71]

In reality, as early as April 1914, the German emissary to Baghdad was emphasizing to his government the importance of the oil facilities at Abadan and Baku. In September and October 1914 the Germans initiated a scheme to use the ethnic instability of Baku to bring oil production to a standstill. It was deemed that the destruction of oil stocks and the disruption of drilling would cripple Russian rail transport within three months, thus severely hampering Russian capabilities on the Eastern Front. This destabilization of Baku did not occur, at least for the time being.[72] Likewise, by late August 1914, contingency plans were made to capture the Karun oilfields and the Abadan oil installations whereby Germany would acquire "an oil source of unending wealth [that] would be of the greatest value for the Reich naval office." It was also deduced that by capturing or at worst destroying the refinery, the Royal Navy would be denied this valuable commodity, the British would be forced to send troops to the Gulf, and the Germans could potentially consolidate their ambitions towards India.

A small German force led by Wilhelm "of Persia" Wassmuss (the German equivalent to Lawrence of Arabia) penetrated British lines in February 1915 and, aided by inadequate local anti-British Arabs, repeatedly cut the pipeline from February through April. British war correspondent Edmund Candler recalled,

The immense columns of smoke and flame where the escaped oil was burning day and night depressed me with an uncomfortable sense of waste.

2.4 The Anglo-Persian Oil Company fields at Karun, Persia, 1912
(Oil Museum of Canada).

The flames leapt up sixty feet in the air in a circumference of twenty with
a roar like breakers, and above them rose a solid column of blue smoke ...
The manager laughed at my economic scruples. "If you were a millionaire," he said, "you wouldn't mind if your butler opened an extra bottle of
port." The oil, it seems, is inexhaustible ... it flows without obstruction to
the refinery at Abadan on the Shatt-al-Arab, 142 miles from the fields ...
the pipes which had been cut in February, were still under repair.[73]

Canadian driller Jim Brown and three of his fellow countrymen tried to
hold off the "German soldiers and their Arab allies as they attacked the
camp." Jim's grandson later recounted his grandfather's ordeal: "Their
attackers killed some of the workers, so they took off into the mountains and hid. The company at first wrote them off as dead because everyone else had left, and people on other rigs had been killed. They lived

up in the mountains on raw birds and raw mutton because they didn't want to build any fires that would be spotted. More than one hundred kilometres from their base, the small group survived for four months before they were spotted and returned to the camp."[74] In June, the British, with the help of the local Persian Bakhtiari tribe (and numerous financial handouts), secured and repaired the damaged pipeline. The grinding advance of IEF D north along the Tigris River towards Baghdad precluded any further attempts by the Turks or the Germans to conduct operations against the Karun/Abadan oil installations.[75]

Throughout the war, the race to secure oilfields to fuel modern warfare on European Fronts began among Britain, Germany, Turkey, and Russia, which itself was being consumed by an accelerating civil war. By late 1917, within the pervasive disorder and anarchy of the Russian Revolution and corresponding civil war, Germany, like Britain and Turkey, had designs on capturing the Caspian oil fields at Baku: "Western armies found themselves at war with Russia, their former ally; and oil became a crucial issue."[76] Alliances vanished and new relationships were forged. Germans fought Turks and the British flew Bolshevik flags. It was into this confused and chaotic "sideshow" theatre of war that Dunsterforce was deployed to safeguard British oil interests in the Caucasus. As mentioned, by late 1917, oil was paramount to British policy in the Middle East and the Caucasus regions. The empire, on which the sun never set was, however, nearing its breaking point.

Chapter Three

The Last Crusade in the Middle East

Historian John Keegan dubbed 1916 "the year of battles."[1] During this year, the intensity and scale of the war dramatically increased. Both the Allies and the Germans launched fruitless large-scale offensives against fortified, entrenched defensive positions. Stalemate and attrition permeated operations on the Western Front, and the horrific nature of the war was fully realized. During the Battle of Verdun (February to December 1916), the French sustained 380,000 casualties, while the Germans suffered 330,000, for a total of roughly 710,000 (of which 306,000 were killed). Shockingly, the Battle of the Somme (July to November 1916) produced even more devastating results. On 1 July, the opening day of the battle, British imperial forces suffered almost 60,000 casualties, including 20,000 dead. The Newfoundland Regiment (battalion) was virtually annihilated at Beaumont-Hamel. Of the 801 men who went over the top, 733 became casualties in less than twenty-five minutes. Campaign casualties for the Allies were 625,000, counting 147,000 killed. The British Empire suffered 420,000 casualties, while the French contributed another 205,000. Estimates for German losses hover between 470,000 and 550,000. In less than five months approximately 1.5 million men were killed, wounded, or missing. The carnage of the war was reaching epic proportions. Paul Baumer, the narrator and main character of Erich Maria Remarque's classic *All Quiet on the Western Front* (1928), provides a human face for these statistics:

> We see men living with their skulls blown open; we see soldiers run with their two feet cut off, they stagger on their splintered stumps into the next shell-hole; a lance-corporal crawls a mile and a half on his hands dragging his smashed knee after him; another goes to the dressing station and

over his clasped hands bulge his intestines; we see men without mouths, without jaws, without faces; we find one man who has held the artery of his arm in his teeth for two hours in order not to bleed to death. The sun goes down, night comes, the shells whine, life is at an end. Still the little piece of convulsed earth in which we lie is held. We have yielded no more than a few hundred yards of it as a prize to the enemy. But on every yard there lies a dead man.[2]

The year of battles took a ghastly toll on the field forces of all nations.

By 1917 the need for manpower to sustain Allied formations became increasingly important as events unfolded on both the Western and Eastern Fronts. By the close of 1917, the Allies faced numerous and immediate, strategic, and operational problems. Unrestricted German submarine warfare wreaked havoc on transatlantic supply lines. The year 1917 witnessed the sinking of 2,676 Allied vessels, a significant escalation from the 1,157 of 1916.[3] Despite the realization of conscription in Britain, New Zealand, and Canada (which was highly controversial among French-Canadians), reinforcements were dwindling, and there were increasing numbers of deserters in the French and Italian armies.

Although the United States entered the war on 6 April 1917 and had the potential to tip the scales in favour of the Allies, it would be months before a significant and competent field force was ready for deployment. After all, the nationalistic American political and military bureaucracy insisted that U.S. troops would take to the trenches only after they had been organized into an all-American entity. Field Marshal Sir Douglas Haig, BEF commander-in-chief, lamented in October 1918, "The American Army is disorganized, ill-equipped, and ill-trained. It must be at least a year before it becomes a serious fighting force."[4] General Erich von Ludendorff, the German quartermaster general, expressed his belief that "the French and British generally fought with caution; the Americans attacked more boldly but with less skill."[5] Britain – and her dominions of Canada, Australia, New Zealand, South Africa, and Newfoundland – and France continued to shoulder the weight of the war. In addition, after the disaster at Caporetto in October and November 1917, the Italians struggled to maintain an offensive-driven army. There was no Allied or German breakthrough on the Western Front – stalemate and attrition continued.

To compound the Allies' problems, they witnessed the capitulation of their Russian ally and the collapse of the Eastern Front in November 1917, eliminating, in one stroke, roughly half of the Entente's potential manpower – an essential commodity in a war of attrition.[6] From mid-1917 on, the Germans began to relocate men and materiel to the Western Front in preparation for a massive offensive. By the time the Treaty of Brest-Litovsk was signed on 3 March 1918, forty-four German divisions had already been relocated. Between November 1917 and 21 March 1918, when the five-stage Kaiserschlacht offensive began, the Central Powers had increased their fighting strength on the Western Front by 30 per cent. By comparison, Allied strength fell by 25 per cent over the same period, as a result of the devastating losses sustained during the Passchendaele offensive and the dearth of immediate replacements.[7] The German offensive threatened to prolong the war indefinitely. In June 1918, the Central Powers still had 51.5 infantry divisions and 7 cavalry divisions in Russia, the Ukraine, the Baltics, and the Caucasus. Turkey expected the 1918 German offensive on the Western Front to reduce British power in the Middle East and, when coupled with the withdrawal of Russian forces, it would allow Turkey to launch an offensive.

Initially, the Allies welcomed the Russian Revolution, believing that democratic rule could revive the morale of a war-weary population. These hopes, however, were short lived. Alexander Kerensky's weak leadership and dispersed power were not strong enough to unite the country, and his Socialist Revolutionary Party could not parry the Bolshevik insurgency. It was actually the German General Staff that tipped the balance of the political scales to the left. They found Lenin in exile in Switzerland and helped him across Germany into Russia. He arrived in Petrograd on 4 April and was reunited with Trotsky. Trotsky too had been in exile, first having been living in France, then arrested and taken to Spain, from where he was sent to Cuba, then secretly redirected to New York, where he took passage aboard a Swedish ship to Stockholm. After his ship had to dock in Halifax, Canada, where he was arrested but again found himself on another Swedish ship, eventually reaching Petrograd through Finland: "The Kaiser's government paid little heed to the chance that Lenin's heirs might become a deadly danger to future German governments ... Modern Americans might draw parallels with the US support of anti-Soviet Islamists and mujahideen in the Afghanistan of the 1980s. In the First World War, too, the immediate demands of war had effects that reverberated long after the peace treaties were signed."[8] The German Foreign Ministry realized that "it is greatly in our interests that Bolsheviks should survive ... we must try to prevent Russian consolidation as far as possible ... As long as the Bolshevik government remains in power, we shall have to try to apply every available means to keep the Bolsheviks from orienting themselves in any other direction, in spite of the severe tests and handicaps which our own political demands (Estonia, Livonia, Transcaucasia, Crimea, &c.) will impose on them. This will cost money; probably a great deal of money."[9] The Germans were quick to realize that, once in power, the Bolsheviks would sue for peace and remove Russia from the war. At last Germany would have its long-desired one-front war in the west. British strategy was intended to counter precisely this favourable German advantage: "It therefore becomes of particular importance to us, even if we cannot ultimately prevent, to delay as long as possible the establishment of an authority favourable to the Central Powers in the ports of Southern Russia. Civil War, or even the continuation of chaos and disorder, would be an advantage to us from this point of view."[10]

With the confusion of politics surrounding the Russian Revolution and Leon Trotsky's "no war, no peace" policy, which delayed the Treaty of Brest-Litovsk, the Germans commenced rapid invasions into southern Russia and the Ukraine. They also captured islands in the Baltic Sea and were advancing through the Baltic provinces towards Petrograd (St Petersburg).[11] Despite the signing of the treaty on 3 March 1918, the Allies feared that Germany would continue to gain ground in the east, unopposed. The German goals were to capture the important natural, industrial, and military resources of an internally embattled Russia, and to penetrate the Caucasus by means of the Berlin-Baghdad Railway, or alternatively the route from Berlin to Batum to Baku to Bokhara while seizing the vital natural resources of the Ukraine and the Caucasus.[12] The Germans also placated the Ottoman Empire in the treaty by dolling out the provinces of Kars, Ardahan, and Batum surrendered during the Russo-Ottoman War of 1877–8. These fears were significant factors in the decisions of the Allies to deploy forces to Archangel and Murmansk, as well as the Dunsterforce mission to the Caucasus, and to initiate intervention in Siberia via Vladivostok.[13]

Winston Churchill later wrote, "The reconstitution of an Eastern front against Germany and the withholding of Russian supplies from the Central Powers seemed even from the end of 1917 vital to win the war." Churchill was also vehemently opposed to Bolshevism: "Of all the tyrannies in history, the Bolshevik tyranny is the worst, the most destructive, the most degrading."[14] To Aleksandr Kolchak, Cossack commander of the anti-Bolshevik forces in Siberia, the treaty was "the heaviest blow ... It was clear to me that this peace signified our complete subjugation by Germany, our complete dependence on her, and the final loss of our political independence."[15] It was clear to Allied leaders, including David Lloyd George, that

> although the Bolshevik Government of Russia had deserted the Entente and signed a separate peace with Germany, it was obvious in these circumstances that the Entente could not afford to abandon Russia to the domination of Germany ... which stood to gain from its treaty spoils ... of foodstuffs and fodder, of oil and minerals. By controlling the Ukraine and the Black Sea, the Caucasus, and penetrating into Siberia, they hoped to escape from the stranglehold of the Allied blockade ... Further, there were very considerable military stores ... at the ports of Archangel, Murmansk, and Vladivostock ... the danger was that these would fall into the hands of Germany and be used against us.[16]

By the end of 1917, the Allied naval blockade was finally beginning to take a toll on the German war machine, and it was worrisome for Allied leaders to think that in the east the Central Powers might gain the oil, food, and resources that the blockade finally began to deny them. "Germany had won the first successes, and the fighting had taken place outside her territory," acknowledges Raymond Aron. "For all that, as the fighting went on she became the probable loser, so greatly did the resources of the Entente, which was mistress of the seas, come to exceed those of the Reich, suffocated by the blockade."[17] Germany aimed to counter this disadvantage, which included the absorption of the Caucasus oil.

The Germans were also advancing unopposed through the Baltic region and the Ukraine with a view to penetrating the Russian interior and the Caucasus to secure the agrarian yields and rich mineral resources (predominately oil, cotton, manganese, and wheat) of a warweary Russia in the midst of political chaos, lawlessness, and civil war.[18] In 1992, Boris Yeltsin's finance minister, Yegor Gaidar, compared the aftermath of the recent collapse of the Soviet Union to the repercussions of the 1917 downfall of the tsarist regime: "A superpower was in anarchy. We had no money, no gold, and no grain to last through the next harvest, and there was no way to generate a solution. It was like travelling in a jet and you go into the cockpit and you discover that there's no one at the controls."[19] Not only were the Germans entrenched in the Ukraine, they also appeared to be on the verge of achieving results in their ambitious scheme to penetrate Central Asia.[20] Removed from the butchery of the Western Front, in the closing year of the war, oil

3.1 Petrol depot on the Amiens-Albert Road during the Battle of the Somme,
September 1916. As the war became increasingly mechanized, petroleum
became a war-winning weapon (Imperial War Museum).

dominated British strategy in both the Middle East and the Caucasus.
This oil also helped fuel the continuation of unprecedented bloodlet-
ting on the fields of France and Belgium.

By the close of 1917, the Allies had suffered dramatic setbacks on
every front, save for the secondary theatre of the Middle East (excluding the evacuation of Gallipoli in January 1916). On the Western Front,
the British and French were mired in the mud of attrition. The 1916
campaigns at Verdun and the Somme had been disastrous in both loses
of manpower and morale. While the 1917 British Offensive at Arras
(9 April–16 May) achieved limited gains, highlighted by the Canadian
Corps' capture of Vimy Ridge, imperial forces suffered 160,000 casualties in just thirty-nine days, followed by another 25,000 at Messines

(7–14 June). During the corresponding futile French Nivelle Offensive (16 April–9 May), French casualties totalled 187,000 and more importantly led to serious mutinies, or "a military strike" across French formations.[21] Undaunted, in late July, Haig ordered British and dominion forces into a morass of mud east of Ypres initiating the Passchendaele Offensive. By the time the Canadian Corps captured the village of Passchendaele on 6 November, and the heights of the ridge on 10 November, BEF casualties totalled 275,000.[22]

While British, Canadian, Australian, and New Zealand soldiers were being swallowed by sludge at Passchendaele, the Italians were routed during the Battle of Caporetto (24 October–19 November). The Italians suffered 10,000 killed, 30,000 wounded, 293,000 missing or prisoner, and almost 400,000 deserters. This battle, also referred to as the Twelfth Battle of the Isonzo (or, to the Central Powers, the Battle of Karfreit), was followed by military, civil, and labour unrest throughout Italy.[23] Only the hasty transfer of ten Anglo-French divisions from the Western Front (units they could scarce afford to part with) stabilized the Italian lines. In addition, recently allied Romania suffered a series of setbacks in late 1916 and early 1917, yielding precious oil, grain, and livestock to the Central Powers. By the summer of 1917, the lesser unoccupied enclaves of Romanian territory settled into stalemate. The Russian Revolution, however, left Romania isolated and vulnerable, and with little alternative it signed an armistice on 9 December 1917. On the Macedonian Front the British launched a 1917 spring offensive around Lake Doiran, with a view to pushing northwards along the Vardar River to penetrate the Bulgarian positions and provide for a general breakthrough across the Balkans. The Battle of Doiran began on 22 April and raged intermittently until 9 May. The British suffered 12,000 casualties (roughly one-third of the attacking force), while the Bulgarians, comparatively safe in their secured high-ground concrete-and-stone defensive bunkers, incurred 2,000 losses. This front remained relatively inactive until another Anglo-Greek-French offensive in September 1918.[24]

The only 1917 recompense for the Allies came in the Middle East. Lieutenant-General Frederick Maude captured Baghdad in March, answering the demoralizing blow of Major-General Charles Townshend's surrender at Kut-al-Amara in April 1916. Similar to General Edmund Allenby's modest parade into Jerusalem in December 1917, Maude was also careful not to be portrayed as a Christian crusader. On the Sinai-Palestine front, Allenby, commander-in-chief of the Egyptian Expeditionary Force (EEF), had been ordered to "occupy Jerusalem as a Christmas present." His forces prophetically occupied Jerusalem on 9 December, the opening day of the 1917 Jewish festival of Hanukkah, which venerates the deliverance of the Jewish people. The atheist Allenby triumphantly entered the holy city on foot with no pomp and little ceremony on 11 December, well before his festive deadline. Allenby, acutely aware of the city's antediluvian roots and its sacred position for numerous faiths, orchestrated his entry as a sign of humility and respect to all adherences, and as a conscious contrast to the kaiser's self-aggrandizing visit in 1898. Allenby's proclamation promised that the holy places of the Jewish, Muslim, and Christian inhabitants of the holy city would "be maintained and protected according to the existing customs and beliefs of those to whose faith they are sacred." He then proceeded to hold a joint assembly of all major civil and religious leaders and dignitaries of the city.[25]

Allenby was the thirty-fourth conqueror of Jerusalem and the first "Christian" since the Crusades. His breakthrough was completed with the defeat of the Turks at Megiddo, 19–25 September 1918, and was, according to Lloyd George, a "brilliant operation." Allenby captured 75,000 Turks, while inflicting another 8,000 casualties. British losses were roughly 5,500. According to the Book of Revelation (16:12–16:16) Megiddo is to be the site of a great clash between East and West shortly before the end times: "The kings of the whole world, to assemble them for battle on the great day of God the Almighty. And they assembled them at the place which is called in Hebrew Armaged'don [Megiddo]." Allenby, who used the term *the Fields of Armageddon* in his dispatches to the War Office, became irrevocably known as "Allenby of Armageddon" – the last of a line of Christian Crusaders – titles that he publicly received with embarrassment and privately renounced with derision.

One week later, Prime Minister David Lloyd George announced to the House that these recent victories would

have a permanent effect on the world ... The British Empire owes a great deal to side-shows. During the Seven Years' War ... the events which are best remembered by every Englishman are not the great battles on the continent of Europe, but Plassey [India, 1757] and the Heights of Abraham [Quebec City, 1759]; and I have no doubt at all that, when the history of 1917 comes to be written, and comes to be read ages hence, these events in Mesopotamia and Palestine will hold a much more conspicuous place in the minds and the memories of people than many an event which looms much larger for the moment in our sight [the disaster at Passchendaele].

3.2 Lieutenant-General Frederick Maude enters Baghdad in a staged photograph, 12 March 1917 (Australian War Memorial).

Lloyd George was a firm believer that through these sideshows and by
"knocking away the props" of allies such as Bulgaria and Turkey, Germany would collapse. The reality, however, was that Germany was the
buttress for Austria-Hungary, Turkey, and Bulgaria.[26] In addition, these
victories, however important for morale and to their confined theatres
of war, did little to mollify the 1917 Allied disasters on the Western
Front. Furthermore, this deteriorating Allied position was amplified by
the dissolution of the Eastern Front, the collapse of any semblance of
Russian military order, and the ensuing revolution, civil war, and Russian power vacuum. In May 1917, Brigadier-General F.G. Marsh was
attached to the Russian VII Caucasus Corps near Lake Urumia and
was asked to "tell them of General Maude's brilliant advance to Baghdad. They listened respectfully and even enthusiastically, but as they

3.3 General Sir Edmund Allenby enters Jerusalem, 11 December 1917 (Library of Congress).

marched past in column of route it was clear they were not for any more serious fighting; they looked like men who had just come off a long bout of drinking, and yet they had no liquor for three years. Their *morale* was gone ... It was after this trip that I became convinced that we could expect nothing more from our Russian allies." He described the scene as a "pathetic picture" with many of his soldiers being raw recruits, with a full "85% unable to sign their own names, absolutely ignorant to what it was all about."[27]

A depiction of the war in the Middle East and the Caucasus from 1914 to 1917 has been rendered in numerous general and specialized studies, and no attempt will be made in this work to detail the tactical military developments in Turkish theatres of war. In summary, the Turks (with or without support from German and Austro-Hungarian troops) quite remarkably held their own on widely scattered fronts. What follows, however, is a situational synopsis of the military exchanges in the Middle East and the Caucasus up to the close of 1917, in order to provide context for the deployment of Dunsterforce.

By 1914, the Ottoman Empire, the world's greatest independent Islamic power, was in irreversible decline. It had suffered recent humiliations in the Balkans and in Libya. Although having been relatively docile over the past decades, it decided to join the Central Powers, after a series of Entente rejections, with the hopes of reclaiming lost territory and past glory in a final imperialist gamble. Ottoman leaders were also well aware of nationalistic undertones throughout the empire, while looking west to Europe for political and economic reform. Dismissing the myth of the Ottomans as the hapless victim of circumstance,

> by the outbreak of the First World War the Ottoman Empire was scarcely the rejected and isolated international player it is taken to be. Rather it was in the enviable position of being courted by two warring camps – one wishing its participation in the war (the Central Powers), the other desiring its neutrality (the Triple Entente) ... Apart from their admiration for Germany and their conviction that it would ultimately be victorious, the Entente had less to offer by way of satisfying this group's imperialist ambition: even the allure of Egypt was secondary to Enver's designs on Russia and the Balkans.[28]

The Ottoman/Turkish Army at the outbreak of war numbered roughly 650,000 men, divided into thirty-eight divisions of relatively unknown quality.[29] The Ottoman Empire's decision to enter the war against the

Allies in November produced numerous problems. Most importantly, it threatened Allied colonies in the region and the vital trade routes between these colonies and their European powers, including Russia's precious oil export links. In June 1914, with war looming, German intelligence operative in Mesopotamia, Baron Max von Oppenheim, known as "the Spy" in British circles, reiterated to the kaiser, "When the Turk invade Egypt, and India is set ablaze with the flames of revolt, only then will England crumble. For England is at her most vulnerable in her colonies."[30] Accordingly, the Middle East became another theatre of the Great War. From the German perspective, "the Ottoman empire could fulfill three functions. It could cut Russia's communications through the Black Sea to the rest of the world, tie down Russian forces in the Caucasus, and 'awaken the fanaticism of Islam' to spark rebellions against British and Russian rule in India, Egypt, and the Caucasus."[31]

The history of the Middle East in the Great War, up to the deployment of Dunsterforce, is extremely complicated but chronologically can be divided into three distinct phases. The first, from November 1914 to the end of 1915, marks a period in which Persia's proclaimed neutrality was violated by Britain, Germany, Russia, and Turkey. In short, Britain, France, and Russia made a pact for a new division of Middle Eastern properties, and certain Persian nationalist organizations such as the Jangalis led by Kuchik Khan, independently or with the aid of Germany and Turkey, sought to drive out foreign forces. The Russians maintained a force of roughly eight thousand men known as the "Cossack Brigade" in northern Persia centred at Kasvin, while brevet Brigadier-General Sir Percy Sykes unofficially led the British South Persian Rifles in the south. After a brief flirtation with victory, the Turks abandoned their Persian campaign in April 1915, in the face of reinforced, superior Russian forces.

In the winter of 1914–15, under Enver's direction, the Turks launched a near-suicidal campaign over the frozen mountain passes of the Caucasus against defensive Russian fortifications. In January 1915, after its resounding defeat at the Battle of Sarikamish, the shattered remnants of Enver's Third Army initiated a headlong retreat. Russian forces gained the initiative and pressed into eastern Anatolia, while urging their allies to open another front against Turkey. In the west, on 2 February 1915, the Turks launched an offensive against the British forces in the Sinai with a view to seizing the Suez Canal, while igniting an Islamic revolution in Egypt. The Turkish force, under the command of the German General Liman von Sanders and the Turkish commander Djemel

Pasha, was relatively small, numbering twenty-six thousand men. The strength was indicative of the Turkish commander's confidence that, with the aid of propaganda, he could instigate a holy war in Egypt. The campaign was a miserable failure and the envisioned jihad never materialized.[32]

By the autumn of 1915, northern Arabs were disillusioned with Turkish domination and, under Sherif Hussein of Mecca, lobbied to revive the long-fallen Arab Empire as an independent state. The British government welcomed his opposition to the Central Powers, and negotiations began in October 1915. However, Britain could not promise independence to Syria and other regions of Arabia, as the result of incompatible French interests.[33] With the advent of the 1916 Sykes-Picot Agreement, the 1917 Balfour Declaration, and the clamour for post-war oil, Arab independence was merely lip service to further British machinations in the region. In desperation, the British were making contradictory and backhanded pledges to allies and interest groups that they never intended to keep. George Antonius, the first serious historian of Arab nationalism, denounced the Sykes-Picot agreement as "not only the product of greed at its worst, that is to say, of greed allied to suspicion and so leading to stupidity: it also stands out as a startling piece of double-dealing."[34] In late 1917, when the Bolsheviks published these secret treaties and agreements, "the British and French were seriously embarrassed because the Sykes-Picot condominium, though phrased in general terms, clearly conflicted with what had been promised" to Sherif Hussein and the Arabs. In addition, Balfour pledged that "nothing shall be done which may prejudice the civil and religious rights of existing non-Jewish communities in Palestine" (which would be 90 per cent of the population). It was clear, however, that his declaration meant, as the *Times* headline read, "Palestine for the Jews."[35]

Although the Russians requested Allied assistance during Enver's fruitless foray into eastern Anatolia, it is doubtful that this request alone influenced the decision to launch the Gallipoli campaign. While Russian pleas abetted the final decision, there were, however, other Allied interests in the area, specifically the Dardanelles. The strategic advantage of this region, without going into lengthy detail, was the geographical benefit of transportation and trade (including Baku oil). By early 1915, the prices of imported staple foods to Britain, particularly meat and wheat, had risen by over 20 per cent, leading to strikes and demands for higher wages. For example, coal miners threatened a national strike in March 1915, demanding a 20 per cent wage increase to "meet the extra cost of living." No less than 80 per cent of Britain's wheat requirements came from abroad, primarily from Russia, with lesser amounts from Canada and the United States. Britain's wartime economy could scarcely afford labour unrest and unchecked inflation of staple consumer goods.[36] On 22 January, the British prime minister, Herbert Asquith, wrote to a friend, "The only exciting thing in prospect (after seeing you on Friday) is what will happen in the Dardanelles. If successful, it will smash up the Turks, and, incidentally, let through all the Russian wheat wh. is now locked up & so lower the price of bread."[37] The industrial and labour unrest of 1911 had unnerved Winston Churchill, who was then Home Secretary. He had witnessed the disastrous effects of the strikes and four years later in 1915 was "deeply concerned about the possible impact that war might have upon public order in Britain ... how much worse might be the economic and social dislocation of war? Churchill, as the minister responsible for maintaining order in both circumstances, inevitably found himself considering this very question."[38] The Dardanelles connected the Mediterranean Sea to the Black Sea, a vital waterway for channelling Russian wheat and oil.

In addition, policymakers also referenced Britain's tradition of hostility with Russia in Central Asia. The rise of Anglo-German antagonism "had only overlaid, but had not abolished, Britain's quarrels with France and Russia." Membership in their mutual alliance undoubtedly added a sense a security for British imperial possessions, specifically India, but it also created a dichotomous war for Britain: fighting to achieve its own war aims, but those of its allies as well. These goals were not always compatible: "All policy-makers were agreed that measures had to be taken to protect the British Empire in the East and that Britain had to assist its Russian ally." A push through the Dardanelles could satisfy both objectives. The outbreak of war in 1914 did not cause the Entente partners to overlook their pre-war disputes. "British desiderata were chosen not only with an eye towards securing Britain's postwar position against Germany," concludes David French, "but also against France and Russia."[39] For British policymakers the ideal outcome of the war was an Entente victory on the Western Front, and a British victory in the greater Middle East.

This resulted in the March 1915 Constantinople Agreement between the Entente powers. Believing that the Ottoman Empire would soon be defeated, the agreement dictated the geographical divisions of the spoils of war. Russia would receive control of the former Turkish holdings of Constantinople (a free port to be administered by Russia), the western shores of the Bosphorus, the Sea of Marmara, the Dardanelles, and southern Thrace. France maintained its demands for Syria (including Palestine), the Gulf of Alexandretta, and the coastal region of Cilicia surrounding the Turkish city of Adana. Britain would be granted control over the neutral zone in Persia, Mesopotamia, and southern Mediterranean ports, free passage through the Dardanelles, and the rump of Turkey in Asia, stretching from Anatolia to the Persian border, to provide a buffer between Russia and the British possessions of Mesopotamia, Persia, and India. The British also stressed that "Arabia and the Holy Places had to remain under Muslim control. It would never do for the British to be seen as despoilers of Islam. But above all else the agreement had to be kept secret." As Foreign Secretary Edward Grey explained to his peers, Britain had to preserve some form of independent Muslim state in the Middle East and "take into account the very strong feelings in the Moslem world that Mohammedanism ought to have a political as well as a religious existence."[40] This agreement also meant that the territorial war aims of the allies could not be postponed until after the cessation of hostilities. The game of bluff, two-faced covenants, and Machiavellian diplomacy had begun, and future (often conflicting) pacts would follow, such as the 1915 consolidation of exchanges between the high commissioner of Egypt, Lieutenant-Colonel Sir Henry McMahon, and Sharif Hussein bin Ali of Mecca, promising an independent Arab state in return for military assistance against the Ottomans; the 1916 Sykes-Picot Agreement; and the 1917 Balfour Declaration.

Another reason for the Dardanelles campaign was that the British believed the war was unpopular in Turkey and was engineered by a small and disliked assembly of pro-German supporters. British strategists concluded that this German-allied regime would be replaced by a pro-British administration at the first instance of military defeat, or, at the least, would be willing to settle for peace to maintain power: "The almost casual way in which the British went about mounting the Dardanelles expedition can only be understood in the light of their belief that the Turks were not a first class Western power but a backward oriental despotism which would collapse immediately the first shots were fired. Too many British decision-makers simply did not believe that the lengthy military preparations necessary to confront a European power like Germany would be necessary in a campaign against the Turks."[41] It was also reasoned that a swift and decisive victory would increase

British prestige and garner support across the Muslim world. The Dardanelles campaign would also force Turkey to relocate troops from Mesopotamia and Palestine, allowing the British to push their offensives in both theatres.

Nevertheless, the benefits of getting through the Dardanelles were so obvious that a naval operation was planned by Winston Churchill, then Lord of the Admiralty. On 18 March, under the direction of General Sir Ian Hamilton, commander-in-chief of the Mediterranean Expeditionary Force (MEF), a combined British and French fleet assembled at the Dardanelles Strait and bombarded coastal defences. With no amphibious landings planned, the naval attempt to force the strait was unsuccessful and was aborted.[42] The plan to take the Dardanelles, however, was not. On 25 April 1915, now known as ANZAC Day, British, Australian, New Zealand, and Newfoundland troops landed on the Gallipoli Peninsula (with the French landing to the south on the Asiatic shore of the straits at Kumkale), supported by a naval bombardment. The campaign proved to be futile and was abandoned by the Allies in January 1916.[43]

During the second phase of the Middle East in the Great War, from the beginning of 1916 to March 1917, the British and the Russians again launched offensives in Mesopotamia and Persia, and for a second time drove out the Turks, as they had done in April 1915. In February 1916, the War Office replaced the India Office in command of the Mesopotamian enterprise. With the advent of the May 1916 Sykes-Picot Agreement, the Middle East was partitioned into British, French, and Russian (and later Italian) spheres of influence. This agreement was based upon the recommendations of the earlier de Bunsen Committee of June 1915, which was established to formally study and forward tangible British war aims in the Middle East following the misaligned Constantinople Agreement of March 1915. "Unquestioned control" of oil resources, including related industry and transportation mechanisms, was one of six key interests promoted in its first detailed report. Emphasis was given to Mesopotamia and a future pipeline to the terminus refinery/port at Haifa, in what became the British mandate in Palestine (now Israel) following the war – a British calculation for the 1917 Balfour Declaration. Britain extended her control over the rest of the southern and eastern regions and eventually occupied Baghdad in March 1917.[44] To Curzon, "The capture of the city would ring through the East and would cause such an impression that it would partially discount any failure at the Dardanelles."[45] The triumph of Baghdad and the final sanction of the principles of the ongoing McMahon-Hussein negotiations were a way of buttressing flagging British prestige in the Middle East following the evacuation of Gallipoli. During the discussions of 1915, the sharif had no intentions of actually rebelling against the Turks until the British position in the Middle East became favourable; the British had merely bought his neutrality for the time being. By 1917, however, British headway in both Mesopotamia and Palestine swayed him to fulfil his prior assurances to provide military support against the Turks. However, the capture of Baghdad, allied to the unfolding unrest in Russia, had unforeseen strategic consequences for the British.

At this time, the war began to exact a toll on civilian populations. In late 1916, widespread famine began to devastate the local populations of Persia, eastern Anatolia, and the southern Caucasus. Local crops withered, and the import of foodstuffs from India, Mesopotamia, and the United States became non-existent, because the few and bucolic local roads and railways were used for war supplies by both sides. In addition, all belligerents, whether Ottoman, British, or Russian, refused to pay for local oil, which greatly aggravated the conditions brought on by the drought and famine. Between 1917 and 1919, it is estimated that nearly half (nine to eleven million people) of the Persian population died of starvation or disease brought on by malnutrition. Those men fit enough to fight, generally took up resistance against the British, who now controlled most of the region.[46] In addition, plagues of locusts on a biblical scale ravaged 75 to 90 per cent of crops in Syria and Lebanon throughout 1915 and 1916, leading to drought and famine, which claimed 350,000 to 500,000 lives in the region by war's end.[47]

The third phase of the Middle Eastern theatre of war falls in the period of April 1917 to January 1918. The Russian Revolution unfolded, causing the Russian armies in Persia and the Caucasus to disband and evacuate their positions. The agreements of 1907 and 1916 between the Allies and Russia became moot.[48] The United States officially joined the Allied war effort in April. With the potential for more manpower on the Western Front, thanks largely to the United States, Britain afforded more troops to General Sir Archibald Murray's Egyptian Expeditionary Force. Maude's successes in Mesopotamia, including the capture of Baghdad in March 1917, drastically changed the situation in the Middle East. If given appropriate troop allocations, Britain could now gain ground in Persia and Mesopotamia. However, in Palestine, Murray delayed any further attacks and subverted the British War Office with spurious reports of his progress. He was replaced by General Sir

Edmund Allenby in June 1917. Allenby, as mentioned, proceeded to launch successful attacks on Gaza in November 1917 and on Jerusalem in December of the same year.[49] With these regions safely under British control, the main railway lines from the Mediterranean ports across Syria, through Arabia to the Persian Gulf were in British hands. Also ports on the Mediterranean, Red, and Caspian Seas, the Persian Gulf, and the Tigris and Euphrates Rivers were open for Allied shipping.[50]

Flushed by these recent victories, on 2 November 1917 the British issued the Balfour Declaration demarcating a Jewish homeland in soon-to-be-conquered Palestine. This was a strategic initiative to protect British interests and to help harden American favour. Having a cordial Jewish state in Palestine would ensure British control of the Suez Canal – the pathway to the Middle East, Central Asia, and India – while protecting oil interests and providing ideal locations for the terminus of pipelines at refineries constructed at Mediterranean ports. It would also appeal to the large Jewish diaspora in the United States, who were becoming a swelling electoral bloc in U.S. cities, principally in the highly populated east. Between 1900 and 1914, as Jewish pogroms engulfed Eastern Europe and Russia, 1.5 million Jews immigrated to America. When America entered the war in April 1917, its Jewish population had risen to over 2.2 million. Today, the United States and Israel are home to 80 per cent of the world's Jews: "The origins of modern Israel – and of the modern Palestinian national movement – date to the years immediately following Balfour's Declaration."[51]

In addition, irregular Arab guerrillas, led by T.E. Lawrence, who took command of these forces in 1916, were wreaking havoc on German and Turkish reinforcements and supply depots in Palestine and Western Arabia, distracting sizeable enemy forces from the main fronts.[52] In early 1918, however, the decaying situation in the Middle East, which was spawned by the collapse of the tsarist regime, became even more threatening to local Allied strategy. With the signing of the Brest-Litovsk Treaty, Russian forces under General Nikolai Yudenich who had been embattled with both German and Turkish forces in the southern Caucasus since 1915, disintegrated. Until the summer of 1917, the Russian line extended from south Russia, through the Caucasus, across the Caspian Sea, through northwest Persia, until its left flank joined General Maude's British forces in Mesopotamia, east of Baghdad. By October 1917, this continuous Allied line was melting away. Russian troops were deserting en masse, and the entire Russian Army announced its intention to withdraw from the area completely. With the advent of the Russian Revolution and the final collapse of the southern Russian forces in November 1917, and the unexpected death of General Maude from cholera that same month, the British faced an entirely new strategic situation.[53]

The Turkish Army, inadvertently acting as a vanguard for German follow-on forces, found nothing between itself and the long-coveted possession of the oil-rich region of the southern Caucasus and began to work their way along the Transcaucasian Railway. A gap, some 450 miles wide, was forming on the right flank of the British Mesopotamian Force, through which Turkish and German agents and troops could encircle the Allied forces and pour into Central Asia. Germany was arming tribes in Persia, who were hostile to the British, and by the beginning of 1918, 300,000 rifles had been distributed:[54] "With no Russian Caucasian army left to oppose them, the Turks had reversed three years of Russian gains in less than two months, restoring the 1914 borders (and going slightly past them) while hardly breaking a sweat."[55] The British were cognizant that these deployments were "to ensure for the Ottoman Government – 1. A powerful military position in the world. 2. Full opportunity to crush and massacre small subject races. 3. Pan-Islamic and pan-Turanian expansion in Central Asia, India and Africa. 4. Facilities for promoting dissention among the Powers."[56] The first comprehensive report detailing pan-Turanian ideology and its religious, geographical, racial, military, and strategic appendages was promulgated on 29 November 1917. The report also contained a section entitled "German Support of Pan-Turanianism," which detailed the financial, propaganda, and clandestine efforts of German agents in the region to bolster German influence and sway under the guise of pan-Turanian backing.[57]

Clearly the British were concerned with any push by the Turks or Germans, individually or collectively, into the Caucasus or Central Asia, "in so far as they are given opportunities by the course of events in Russia," thereby fashioning an environment "intensely prejudicial to the position of Great Britain in India."[58] The newly appointed commander of the MEF, Lieutenant-General William Marshall (who replaced the deceased Maude), did not have sufficient forces to repel the inevitable onslaught. Alterations were desperately needed to safeguard British interests and operational intentions in the Middle East and the Caucasus.

The situation in the southern Caucasus and in neighbouring northwest Persia – east of the Turkish border – was extremely important to the Allies, specifically the British. Throughout the war, India was threatened from the Northwest Frontier, aggravated by the hostility of a considerable portion of the Afghan population, lured by German agents and bribes. As part of the kaiser's plan to ignite jihad in India against the British Raj, a secret emissary was sent to Afghanistan to convince Emir Habibullah to instigate a holy war in India. This 1915–16 mission operated at the "vortex of four clashing empires – the German, Ottoman, Russian, and British." Led by diplomat Werner-Otto von Hentig, the mission "wound its way from Berlin to Vienna to Constantinople to Baghdad ... to Herat and Kabul."[59]

In central Persia, Hentig was joined by the resourceful and wily Oskar Niedermayer, often referred to as the "German Lawrence." This picaresque enterprise, however, was plagued by complications from the outset, and as early as November 1914, British spies had full knowledge of the German-Afghan initiative. More importantly, in March 1915, British agents seized a diplomatic codebook in western Persia abandoned by Wilhelm Wassmuss, an elusive German agent, allowing them to intercept messages from German consuls in the Ottoman Empire and also those sent by Hentig and Niedermayer. The greatest difficulty for these German emissaries, however, was to convince the emir to abandon his bonds with the British, which had been validated through a 1905 Treaty of Friendship.[60]

Knowing German intentions, the British began to flood Kabul with propaganda and sent the emir personal messages regarding the progress of the German party, spotted with disinformation. King George V wrote a personal letter to his Afghan peer on 24 September 1915, "My Dear Friend, I have been much gratified to learn ... how scrupulously and honourably Your Majesty has maintained the attitude of strict neutrality which you guaranteed at the beginning of the war, not only because it is in accordance with Your Majesty's engagements to me, but also because by it you are serving the best interests of Afghanistan and the Islamic religion [and] still further strengthen the friendship which I so greatly value, which has united our people since the days of your father, of illustrious memory, and of my revered forebear, the great Queen Victoria." In an accompanying letter from Charles Hardinge, the viceroy of India, the emir was informed that his annual subsidy would be increased by £25,000 (from £400,000 to £425,000). In reality, Habibullah still had £800,000 of unspent credit in Delhi, in addition to sizeable investments in London.[61]

In the meantime, Niedermayer and his motley crew of twenty-five "dried up skeletons" evaded British and Russian pursuers, and after seven perilous weeks in the Persian desert (marching some 30–40 miles per day in temperatures upwards of 50°C), crossed the Afghan frontier on 19 August 1915. Kabul, although in sight, still lay some four hundred miles east, with the gates to India only two hundred miles beyond. On 2 October, one year after Niedermayer had left Constantinople, the Germans entered the Afghan capital. Habibullah, however, was intelligent, cautious, and a savvy veteran of Great Game politics. Having just received the entreaty from King George and a raise in pay, he was in no hurry to hold audience with the German envoys, who spent the next twenty-four days in cordial, albeit guarded, house arrest: "Habibullah's caution was wholly in character. He had not survived as sovereign of his realm for fourteen years in between the British and Russian empires without learning how to play the powers off against one another. Far from the provincial tribal Islamic headman the Germans had imagined him to be, the Emir was European in both his dress and his manners, and evidently well informed about the world war."[62] The emir was obviously well aware of his opportunity to play the game with a new set of pawns: Britain and Germany.

At last on 26 October, Habibullah's Rolls-Royce (the only car in Afghanistan) collected Hentig and Niedermayer and shuttled them down the paved road (again the only one in Afghanistan) to his palace. Over the course of the next two months, the emir held daily meetings with his guests, listening to their propositions. He maintained his poker face, however, refusing to play his hand by rarely saying a word in response. Although his manners were beyond reproach, Habibullah treated the Germans as if "we were businessmen with various goods [to sell], from which he wished to determine which would be good or useful to him."[63] The emir was receiving intelligence from the British, who were generally pleased with his policy of "masterly inactivity."

Finally, on 24 January 1916, Habibullah signed a treaty with the Germans; the crowning moment of his brilliant self-serving scheme. To replace his British subsidies, which would be forfeit if his forces invaded India, he secured a sum of £10 million (£5 billion today), in addition to the promise of 100,000 modern rifles, 300 artillery pieces, and other contemporary military equipment. Lastly, he assured Hentig and Niedermayer that the invasion would begin when a force of 20,000 well-armed Turkish and German soldiers arrived to cover the rear against an inevitable Russian attack – which both parties knew was logistically impossible. Niedermayer was rightly "convinced that any attempt to induce Afghanistan to go to war against India is futile as long as it is based only on diplomatic activities."[64] The following day, Habibullah summoned the British agent and declared his continued loyalty and neutrality and belatedly replied to King George reaffirming this position. By playing both nations, Habibullah ensured that he would be on the winning side, regardless of who actually won the war. The treaty with the Germans was merely an insurance policy, for if the untenable terms, calculatingly imposed by the emir, were ever met, the Central Powers would have to be categorically winning the war.[65]

Habibullah continued to delay until the Germans had finally given up hope of cooperation and of an Afghan invasion of India. With the sweeping 1916 Russian gains in Anatolia and Persia, the Arab revolt in Mesopotamia, and the failure of the German offensive at Verdun on the Western Front, both Germany and the Ottomans had more immediate concerns. On 15 February 1916, the Russians seized the impregnable fortress of Erzurum, sending the Turkish Third Army into a hasty retreat towards Ankara: "It was a bitter blow to Turco-German prestige. Any chance Niedermayer still had of inducing Emir Habibullah to launch an Afghani holy war against British India most likely perished in the snows of Erzurum."[66] As a result, Niedermayer and Hentig left Kabul towards the end of May 1916, and with them the kaiser's hopes of igniting rebellion in India via Afghanistan.

Hentig escaped east with stops in Shanghai, Honolulu, San Francisco, Halifax (Canada), and Bergen (Norway) before reaching Berlin. Niedermayer also eventually made it back to Tehran, having been beaten, robbed, and left for dead in the Persian desert by his Turkish escorts. He reported to the German Embassy, "Our next and most important objectives are the Caucasus and northern Persia." He would reappear in Mesopotamia in early 1917, coming face-to-face with his British counterpart, Lawrence of Arabia, as part of the German-reinforced Turkish Yildirim Army (Lightning Army) or Heeresgruppe F, initially commanded by General Erich von Falkenhayn and later by General Liman von Sanders. This unit attempted without success to crush the Arab revolt and deny British advances in Palestine and Mesopotamia.[67] Nevertheless, during 1915–16, the danger posed by their mission to Afghanistan was viewed as a great threat in British circles. According to Brigadier-General Sir Percy Sykes, commander of the South Persian Rifles, "The German Mission to the Emir created a crisis of the first magnitude in Afghanistan and was a source of the gravest anxiety in India."[68] Any advance on India by Turkey would influence the fortunes of not only India, but the entire British Empire. India was the source of considerable wealth in raw war materials vital to the Allied war effort.

To avoid such a catastrophy, the strategic solution was to limit Turkey's access to the transportation routes leading south to India, the majority of which were in the Middle East. The main cities on both the Tigris and Euphrates Rivers, including Mosul, Baghdad, Fallujah, and Basra, and the northern Caspian ports of Enzeli and Baku, were vital ground in halting any southeast Turkish or German advance. The British also needed to protect the road from Baghdad to the port of Enzeli. The road, 630 miles long, climbed through a succession of mountain ranges and desolate regions and was frequently raided by Turkish or hostile Persian forces being encouraged by German/Turkish agents. In addition, hostile Jangali tribesmen under Kuchik Khan controlled all approaches to Enzeli. The protection of this route was under Marshall's mandate, but he could not devote any resources to its security, given his obligations in Mesopotamia and his already overextended forces.

With the Russian departure and Marshall's MEF and Allenby's EEF lacking the capacity to expand operations beyond their current area of operations, it was necessary to insert secondary forces to meet strategic objectives in the Middle East. The Russian force that had long held the Caucasus-Persian front fluctuated between 125,000 and 225,000 soldiers.[69] The Allies could not spare reinforcements from any theatre, including those in Palestine or Mesopotamia, to replace these numbers. Highly mobile and highly trained special forces seemed to be the only alternative. As mentioned, there were a number of other relatively obscure Allied "sideshow" campaigns within volatile, post-revolution Russia.[70] The necessity for Allied intervention into both northern and southern Russia was a reaction to the overall strategic situation, which had been significantly transformed during 1917. Within this paradigm Dunsterforce was deployed to northern Persia and the Caucasus in 1918 to safeguard British oil interests.

Chapter Four

The Black Blood of Victory

On 21 November 1918, ten days after the Armistice, the imperial government hosted a banquet for the Inter-Allied Petroleum Conference in London, chaired by Lord Curzon. Curzon had worn many distinguished hats as the leading expert on Persia in the Foreign Office, and the viceroy of India, during which tenure he supported and used diplomatic leverage to buttress D'Arcy's initial Anglo-Persian Oil Company venture. He had been a member of the War Cabinet and was soon to become the foreign secretary. During his opening remarks Curzon pronounced to his guests that during his visits to the front lines of France and Flanders, "one of the most astonishing things was the tremendous army of motor lorries." He then declared, "The Allied cause had floated to victory upon a wave of oil." Following Curzon's address, Senator Henry Bérenger, director of France's Comité Général du Pétrole, stressed that oil, "the blood of the earth [was] the blood of victory ... Germany had boasted too much of its superiority in iron and coal, but it had not taken sufficient account of our superiority of oil. As oil had been the blood of war, so it would be the blood of peace. At this hour, at the beginning of the peace, our civilian populations, our industries, our commerce, our farmers are calling for more oil, always more oil, for more gasoline, always more gasoline. More oil, ever more oil!"[1]

During the final years of the war, oil became key to feeding the war machines of all nations, and also became a crucial issue during the negotiations of the peace. With the advent of the Russian Revolution and the corresponding power vacuum in Russia and its peripheral states, Baku became the principle petroleum target for competing belligerents and allied nations. The quest for this all-important resource led to heightened acrimony between Britain and France, and between Turkey and Germany, all rivalling against an incapacitated Russia, which was reduced to a mere brokering power in the midst of internal chaos and violent political dissidence. Specifically conquering oil regions had not been a primary concern or war aim for any nation prior to 1916. Following the shattering battles of that year at Verdun and the Somme, and an increasingly mechanized war, oil emerged as a core strategic component in the evolution of the progression of the war and seeped into the war aims of its contributing nations.

For Germany, its acute shortage of oil became a serious hindrance to its protracted military capabilities. In 1914, strategic planners did not account for increasingly industrial and mechanized warfare paralleling the importance of oil until 1917, at which point any gains made in securing oil from Romania and Russia were too little too late. By late 1916, the Allied naval blockade had starved Germany of its foreign oil supplies. Prior to the collapse of the Eastern Front, Romania was the only viable source available, as it was the largest European producer after Russia. Romania, however, only accounted for a mere 5 per cent of total European output. By comparison, Baku alone produced 75 per cent. Before the war, Germany and its banks had secured large interests in Romanian oil. Romania, however, remained neutral until August 1916, at which time it joined the Allies, vying to profit from the hard-fought gains of the Russian Brusilov Offensive (June to September 1916). Despite the drastic setbacks incurred by Austro-Hungarian and German forces during this Russian advance, and the availability of Romania's oil to Allied coffers, the entry of Romania into the war was in a sense a blessing for the Central Powers, as it provided the opportunity to obtain a secure supply of oil. German forces immediately counter-attacked, and as General Ludendorff remarked, "As I now saw quite clearly, we should not have been able to exist, much less carry on the war, without Rumania's corn and oil."[2]

While Romanian and Russian forces were barely hanging on, the British fully realized that "no efforts should be spared to ensure, in case of necessity, the destruction of the supplies of grain and oil, as well as the oil wells."[3] By 23 November, hope for a Romanian victory, or at best a stalemate, vanished as German forces under General Erich von Falkenhayn, in command of a young Lieutenant Erwin Rommel, forced the Transylvanian mountain passes into the Wallachian Plains towards the oilfields at Ploieşti, while to the south General August von Mackensen's forces crossed the Danube River. The British responded.

4.1 The kaiser touring the Ploieşti oilfields in Romania with General August
Mackensen to his left, March 1917 (Imperial War Museum).

Under the command of Colonel John "Empire Jack" Norton-Griffiths,
the great colonial railway, harbour, and sewage engineer (and the con-
tractor for the Baku aqueducts), British agents were ordered to sabotage
all oil installations in Ploieşti. The first fields were ablaze on 26 November. After the demolition of more wells the following day, Romanian
workers protested directly to "Empire Jack." His response was simply
to unholster his revolver and shout, "I don't speak your blasted language!" According to Norton-Griffiths, by the time the Germans captured the oil fields on 5 December, every vestige of Romanian oil (over
seventy refineries and 800,000 crude tons) had been destroyed under
his mission "to lay waste the land." As the builder of engineering mar-
vels across all corners of the globe from railways in Angola, Australia,
and Chile to harbours in Canada, to sewage systems in Manchester,
to subways in Chicago, he was personally sickened by his venture.

Nevertheless, his mission denied the Germans this vital commodity.[4] It was five months before the Germans extracted any oil, and by the close of 1917 oil production was only a third of what it had been in 1914. By 1918, however, the Germans had reached 80 per cent (1.34 million tons) of the 1914 production.[5] Ludendorff grudgingly remarked that Norton-Griffiths's efforts "did materially reduce the oil supplies of our army and the home country. We must attribute our shortages in part to him." Romanian oil, he added, "made just the difference between shortage and collapse" for the time being.[6]

Nevertheless, Germany still desperately needed more oil to continue total war. In 1914, the Galician oilfields provided 60 per cent of Germany's oil. During the 1915 German/Austro-Hungarian Gorlice-Tarnow Offensive (May–September 1915), however, Russian troops destroyed all oil installations during the "Great Retreat." In 1916 the oilfields of Galicia produced only 554,000 tons (down from 1910 production of 2 million).[7] For the Central Powers, the Galician and Romanian wells, and the 10,000 gallons a day produced at the Quaiyara fields of the Mosul *vilayet*, which had captivated Major Hubert Young before the war, could not meet the demands of an increasingly mechanized and mobile war.[8] Nor were hijacked shipments from the United States, redirected to Germany from Scandinavia, thus circumventing the blockade: "The barrels are brought down to the wharf ostensibly for shipment on vessels sailing for neutral ports, but on the other side of these are moored vessels bound for Lubeck and other German ports. The barrels are merely passed across the decks of the vessels which are supposed to receive them, and placed on board the vessels bound for Germany."[9] Germany was surrounded geographically by neutral countries: the Netherlands, Denmark, and Sweden, "any one of which could act as an entrepôt for German trade; thus if the blockade was to be effective some way of plugging the gaps in it would have to be found."[10] It was also confirmed that Shell's three Scandinavian subsidiaries, most notably the Anglo-Swedish Oil Company, were supplying oil to the Germans. In late 1915, the Admiralty reported, "Sweden is the principal offender, and the chief source of supply for the Germans at present, and goods are flowing through her ports in enormous quantities."[11]

Consequently, the APOC incorporated any "enemy oil property" suffused with German capital as a "war measure," including British Petroleum (which had been under contract to distribute Shell oil), the Homelight Oil Company, the British Creosote Company, and the Petroleum Steamship Company. As a result, the APOC reaped an additional

850 distribution depots and eleven tankers.[12] In addition, in September 1915, the British Cabinet had set aside an initial £400,000 for British shipping firms to commission all neutral oil tankers in an effort to stop cargoes from reaching Germany.[13] The Royal Navy had also been seizing Standard Oil vessels flying the German flag (under its German subsidiary Deutsch-Amerikanische Gesellschaft), and confiscating their precious petroleum consignments.[14] To Churchill, it was "most important to attract neutral shipping to our shores, in the hopes especially of embroiling the United States with Germany ... For our part, we want the traffic – the more the better; and if some of it gets into trouble, better still."[15] British harassment of Standard Oil's "German" freighters continued into early 1917. This led David Lloyd George to note, "The lack of sufficient rubber, lubricants and petrol, reduced seriously the mobility of the German Army."[16]

Germany increasingly looked to the Middle East and the Caucasus as a source of oil. In the spring of 1916, British operatives intercepted German-Ottoman communications outlining "articles on the importance of Persian and Turkish oil. These indicated the significance that Germany attached to securing possession of the Mesopotamian and Persian oilfields, which was an important objective of Turco-German military operations in the Middle East."[17] In reality, Germany and Turkey had very different strategic designs to achieve the same goal – securing the Caucasus oil. Although allies, acrimony between Germany and Turkey was immediate, and strategic priorities continued to diverge during the course of the war, leading to actual military conflict in the Caucasus by the summer of 1918. Throughout the war, Turkey placed greater importance on its eastern Anatolian and Caucasus front to promote pan-Turanian ideology, draining crucial manpower from Mesopotamia and Palestine, which the Germans believed to be the vital ground. Although Germany buttressed Ottoman forces in the Middle East, it was engaged in a two-front war in Europe and could scarcely afford to redirect any significant resources to these theatres of war. With its own designs on the Caucasus, Germany was furtively attempting to pull Ottoman forces away from this front, to allow for future German advances into the region.

The refusal of Ottoman leaders to concede to German demands to concentrate Turkish forces in Mesopotamia and Palestine created a rift in military hegemony, but also allowed the British to dominate these theatres of war from 1917 onwards. According to the chief of the General Staff, Field Marshal Paul von Hindenburg, the capture of Baghdad "killed many German dreams" of the Berlin-Baghdad Railway, in what Ludendorff described as a "crushing blow." The Germans now set their sights upon the Berlin-Batum-Baku-Bokhara route to the Indian frontier.[18] In July 1918, the newly appointed chief of the Imperial General Staff (CIGS), General Sir Henry Wilson, advised the Imperial War Cabinet that it was only "a question of time before most of Asia became a German colony, and nothing can impede the enemy's progress towards India, in defence of which the British Empire will have to fight at every disadvantage." Wilson had replaced Sir William Robertson as chief of the Imperial General Staff in February 1918 after Robertson's resignation in the midst of heated "duelling" with Lloyd George. Robertson, however, a former senior intelligence officer with the Indian Army of the British Raj, stressed that geography alone made any advance on India by this route quite improbable.[19]

Although the Russian Revolution transformed the strategic parameters of all belligerents in the region, Turkey adhered to its 1914 position of a pan-Turanian drive through the Caucasus and into Central Asia to revive the Ottoman Empire and unite Turkish peoples under one flag. Baku oil was a windfall of this design. However, by this time Baku oil was a war aim for both Britain and Germany and gave strategic leverage to Lenin and his Bolshevik revolutionaries: "If Lenin and the Bolsheviks succeeded in knocking Russia out of the world war, perhaps Germany's *Drang nach Osten* could resume after all, without the Turks who had resolved on sabotaging it. With their hearts broken by the fall of Baghdad, German war-planners now set their sights on the oil fields of Baku."[20] In fact, in April 1917, at the onset of the Russian Revolution, the German Foreign Office ordered a complete study of Baku oil. At the same time the Admiralty staff in Berlin prepared a revised German war aims document stressing the need to secure "permanent German influence in Asia via Caucasia in the direction of India."[21] In May 1918, Ludendorff ordered the creation of a German base on the Caspian Sea, "*um von dort im Zusammenwirken mit Afghanistan die Englische Herrschaft in Indien zu treffen*"[22] (in order to use it, in conjunction with Afghanistan, to take the English rule in India). At the outbreak of hostilities in 1914, however, Russia struck first.

The Russian Army of the Caucasus under General Nikolai Yudenich launched a sustained offensive at the beginning of November 1914, marching into Ottoman Armenia. A division of local Armenians quickly mobilized in support of Russia, much to the wrath of Young Turk leaders, and by December Yudenich's forces had penetrated over fifty miles into Ottoman territory. Enver Pasha, the Ottoman minster of war, was fanatical in his pan-Turanian ideology. He was determined to strike back and recover Russian lands in eastern Anatolia and the Caucasus with a high Turkish population and those (Kars, Ardahan, and Batumi) forfeited by the 1877–8 Russo-Turkish War, which boasted a Muslim population of almost 80 per cent. Enver was convinced that if Sarikamish fell, the entire Russian front would collapse, and the "liberated" Muslims of the Caucasus would unite with Turkish forces, followed by those of Transcaspia, Turkestan, and finally India. General Liman von Sanders, the senior German military attaché, not only refused to command this venture, but derided Enver for his "foolish plan" and regarded him as a "buffoon in military matters."[23] Enver had commented to Sanders that he "contemplated marching through Afghanistan to India." India itself was not a pan-Turanian objective, but "*British India* had long been an objective of Britain's rivals, including Germany and Russia."[24]

When Enver arrived at the front on 13 November, he revealed his concept of operations to the Third Army commander Hasan Izzet Pasha, who had been his instructor at the Imperial Military Academy. Enver attempted to rally his officers with pan-Muslim rhetoric. "Every simple soldier knows that he is fighting not merely for 30,000,000 Turks," he exhorted, "but also for the lives of 300,000,000 Mohammedans."[25] Izzet was less than enthusiastic and pleaded to postpone the operation until after the worst of winter. After a series of arguments, Enver derided Izzet for failing to follow orders and told him that if he had not been his teacher he would have executed him. Instead, Izzet was conveniently relieved of command and replaced by the self-appointed Enver, who, against the objections of his subordinate officers, launched his reckless offensive the following week.[26] On the eve of battle, Enver soberly addressed his troops: "Soldiers, I have visited you all. I saw that you have neither shoes on your feet nor coats on your backs. Yet the enemy before you is afraid of you. Soon we will attack and enter the Caucasus. There you will find everything in abundance. The whole of the Muslim world is watching you ... Our supply base is in front of us."[27]

The frostbitten, starving, and typhus-ridden Turkish forces, numbering some 112,000, struggled through high mountain passes with temperatures plunging to –40°C and snowdrifts reaching nine to thirteen feet deep. Most of the artillery was abandoned because of impassable terrain, and the severely underequipped units, utterly lacking logistical support and supply, frequently got lost or wandered without knowledge of flanking formations. The Third Division (made up of the IX, X, XI Corps) was short 5,376 service animals (horses and oxen), 809 wagons, 40,000 uniforms, 9,500 rifles, 23,428 shrapnel shells, and 3,340 corresponding fuses, in addition to officers and other basic military kit.[28] It was reported on 29 November that X Corps alone was short 17,000 overcoats, 17,400 pairs of boots, 23,000 groundsheets, and 13,000 rucksacks.[29] Nevertheless, piecemeal Turkish forces repeatedly attacked the main fortified Russian position at Sarikamish between 22 December 1914 and 17 January 1915 with shattering losses. By mid-January the remnants of Enver's devastated and demoralized forces straggled back into eastern Turkey (forced to march as naval transports were sunk by the Russian Black Sea Fleet). Estimates vary, but Third Army losses range from 80 to 90 per cent (or roughly 95,000), while Russian losses are reported to be around 30,000 out of roughly 60,000 to 75,000 engaged.[30] A German officer attached to the Ottoman General Staff reported to Berlin that Enver "suffered a disaster which for rapidity and completeness is without parallel in military history."[31] In essence, the Third Army ceased to exist. Its combat strength on 28 January was reported as a meagre 12,400 men.[32]

Undaunted, Enver ordered another ill-fated offensive on 15 January, when he directed 25,000 men of the Fourth Army to attack across the Suez Canal. This campaign, launched on 2–3 February, and designed to incite local jihad against the British, which never materialized, was also a miserable failure. With the Allied naval assault in the Dardanelles of February–March 1915 and the subsequent April amphibious landings at Gallipoli, Constantinople was directly threatened, not only from this force, but also from the Russians in the east, who were penetrating from the Caucasus through eastern Anatolia. The disaster at Sarikamish and the retreats from Basra and the Suez drastically reduced the strategic offensive capabilities of the Ottoman army. Furthermore, Gallipoli, in combination with British advances in Palestine and Mesopotamia and Russian gains in eastern Anatolia, kept Ottoman forces diffident and defensive for the next two years.

Fighting in the Caucasus then settled into a stalemate. Change came in the early spring of 1916 when Russian forces, including at least 150,000 Armenians (Armenian irregulars captured Van in May 1915), took the fortress city of Erzurum, the critical port of Trebizond, and Erzincan, the primary road, river, and rail junction in Anatolia. The Russians continued to penetrate deep into Ottoman territory, where they remained until late 1917. The Russian capture of the bastion of

Erzurum, with its series of intricate forts, in February 1916 was feted in the climax of John Buchan's cloak-and-dagger novel, *Greenmantle*, and was publicly celebrated in Britain. By this time, Turkish forces in the east had suffered roughly 330,000 losses and were disorganized and demoralized. Campaigning ceased during the winter months and if the planned Russian offensive had resumed in the spring of 1917 and the tsarist regime had not collapsed in March 1917, "the Turkish armies in the east would have collapsed completely."[33] Russian forces had the potential to march on Constantinople itself and hasten the fall of the Ottoman Empire.

In any event, the collapse of the Russian Army of the Caucasus by the autumn of 1917 provided Enver with a chance for redemption from his 1915 fiasco in that region. Once more, relatively unopposed as he believed, he could unleash his pan-Turanian plan of uniting Turkish peoples under his empire. His vision would be realized by seizing the ground lost in the last Russo-Turkish War (and then some), by driving through eastern Anatolia, through the Caucasus seizing Baku, before marching into the steppes of Central Asia and India.[34] Lloyd George noted, "The real political aims of Turkey at this time were Pan-Turanian. They particularly wished to expand in Trans-Caucasia and Cis-Caucasia, regions inhabited by kindred tribes ... the Turks were comparatively little interested in the alien Arabs, and throughout the War they tended to direct their major efforts towards the Caucasus."[35] While pan-Turanian ideology fed Enver's second attempt to unite the Turkic peoples under a grand empire in the spring and summer of 1918, Baku oil was at the forefront of his resurrected Caucasus crusade. Enver, however, was not alone in trying to profit from the internal Russian strife to conveniently arrogate Baku's precious oil.

In the summer of 1918, Maurice Hankey, secretary of the Imperial War Cabinet, remarked that oil had become a "first class British War Aim." In May 1917, Lloyd George had placed the Colonial Secretary Walter Hume Long in "charge of all oil questions." The energetic and able administrator quickly formed the Petroleum Imperial Policy Committee, under the former colonial secretary Lewis Vernon Harcourt and his aide, professor of mining engineering and Britain's leading petroleum expert, John Cadman. The committee's assignment was to take stock of supplies, future necessities, and potential oil supplies, all within the greater geopolitical context of the war.[36] Long stressed, however, that the single most important task of the committee was "to consider what steps should be taken to secure control of as much as possible of

4.2 Hand-dug oil pits near Mosul, ca 1911 (Library of Congress).

the world's supply of natural petroleum … It is absolutely vital to the British Empire to get a firm hold of all possible sources of petroleum supply."[37] Mirroring the British organization, the French established the Comité Générale du Pétrole chaired by Senator Henry Bérenger.

Harcourt frequently consulted the Admiralty – the main oil-consuming sector. The Royal Navy consumed 9.1 out of 10 million tons of oil imported into the United Kingdom during the war. Pointing to the Mosul-Baghdad area on a map, Captain Hall of the Admiralty Intelligence branch bluntly asserted, "The ultimate success of the war depended on what we did there" – an obvious reference to the need to control the rich, yet relatively unexploited, oilfields of Mesopotamia. The First Sea Lord, Sir Henry Jackson, wholeheartedly agreed that Mosul must be brought into the British sphere by either diplomacy or force of arms. Jackson had impressed this notion upon senior politicians as early as 1916 in a committee on future war aims. Long agreed with his assessment and also urged the government to investigate shale oil from Scotland and also potential sources in Mesopotamia.[38]

British policy was to maintain a six-month stock of reserve oil. By August 1917, however, inventory was only two months, and a shortage of oil was constraining the operational mobility of the Royal Navy. Long reported that the current stocks were "by no means sufficient for real National safety ... and the question of supply has from time to time given cause for very great anxiety."[39] Long did add one positive and foreshadowing caveat to the creation of an Anglo-American oil monopoly: "As practically the whole of the tank tonnage now in commission is British or American owned we are able, in association with the United States, to regulate the whole-oil trade of the world." As such, as early as the summer of 1917, a unified British-American oil policy to jointly control the world's most precious resource was formally being addressed.

Nevertheless, the German submarine campaign targeting these tankers, coupled with the increased need for oil due to the dramatic mechanization and industrialization of the war, had created, as reported by the *Times* of London, "a dearth of petrol."[40] For example, in June 1917 Britain consumed 395,000 tons, but in June 1918 consumption had risen to 477,000 tons. Oil consumption of the Royal Navy increased from a monthly average of 80,500 tons in 1914 to 190,000 tons in 1917, as by this time a full 48 per cent of the British fleet was oil-driven. Without American imports, Long noted, "our modern oil-burning fleet cannot keep the seas." It was estimated that total annual British requirements for 1918 would exceed 6.5 million tons.[41] During the summer of 1917, a series of "desperate" telegrams were sent from London to Washington pleading for more petroleum. "Oil is probably more important at this moment than anything else," wrote Long in October 1917. "You may have men, munitions, and money, but if you do not have oil, which is today the greatest motive power that you use, all your other advantages would be of comparatively little value." Although domestic restrictions on oil use had been put in place in early 1916, such as a ban on "pleasure driving," these minor stopgap measures could in no way fuel the needs of the navy and of modern war on the Western Front. Following the 1916 oil-rationing program, civilian savings averaged only 20,000 tons per month. The shortage of oil was so acute that it was even proposed, although summarily rejected by the Admiralty, to cease construction of oil-fired ships and revert to coal or to conduct experiments with an ethanol-based fuel.[42]

Another reason for the suggested naval restructuring was the realization that naval war depended on the numerous benefits of oil-fired ships. Following the Battle of Jutland (31 May–1 June 1916), during which the British lost three battle cruisers, three armoured cruisers, and eight destroyers, the Grand Fleet was harnessed to avoid fleet-to-fleet engagements and remained reclusive. The Admiralty deduced that it "would be wrong to gamble with the safety of the Grand Fleet because the whole of the allied cause rested upon it."[43] In July 1914, two weeks before hostilities with Germany commenced, Admiral Sir John Jellicoe, commander of the Grand Fleet at Jutland, advised Churchill, "It will be seen therefore that far from the British ships showing a superiority [to German ships], the exact opposite is usually the case and assuming equality in design it is highly dangerous to consider that our ships as a whole are superior or even equal fighting machines." After Jutland, it was deduced that coal-fired capital ships could not provide the decisive advantages that oil-burners could. As Jon Sumida attests, "The loss of three battle cruisers at the battle of Jutland in 1916, on the other hand, raised fundamental questions about the soundness of pre-war British naval technology, particularly with regard to capital ship design and fire control."[44] Oil-fired ships, however, required oil.

The petroleum crisis in France was even more acute. Bérenger warned Prime Minister Georges Clemenceau in December 1917 that France would be dry of oil by March 1918 and that current supplies were so low that it was doubtful if France could maintain a prolonged defensive, like that at Verdun, for more than three or four days. Prior to the war, Clemenceau did not share the British zeal for petroleum and supposedly stated, "When I want some oil, I'll find it at my grocer's."[45] Facing a critical shortage, however, Clemenceau now directly appealed to U.S. President Woodrow Wilson for an additional "hundred thousand tons of tanker capacity." He added that at present, oil was "as vital as blood in the coming battles [and] a failure in the supply of gasoline would cause the immediate paralysis of our armies." He ominously added that a continuing deficiency of oil might "compel us to a peace unfavourable to the Allies … The safety of the Allied nations is in the balance." Additional American oil was quickly made available to both France and Britain.[46] The problem facing the Allies was not only the basic supply of oil, but also limited transportation. Therefore, by June 1917, Britain adopted for use the ballast tanks of 443 ocean liners and cargo ships as fuel-carrying "double-bottoms," which transported an annual 500,000 tons of oil, the equivalent to fifteen full-capacity tankers. This solution, however, had consequences. This oil supplanted agricultural imports from the United States and Canada, which decreased by

1.25 million tons over the next year, prompting supplementary stringent rationing regulations in the United Kingdom.[47]

Furthermore, in February 1918 an Inter-Allied Petroleum Conference, consisting of the United States, Britain, France, and Italy, was created to coordinate and control all oil shipping, distribution, and supply. This effective organization, coupled with the introduction of the convoy system to negate unrestricted German U-boat operations, and the supply and demand competition between Standard Oil and Royal Dutch Shell, solved the Allies' immediate oil crisis. Standard Oil NJ alone supplied 26 per cent of all Allied oil. Nevertheless, the war was ongoing with seemingly no end in sight. At this time, the Allies were by no means assured victory, and the outcome of the war still hung precariously in the balance. America, however, had entered the war in April 1917, and although its oil production had increased from 35.43 million tons in 1914 to 45.56 million in 1917, internal use rose dramatically to fuel its own military, industrial, and domestic needs. In fact, the United States was supplying the Allies with so much oil (80 per cent) that a gasoline famine gripped the country in 1918, a year that saw the highest gas prices, in inflation-adjusted terms, in the history of the United States. The American price per barrel annual average rose from $0.81 in 1914 to $1.98 in 1918. Appeals went out for "Gasolineless Sundays" on which day people would refrain from driving. President Wilson sardonically quipped, "I suppose I must walk to church."[48] The relatively secure immediate supply of oil was a key Allied advantage; however, other sources, apart from American, were still essential to continue the protracted war on the seas and on the bloodied battlefields of Europe and the Middle East. For example, British oil production in Persia, although increasing ten-fold during the war, was only eighteen thousand barrels per day by 1918.[49]

The quest for oil in conjunction with the crisis in Russia altered the structural foundation of the British wartime government. Prior to the Russian Revolution, British policy on the Caucasus had been promulgated and implemented by numerous committees, each vying for dominance, expansion, and funding, creating a muddled strategic doctrine. As events unfolded and oil became a prime objective, the War Cabinet and senior politicians, frustrated with the lack of a coherent policy or course of action, sought to create a single committee in response to new threats and evolving British interests. On 7 March 1918, the War Cabinet released a secret memorandum, written by chief of the Imperial General Staff Wilson, criticizing the ineffective inter-committee cooperation,

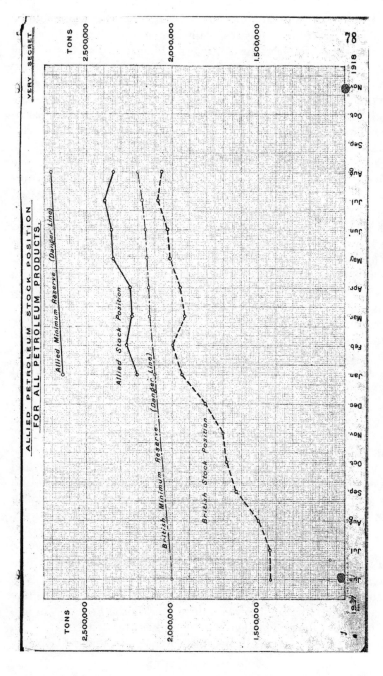

4.3 Allied Petroleum stock position for all petroleum products, August 1918 (National Archives, United Kingdom).

citing that "important measures have been rendered impossible or delayed with grave consequences by the lack of co-ordination involved by the present machinery. The existing machinery consists of:– (a) The Russian committee, (b) The Persian committee, (c) The Middle East committee. The above committees meet nominally about once a week, but in practice meetings are liable to be postponed owing to pressure of work of individual members. The composition, status and executive powers of these committees vary." The document concluded with the adamant recommendation, "In view of the situation created by the collapse of Russia and of the two main objectives of the enemy, i.e. the exploitation of Russian resources and the penetration for military purposes of Central Asia, it is vitally necessary that Allied policy in the East no less than in the West should be regarded from the standpoint of the single front."[50] This opinion was shared by the secretary for war, Lord Milner, who personally approached the prime minister on 20 March to lobby for a single "Eastern Committee."

The following day, a unified Eastern Committee was created with "executive functions," chaired by Lord Curzon. The primary members, aside from Curzon and Wilson, were Arthur Balfour (foreign secretary), his assistant director Lord Robert Cecil, Charles Lord Hardinge (permanent undersecretary of the Foreign Office), Edwin Montagu (secretary of the India Office), South African General Jan Smuts, and Major-General Sir George Macdonogh (director of military intelligence). It should be noted that neither Prime Minister Lloyd George nor Milner, although consulted, sat on the Eastern Committee. Nevertheless, both men supported a peripheral strategy to hasten the end of the war and to promote British interests in the Middle East and the Caucasus, including oil.[51]

Both Curzon, former chairman of the Middle East Committee and now head of its more sweeping successor, the Eastern Committee, and Maurice Hankey, secretary of the War Cabinet, supported the acquisition of oil-producing regions as a primary war aim, after approaches had been made to them "by people with knowledge of oil production."[52] While these lobbyists remained anonymous, likely the vital player for obtaining support for the Admiralty's oil war aim was Admiral Sir Edmond Slade, who was a leading authority on the Persian Gulf area and was instrumental in planning the Royal Navy's transition from coal to oil. In 1913, he was sent to the Middle East by Churchill to investigate the potential government investment in the APOC, of which Slade himself eventually became a major shareholder. On 29 July

4.4 Lord George Curzon in his position as viceroy and governor general of India, 1905 (Library of Congress).

1918, Slade produced and promulgated the linchpin document, *Petroleum Situation in the British Empire*: "The case as stated in the paper is sufficiently alarming to make the question one for immediate decision else we may find ourselves out-manoeuvred not only by the enemy but by neutrals or even by our present Allies."[53]

Slade's elaborate paper was extremely well-prepared and supported by comprehensive statistics and research, including findings of the 1917 U.S. Geological Survey. The title itself is perhaps misleading, as Slade presented a very well-defined study and outlook for global oil production and potential, summarizing that, for Britain, "it is obvious that the sources of supply from which we drew our require- ments before the war will not be sufficient to give us this enormously increased amount and we must look to other sources from which it can be drawn."[54] He argued that not only would vastly augmented oil stores be needed for military purposes, but domestic use, including industry and the rise in personal motor cars, would also skyrocket in coming years. Between 1914 and 1920, automobile registration in the United States increased dramatically. In 1914, there were 1.3 million officially registered automobiles in America. By 1920, this number had risen to 27 million vehicles, double the per-capita rate of Canada, its nearest rival. In fact, by 1927, the United States accounted for 85 per cent of global automobile production, and the country boasted 143,000 gasoline sta- tions. The United States was also the first to achieve mass motoriza- tion, with one automobile for every 5.3 Americans (18.9 per cent) that same year, while the mechanized countries of Europe – Britain, France, and Germany – could boast only one car for every forty-four people (2.3 per cent).[55] In conjunction, between 1900 and 1919, 225,000 miles of surfaced highways were constructed in the United States, bringing the total up from 125,000 to 350,000. This increased the need for petroleum, as asphalt is a significant by-product of the refining process.[56]

Oil production within the British Empire was paltry at best, as Can- ada was not yet a top producer, and the little that Canada produced was used within the country, and the "Burmah fields are not capable of great expansion." In 1913, Russia and Romania supplied Britain with 19.3 per cent of its oil, sources that by 1918 were no longer viable and could not be counted upon following the war (not to mention a decreas- ing annual production in both nations). The United States supplied 62.3 per cent that same year and made up the difference during the war by supplying the United Kingdom with 80 per cent of its oil between 1914 and 1918.[57]

The dilemma, according to Slade, was that U.S. production had peaked and was in decline, while U.S. domestic use was increasing dra- matically: "It is therefore safe to assume the United States authorities will not sit still and see the Petroleum resources of their country endan- gered ... the amount of Petroleum that we shall be able to draw from the United States will be greatly diminished if not entirely stopped." Furthermore, he argued that the 4.1 per cent imported from Mexico would be reassigned to the United States, who, by proximity alone, not to mention U.S. investment would, and with its own declining

Table 4.1 Sources of British oil, 1913 (tons)

Source	Total output	Exportable surplus	British imports	% of total British intake
United States	33,150,000	7,120,000	1,100,000 (16%)	62.3
Romania	1,880,000	940,000	230,000 (19%)	11.6
Russia	8,370,000	670,000	130,000 (19%)	7.7
Dutch Indies	1,500,000		125,000 (8%)	7.7
Mexico	3,480,000	1,740,000	70,000 (4%)	4.1
Others				6.5

Source: NA CAB/24/59, "Petroleum Situation in the British Empire," 29 July 1918.

production, import all of Mexico's low-grade exportable surplus. The massive wartime industrial boom in Canada would also likely see Canada tap into both the Mexican and U.S. markets, not to mention retaining its domestic oil.[58] In fact, the U.S. director of the Bureau of Mines reported to Wilson in 1917, "Within the next two to five years the oil fields of this country will reach their maximum production, and from that time on we will face an ever-increasing decline," causing Wilson to lament, "There seems to be no method by which we could assure ourselves of the necessary supply at home and abroad."[59] On the basis of his pre-war 1913 British oil import statistics, Slade concluded that, given these factors, only 14.2 per cent of oil imports from the Dutch East Indies and other sources remained viable in 1918. Even these he argued were not secure, given their ownership by Royal Dutch Shell and geographic distance from the United Kingdom. Exportable oil from the Dutch colonies, which had reached its zenith, would be grabbed by countries like Japan, Australia, and India, in closer proximity to the root source.

Germany was also wanting oil "in order to make up for the loss of Petroleum from the failing Galician fields ... We have the object lesson of German penetration into the shipping and other commercial interests and we must not allow it to be repeated ... it is quite obvious that if Germany cannot obtain the coveted control directly as the result of a victorious war, she will endeavour to obtain it through peaceful penetration." Slade proceeded to stress the importance of the Middle East as the foremost region for potential oil wealth:

In Persia and Mesopotamia lie the largest undeveloped resources at present known in the world ... If this estimate is anywhere near the truth, then it is evident that the Power that controls the oil lands of Persia and Mesopotamia will control the source of supply of the majority of the liquid fuel in the future ... We must therefore at all costs retain our hold on the Persian and Mesopotamian oil fields ... and we must not allow the intrusion in any form of any foreign interests, however much disguised they may be. We shall then be in a position of paramount control ... and enjoy all the advantages that this will give us if we find ourselves forced into another war. These advantages are very great and we cannot expect to enjoy them without making some sacrifices for them and we must be prepared to defend our claim against everybody. Conventions and Treaties are only paper and can be torn up and are not sufficient safeguard. We must have absolute security in this matter ... So far as the conduct of the war is concerned, the retention and development of the Persian oil lands is absolutely essential to the carrying on of the Mesopotamian expedition ... In conclusion the policy I would urge upon the Admiralty is:–

1 To press the Government to take the most energetic measures to prevent the enemy in any way from endangering the oil fields and works in Persia. This is indispensable to the success of the war.
2 To push forward as soon as possible the further development of the oil lands of Persia and those in Mesopotamia by purely British interests.
3 To push forward the exploration and development of all possible oil lands in the British Empire by purely British interests.
4 To encourage and assist British Companies to obtain control of as much oil lands in foreign countries as possible, with the stipulation (to prevent control being obtained by foreign interests) that the Oil produced shall only be sold to or through British oil distributing Companies. These oil lands can be developed to assist to provide our requirements in peace whilst our own resources in British territory can be conserved for war.
5 To exclude from participation in British Petroleum business all foreign interests in any shape or form, such participation being only a stepping stone to ultimate control and a very great danger in any future war.

The cover page to Slade's report written by the First Lord of the Admiralty, Eric Geddes, for submission to the Imperial War Cabinet concluded, "It is understood that a discussion will shortly take place on War Aims which must include the retention or otherwise of Mesopotamia, and it is hoped that in reviewing this question the extreme importance of that country in regard to the Petroleum situation will not be lost sight of."[60] In a subsequent letter, Geddes reminded the Cabinet, "The oil bearing districts of Mesopotamia and Persia are of very great national importance to us."[61]

Slade's argument was not only methodical, provident, well researched, well supported, and well written, it was also very convincing. Hankey, who received the report on 30 July, instantly began to campaign for the Admiralty's position within Whitehall, pressing for greater resolve and action in the Middle East and the Caucasus. Responding to Geddes on the same day, Hankey confirmed that the oil situation "appears to me to have a most important bearing on two questions which are about to be considered by the Imperial War Cabinet and the Committee of Prime Ministers respectively, namely, (1) The question of War Aims, and (2) The question of the Future Campaign." Hankey then elaborated:

As regards War Aims, if this information is correct, the retention of the oil-bearing regions in Mesopotamia and Persia in British hands, as well as a proper strategic boundary to cover them, would appear to be a first-class British war aim. As regards the future campaign, it would appear desirable that before we come to discuss peace, we should obtain possession of all the oil-bearing regions in Mesopotamia and Southern Persia, wherever they may be ... you will have seen that both Palestine and Mesopotamia have rather become "dead ends," because of the new line of penetration to the East which the enemy has opened up through the Caucusus [sic] towards the Caspian and from thence through Turkestan or Persia towards India. The acquisition of further oil-bearing country, however, might make it worthwhile for us to push on in Mesopotamia.[62]

The following day, 1 August, Hankey wrote to both Arthur Balfour, secretary for foreign affairs, and Prime Minister David Lloyd George. To Balfour he stressed,

Oil in the next war will occupy the place of coal in the present war ... The only big potential supply that we can get under British control is the Persian and Mesopotamian supply. The point where you come in is that the control over these oil supplies becomes a first-class British war aim. I write to urge you that in your statement to the Imperial War Cabinet you should rub this in ... Admiral Slade tells me there are important oil deposits in Mesopotamia north of our present line ... as they might have an important influence on future military operations.[63]

In his letter to the prime minister, Hankey took a more pragmatic approach, admitting that while "there is no military advantage in pushing forward in Mesopotamia ... the argument is that the German gun is now aimed at India, across the Caspian Sea, instead of, as formerly down the Baghdad Railway. From Mesopotamia we cannot affect their advance across the Caspian ... in Mesopotamia where the British have an enormous preponderance of force. Would it not be an advantage, before the end of the war, to secure the valuable oil wells in Mesopotamia?"[64] On the same day, however, Hankey wrote to Admiral Rosslyn Wemyss. The admiral forwarded Slade's report with his own cover letter, no doubt influenced by Hankey. Wemyss's cover letter urged the "importance of these oil wells as a war aim ... it is supremely important for our future to get this oil."[65]

On the 2 August, the Admiralty itself produced a report, "to show the great importance of petroleum as fuel for the future," based upon known and potential oilfields in Mesopotamia and Persia referencing all available studies, including the aforementioned Mosul report submitted to the kaiser by German engineers in 1898. If Baku could not be held, they argued, these regions became increasingly vital to British strategic interests. The Admiralty's report also contained a meticulous "Map Showing Important Oil Occurrences in Mesopotamia and Part of Persia," which was shown to Lloyd George (unfortunately, this map is too large to reproduce).[66] In addition, on 9 August, the Royal Air Force also opportunely submitted a report to the War Cabinet in support of Slade's recommendations:

The whole future of air power is dependent upon adequate supplies of liquid fuel. No other form of fuel is as yet in view. Air power is still in its infancy. Its development as a striking force is just beginning. Air force will in the near future be the first line of offence and defence. Air warfare will clear the way for sea warfare and land warfare. I do not think that it is an over-statement to say that the very existence of the Empire will depend in the first instance upon aerial supremacy. Admiral Slade has shewn clearly in his paper that in Persia and Mesopotamia lie the largest undeveloped resources of liquid fuel in the world. In view of the paramount importance of liquid fuel, both to the Royal Air Force and to the Navy, it is essential that steps shall be taken to monopolize all possible supplies of petroleum and kindred oils. Further, the areas in which it is contained must be safeguarded by a very wide belt of territory between it and potential enemies.[67]

With these additions to Slade's already meticulous study, the issue of oil entered all levels of British military and economic policy and planning for the duration of the war and into the peace, although marginalized scepticism persisted.

While Balfour acknowledged the benefits of seizing the oil regions of the Middle East while the war was still ongoing, he was wary of promoting Hankey's oil crusade, believing that Britain's allies, chiefly the United States and President Wilson, would regard this manoeuvre as a "purely Imperialist War Aim." Throughout the war Balfour had outwardly expressed his belief that the war should not be used as a medium to expand the British Empire. Undaunted, Hankey wrote Balfour again, on 12 August, the day before the crucial Cabinet meeting on war aims. The argument Hankey gave in response to Balfour's fear of upsetting the United States was the "great importance to push forward in Mesopotamia at least as far as … is necessary to secure a proper supply of water. Incidentally this would give us most of the oil-bearing regions." In short, these regions contained the headwaters of both the Euphrates and Tigris Rivers, and their control was essential to ensure adequate water supplies of lands to the south already under British control. Furthermore, he argued, if these areas were not to be under Ottoman rule, "it is almost unavoidable that we should acquire the Northern regions of Mesopotamia … If these regions are not to be under the control of the Turk, under whose control are they to be? I submit there is only one possible answer, and that is that, in some form or another, they will come under British control."[68]

Hankey's tireless efforts paid dividends the following day, when Balfour announced that Britain was the only logical choice to control Mesopotamia, because all other nations were weakened, specifically Russia and Turkey, and that Mesopotamia should be the exception to his belief that the British Empire should not capitalize on the war to promote expansion. "I do not care under what system we keep the oil," Balfour added, "but I am quite clear it is all-important for us that this oil should be available." Following Balfour's address, both the Admiralty and the Air Staff presented their papers in favour of seizing the oil rich regions of northern Mesopotamia. Finally, Lloyd George alluded to the benefits of capturing Mosul before the cessation of hostilities and gave the green light for its occupation. He reasoned that the *vilayets* of Basra, Baghdad, and Mosul must be administered by the same government (thereby removing any French claims).[69] As Stephen Roskill has acknowledged, "Though Hankey's views on post war oil policy were without doubt as overtly 'imperialistic' as Balfour stated, the British government's aims after the war did in fact follow closely the lines proposed by Hankey ... The end of the war by no means terminated the rivalry between the international oil companies, and the involvement in them of the British government through the powerful interests of the Admiralty."[70]

The dilemma, however, was that the northern half of the Mosul *vilayet* was in the French sphere of influence under the May 1916 Sykes-Picot Agreement, which partitioned the greater Middle East into British, French, Russian, and later Italian zones of "control" or "protectorates." This document hammered out by British representative Sir Mark Sykes and his French counterpart François Georges Picot, was chastised by British politicians for callously "surrendering" Mosul to the French. Thereafter, the British tried at all turns to undermine the agreement, especially after the capture of Baghdad. In 1913, Sykes prophetically warned Parliament that the "break-up of the Ottoman Empire in Asia must bring the powers of Europe directly confronting one another in a country where there are no frontiers [defined borders]. The very awkward geographical situation troubled the mind of Alexander the Great, the mind of Diocletian and the mind of Constantine."[71]

For Hankey, the outcome of the 13 August 1918 Imperial War Cabinet was a victory for British oil interests and for oil as a "first-class British war aim."[72] This included the vital oil at Baku. "In Baku, the Entente were supporting an anti-Soviet Government, since Lenin had conceded to the Germans the exploitation of the Caspian oil resources," Lloyd George later remarked. "We found it necessary to intervene in order to hold the Central Powers in check and prevent them from securing valuable supplies. This was in the south, around the Caspian, where were the oil-wells of Baku ... If Germany succeeded in provisioning itself freely from these sources, the whole effect of our blockade would be lost ... Had their hopes been realised, the War might have had a different outcome."[73] The Germans assured the Bolsheviks that they would restrain the spring 1918 Turkish offensive directed at Baku in exchange for 25 per cent of its oil. To this, "of course, we agreed," said Lenin. This arrangement was relayed to the Bolshevik Baku Commune, ordering it to acquiesce to this "request." The local importance of this oil was too dear, however, and the committee adamantly responded, "Neither in victory nor in defeat will we give the German plunderers one drop of oil produced by our labor."[74]

Furthermore, on 2 October, General Marshall was ordered to capitalize on Bulgaria's departure from the war confirmed on 29 September by the Armistice of Thessalonica. He was told, "As much ground as possible should be gained up the Tigris. Such action is important not only for political reasons but also to occupy as large a portion of the oil bearing regions as possible. At the same time, the work on the L. of C. [lines of communication] to the Caspian should not be retarded in any way as the development of this route is looked upon as of primary importance."[75] Marshall began to organize for a push north to capture Mosul and its oilfields.

At the 1917 Inter-Allied Conference in Paris on 25–6 July, Lloyd George had proclaimed to his colleagues, "If the Central Powers should succeed in obtaining possession of the vast stores of Russian wheat and oil, so essential to their continued prosecution of the War not only for themselves but also their allies, it would mean the prolongation of the struggle, perhaps by years." By the close of 1917, Germany was increasingly suffering from the effects of the naval blockade and of a protracted war. The domestic grain yield for 1917 decreased by 48 per cent as compared with 1914, while the potato harvest fell by 15 per cent over this same period. Oil shortages plagued industrial, military, and civilian circles, rationing of all commodities was sweeping, and hoarders were harshly punished. Ersatz substitutes supplanted a variety of foodstuffs and heating oils, cooking oils, and lubricating oils. Petroleum and high-quality oils were reserved strictly for military use, most notably for aircraft. By this point, even aircraft were dependent mainly on the heavy and ineffective benzol fuel. Lack of oil drastically hampered the German war economy both on and off the battlefield, and civilian morale was declining to the point of dire misery, as resources became increasingly scarce.[76]

Allied leaders agreed that some form of intervention was necessary to secure the vast Allied war materials stockpiled at the ports of Archangel, Murmansk, and Vladivostok, and to prevent German exploitation of Russian natural resources, chiefly in the Ukraine and the Caucasus. In southern Russia, the Allies were faced with the dilemma of "how best to prevent Germany from revictualling herself afresh from the corn lands and the oilfields which would be laid open to her if she succeeded in penetrating to the Don and the rich provinces of the Caucasus." It was decided that one of the "main objectives in the East" was to "prevent Germany and Turkey from gaining access to the oilfields of the Caspian."[77] So began the "Adventures of Dunsterforce."

On 6 December 1920, soldier, diplomat, and acclaimed scholar on the Middle East, Brigadier-General Sir Percy Sykes concluded a lecture

CANNON-FODDER—AND AFTER.

KAISER (*to* 1917 *Recruit*). "AND DON'T FORGET THAT YOUR KAISER WILL FIND A USE
FOR YOU—ALIVE OR DEAD."

[At the enemy's "Establishment for the Utilisation of Corpses" the dead bodies of German soldiers are treated chemically,
the chief commercial products being lubricant oils and pigs' food.]

4.5 "Cannon-Fodder – and After." Cartoon from *Punch!* mocking
Germany's shortage of petroleum, 25 April 1917.

at the Royal Geographical Society in London, addressing a brimming room: "We have heard a most interesting lecture to-night, but in reality it is a great deal more than that. I think that when the history of the Great War is finally written and we gain some distance from the events, this will be looked upon as the great adventure of the Great War … He took an expedition to Baku, and denied the oil of Baku to the Turks for six weeks. He also did what was of greater importance, he prevented the Turks and their German masters from joining hands … and this would have been a most appalling menace to the Indian Empire."[78] The guest speaker being applauded was Major-General Lionel Dunsterville, commander of an undersized, elite secret unit made up of choice soldiers from the British Empire that took on his name – Dunsterforce – operating in Mesopotamia, Persia, and the Caucasus between December 1917 and September 1918. "Indeed, oil was the pivotal question," reiterated Sykes. "In consequence, to deny Baku to the enemy, even for a while, was of great importance. Major-General Dunsterville was appointed to carry out this extremely difficult task."[79]

The conditions and geography of the Middle East and Caucasus in which Dunsterforce travelled and fought were unrelenting, austere, and hazardous. Forced marches of ten to thirty miles per day under blistering temperatures topping 50°C or plummeting to -40°C in mountain passes exceeding ten thousand feet became routine. These hearty imperial soldiers were blasted by wind and sandstorms, ravaged by flies, mosquitos, snakes, and scorpions, in addition to the conventional concerns of thirst, hunger, disease, and combat. They were unwelcome and unsolicited strangers in exotic lands in the midst of drought, famine, genocide, ethnic cleansing, and civil war. Local tribes who were friends one day were foes the next, changing sides with the ebb and flow of the fortunes of war. Isolated from immediate reinforcements or a reliable supply line, the men of Dunsterforce trudged forward from Basra to Baghdad to Baku, covering some thirteen hundred miles by every mode of transportation available, including boat, rail, horse, camel, car, and foot. They were ostensibly wandering orphans of the war and dubbed by one participant as "no man's child."

Along the way, they encountered German spies, rescued American missionaries, viewed the lands of biblical narrative, toured the ruins of ancient empires, dined with sheikhs, mingled with locals of various ethnicities and faiths, ministered to starving Persians and refugee Armenians and Assyrians, and built roads to alleviate famine and the passage of Christian refugees fleeing ethnic annihilation. The soldiers

of Dunsterforce battled Turkish forces, the "Savage Division" of jihad-
ist mercenaries, and rogue Kurdish and Jangali guerrillas. They fought
alongside Bolshevik soldiers of the Red Army, volunteer Armenian
units, disavowed Russian Cossacks, and flew Serbian and Bolshevik
flags, all in an attempt to protect Baku's precious oil from Turkish or
German appropriation.

The story of Dunsterforce is inseparable from British oil interests and
has yet to be written in any great detail or clarity. Secondary sources
predictably recite the same account, which only shadows the peripher-
ies of the mission and its place in the broader context of Britain's oil
war. What has been written is recycled from previous works, which
in turn rely on Dunsterville's own account, *The Adventures of Dunsterforce* (1920). His work, however, must be read and cited with caution. As John F. Kennedy eloquently articulated after his failed 1961
Bay of Pigs invasion, "Victory has a thousand fathers, but defeat is an
orphan."[80] Dunsterville was discredited following his mission, and he
spent the remainder of his life trying to clear his name and capitalize on
his boyhood relationship with Rudyard Kipling. The character Stalky
in Kipling's fiction *Stalky and Co.* (1899) is a romanticised portrayal of
Dunsterville as a youth, bordering on fiction, during their time at the
United Services College in North Devon.

As if representing Dunsterville himself, Richard Hannay, Buchan's
Greenmantle hero, after hearing his initial briefing, simply asks his superior officer, "And the mission you spoke of is for me to go and find out?"
Nodding, his senior intelligence officer stoically states that the Turco-
German threat is "moving eastwards ... It is life and death. I can put it
no higher and no lower. Once we know what is the menace we can meet
it. As long as we are in the dark it works unchecked and we may be too
late ... but if the East blazes up ... there will be hell let loose in those
parts pretty soon. Hell, which may spread. Beyond Persia, remember,
lies India ... The stakes are no less than victory and defeat ... That is the
crazy and impossible mission."[81] Oil was the exclusive aim of Dunsterforce's mission.

Chapter Five

The Deployment of Dunsterforce

On the evening of 28 January 1918, newly promoted twenty-four-year-old Sergeant Crofford Campbell sat in his small hotel room with a view of the Tower of London listening to the explosions of a German Gotha bomber air raid. Rather than being unnerved, Crofford, who had enlisted in the Canadian Expeditionary Force in October 1914, and was wounded at the Somme in 1916, thought little of the event, having served since September 1915 on the Western Front. While awaiting orders from the "War Office for special duty," he simply recorded in his pocket-sized diary, "Air raid commenced at 8 PM and lasted well after midnight."[1] Crofford and another 300 men scattered on leave throughout London, constituting what was known only as the "hush-hush army," were actually listening to the worst single bombing incident of the war. The "X87" German raid killed 58 civilians, while wounding 173 others. One 660-pound bomb hit the Odhams Print Works, killing 38 and wounded another 91.

Unbeknownst to these men, the planning and actual deployment of what was officially known as the British Mission to the Caucasus was already underway. This secret force, soon to be dubbed "Dunsterforce," after its commanding officer, Major-General Lionel Dunsterville, had, after deliberation, been sanctioned by the War Office on 19 December 1917. This group of men, made up of Canadians, Australians, New Zealanders, South Africans, Russians, and British soldiers, would embark on one of the most capricious, strange, and muddled missions of the Great War. In the process, they would traverse the lands of biblical narrative, look upon ancient monuments erected by legendary rulers of glorious empires, and bear witness to the plights of the Persian famine and the Armenian people. The objective, however interpreted, was still oil.

Religious and ethnic violence between the Christian Georgians, Assyrians, and Armenians and their Islamic counterparts coincided with the spread of Islam into the Caucasus between 632 and 661 CE.[2] While many local tribes converted to Islam, such as the Circassians, in other regions, most notably the southwest, adherence to Christianity was upheld. During the mid-1500s under Suleiman the Magnificent the Ottoman Empire stretched into the southern Caucasus, creating a "checkerboard" pattern of interspersed enclaves of Muslims and Christians living a precarious coexistence. While ethnic violence was habitual, memories of the clashes between Armenians and Azerbaijanis from 1894 to 1896 and 1905 to 1909 lingered long into the First World War. Corresponding violence erupted in Bosnia, Albania, Macedonia, and Kosovo between 1908 and 1913. The massacres of 1905 began during the Russian revolution of that same year, which included widespread workers' strikes, civil unrest, and military mutinies. Strikes and ethnic violence in Baku devastated oil production, which had reached its zenith in 1901 accounting for nearly 52 per cent globally. Following this Azeri-Armenian War, ethnic hostility and suspicion permeated the Caucasus, most notably in Baku, and oil output stagnated.[3] During the First World War, this xenophobia would spawn unprecedented mass murder.

The Armenian "genocide" remains a highly controversial political issue, and the historiography, while vast, is emotionally driven and peppered with propaganda, dis-information, and outright fiction. Blame, denial, validation, and argumentation over lexis, specifically the use of the label *genocide* to imply an act of premeditated and calculated state-sponsored extermination – akin to the now-infamous 1942 Wannsee Protocol – permeate discourse. Shortly after enacting the 1935 Nuremburg Laws, Hitler professed to his inner circle, "Who, after all, speaks today of the annihilation of the Armenians?"[4] What cannot be denied, however, is that hundreds of thousands of innocent Armenians and Assyrians, including women and children, died at the hands of the Turks (and to a lesser extent the Kurds and Circassians) during the Great War, "with profound historical, moral, and practical consequences which persist into present day."[5]

Reliable documentation is incontrovertible, and the genocide was witnessed by scores of objective observers, many of whom wrote immediate narratives, diaries, letters, and reports. German military attachés, horrified by the slaughter and starvation, wrote detailed dispatches to their superiors in the hopes that pressure could be brought to bear on the Ottomans, while clearing Germany of complicity and international condemnation. General Ludendorff remarked, "Turkey plunged into a war of murder and looting in the Caucasus." General Paul von Hindenburg remembered, "The atrocious events ... which transpired in the entire domain of the Ottoman Empire and towards the end of the war occurred also in the Armenian part of the Transcaucasus."[6] Ambassadors from Germany, Austria, Britain, and, most notably, Henry Morgenthau, the ambassador for (at this time) neutral America, wrote meticulous reports and records, as did a variety of missionaries and aid workers, not to mention Armenians themselves.[7] In August 1916, the British foreign secretary, Sir Edward Grey, was presented with an exceptionally vivid report of over seven hundred pages, compiled by historian Arnold J. Toynbee and former politician and academic James Bryce. This vast collection of candid evidence, entitled *The Treatment of the Armenians in the Ottoman Empire 1915–16* (also known as the "Blue Book"), contained letters, accounts, and diaries of observers from a host of countries and denominations, as well as Armenian testimonies. "It is a terrible mass of evidence," wrote Grey upon its completion, "but I feel that it ought to be published and widely studied by all who have the broad interests of humanity at heart. It will be valuable, not only for the immediate information of public opinion as to the conduct of the Turkish Government towards this defenceless people, but also as a mine of information for historians in the future."[8]

What has been overlooked was that the Ottoman authorities were convinced that the European powers would use Christian minorities as a political, if not moral, excuse to dismantle piecemeal and then colonize Ottoman territory. Philip Jenkins, a pre-eminent scholar of theology, reiterates,

> While this fact does not for a moment justify the violence, we should recognize the Turks were reading European ambitions with deadly accuracy ... While the Russians wanted to organize an amicable partition of Ottoman lands, rival powers like British and French dreaded the expansion of tsarist power into the Mediterranean world ... Conceivably, as in Algeria, European rule could lead directly to the mass settlement of white Christian immigrants, leaving Muslims as dispossessed strangers in their own countries ... Further raising tensions, Western powers began to care deeply about the promising oil discoveries that were making news in Ottoman-ruled Mesopotamia and Arabia (and in neighboring Persia).

In contrast to the Ottoman rationale, the Armenian persecution gave perceived justification, whether moral or imperialist, to ambitious

European powers, as the details of the horrific violence spread across the globe, angering its Christian populations.[9]

In 1914, the Armenian population of the Ottoman Empire was roughly 1.68 million, including 1.5 million living in the *vilayet*s of eastern Anatolia bordering the Russian Caucasus, home to another 1.3 million Armenians. An additional 900,000 made up the diasporas in Persia, Egypt, India, Europe, and the United States.[10] At the outbreak of war, Armenians began migrating from Ottoman territory into the Russian Caucasus or Persia. By December 1915, the British consul at Batum reported the number of known Armenian refugees in the Caucasus to be 173,038, although the actual figure is likely closer to 250,000.[11] Other Armenians, predominantly young men, enlisted in the Russian army, or, as irregulars, initiated sporadic attacks and bombings against Turkish soldiers and administrators. Following Enver's disastrous winter campaign to force the Caucasus and the final defeat of his Third Army at Sarikamish in January 1915, the situation escalated quickly. With the inevitable Russian counterattack that would accompany the spring thaw, Third Army commanders feared a simultaneous Armenian insurrection behind its lines. Morgenthau repeatedly tried to intercede on behalf of the Armenians, going so far as to offer Turkish officials a new homeland for the Armenians in the western United States. "There is no use arguing," he was told. "The Armenians have openly encouraged our enemies. They have assisted the Russians in the Caucasus, and our failure there is largely explained by their actions."[12] Unfortunately, for the non-combatant Armenian populations there was some truth to this. "I came into this world a Turk," declared the physician Mehmed Reshid, the "executioner governor" of the Diyarbekir *vilayet*, to the southwest of Lake Van. "Armenian traitors had found a niche for themselves in the bosom of the fatherland; they were dangerous microbes. Isn't it the duty of a doctor to destroy these microbes?"[13]

As a result of these concerns, on 25 February 1915, in near panic, Mehmed Talaat, minister of the interior, issued Directive 8682, entitled "Increased Security Precautions." Essentially, the directive ordered all Armenians to be disarmed, including 40,000 in the Ottoman Army, who were relegated to "labour" battalions and were literally worked to death. Many Ottoman units and Muslim civilians interpreted the directive to serve their own purposes and began punitive raids on Armenian communities, raping, burning, and looting in the process. In April, the Armenian leadership and aristocracy in the Ottoman capital of Constantinople (Istanbul), along with 5,000 others, simply vanished.

The remaining 140,000 were removed from public positions, stripped of their wealth, and languished in ghettoized poverty.[14] At this time, Armenian guerrillas began attacking Turkish patrols outside the city of Van in what Ottoman officials labelled "open rebellion." Ottoman forces advanced on Van and laid siege to the city, swollen with an additional 15,000 Armenian refugees from the surrounding area who had escaped Turkish retribution. In the midst of fierce fighting, Muslim civilians inside Van were killed or fled in a mass exodus: "The fighting in and around Van was merciless. While Ottoman regulars and Kurdish militiamen besieged the town, tribesmen roamed the outlying areas. Armenian males twelve years or older were targeted for death, and Armenian women liable to kidnapping and rape. On order of Van's governor, Djevdet Bey, Armenian men had horseshoes nailed to their feet and were force-marched through the streets before being killed. Inside the town, well-armed rebels held the advantage, and they, too, gave no quarter, exacting retribution on Muslim women and other non-combatants."[15] As anticipated, Russian forces (containing a high number of Armenians) under General Yudenich arrived to break the siege on 23 May, forcing a Turkish retreat.

Turkish reaction was immediate. On 30 May 1915, the infamous "Regulation for the Settlement of Armenians Relocated to Other Places Because of War Conditions & Emergency Political Requirements" (Tehcir Law) was ratified by Talaat's Ministry of the Interior under the oversight of the Department of Settlement of Tribes and Immigrants. The military was in charge of corralling an unwilling Armenian population, while local officials were responsible for arranging transportation, accommodation, nourishment, and health care en route to their new homes in the deserts of northern Mesopotamia and Syria. All of this was to occur during a war in which the Ottoman army was already in dire need of these military necessities.[16] This legislation, argues Roger Ford, "enabled the Ottoman government to round up all Armenians ... and concentrate them in camps prior to 'resettling' them in the extremely inhospitable desert areas of Syria and northern Mesopotamia – a textbook example of what we have come to call ethnic cleansing."[17] Historian Efraim Karsh asserts, "The forceful relocation of almost an entire people to a remote, alien, and hostile environment amid a general war was tantamount to a collective death sentence. In the end, whatever their initial intention, the Ottomans' actions constituted nothing short of genocide."[18]

Deportations began in the northeast *vilayets* bordering the Caucasus, and in Ankara in July, followed by the western *vilayets* in September.

5.1 Armenian widows with children and orphans in eastern Anatolia, September 1915 (Library of Congress).

Most healthy Armenian men (still living) were already being used as slave labour, or alternatively continued to fight in either the Russian army or as members of independent guerrilla formations. Over 175,000 Armenians served in Russian forces during the war.[19] Of the deportees, therefore, the majority were women, children, and the elderly, who died from rape, murder, torture, starvation, dehydration, disease, and other acts of barbarism. Many who did survive were sold into slavery or prostitution, with young males converted to Islam. They were also preyed upon by gangs of Kurds and criminals released from prison for this sole purpose. In societies founded on personal and family honour, rape is a weapon used to systematically destroy the essence of cultural cohesion by shaming religion and race.[20]

While the Armenian pogrom had essentially run its course by the end of 1916, between March and September of 1918 Baku would be the setting for further Armenian-Muslim massacres. Like all else concerning this topic, the Armenian death toll is also hotly contested. Figures range from 300,000 (the figure acknowledged by modern Turkey) to 1.5 million (claimed by Armenian apologists). The most reliable and meticulous studies of the statistical and empirical data not surprisingly find middle ground and place the number of dead between 665,000 and 850,000 – roughly half of Anatolia's 1.5 million Armenians.[21]

In addition, the 565,000 Christian Assyrians living in the Ottoman Empire and in Persia suffered the same fate as the Armenians, with comparable results. During the first offensive into northern Persia in early 1915, Ottoman forces ravaged Assyrian communities. Months later, during their retreat in the face of successful Russian operations, they turned on their own Assyrian enclaves. While Assyrian fatalities are not known, most estimate 250,000 dead. Coptic Christians in Egypt, fearing the same fate at the hands of their Muslim brethren, organized the secular Wafd (Delegation) Party. Between 1915 and 1917, the Christian enclaves of Syria and Lebanon were also victims of murder and systematic starvation, which claimed upwards of 300,000 lives, before the British occupation in September 1918.[22]

Within this cultural upheaval in Syria, Michel Aflaq emerged as a leading voice of Arab nationalism and founded the Ba'ath (Renaissance) Party, which drew support from controversial Muslim groups such as the Alawites. The Ba'athists have played a pivotal role in the modern histories of Iraq and Syria, most notably under the regimes of Saddam Hussein and Bashar al-Assad. Since the First World War, rapid religious demographic transformation in the Middle East has combined with "a global Islamist revival to fuel the success of potent movements such as Hamas and the Muslim Brotherhood ... Saddam's lunatic invasion of Kuwait in 1990 set the stage for the destruction of his regime and the expulsion or exile of most Iraqi Christians ... Syria's minority populations commonly express their fears that they too might suffer a comparable fate ... In Egypt similarly, recent political and religious upheavals have even raised doubts about the continued survival of Egypt's Copts."[23]

During the pogroms of the war, Muslims also suffered at the hands of the Armenians and Russians. A disguised Armenian priest, Grigoris Balakian, travelled throughout Anatolia to document the destruction of his people. In addition to witnessing the Armenian plight, he recorded

the survivors of the hundreds of thousands of Muslims who had fled the Russian armies and the Armenian volunteer regiments. Decimated by starvation and epidemic, these Muslims would die in the severities of the coming winter. I passed through the Turkish neighbourhoods along the river and came upon thousands of Turkish and Kurdish refugees – women, girls, and children – on the flagstone pavements in front of the mosques. They were living ghosts, reduced by starvation to skeletons; for clothing they had only rags hanging from their shoulders, and the dirt that covered them rendered them unrecognizable. There was no visible difference at all between these refugees and Armenian exiles.[24]

It is likely that 40 per cent of the Muslim population of eastern Anatolia perished during the war: "Throughout the empire and its borderlands Muslims, too, suffered at the hands of both the Ottoman state and its wartime enemies. Kurds, formerly employed by Ottoman authorities as irregular troops, were also deported from sensitive borderlands or simply slaughtered. Muslims were attacked, moved about, and killed by Christian states and empires in both the Balkans and the north and south Caucasus. In round figures, these regions were emptied of more than a million Muslims during the First World War alone."[25]

Allied leaders were well aware of the ethnic strife in Anatolia and the Caucasus, and the atrocities committed against the Armenians were used as a powerful propaganda tool, most notably in the United States, which contained the largest Armenian diaspora. Sean McMeekin notes, "The wholesale removal of the Armenian population of eastern Anatolia in 1915, whether pre-meditated or carried out in the opportunistic fog of war, had an important strategic dimension [and] gave the Great Powers an excuse to intervene."[26] The British furtively used the Armenian incident for imperial advantage by associating "the liberation of Armenia, a desolated country where Britain had no long-term territorial interests ... with the liberation of strategically important, oil rich and fertile Mesopotamia."[27] With the design of Dunsterforce, Britain was now prepared to back irregular Armenian formations against further Ottoman penetration into the Caucasus in order to protect Baku's prized oil. The War Office also pleaded with the Russian provisional government to transfer all Armenians under its command to the Caucasus to join their thirty-five thousand brethren already under arms, while requesting that the U.S. administration draft Armenian Americans for service in the Caucasus as well.[28]

As early as 20 October 1917, General Sir William Robertson scrutinized the situation in the Caucasus, remarking, "The Armenians are the only large body on the Russian Asiatic front whose interests are vitally bound up with the success of the Allied cause."[29] On 30 November the

British minister in Tehran, Sir Charles Marling, received a deputation from Tiflis consisting of Georgian and Armenian leaders. In essence, they asked for funds to continue to operate forces against the Turks on the Caucasus front. Marling wired the Eastern Committee with the opinion that the "country could be secured as a stronghold against Maximalist influences if money were forthcoming, but if it were not, then Caucasian troops (which members of the deputation asserted to be the best trained and most loyal) would probably leave the front ... which would leave open the whole range of the Persian and Caucasian fronts."[30] Curzon added, "It must be borne in mind that the Allies are pledged in the most categorical manner to secure the liberation of Armenians from the Turkish yoke, and should that pledge be broken, not only shall we be dishonoured before the world, but the Armenians, handed back to their oppressors, will, in so far as they have not already been destroyed, disappear from the list of peoples."[31] Mark Sykes, British author of the 1916 Sykes-Picot Agreement and Curzon's trusted advisor, agreed that that the "Armenian Question is the real answer to pan-Turanism just as free Arabia is the answer to Turkish pan-Islamism."[32]

On 14 December, Lieutenant-General Sir George Macdonogh, senior intelligence officer (soon to take command of the newly minted Military Intelligence and Operations unit), explained to the War Cabinet that

> he had communicated the decision of the War Cabinet promising assistance to the Armenians, and had received from General Shore [commander of the British Military Mission to the Caucasus based in Tiflis] a telegram to the effect that the Armenian fraternity had collected a sum of between 5 and 10 million roubles, and giving figures for the cost of mobilising 20,000 men and maintaining 40,000 men for three months. The Director of Military Intelligence stated that the most valuable help in this part of the world might be expected from the Armenians, who had every reason to fight the bitter end.[33]

During a special committee of the War Cabinet on 19 December, Robertson urged that "definite encouragement should be given to the Government in Tiflis, and an endeavour should be made to constitute an Armenian Army, which should be given financial support." It was also promulgated that the Persian and Caucasus fronts would be placed under one command and mission made up of select officers and NCOs to train and lead Armenian, Georgian, Persian, and other local troops and resources with a view to checking Turkish and German penetration on these fronts:[34] "We started another adventurous policy – sending a minute force up from Mesopotamia to the Caucasus with instructions to endeavour to organise the Georgians and Armenians for resistance to the Turks and to secure the flank of the Mesopotamia Force."[35] This mission was then officially sanctioned as the British Military Mission to the Caucasus – soon to be known variously as "the Baghdad Mission," "the Hush-Hush Army," and finally as Dunsterforce.

Dunsterforce was one of three "hush-hush" missions designed and deployed to safeguard British interests in the Middle East, the Caucasus, Central Asia, and India. According to Lloyd George,

> There can be no question that throughout 1918, the Germans looked to Russia, not merely to supply them with substantial territorial gains to reward them for their war effort, but still more as a vitally important source of foodstuffs and fodder, of oil and minerals … In Russian territory where, after the collapse of Russia and the Treaty of Brest-Litovsk, we found it necessary to intervene to prevent them from securing valuable supplies. This was in the south, around the Caspian, where were the oil-wells at Baku … the road to that valuable region lay open, both the Germans and the Turks began a race for it. Our concern was to prevent either of them from winning.[36]

Following the 19 December meeting, the Eastern Committee of the War Office, under the direction of General Robertson and Lord Curzon, began organizing special military missions to combat the threat of a German and/or Turkish push southeast through the Caucasus into Central Asia and India: "The situation in Trans-Caucasia and Persia grows very menacing … We are now confronting a coalition of forces which is out to produce a world revolution, a holy war, and a pan-Turanian rising … anarchy is a bad neighbour for Afghanistan and India."[37] The War Office agreed that it was "time to push about like the devil in the Caucasus … and turn the tables upon the Germans in that part of the world … especially of those great parts of Turkey-in-Asia which lie beyond Asia minor properly speaking, would not only add greatly to her economic strength but would put her in a geographic-strategic position between Asia and Africa, which would make her, in effect, Mistress of both these Continents … The even more serious crisis … to fuel and petrol might be solved."[38] In June 1918, Curzon provided the Imperial War Cabinet with a bleak situation report: "German ambitions, which had received an immense impetus since the collapse of Russia and the Treaty of Brest-Litovsk, lay along two main lines of advance: a northern line through the Black Sea, the Caucasus, the Caspian and Turkestan, to the borders of Chinese Turkestan; and the southern through Palestine, Mesopotamia, and through Persia and Afghanistan against India. The whole area between these lines was a theatre of actual or probable warfare."[39]

The Eastern Committee duly noted, "It is a race against time ... Trans-Caucasia seems thus to be both the most promising and by far the most vital from the point of view of British interests."[40] Three distinct missions were therefore designed to negate these possible disadvantages. The largest and western-most force, Dunsterforce, was to move through Persia from Baghdad, reach the ports of Enzeli and Baku, on the western shore of the Caspian Sea, and establish contacts with pro-Allied elements of the local populations from a headquarters based at Tiflis. The select officers and NCOs of the mission were to then train, organize, and lead these local militia forces financed by the British.

A second, smaller mission, under command of Major-General Sir Wilfrid Malleson, dubbed "Malmiss," was to operate east of Dunsterforce, after which it was modelled. On 4 January the War Office questioned the India Office, "Do you think it is practicable to set up British organization in Turkestan like Dunsterville's in the Caucasus?" The mission was authorized in April, as "War Office consider that, in view of proposed intimate connection between Turkestan and Caucasus, preparation and despatch of suitable Mission to former should be undertaken without delay."[41] Officially known as the British Mission to Meshed, its objective was to travel north along the Persian-Afghan frontier to safeguard the cities of Meshed and Ashkhabad, the latter being situated west of the Caspian port of Krasnovodsk on the Transcaucasian Railway. Secondary tasks of Malleson's covert force were to "take counteraction against enemy agents endeavouring to penetrate Afghanistan and Baluchistan from the west, to keep an eye on developments in Herat and to take advantage of any possibilities to deny the use of the Central Asian railway to the enemy in the event of Baku being occupied by Nuri Pasha's army." The penny-packet force reached its destinations in July.[42]

Major-General Sir George Macartney was placed in command of the third and smallest special force consisting of sixteen "cavalry guides." His mission, operating yet farther east, was to proceed via Chinese Turkestan (Kashgar) into Russian Turkestan to the city of Tashkent, again a vital stop along the Central Asian railway. Sanctioned by the

India Office, Macartney was unaware of the Malleson and Dunsterville missions operating to his west. A splinter operation from this force consisted of three men led by Colonel Frederick M. Bailey, who reported on the developments on the Russian and Chinese Turkestan/Kashgar frontier. Bailey was also to ascertain Bolshevik intentions in India, while "keeping an eye" on the some 40,000 German and Austro-Hungarian POWs roaming the area – the remnant of a far greater number (upwards of 110,000) released after the Treaty of Brest-Litovsk.[43] Dunsterforce, however, was given the most critical and dangerous assignment, as its zone of operation was closest to the Turkish threat and was under what the Russians labelled before the war "German orientation." The safeguarding of Baku oil was also of the utmost importance.

Seldom has any portion of the world been occupied by such a mosaic of conflicting parties and interests as the region in which Dunsterforce operated in 1918. The Caucasus, although part of Russia, "was not ethnically Russian, but nor was it – if viewed as a whole – anybody else's."[44] There were numerous groups, ethnicities, religious movements, and external nations battling for the regions of the southern Caucasus by early 1918, "and during the First World War, when the combination of intercommunal ill-feeling, foreign invasions, and state-organized genocide decimated [sic] the regions' local populations, both Muslim and Christian. As it happened repeatedly in Caucasus history, the victims of one era became the perpetrators in another."[45]

Nationality and Main Objective and Interests

- Turks: To conquer Transcaucasia and its resources, and promote pan-Turanian ideology
- Anti-Bolshevik Russians: To control the Caspian Sea and link up with British forces
- Bolshevik Russians: To make peace and return home
- The Trans-Caucasian Republic (formed April 1918, consisting of Georgia, Russian Armenia, and Azerbaijan): To obtain independence from both Russia and Turkey
- Armenians: To escape Turkish brutality and oppression, and promote Armenian autonomy.
- Germans (penetrating the Ukraine): To penetrate the Caucasus, Persia, and Afghanistan to control natural resources and trade routes, in addition to supporting unrest against British rule in India

- Persians (neutral): To be void of all foreign parties, equally suspicious of all invaders' motives
- British: To prevent the Turks/Germans from overrunning the Middle East and the Caucasus, while protecting India, natural resources, trade routes, and oil interests[46]

Following the Russian Revolution, aside from the Turkish 1915–16 "relocation campaign" of Armenians, the ethnic and religious strife and violence in the Caucasus rapidly intensified. It was into this genocidal maelstrom that Dunsterforce marched. According to American Robert H. McDowell, who served in Persia and the Caucasus from 1917 to 1921 in the positions of British consul at Hamadan, an agent with British Military Intelligence Branch, and with the American War Relief Agency,

As I saw them in the Caucasus the civil wars were struggles between people who had been close neighbors for centuries, though they differed in nationality, religion or historical tradition. The conflicts were terribly aggravated by the thousands of refugees who were without food and shelter because of the destruction, massacre and rape they had suffered elsewhere. To the wandering hordes this was not a war to gain food or shelter but to destroy them, not to attain security but to annihilate the enemy. The civil wars were primitive wars fought with the modern weapons brought with difficulty from the frontlines of the World War ... I heard of captured men, women and children having been herded into a church or mosque and burned alive ... I saw bodies of women with their breasts cut off, pregnant women with their bellies split open, men with the penis cut off and stuck into the mouth to add insult to injury. From what I observed in the Caucasus I am inclined to draw a general conclusion that the intensity of the local civil conflict in 1918, 1919 and 1920 was a principal factor in the defeat of the White armies by the Red Army.[47]

Naturally, with the turmoil created by interest groups and factions operating in the region, it was necessary for the commander of the "hush-hush" force to be familiar with Russian culture and language, as well as the state of affairs in the region. Dunsterville met these criteria: "My own knowledge of the Russian language and known sympathy with Russia had probably a good deal to do with my selection for the task."[48] He was widely travelled, had a vast amount of knowledge of Russian institutions, and was fluent in Russian dialects. "The learning of language is easy to some, but terribly difficult to others,"

Dunsterville noted. "Ignorance of each other's language is the cause of half the trouble in the world." He was fluent in Urdu, Punjabi, Pashtu, Persian, Russian, German, French, and Chinese.[49]

By this time Dunsterville was already a legendary figure, thanks to his childhood friend Rudyard Kipling, who immortalized him as the bold leader "Stalky" in the boyhood picaresque adventure tale *Stalky and Co.* (1899).[50] Dunsterville and Kipling (both Anglo-Indians) had been classmates at the United Services College in north Devon, better known as "Westward Ho!" The college was founded in 1874 by a group of military officers who could not afford the prohibitive costs of the more aristocratic schools of Eton and Harrow. Dunsterville's father (and grandfather) was a general in the Indian Army of the British Raj and was one of the school's founding members. "Stalky & Co. is a work of fiction," Dunsterville later wrote, "and not a historical record. Stalky himself was never quite so clever as portrayed in the book. But he represents, not an individual – though his character may be based on that of an individual – but the medium of one of the prevailing spirits of this most untypical school."[51]

After graduating from Sandhurst, Dunsterville was commissioned in 1884 and prior to the war served predominantly in the backwaters of the British Empire. While his peers fought and were promoted in Britain's major campaigns of the era (chiefly the Anglo-Boer Wars, 1880–1, 1899–1902), Stalky faded into obscurity with postings to Malta, Sudan, Waziristan, China, and India, eventually taking command of the 20th Punjabis as a colonel in 1908: "By some mischance he had missed, not only the campaigns in Burma, Egypt, and South Africa in which the successful generals had made their names, but also the more spectacular events in the campaigns on the Indian frontier. He had seen much service with the Sikhs but not in the affairs which caught the public eye. Perhaps, too, peculiar talents which impressed the other boys in Number Five Study at Westward Ho! were not so much esteemed by the bureaucrats in Simla and Whitehall."[52] Throughout his career he was seemingly always passed over by military authorities and was chronically short of private funds. Kipling frequently lent his old friend money, and although Dunsterville meticulously accounted for and repaid his debts, at the outbreak of war he found himself back in England with the prospect of an early retirement on a meagre pension.

When he volunteered his services in August 1914, he was bluntly told by the War Office that "Indian Army colonels were not particularly wanted." He was assigned to train-conducting duty in the rear echelons of France, shuttling men and supplies to the front, a task usually given to much more junior officers. In April 1915, he sailed with his wife and daughter to take command of the 1st Infantry Brigade at Jhelum on the Northwest Frontier of India, where he conducted small operations against hostile tribes. "On the frontier," he recalled, "it is often hard to tell friend from foe." Kipling supported the war effort publicly and in his writing, and his eighteen-year-old son John was killed in September 1915 at the Battle of Loos. Kipling also had high-profile political and military connections and lobbied for a superior position for his friend Stalky.[53] Dunsterville nevertheless remained in his position in India until his selection, in December 1917, at fifty-three years of age, to lead the force that would take his name.

On Christmas Eve 1917, while in command of the 1st Infantry Brigade on the Northwest Frontier of India (now Pakistan), Dunsterville received secret orders to present himself to Army Headquarters at Delhi, with a "view to proceed overseas on special work."[54] His stay in Delhi was brief, as the War Office was pushing to expedite the insertion of this special force into the Caucasus. After the selection of his General Staff, he embarked at Karachi on 6 January 1918, reaching Basra in Mesopotamia six days later, with the mission "to organize, train and eventually lead the Armenians, Georgians and Tartars (these being the people of the Southern Caucasus) for the prevention of the spreading of German propaganda to Afghanistan and thence to India, the protection of the BAKU oil fields, the prevention of the Cotton crop stored at KRASNOVODSK getting into German hands and to provide an additional force to operate against the Turks from the East, and to hold the BATOUM – TIFLIS – BAKU – KRASNOVOSK line to Afghanistan."[55]

The Christian Georgians, Armenians, Assyrians, and Russians feared Turkish occupation and wholesale slaughter of their peoples if Turkish forces occupied their homelands. The population of the greater Caucasus of roughly nine million was at this time 60 per cent Christian and 35 per cent Muslim, with the remaining 5 per cent divided among Jews, Buddhists, and pagans. In fact, the region was home to no fewer than eighteen distinct "races" and forty-eight different languages and dialects.[56] Peter Hopkirk claims that the Caucasus was inhabited by "no fewer than forty-five different nationalities and ethnic groups … In a region so riven by hatred, jealousy and mistrust – and no less so today – this [Dunsterville's mission] might appear little better than suicidal."[57] Muslims engaged in agriculture, subsistence farming, and unskilled labour in the oilfields. In contrast, 71 per cent of business-owners, merchants, and skilled labourers were Armenian. While there were homogenous regions such as Orthodox Georgia, or the predominantly Muslim Azerbaijan, in the south and west these disparate religious populations often lived in adjacent communities, or in ghettoized neighbourhoods within major centres, much the same as Orthodox Serbs, Catholic Croats, and Sunni Muslim Bosniaks of the former Yugoslavia – which climaxed in an ethnic-cleansing crescendo between 1991 and 1995.

During his discussions in Delhi, however, Dunsterville had dispatched a special request, through the War Office, to all corps commanders on the Western Front. Interestingly, special attention in the message was given to the commanders of the Canadian, Australian (and New Zealand), and South African contingents. Sir Edward Kemp, the Canadian minister of overseas military forces, reported to his prime minister, Sir Robert Borden,

> The Imperial authorities were confronted with a difficult and hazardous situation owing to the demoralization and retirement of the Russian Army in the Caucasus which was operating on the Eastern or right flank of the British Army in Mesopotamia. I was asked to furnish them with 15 level-headed Officers and 26 Non-Commissioned Officers, to co-operate with the British Officers and Officers from other Dominions in organizing a somewhat mixed and irregular army of different nationalities which inhabit the territory ... The population of this area is of a very mixed character, but to a considerable extent it is antagonistic to the Turk, and included in it is a certain number of Armenians.[58]

On 3 January, the Australian Corps commander, Lieutenant-General Sir William Birdwood, his Canadian counterpart Lieutenant-General Sir Arthur Currie, and South African leader General Jan Smuts all received the same letter from the Eastern Committee of the War Office. The request, hand-delivered by Dunsterville's second-in-command, Colonel John J. Byron, to whom the task fell of recruiting and organizing the mission in Europe, stressed that cooperation was needed for "a very important and difficult mission." Like Dunsterville, Byron's past experiences lent themselves to this senior appointment.

Born in Ireland, Byron immigrated to Australia in his early twenties. He was commissioned in the Queensland Defence Force in 1885 and was promoted to lieutenant-colonel in command of the Queensland Permanent Artillery in 1896. During the Boer War, he took part in the advance on Kimberly and was wounded at Magersfontein. In February 1900 he was promoted to aide-de-camp to the British commander-in-chief Lord Roberts and saw further action at Paardeberg and Driefontein. Mentioned in dispatches twice, Byron was appointed Companion of the Order of St Michael and St George in 1901. Following the war, he stayed on in South Africa to manage the Duke of Westminster's estate in Orange Free State Colony. He served in the colonial legislature from 1907 until the creation of the Union of South Africa in 1910, at which point, until his death in 1935, he served as either a senator or as a member of Parliament. Prior to his assignment under Dunsterville, he had served in both the German South-West Africa and East Africa campaigns, before commanding a British artillery group on the Western Front.

Given his military record, his colonial roots, and his service in command of colonial soldiers, Byron had an intimate knowledge of, and friendships with, many of the commanders and soldiers of the dominion forces.[59] This was recognized in the Eastern Committee letter to dominion commanders:

> We realize how difficult it is for you to spare good officers, and especially the kind of officers we want but from Colonel Byron's explanation you will realize what a big question is involved – nothing more or less than the defence of India and the security of our whole position in the East. If we only stem the rot in the Caucasus and on the Persian frontier and interpose a barrier against the vast German-Turkish propaganda of their Pan-Turanian scheme, which threatens to enflame the whole of Central Asia including Afghanistan, our minds will be at rest as regards Mesopotamia and India, the latter of which is practically bled white of Indian troops.[60]

Dunsterville, now en route to Mesopotamia, had requested 150 officers and 300 NCOs possessing "the spirit of adventure, undoubted courage, and the ability to quickly estimate difficult situations. They must be of strong character, adventurous spirit, especially good stamina, capable of organizing, training and eventually leading irregular troops." The letter received by the dominion commanders was different from that sent to British corps commanders. Given these criteria, it was believed dominion troops would be better suited, as they had earned the reputation as superior, tough, spearhead forces of the British Expeditionary Force on the Western Front. Influenced by the nature of their countries of origin, and what was perceived by the British to be sturdy physiques due to "hard living," they would stand up better under the conditions of the mission. The process of selecting these "specially qualified officers and other ranks from the Dominion Forces" who were active on the Western Front was the same throughout dominion formations.[61] The Canadian selection system can serve as the model.

On 5 January, two days after Currie received notification, a message was sent from Canadian Corps Headquarters directly to brigade commanders asking for volunteers to partake in "a hazardous enterprise in a foreign theatre of war."[62] The officers were given no other specific details about the mission, but those who accepted the call believed that no duty could be worse than spending another winter in the trenches of the Western Front. On 7 January, another request was sent to brigade commanders for the officers who volunteered for the mission to be sent immediately to see Currie at Canadian Corps Headquarters at Camblain l'Abbé. The following day a parade was held, and after each volunteer was interviewed, fifteen officers were selected. According to volunteer Captain Robert Harrison, "Lt-Gen. Sir Arthur Currie at this time gave no inkling of the country in which the operations were to take place ... speculation was rife amongst these concerned as to their destination."[63]

The senior Canadian, Lieutenant-Colonel John Weightman Warden, recalled the selection process. Warden, born in Nova Scotia, was a veteran of the Boer War, had been wounded during the Second Battle of Ypres in April 1915, won the Distinguished Service Order in January 1917, and was the commander of the 102nd (North BC) Infantry Battalion. Warden mentioned in his 8 January diary entry that he "volunteered for service with a secret mission to the east & interviewed [by] Corp. Comdr Lt Gen Sir Arthur Currie & Col. Byron who was O.C. mission. Corp. Comdr consented to my leaving & issued an order for me to be seconded [transferred] to the Imperials." "Honest John," as he was affectionately known by his troops for his "childlike simplicity of character combined with exceptional soldierly qualities,"[64] added that the only reason he relinquished command of his beloved battalion was that he "could not stand" his brigade commander, Brigadier-General Victor Odlum, or Major-General David Watson, his divisional commander: "Both very mercenary men & political ... who used their Comds to make to gain Public notice & repute ... most averisious [sic] decoration hunter, as are most of the staff."[65]

These fifteen men were invited to suggest the names of NCOs who showed strong leadership and who might work well in an irregular force. From the nominations forwarded by the selected officers, twenty-nine self-reliant and distinguished NCOs were hand-picked from across the Canadian Corps. These forty-four men were told nothing of their destination – simply that they would leave for London in a week. In fact, unlike the officers, the NCOs had not been told anything at all, not even that they had volunteered for a "hazardous enterprise in a foreign theatre of war." They were simply told to "report to the Battalion Orderly Room where they received transportation to London. They were sent to the Divisional Baths, issued with clean underwear, and given a little money." Each Canadian volunteer was given a route letter with directions to report to the Ministry of Overseas Military Forces of Canada at Argyle House no later than the morning of 14 January for further instruction.[66] This process was repeated in the Australian Corps and the South African and New Zealand Divisions at roughly the same time.

Like Currie, Birdwood received the letter from Byron on 3 January and proceeded to send out requests to his five divisional commanders for "cream of the cream" officers. By 8 January, twenty officers had been selected following interviews with both Byron and Birdwood. Once gathered at Australian Corps Headquarters at the old Chateau deFlêtre, Byron addressed the group: "Gentleman, are you prepared to undertake a desperate venture which will probably cost you your lives?" He continued, "But, if successful, [it] will mean everything at this stage of the war to the British Empire." The first question offered from the group was simply, "Well, what's the job?" To which Byron replied, "I am sorry, but I cannot tell you." Naturally the next question was, "Well, where is the job?" The answer was the same, after which point Byron curtly refused to address any more questions. The officers were ordered to precede to Australian Imperial Force (AIF) Headquarters at Horseferry Road, Westminster, London, by 12 January.[67] Meanwhile, on 10 January, Birdwood received instruction to provide forty NCOs of "relatively similar qualities." Upon objecting, on the grounds that he was already lacking trained senior NCOs, the request was reduced to twenty men, who arrived in London on the twentieth. The eleven officers and twenty-three NCOs selected from the New Zealand Division, dubbed the "little band of stalwarts," arrived in London on the thirteenth.[68]

According to Major M.H. Donohoe, Dunsterville's intelligence officer, the soldiers assembled were indeed elite:

With few exceptions our party consisted of Dominion soldiers gathered from the remote corners of the Empire. There were Anzacs and Springboks,

Canadians from the far North-West, men who had charged up the deadly shell-swept slopes of Gallipoli, and those who had won through at Vimy Ridge. They were, in fact, a hardened band of adventurous soldiers, fit to go anywhere and do anything, men who had lived on the brink of the pit for three years and had come back from the Valley of the Shadow of Death … the cream of the fighting men from the South African contingent and from the magnificent Australian and Canadian Divisions. I do not recall a single officer or N.C.O who had not won at least one decoration for bravery.[69]

Dunsterville agreed with this assessment: "All were chosen for special ability, and all were men who had already distinguished themselves in the field. It is certain that a finer body of men have never been brought together, and that command was one of which any man might well be proud."[70]

Having disembarked at Basra "after a beastly rough voyage" on 12 January 1918, Dunsterville travelled to Baghdad, reporting to General Headquarters Mesopotamia on 18 January, where further orders from Robertson (dated 14 January) awaited him.[71] Although under the direct command of the War Office, not the commander-in-chief of the Mesopotamian Expeditionary Force (MEF), Lieutenant-General William Marshall, with whom he was staying while in Baghdad, the two sat down to review the orders and the possible courses of action and coordination of their respective forces. Dunsterville was promoted to major-general, appointed chief of the British Mission to the Caucasus, and also British representative at Tiflis. In reality, he received one promotion that vaulted him from a colonel, commanding a brigade of the Indian Army, to a major-general commanding soldiers from across the British Empire. The mission of his new command was entwined in British geo-political and petroleum-economic strategy in the Middle East and the Caucasus, in the midst of the military and political chaos of the Russian Revolution. Having arrived in Baghdad, Dunsterville flippantly noted in his diary, "Owing to the secrecy of my arrangements, I am called the Commander of the 'Hush, Hush Army.' I blossomed into a Major-General yesterday – as it was obviously foreseen Daisie [his wife] had made the holes for the new resplendent stars."[72] He was ordered to proceed to Tiflis, via Baku, as soon as possible.

Marshall, not privy to original War Office plans, was against the mission from its inception. Informed of the operation on 3 January, he regarded Dunsterforce as a "mad enterprise," suspecting from the outset that his already undermanned MEF would be called upon to provide augmenting men, transport, and reinforcements. "Presumably, the idea of the Dunsterville mission and its objective emanated from the Eastern Committee of the War Cabinet," he later recalled. "I was not consulted in the matter and knew nothing of the political reasons which prompted its dispatch, but, had the Eastern Committee done me the honour of asking my opinion, I should certainly have advised against the whole project." Marshall viewed the threat to India as purely fictional, "rumours, which I entirely disbelieved." He considered the Eastern Committee distraught: "Bogies created by the enemy or by our own too lively imaginations are apt to become a nuisance if encouraged."[73]

In practical military terms, Marshall rightly understood that any Turkish or German push through Persia or Afghanistan to the gates of India was impossible, given the lack of transportation routes, the rugged, inhospitable terrain, and what would be an unmanageable supply line. Nevertheless, he was ordered to support Dunsterforce and collaborate in aiding the mission, despite the fact that Marshall had no direct relationship to, or control over, Dunsterville in the chain of command – a sore point for the senior MEF commander: "The Dunsterville mission had nothing to do with me, it was not under my orders, and I did not then realise that it was going to involve us in an invasion of Persia, a neutral country which did not want us there at all." Although dutifully obedient to his vague orders, Marshall adamantly replied on numerous occasions that while he would cooperate with Dunsterville, he would not, and could not, bolster Dunsterforce by draining manpower from his MEF.[74]

Meanwhile, the volunteers of Dunsterforce, released from their units on the Western Front, trickled in to the Tower of London, where they had been ordered to report by their national headquarters. The Canadian and Australian officers arrived first between 12 and 14 January, followed by men from the other dominions. This colonial collective, augmented by British soldiers and fourteen Russian officers and one Persian, met at the Tower on 14 January to undergo strict medical evaluations (one officer and five other ranks of the Canadian party were released as medically unfit with venereal disease and were replaced with one officer and two other ranks from the Canadian Depot in London). Once medically processed, all officers below the rank of captain were thereby promoted to that rank, and junior NCOs to the rank of sergeant. They were also told that they would be paid at national rank rates, as those of the dominions exceeded the standard imperial pay rates. [75]

The following morning, still unaware of their destination or mission, each man was given £25/10s (and an additional £3 for mess kit) and a detailed list of summer and winter clothing and equipment that was to be purchased during a five-day leave – confusing the possible destination all the more:

(1) Winter Kit £20
    Leather or fur jerkin (to be worn under British Warm[76]) or alternatively a fur coat
    Fur gloves
    Field boots large enough to take extra socks
    Fur cap with ear flaps
(2) Summer Kit £5.10.0
    Khaki [pith] Helmet
    2 suits Khaki Drill
    2 pairs of sun goggles fitted with side flaps to keep out dust
    Spine pad
    Gauze Underclothing
    Mosquito net[77]

According to Australian Captain Stanley G. Savige, "What hope had we of even guessing where we were bound for, when given orders to buy outfits of such complete contrast, together with a supply of medicine, all of which had to last us for two years? Seeing that we were not prophets or seers, we simply read through the list, looked at each other and said, 'Well, how about a spot?' and then booked seats for the theatre." A rancorous Savige went on to mention that after "accumulating all this gear" he spent nearly £80, the difference "coming from our own pockets." Many men also purchased weapons and other equipment.[78]

The secret destination was the hotbed of many conversations among the soldiers. Many believed that they were destined for Norway or Siberia. Others assumed they were bound for Ireland or Quebec to quell the Catholic minorities' violent opposition to the war and their bid for self-rule.[79] Many assumed they were headed for northern Italy, given the recent Italian disaster at Caporetto. Other fallacious reports ranged from East Africa to Egypt to China. Canadian Sergeant David F. McWhirter recalled that on the basis of heightened rumour that they were destined for China, Sergeant "Jimmy Murray began teaching us the Chink lingo that he'd picked up in a chop suey joint in Calgary."[80] One can only imagine the entrancing conversations between these comrades over pints in London pubs concerning their ultimate destination. One also wonders, after these outings, how secret Dunsterforce really was.

The group reassembled at the Tower on the twentieth after five days' leave. The next five days were spent in lectures on hygiene, administrative procedures, and travel conditions, although the destination was still not revealed. On the twenty-fifth, they gathered in parade formation by nationality to be inspected and addressed by the chief of the Imperial General Staff, Sir William Robertson. Following his review of the rank and file, other dignitaries made brief remarks, including Andrew Fisher, the Australian high commissioner to Britain: "Now Boys, you're going on a great stunt – live clean!" The six-foot-five Robertson closed the parade with a brief farewell address: "Gentlemen, I am indeed pleased to see you, for I recognize that before me I see gathered from the Imperial Army and the troops of the various dominions, the cream of the British Army, and in whatever you undertake, I wish you good luck and God speed."[81] The members of this hush-hush force were granted leave for three days, still no wiser as to their destination, only that they would be "embarking on one of the most dangerous missions that British troops had ever been asked to attempt."[82]

In private circles, however, Robertson was against the deployment of troops to ancillary theatres, circumventing the main effort on the Western Front, and urged restraint in "frittering away our reserves to meet what may prove to be subsidiary attacks." He complained in private that 20 per cent of the war effort planning was spent assessing peripheral operations, instead of focussing on the key theatre of the Western Front. To Robertson, squandering troops on "sideshow" campaigns, including the Caucasus, was futile, as "only by beating the Germans shall we win. We must therefore put our men and munitions where they can be used against the Germans." The Dunsterforce mission, as Robertson stated, was intended to be "sacrificial." Robertson was a former chief of intelligence for the Indian Army and former director of the foreign section of the Directorate of Military Intelligence. Like Marshall, he stressed on numerous occasions that geography alone made any realistic threat to India on the imagined German-Turkish route quite impossible.[83]

While Robertson viewed an invasion of India improbable, the Mesopotamian campaign was the only theatre of war removed from the Western Front that he did not view as a "sideshow." Robertson rightly understood the value of Mesopotamian oilfields for this (and future conflicts). Also, as he told the War Cabinet, he did not "think the Mesopotamian Campaign was a side show because as long as we keep up a good show there, India and Persia will be more or less all right whereas anything in the nature of a setback there might cause trouble in those countries." Robertson understood, as did senior politicians, that any threat to British prestige in the region could have adverse consequences in imperial possessions in the region – it was a threat the War Cabinet took seriously.[84]

Reconvening at the Tower, the group was finally briefed on their assignment. Lieutenant-Colonel Richard A. Steel, director of military operations inside the Military Intelligence Operations branch within the department of the chief of the Imperial General Staff at the War Office, began, "Gentlemen, I am now addressing the flower of the British Army on the Western Front. You have been specially selected for this adventurous expedition, and it is quite possible that you might be sacrificed on the altar of British prestige in the Caucasus Mountains." He continued,

> The capture of Baghdad by the British in March 1917 had been offset by the Bolshevik Revolution. The Russian Front which had extended southward through the Caucasus Mountains, across the southern end of the Caspian Sea, and down into Persia, where it linked up with the British Mesopotamian Force at Khaniquin, had now collapsed. The Russians were crowding back home, totally demoralized, leaving a wide-open door to the eastward advance of the Turks and the Germans. The age-old necessity of protecting India demanded some sort of barrier to replace the defecting Muscovites. But the British were expecting a German offensive in France; Allenby was completely occupied in Palestine; the Mesopotamian Army had no troops to spare. The situation was menacing. When things were at their blackest, however, a War Office visionary had a brainstorm. Somewhere in the mountains of Kurdistan, Circassia, Armenia and Georgia there were thousands of enthusiastic warriors who would snap at the chance of squaring off their own private grudges against the Turk, if only they could be entered on the British pay-roll and given good leadership. That was the proposition – to penetrate into the Caucasus Mountains, raise an army, and use that army, against the Turks.[85]

They were also told that Major-General Lionel Dunsterville, already in Baghdad, would be leading the operation, and "everything he [Steel] said at that time [was] being treated with the utmost secrecy," remembered Captain Harrison.[86] To Savige and the others, this mission "did not leave much wanting in the way of adventure."[87] In a sense, the design of this mission was a precursor to the training units formed by NATO and the United States in Afghanistan and Iraq to train Afghan and Iraqi army and police forces.

Following Lieutenant-Colonel Steel's briefing, administrative and pre-deployment matters were taken care of. The men were given an advance of forty-five days' field allowance and thirty days' pay. They were also told that "from the date of leaving Baghdad a special detention allowance of 1. [shilling] a night will for the present be issued in lieu of Field Allowance to enable you to provide your own accommodation and food. When other arrangements for the provision in kind of food and accommodation become possible this allowance will cease and the usual field allowance will be resumed."[88] They were dismissed and told to report ready for embarkation the following morning. That night Sergeant Crofford Campbell and his comrades, enjoying their last night in London, pondered their mission to the sound of explosions, sporadic anti-aircraft fire, Gotha bombers, and air-raid sirens.

The following morning, the volunteers of what was now being labelled Dunsterforce gathered at Waterloo station at 11:30, destined for the Channel port of Southampton. Australian Captain Roy Stewart recalled the many women, family members, and dignitaries seeing the party off. It was his fourteen Russian comrades, however, who caught his attention: "They were very aristocratic, handsome and highly educated fellows – all good linguists, and some of them expert in scientific subjects such as chemistry, physics and mathematics. A bevy of the most beautiful women I have ever seen came down to Waterloo Station to farewell them."[89] Among the dignitaries were the commander of Canadian Forces Britain, Lieutenant-General Sir Richard Turner VC, and his fellow Canadian brigadier-general, H.F. McDonald.[90]

The group reached Southampton at roughly 5 p.m. and boarded the troopship *Viper*, arriving in Cherbourg later that evening. The following morning, the party disembarked for a rest camp at the nearby Chateau de Tourlaville, where they were joined by twenty British sergeants. "Of all the mingling of men that this world has ever seen there was never a finer gathering of real men," Captain Savige wrote. "There one rubbed shoulders with Canadians from out West, the South African from the lone veldts, and the New Zealander from good old Pig Island, and I suppose they thought as much of the Australians as the Australians thought of them."[91] Indeed it was an eclectic and diverse group of men from all walks of life. There were sailors, professional soldiers, engineers, bankers, farmers, cowboys, police officers, students, and skilled tradesmen among other pre-war vocations. Many had seen service in the Boer War, others in the Boxer Rebellion. Canadian Sergeant Leon Bedat (born in France), who was covered in oriental tattoos, had served in the Spanish-American War and the Boxer Rebellion with the U.S. Navy, and had spent "14 months with Venezuala [sic] rebels."[92] Others had participated in the Klondike gold rush, some had led safaris in Zululand, while another claimed to have been on the staff of the Mexican revolutionary Pancho Villa.[93] Colonel W.W. Donnon, an experienced British agent in the Middle East and Asia, was in command of the party while in transit.

The next leg of the journey saw the group leave Cherbourg the following afternoon aboard a train for the port of Taranto on the heel of Italy. The nine-day journey was spent playing cards, reading, chatting, playing instruments, and singing in cramped quarters of anywhere from four to eight men per compartment. Although this train had priority over all others, the going was slow. Stops were made along the way at refreshment stands at convenient stations, and every two to three days the men were put up at rest camps along the line to bathe, eat, and sleep. "This indeed was a welcome change from being crowded four together in about a fifth-class railway carriage in which we attempted to live, eat and sleep," recalled Savige. "The opportunity of a hot bath and the purchase of ... food was not missed on arrival at one of these camps."[94] The route passed south through Caen, Paris, to Marseilles, east along the Riviera across northern Italy, before turning south again through Brindisi, arriving at a staging area three miles from the port of Taranto on the evening of 8 February. In fact, Josephine Gilmore, a nursing sister and wife of Canadian Captain Adam Harrison Gilmore, made the journey from Cannes to Monaco with her husband aboard the troop train, in direct violation of several military regulations. Warden was delighted at meeting his old friend General Jan Smuts (bound for Egypt and Palestine) at the Taranto harbour for the "first time since 1904 in S.A. He remembered me at once."[95]

Although there were no discipline problems out of the ordinary, the second-in-command while in passage, Canadian Lieutenant-Colonel Warden, was not pleased with the quality of the average soldier under his leadership: "A very lively party thus far but do not care for many of the officers and N.C.O.s. I do not think they are the right kind for the work we are to carry out ... However do we manage to hold our own in this war? For incompetence & unqualified ignorance of his duties in war, the average English officer is easily the winner of first place." He continued, "The colonials were very drunken and were really hard tickets. I am perfectly convinced that our Canadians were selected in order to get rid of them, and not for their efficiency in their units. I think it is most disgraceful." In fact, Roy Casey, one of Warden's fellow Canadians, was approached for the mission while in the custody of military police awaiting court martial for repeat offences of absent without leave and drunken and disorderly conduct. Given the choices, he "volunteered" for the assignment rather than face a trial and the ensuing punishment. During an eight-hour break in Florence, Warden noted that the British Army postmaster "was very insulting in his remarks. He never had colonials through before & was afraid of them."[96]

Following two days' rest at a relaxed and modern naval base at Taranto, the party boarded the comfortable P&O liner *Malwa* to run the gantlet of German U-boats across the Mediterranean to Alexandria.[97] Warden noted that on 10 February, the day of boarding was "the limit for absolute incompetence. I have never met the like of the Englishmen called officers such as these were here." The ship was also ferrying colonial soldiers bound for India, British sappers destined for Aden, and forty Irish nursing sisters en route to East Africa, much to the delight of the troops. These nurses were a "very respectable lot, well bred & very well trained," according to Lieutenant-Colonel Warden.[98] To Savige and the other men, with the nurses on board "life was worth living," most notably during the anti-submarine blackouts ordered every evening.[99] "The Australians on board had proved themselves to be as deadly effective in love as they are in war," wrote Intelligence Officer Major M.H. Donohoe.[100] Weighing anchor on the twelfth, escorted by three Japanese destroyers, the three-day voyage was spent in Russian and Farsi (Persian) language classes, instruction of Persian and Middle Eastern history and culture, lifeboat and safety drills, and sporting events between national contingents. The group was also briefed on the progression of the war in Persia and the regulations regarding its official neutrality.

At the outbreak of war the Russians controlled north Persia; however, the Persian gendarmerie of roughly seven thousand was controlled by Swedish officers harbouring German sympathies. With the initiation of hostilities in 1914, Russian and Turkish forces clashed in northwest Persia, resulting in the Turks being pushed back into eastern Anatolia. The Russians maintained control of vital transport routes, including the Kasvin-Kermanshah road. In June–August 1916, the Turks launched a

briefly successful eastward offensive from Baghdad directed at Kermanshah and Hamadan. Sporadic fighting continued in northwest Persia until the British capture of Baghdad in March 1917, at which time
the Russians nullified any previous Turkish gains in Persia and eastern
Anatolia and began to drive further into Ottoman territory. At this time
the contiguous Russian line extended roughly 450 miles from the Caspian Sea to Khanikin on the Mesopotamian frontier, where it joined the
right flank of Marshall's MEF.

In southern Persia, the seven thousand men of brevet Brigadier-
General Sir Percy Sykes's South Persian Rifles patrolled major routes and
towns to counter the gendarmerie and tribal opposition, and to uncover
German and Turkish propaganda and covert operations. Sanctioned by
the Persian government in March 1916, this force based in Shiraz was
composed primarily of Indian and local soldiers under British officers. In
addition, a small Indian force based in Seistan under Brigadier-General
R.H. Dyer patrolled the eastern Persia cordon. With the onset of the Revolution, the Russian line slowly melted away, exposing the right flank
of the MEF while rendering the approaches to India vacant. Plugging
this gap, the men of Dunsterforce were told, was to be their mission, in
addition to safeguarding the precious oil at Baku.[101] "The position was
almost desperate and demanded measures involving the greatest risks,
but British initiative rose to the occasion," wrote Sykes.

> It was decided to meet the enemy as far as possible from the frontiers
> of India and ... to despatch a mission across northwest Persia and the
> Caspian to the Caucasus, with the object of inducing the inhabitants of
> the latter region to fight for their homes and thereby prevent the Turks
> and their German masters from taking Baku. The occupation of the enemy
> of this town ... would not only have constituted an important advance
> along the Batum-Baku-Tashkent line, but would have made secure their
> control of the priceless oil fields ... Indeed, oil was the pivotal question.
> In consequence, to deny Baku to the enemy, even for a while, was of great
> importance.[102]

Arriving at Alexandria on the afternoon of 15 February, the group's
rail travel to Suez was delayed until the following evening, allowing
the men to spend the following day sightseeing, shopping, and taking leisure in the bars and brothels, seemingly favoured by the Canadians and Australians above all else. Most, however, were curious to
see the places that "one read of in Bible hour" as children, including

the catacombs, palaces, tombs, and "remains of the ancients." Many remarked on the squalor of the streets, and of the ethnicities (Arabs, Persians, Jews, and various Europeans) they rubbed shoulders with in the markets and bazaars.[103] Here, the party took on an additional twenty officers and forty NCOs from Allenby's EEF, including two officers and five NCOs from the Australian Light Horse.[104]

An overnight train trip, "obtaining a fleeting glimpse of the Pyramids,"[105] carried them from Alexandria to Port Said, where they boarded a decrepit transport, the "old tub" *Nile*, which shuttled them down the Red Sea, through the Indian Ocean, and up the Persian Gulf to Kuwait, to the destination of Basra. The cabins, reserved for officers, were infested with rats and cockroaches, the holds for the NCOs were wet and damp, the ship was overcrowded with additional troops and "coloured labourers," and the Lascar crew (Indian sailors) had recently battled a bout of smallpox. The steamer was "indescribably filthy and had been running in the China trade for a quarter of a century," and had also seen service at Gallipoli and throughout the Middle Eastern theatre of war.[106] Throwing rank to the sea, most officers and NCOs opted to intermingle and sleep outdoors on the grimy decks. Warden and Campbell both record in their dairies that the *Nile* was "a very, very dirty ship, the worst I have ever traveled on." Nevertheless, electing for fresh air in lieu of the dank interior, men delighted in the biblical landscapes throughout the journey. "Mt Sinai and the Holy Lands can be seen in the distance," recorded Warden. "Also the place where Moses is supposed to have stopped the Red Sea & brought the Israelites through on dry ground. *I think* the tide was out at the time!" Sergeant Campbell, as did Warden, commented at passing the "12 Apostles and through the Gates of Hell" (the common references to the Halba Desert Island chain, Eritrea, and the narrow southern mouth of the Red Sea leading to the Gulf of Aden [Manab Strait], separating Yemen, Eritrea and Djibouti).[107]

Language and historic-cultural lectures continued during the voyage to include the Caucasus, in addition to Russian, Persian, and Arabic. "I have sometimes thought since," wrote Major Donohoe in 1919, "that to the Gods on High our ship must have appeared a sort of floating Tower of Babel, so intent on speaking strange tongues were each and all ... what one Anzac aptly described as 'this upside-down language.'"[108] During downtime, sports rivalries blossomed on deck, chiefly between the "Aussies and Canuks."[109] The journey, however, was not without incidents. Two men mysteriously disappeared overboard, and two British marines who were headed for India broke into the canteen, stealing alcohol and cigarettes. The culprits were never located and Warden bitterly complained, "I am positive we have many who will make a mess of things for us amongst the inhabitants where we are going." In contrast, both Captains Harrison and Savige identically record in their journals that "the trip to Mesopotamia was uneventful."[110]

On 1 March the party sighted Kuwait (City), which they could admire only from a distance. A smaller hospital ship, the *Erinpura*, docked alongside the *Nile*, to transport them some eighty miles up the shallow Shat-el-Arab to Basra. "She was spick and span," wrote Donohoe, "and the general air of cleanliness was so marked after the filthy tub that had conveyed us from the Suez that we trod her decks and ventured into her cabins with an air of apologetic timidity."[111] The men welcomed the "very clean & tidy" ship with "food well cooked & tasty. What a contrast to the S.S. Nile!" recorded Lieutenant-Colonel Warden, who went on to describe the journey to Basra in vivid detail:

> Passed up river Shat-el-Arab which is the river Tigris & Euphrates in one. They join at Kurna (the site of the old Garden of Eden 100 miles upstream). No boat over 18ft of draught can enter the river owing to a Bar at its mouth. 30 miles up on the left bank is the Anglo-Persian Oil Co's plant & a mile father up is the Castle of the Sheik of Mahamerah's [sic], where he lives. He is the most powerful sheik in Arabia, Mesopotamia, or Persia & most friendly to the British. The country is very flat & and river banks dyked (called Bunds) all the way. Date Palms growing along its banks, for Arabs living along the river. Passed the three large steamers sunk by the Turks just above Sheik's Palace in order to block the river, but out swang downstream before sinking & left the channel clear. Arrived at Basrah at noon.[112]

Captain Savige also presented a vivid picture of this journey:

> At daybreak we all turned out to get a view of the magnificent river of Mesopotamia. For miles it is about a mile and a half across, and as we moved slowly upstream, place and place of interest came into view. The banks are lined with date palms which grow in great abundance. Numerous vessels of every description moved either up or down the river – transports of troops, cargo vessels with Army Service Stores, and the hospital ship laden with the sick and wounded. Hugging the banks were huge Arab dhows, laden with the merchandise of the country, being towed by natives who hauled these primitive barques with great ropes attached

either round the head or to the waist. Now and then a smaller canoe, propelled by poles, would be passed. All of this was indeed a restful change to the eye after being a couple of weeks at sea.[113]

Many also commented on passing the colossal Anglo-Persian oil refinery at Abadan at the mouth of the river.

This group of Dunsterforce finally disembarked at Basra on 2 March 1918. Almost two months had passed since they had left their units on the Western Front. Their next destination was Baghdad, to join their commander Major-General Dunsterville, who was laid up with a case of "real bad influenza." Always the hopeless romantic of a bygone Don Quixote era, Dunsterville mused in his diary from his Baghdad bed, "My task is as difficult for one man as any Napoleon undertook. I am as strong as Napoleon in my confidence in myself, but unlike him … I find it impossible to place myself on a pedestal, this was a great asset to him – in fact, it made him … These long journeys are full of dramatic change. I am just awaiting to jump off into darkness and eternity for a space, with a fair hope of emerging on the far side, and here I have a pantomime with string band and as I stand on the verandah at night, the romantic Tigris flowing as it has flowed for many thousand years, and the moon-light on the water, and everything good the world holds."[114]

Basra to Baghdad to Baku

The region of Basra had been home to the Sumerian civilization beginning around 6,000 BCE. These ingenious peoples dug irrigation canals,
travelled the river systems for transport and trade, and developed the
first city states by 4,000 BCE. Babylon, the legendary city of the seven
ancient wonders of the world famed for its hanging gardens, sat on a
tributary of the mighty Euphrates River. It gained wealth and prestige as
the capital for a succession of mighty empires, each violently displaced
and replaced. The Babylonians were followed by Assyrians, Persians,
Greeks, Romans, and finally by Islamic Arabs. Eventually abandoned,
its remnants were sequestered beneath the mud deposits of the biblical
river. According to Dunsterville, it was the "land of Chaldaea, Babylon,
Nineveh and Abraham – fallen Empires all around are represented by
mud heaps ... under us it will again blossom into the Garden of Eden."[1]
The modern city of Basra was founded by Arab merchants in 638 and
became famous as the fabled home of Sinbad the Sailor of *One Thousand
and One Nights* (Arabian Nights) – translated into English by Richard
Burton in 1885. By 1918, Basra was the vital economic hub on the Persian Gulf: the gateway to the interior river systems of Mesopotamia
and Persia, the exporting port for Anglo-Persian oil, and "the key to
Mesopotamia," as General Sir Edmund Barrow, the military secretary
at the India Office, remarked on the eve of war.[2]

Since capturing Basra from the Turks in November 1914, the British,
under Major-General George McMunn, initiated drastic urban reforms,
including the construction of paved roads, wharves, hospitals, ele-
vated cemeteries, churches, hotels, electric power and fuelling stations,
administrative buildings, a cinema, and even a horse-racing track. The
modernization of Basra was, indeed, a herculean task. However, in

keeping with true British zeal and design, as the joke went, Basra, like all imperial outposts soon sported, among other necessities, a cricket pitch, a football field, and a church.[3]

Covered in omnipresent dust, the city was sited amid rancid, malodourous marshes and low-lying, tide-infused swamps, spawning malaria-ridden mosquitoes. Sanitation was non-existent, generating a fly population that greatly exceeded the sixty thousand inhabitants: predominantly Arab, with high concentrations of Armenians, Jews, Indians, Greeks, Chaldeans, Persians, Kurds, Russians, and a host of traders, diplomats, missionaries, and adventurers from European nations and the United States. According to an Arab proverb, when Allah made Hell, he did not find it caused enough suffering, so he then created Mesopotamia – and added flies. The diary entries of the men of Dunsterforce certainly support this lore.[4] Drinking water was scare. The smaller tributaries were utterly polluted and the small number of wells yielded water too salty for drinking. The main waterway produced the only water reasonably fit for consumption. It too, however, was shared with animals and used for the chores of washing and the discarding of human waste and other refuse. Under Turkish rule, the city had been allowed to fester in squalor with a "total absence of any sanitary system or method, and the presence of numerous disease-ridden brothels." Major Donohoe recalled his "wonder and bewilderment that the entire population has not long ago been wiped out by disease."[5]

The Dunsterforce party disembarked at Basra on 2 March, having already travelled an astonishing 5,500 miles since leaving London. The group was fragmented into two camps, the majority housed in the central former Turkish barracks (now British Headquarters) near the river at Ashar, with the remainder occupying a tented camp on an open plain of high ground at the Medical Reinforcement Depot at Makina, roughly two miles from the city centre.[6] As the following day was a Sunday, the men had the day off to wander Basra. They perused the grand bazaar (which was the heartbeat of the city) not far from the main barracks, sampled local cuisine, and gawked at the "expert native boys" who poled the *bellem* (resembling a gondola), shuttling people and goods across the canals and streams. "These canals teem with small native boats," wrote Savige. "Propelled by poles … it has become an art in which only the native, reared from childhood to his job, is the only proficient handler of such craft."[7] Others watched the women street-dancers. Sergeant Campbell was awestruck when taking tea to hear "an Arabian band play our national anthem."[8] As Savige described typical Basra,

6.1 "Mesopotamia Day" poster raising funds for British imperial troops of the forgotten theatre, April 1916 (Library and Archives Canada).

6.2 Sergeant Crofford Campbell (*far right*) and fellow Canadians of Dunsterforce in Persia, 1918 (Campbell Family Private Collection).

One walks along its narrow, winding streets which are roofed from one
side to the other ... The streets themselves are hardly wider than a foot-
path, yet strings of mules, horse-drawn carriages and horsemen move
rapidly along ... shouting at the top of their voices. The shops are small
and crammed with tawdry ware ... cheap Manchester goods and cheap-
jack Birmingham ware exhibited in great profusion. The women in most
cases are heavily veiled, but, like other parts of the world, with the advent
of Western civilization, the superstition of the East is being thrown off, and
gradually women are doing away with their face coverings.[9]

The upriver journey to Baghdad was delayed by lack of transportation,
furtively withheld by General Marshall, who assumed responsibility for

Dunsterforce (taking over from the War Office) on 12 March. Marshall fallaciously cited weather as the key hindrance in a report to the War Office: "Though for some time the bad weather enabled me to postpone the evil day, I eventually received orders to carry out this, in my opinion, mad enterprise."[10] The seemingly unnecessary delay was noted by senior officers. "During this period we merely killed time," wrote Warden, "Not a word during this period of our nominal chief General Dunsterville ... The delay was inexplicable, there seemed to be every possible means adopted to waste time."[11] The days of waiting were spent in drill, including, curiously, sword drill (solely done to occupy time and keep the men out of trouble), and with leisure, and by fighting off the ever-present mosquitoes and flies. Language, cultural, and historical classes also continued to be taught. Routine parades and inspections were conducted by "every General within fifty miles," including McMunn and newly promoted Brigadier-General Byron. Downtime was spent in the usual, perhaps wayward, pursuits of a young soldier, and also at the cinema, playing sports, or aimlessly wandering the maze-like streets. The Gymkhana Club, a pseudo officers' mess, adjacent to the camp at Mekina, invited the "hush-hush officers" to join as honorary members. "If ever a piano required attention," wrote Savige, "it was after this party left, as night after night until well on into the early hours of morning, its soul was worked out of it by some pianist."[12] Following three days of rain, which turned the Mekina camp into a morass, the sun and humidity put a strain on training, while also reinforcing the "night raiding parties ... of mosquitos."[13]

The most notable event of the respite in Basra was the undertaking of the only Persian officer of the group that left London. Captain Ali Akbar suggested a visit to Sheik Khazal Khan of Mohammerah, known to be pro-British as the result of his vast wealth accumulated in connection to the Anglo-Persian Oil Company. After cordial discussion during the first exchange, twenty officers, predominantly Canadian, were invited to attend the wedding of the sheik's choice son on the following day. On the afternoon of 5 March, these twenty men under command of Lieutenant-Colonel Warden made the eighteen-mile river journey to participate in the festivities at the palace:

We arrived at 7pm ... he met us personally & introduced us to the son which is the Bridegroom & heir & several other sons. (He has 35 wives and about 100 children) ... the wives & daughters are not allowed out of the Harem. Women are mearly [sic] for man's use & not a companion here in this country. The Sheik pays no dues to the Shah of Persia but draws a fat one – 20,000 pounds – from England ... Several other guests were present among them the British Consul & wife & several of the officials of the Anglo-Persian Oil Coy & Bank Staff. I however was the principle [sic] guest & sat on the Rt hand ... dinner (twelve courses), native Persian dancers (very suggestive), fireworks, theatres & concerts ... in this case it ends in a day or two after over a month's run ... We enjoyed ourselves very much. The Sheik informed me I was the Sheik of Mahamerah & everything he had was mine. I was therefore the possessor of 35 wives just for the night, but I did not get the opportunity to visit them. However, I beat him for numbers, as I had his 35 & my own one at home ... arrived back at 6 am.[14]

The remaining days were spent in drill, training, and packing stores.

For lack of transport, the men of Dunsterforce were shuttled to Baghdad in two parties. The first contingent of sixty-five men, including Byron and his senior staff, left on 10 March and arrived in Baghdad nine days later. The second, larger party embarked on the seventeenth, on barges crewed by the twenty-eight men of the First Overseas Canadian Pioneer Detail of the Inland Water Transport Section. "The navigation of the Tigris even in peacetime, is a hazardous undertaking," wrote Donohoe. "The despatches of the victorious generals in Mesopotamia ... have entirely overlooked the great contribution of the men of the Tigris River Flotilla, who have apparently been left without reward or recognition ... The admirable part played by these river skippers of the Tigris has never been told, and so has never been properly appreciated by their countrymen at home." The second party arrived in Baghdad on the twenty-eighth.[15]

The trip for both contingents was relatively uneventful, with classes continuing in Russian and Persian, and sports competitions on deck. The only inconveniences were the usual mosquitoes and flies and the capricious weather, ranging from hail to rain to days reaching 58°C. The trip to Baghdad offered the soldiers glimpses of historic sites only previously read about in the Bible and other books, or discussed at Sunday school. First, they passed the purported site of the Garden of Eden at Qurnah (where the two great rivers meet). They were also shown, by some self-proclaimed Bible expert onboard, the alleged "tree of knowledge of good & evil." Further up the Tigris, a large blue-tiled dome surrounded by a blue porcelain wall and palms marked Ezra's tomb, revered by both Christians and Muslims. The Book of Ezra describes how in 540 BCE, after being freed by the Persian King Cyrus the Great, he led a group of Judean exiles living in Babylon to their home city of Jerusalem (Ezra 8:2–14). Here, he enforced observance of the Torah – the first five books of the Old Testament – and cleansed the community of mixed marriages. After passing through the "Devil's Elbow," the most dangerous section of the Tigris, the flotilla anchored at the fertile green Amara (known for its brass and copper artisans) for the night, some taking the opportunity to stroll along the 1915 trench lines and earthworks, and visit the purported site where Adam and Eve made their exit from Eden at the "Garden of Tears."

The men were also given a few hours to wander the battlefield of Kut-el-Amara, where, after a 147-day siege, Major-General Charles Townshend surrendered his British-Indian force of 11,800 (6th Poona Division) on 29 April 1916.[16] The event was hailed as the worst British defeat since the 1781 surrender of Yorktown to the Americans, or "Black Week" in December 1899, during which the British suffered three crucial defeats at the hands of the Boers, preceding the 118-day siege of Ladysmith (30 October 1899–28 February 1900). "I regret to have to say," concluded Curzon, "that a more shocking exposure of official blundering and incompetence has not in my opinion been made, at any rate since the Crimean war."[17] While Townshend lived out the war in luxury on the island of Halki in the Sea of Marmara and attempted to broker a peace treaty with the Ottomans in October 1918 to save his reputation, 65 per cent of the British and 50 per cent of the Indian POWs died in captivity of disease, starvation, and mistreatment, including rampant sexual abuse. "He sacrificed many thousands of lives in the attempt to hold his position when he had plenty of opportunity to evacuate," recorded Warden without pretence or romance.[18] Not all walking these former front lines shared his interpretation. "The Turks, to commemorate for all time their victory, commenced building a giant obelisk on a big rock formation, and at each of the four corners was placed a captured British gun," wrote Savige. "Unfortunately for themselves, they were not granted sufficient time to complete their emblem of triumph, as the relieving force under General Maude soon turned out gloom into sunshine and re-captured Kut."[19]

Similarly, the men were given opportunity to meander around the ruins of Ctesiphon some twenty miles south of the outskirts of Baghdad. Settled as the capital of the Parthian Empire around 600 BCE, the city was occupied throughout history by empires and invaders including the Persians, Greeks, Romans, and finally by Arabs in 637 during the Islamic conquest of Persia. Aside from the ruins of the massive white palace built around 600 by Khosrau II, the twenty-second Sassanid king of Persia, the only standing structure of the ancient city and palace itself was the great vaulted arch (begun in 540 by Khosrau I, the largest ever constructed in Persia). It is also a Shia Muslim holy site, purportedly the burial place of the Prophet Mohammed's barber Salman Pak. "There are many ruins of ancient cities built from 3000 to 5000 B.C.," recorded Warden in his diary. "We are now travelling through the oldest part of the world. There are traces giving conclusive proof that there were a highly civilized race of people inhabiting this part of the world 6000 B.C. & and long before the dawn of history. This was a flurishing [sic] commercial busy place, now a land of desolation & waste ... with a little dyking & irrigation worked out properly, this can be made one of the richest countries in the world."[20]

The contingents arrived in Baghdad on 19 and 28 March respectively. Dunsterville was not present to greet his men. Upon reporting to MEF headquarters, Colonels Donnan and Warden entered General Marshall's office. As he tapped his pencil on his desk, the truculent general looked up quite annoyed, surveyed the group, and asked caustically, "Who are you and what are you here for, anyway? I have no instructions for you." Upon leaving the headquarters, Warden quipped to Donnan, "If that is the sort of treatment that is to be accorded to us by senior officers, I do not think our expedition will be much of a success. In fact, I am afraid it will be a dead fizzle."[21] According to Major Donohoe,

No one knew quite what to do with us, and General Headquarters was seemingly divided in mind as to whether we should be treated as interlopers, and interned for the duration of the War, or left severely alone to work out our own salvation, or damnation, as we might see fit. The latter view carried the day, and our welcome in official quarters was therefore distinctly chilling. The difficulty chiefly arose, it appears, because General Dunsterville ... had been given a separate command, and was independent of the General commanding-in-chief in Mesopotamia. Jealousy was created in high quarters. There was a spirited exchange of telegrams with the War Office, in which such phrases as "Quite impossible of realization," "Opposed to all military precedent," are said to have figured prominently.[22]

While a nuisance to Marshall, the fragmentary arrival of this ragtag force under secret orders intrigued other soldiers stationed at Baghdad.

Lieutenant-Colonel John Edward Tennant, a Royal Air Force squadron commander, speculated about their purpose and destination:

> Clouds were gathering over the Caspian in the north, and a phantom army of officers, N.C.O.s, and men from overseas was arriving at Busrah. Volunteers from the Mesopotamia and all scenes of war began to accumulate at Baghdad. Australians, New Zealanders, Canadians, and English, they were known as the "Hush Hush Army." We were not allowed to talk about their mission, but we knew that some swashbuckling game was afoot, for they were as tough a looking crowd of cheery customers as our race could produce; veteran fighters all, and a formidable enough gang to back any man into battle. General Dunsterville, the original of Kipling's "Stalky," arrived to lead them. They were to cut themselves away from Mesopotamia, migrate north through Persia into Armenia, and there muster the Armenians and train them into an army to march against the Turk or Bolshevik, thus securing our threatened right flank. It was a daring enterprise. They faded away over the mountains as silently as they had come.[23]

This motley collection of soldiers dubbed "nobody's child" by Warden, had made their way from the Western Front to Baghdad over the course of almost three months. Meanwhile, Dunsterville and his small staff had already initiated the mission, tumbling into a political and military landscape that was radically transformed.

By this time, the service and support elements and peripheral players to his mission had been dispatched across Persia and the Caucasus. At this point, Dunsterville was the responsibility of the War Office and the Chief of the Imperial General Staff General Sir William Robertson, who was soon replaced by General Sir Henry Wilson in February 1918. In effect, the Eastern Committee of the War Office, steered by Curzon and Arthur Balfour, had strategic jurisdiction over Dunsterforce. The operational level was controlled by the Military Intelligence Operations (MIO) branch (formed on 30 January 1918) of the Department of the CIGS, headed by Lieutenant-General George Macdonogh, and his subordinate Lieutenant-Colonel Richard A. Steel, a figure familiar from the previous chapter.[24]

The MEF commander General Marshall, who was at odds with both Dunsterville and his secret campaign, was ordered to support the mission from his headquarters at Baghdad. Eventually, Marshall wielded great influence over the conduct of Dunsterforce. He tried to sabotage the mission at every opportunity, particularly after its reassignment from the War Office/MIO to his MEF command on 12 March (as did the British minister in Tehran, Sir Charles Marling, who was also suspect of the operation).[25] "Had the Eastern Committee done me the honor of asking my opinion," wrote Marshall, "I should certainly have advised against it. Persia was a neutral country which did not want us there at all ... From a purely military point of view the creation of another 700 miles of communications, and most of that distance through mountainous country with a mere track as a road, seemed to me to be madness." He even contemplated resignation but deemed it to be unpatriotic during a time of crisis and war.[26]

British consuls at various locations also played a vital role in the facilitation of Dunsterforce, particularly Major Ranald MacDonell, who split his time between Tiflis and Baku and was heavily involved in espionage; Robert H. McDowell at Hamadan; Lieutenant-Colonel Roger L. Kennion in Kermanshah; and C.B. Maclaren at Resht/Enzeli. These men, in addition to their regular duties, often acted as intermediaries or spies for Dunsterville, secured and shared important information and intelligence, warehoused supplies, stores, and money, and provided safe houses for members of the expedition.[27] "In friendly territory, of course, my status was overt," wrote McDowell, "while in territory in the Caucasus controlled by either German or Bolshevik forces my cover was that of a refugee from the Near East, one of the hordes of people, native and foreign, disrupted by civil war and wandering through the region in search of food or safety."[28]

Brigadier-General Offley Shore, who had been the senior British attaché to Russian forces in the Caucasus and commander of the British Military Mission to the Caucasus, remained at his headquarters in Tiflis following the Russian Revolution. In his opinion, "Success depended on the rapidity of Major-General Dunsterville's arrival in Tiflis."[29] Shore was joined in early February 1918 by Captain Edward Noel, an experienced intelligence officer sent by Marling to gauge the overall situation. Shore insisted upon dealing directly with the War Office, circumventing his direct superior, Marling, in Tehran. Noel was inserted in Tiflis by Marling to counter Shore's withholding of information. Together Noel and MacDonell undertook numerous intrepid clandestine operations on the line between Tiflis and Baku, as well as supplying Armenian forces with money and weaponry to prolong their rearguard actions against the advancing Turks. "Noel ... was, I think, one of the bravest people I have ever met," wrote MacDonell, " – that is, if a complete lack of any fear of consequences and the absence of any appreciation of

what it known as personal safety constitutes bravery."[30] Unlike Shore,
Captain Noel repeatedly told his superiors that the British were placing
too much stock in the use and abilities of the Armenians in countering
Turkish and German advances in the Caucasus. "The duties of Captain Noel and others, who I was subsequently to meet," remembered
MacDonell, "were to prepare, devise or create a situation that would
enable General Dunsterville and his force to take charge. At the time
anti-British feeling ran high, so the task looked pretty hopeless."[31]

In addition, an intricate network of adroit British spies littered the
region, often working independently without support for months, while
traversing vast territory, sporadically checking in at a British consul,
bank, private business, or mission to unload intelligence. These agents
in possession of large sums of money were "far more than 'spies' in the
accepted sense. The acquisition of information that might direct and
guide policy and strategy was only one aspect of their task and it was
not the most important one. They were heavily involved in politics ...
making arrangements behind the scenes and playing 'the more delicate
threads' with people the British Government did not wish it known
they were negotiating with ... committing Britain to policies that were
not necessarily approved in detail by the government."[32] According to
Sir Walter Bullivant, Buchan's fictional head of intelligence in Greenmantle, "We have had our agents working in Persia and Mesopotamia
for years – mostly young officers of the Indian Army. They carry their
lives in their hands, and now and then one disappears, and the sewers
of Baghdad might tell the tale. But they find out many things, and they
count the game worth the candle."[33] The most famous of these "gentleman adventurers" were Colonel G.D. Pike, who replaced Shore (gladly
supplanted by the War Office) in mid-February, and Captain Reginald
Teague-Jones (alias Ronald Sinclair).[34] The Germans, not to be outdone,
also had very capable and experienced agents traversing Persia, the
Caucasus, and Afghanistan, bidding to sway the local populations to
their favour with the hopes of inciting an Islamic rebellion against British ascendancy in this area and also in India.

The War Office also placed a veteran intelligence officer, Lieutenant-
Colonel C.B. Stokes, under the command of Dunsterville, who decided
"it important to work up our information from the Teheran side and
accordingly posted him to the capital, where he could ... liaison between
my force and the diplomatic representative."[35] As mentioned, Major
M.H. Donohoe, who made the original journey from London, was the
intelligence officer embedded with Dunsterforce.[36] Lieutenant-Colonel

Alfred Rawlinson, after receiving orders from the War Office to proceed to Persia, was "placed on special duty as an expert in camouflage and extemporized motor machine-gun work, in which he excelled." Rawlinson, an artillery officer by trade, was also in command of the limited artillery attached to Dunsterforce. Alfred's brother was General Henry Rawlinson, Fourth Army commander on the Western Front. Their father was Sir Henry Rawlinson – major-general, orientalist, and politician. Henry, a renowned expert in ancient Persian language and culture, spent considerable time in Mesopotamia and Persia and is credited with deciphering the cuneiform language of Persia and Assyria (thirtieth century BCE to first century).[37]

Also within Dunsterville's sphere of influence were, as mentioned earlier, Brigadier-General Sir Percy Sykes and his seven thousand–odd South Persian Rifles operating in southern Persia, the mission of Malleson, situated east of the Caspian port of Krasnovodsk on the Transcaucasian Railway, and those of Macartney and Bailey operating yet further east. The force offering Dunsterville the most direct assistance, however, was that of the avaricious, yet fiercely anti-Bolshevik, Ossetian Cossack Russian commander Colonel Lazar Bicherakov. He was a stout veteran of the Eastern Front, had been shot six times, and had only partial use of his hands because there was a bullet lodged in his spine. Bicherakov was an archetypal soldier, a charismatic and natural leader who possessed an intrinsic martial capacity and a true affinity for war. His mercenary force, consisting of some twelve hundred loyal Cossack cavalry, patrolled northwest Persia and the southern Caucasus region, handsomely paid and liberally supplied by the War Office via Dunsterville (who began his operation with an initial sum of £300,000). While Dunsterville found in Bicherakov a kindred spirit and "a truly heroic figure," his superiors were sceptical about Bicherakov's loyalty and intentions.[38] Many believed that his fidelity rested solely upon the acquisition of personal wealth. Another concern was that when tasked for combat, Bicherakov would auction his force to the highest bidder, or, without firing a single shot, simply return home and vanish with his fortune amassed at British expense. Dunsterville's intelligence officer, Major Donohoe, quickly realized that Bicherakov and his Cossacks "were stout fighting men of the mercenary type ... they were willing to make war on our side as subsidized auxiliaries. In short, these heterogeneous cohorts were for sale ... and the British taxpayer bought them at an inflated price."[39]

While the supporting players to Dunsterforce and its main body from the Western Front were being assembled and deployed, the political landscape of the Caucasus was anything but stable, predictable, or certain. Following the Russian Revolution, a Transcaucasian Commissariat was formed on 11 November 1917, four days after the Bolshevik coup d'état, in order to safeguard the political and geographical integrity of the Caucasus region, which the Russians had been fighting for over the course of the war. This political body based in Tiflis was made up of twelve members representing each of the major ethnic groups in the region – three Armenians, three Georgians, three Azerbaijanis (or Azeri Tartars), two non-Bolshevik Russians – headed by Georgian Menshevik Evgenii G. Gegechkori. From the outset, the commissariat rebuffed Bolshevik representation, while refusing to recognize Lenin's regime. Rightly, the Caucasian representatives, who formed a *Seim* (general assembly) in January 1918, believed that the Bolsheviks would use their territory as leverage in negotiations with the Central Powers. Representatives from the Caucasus were denied representation at all peace negotiations, including those surrounding the tenets of Brest-Litovsk. Indeed, the Bolsheviks were arranging a peace and transfer of lands in the Caucasus and the three Russian provinces (Ardahan, Kars, and Batum) in eastern Anatolia to Turkey, over the heads of the politicians and people most immediately threatened by the collapse of the Anatolian, Persian, and Caucasus fronts. Germany was prepared to allow the transfer of these lands to the Ottomans but flatly rejected further proposals that Turkey be permitted to advance farther northeast across the 1877 frontier into the southern Caucasus. The Germans believed that by acquiescing to these Turkish demands, they would be mollified to some degree and would not interfere with German designs on the Caucasus.[40]

Immediately the commissariat engaged in separate peace talks with the Ottoman regime in the town of Erzincan beginning on 25 November 1917. On 18 December, a peace treaty was ratified between the parties, although the text was careful not to recognize any sovereignty of the Caucasus. It also included a clause forbidding strategic regrouping of military forces, a condition the commissariat stressed so that Ottoman forces in the Caucasus could not be redirected for use against the British in Mesopotamia and Palestine.[41] Defending the Caucasus were ten thousand Georgian soldiers of questionable morale and reliability, and no more than twenty-two thousand Armenian soldiers secretly armed and funded by the British through the military mission at Tiflis.[42] In a twist of fate, the commissariat had no need to worry. The Middle Eastern theatres were secondary to the main Turkish pan-Turanian drive through the Caucasus to Baku, and onward into central Asia, which would begin the following month, despite strong German objections. According to the German Foreign Ministry, "Before the war ... we went to great pains, against Russia's resistance, to clear ourselves a path to Persia across Transcaucasia, and we have spent millions on creating a pro-German Caucasian state to give us a bridge to Central Asia."[43] Fissures in the German-Ottoman alliance, which had thus far been dormant, began to be manifest.

The duties of the commissariat were made all the more trying by food shortages, a deluge of wandering, starving Armenian, Assyrian, and Kurdish refugees (upwards of 400,000 to 500,000), and thousands of peripatetic Russian soldiers who raped and pillaged towns on their passage home seeking food, fuel, and plunder. These Russian soldiers also sold their weapons and military stock (some supplied by their allies) to the highest bidder (without prejudice of political, ethnic, military, or moral motives) – Armenians, Bolsheviks, Jangalis, Tartars, or Turks.[44] "The trains were always greatly overloaded, with the car roofs carrying not only troops but cases and even artillery pieces and armored cars," wrote British agent Robert McDowell from Hamadan. "In some instances, despite their pleas, railway personnel were forced at gunpoint to drive into tunnels where material and men on the roofs were swept off in bloody slaughter ... At times the men became rough and I saw many a simple argument end with a skull crushed under the rifle butts or boots of comrades. Repeatedly I saw signs reading to the effect 'Comrades, do not throw people off the train while it is moving. It gives us a bad name.'"[45] Brigadier-General Sir Percy Sykes recounted similar chaos around Tabriz in northern Persia: "Some of them took to highway robbery and others lay about drunk, so long as wine or spirits were procurable ... plundering and pulling down houses as they went, in order to secure food and fuel. The Russian soldiers wandered through here in their thousands, sold their rifles, ammunition, stores, horses, and, in fact, anything that would fetch money. Horses went for a few shillings, but fodder has been at such a terribly high price that beasts were dear as gifts."[46] General Marshall shared this opinion: "All the swine up there [Caucasus] are fighting and murdering one another and there isn't an hour of fight in the Russians who are now just like frightened children and simply want to run home for fear of the unknown."[47] In addition, roving Armenian soldiers, formerly employed by Russia, formed organized militia units and began ravaging Kurdish and Muslim communities in eastern Anatolia, northwest Persia, and the

Table 6.1 Baku election results, November 1917

Party	Votes
Bolshevik	22,276
Musavat	21,752
Dashnaktsutiun	20,314
Social Revolutionary	18,789
Kadet	9,062
Muslims of Russia	7,841
Menshevik	5,667

Source: Hovannisian, *Armenia on the Road to Independence, 1918* 147.

southwest Caucasus, while preparing to withstand the inevitable Turkish advance into their Anatolian and Caucasus homelands.

Even more confusing was the political condition at Baku, driven by ethnic and sectarian divides. In summary, no single political party was powerful enough to control civil or economic administration of the cosmopolitan, proletarian, oil-rich city housing numerous ethnicities including Azerbaijani Muslims (35 per cent), Russians (25 per cent), and Armenians (15 per cent).[48] The November 1917 elections to the Constituent Assembly yielded no consensus for political command and control.

Thus, while Bolshevik Armenian Stepan Shaumian chaired the Baku Soviet, he frequently professed that since his party alone could not "master Baku, it was necessary to rely on other elements."[49] In essence, the Bolsheviks, Dashnaks (Armenians), Mensheviks (Russians), and Social Revolutionaries (Russians) formed a tenuous anti-Ottoman alliance, alienating the Musavats (Azerbaijani Muslims). The deep-seated hatred between the city's Armenian and Muslim populations, relatively dormant since 1909, was seething and reaching a violent breaking-point, which would eventually come in March.

The British administration was keeping a watchful eye on the events transpiring throughout Russia, including those of the Caucasus. On 5 January 1918, Prime Minister David Lloyd George gave his now-infamous "British War Aims" speech. He promoted "separate national conditions" for Arabia, Armenia, Mesopotamia, Syria, and Palestine, and the internationalization of the Black Sea–Mediterranean passage. As for the ongoing situation in formerly allied Russia, "Much has been said about the arrangements we have entered into with our Allies on this and on other subjects. I can only say that as new circumstances, like the Russian collapse and the separate Russian negotiations, have changed the conditions under which those arrangements were made, we are and always have been perfectly ready to discuss them with our Allies."[50] In short, any measures made prior to the Russian Revolution were now void, including those concerning the Middle East.

More importantly for future Allied relations, the British now viewed the 1916 Sykes-Picot Agreement as untenable (and perhaps always did) and no longer validated French privileges to the untapped oil fields of Mosul. "The general position has so much changed since the Agreement was entered into that its provisions no longer appear suitable to president conditions," Balfour explained to the Italian ambassador in London. "Not only has the military position in Mesopotamia, Palestine and Syria completely altered, but two political changes of vast importance have taken place. The United States have come into the war and Russia has gone out."[51] With oil now occupying the top tier of British war aims, any French ambitions in Mesopotamia or the Caucasus that would undermine British oil interests, were deemed unacceptable by British planners: "From the military point of view it would be most undesirable for the approaches to India from South Russia, the Black Sea, and Turkey in Asia, which converge at Baku, to be placed at the disposal of an ambitious military Power [France], which although friendly at the moment, is our historical world rival. In fact, it does not appear to the General Staff that any other Power except herself can be permitted by Great Britain to function in this manner."[52]

In addition, the Eastern Committee's report of mid-January 1918 provides insight into the British rationale, while also encompassing the general confusion and chaos befalling the Caucasus. The report accurately predicted the German intention of "switching off the Baghdad line to India, and turning towards the line of the Turanian peoples." It also correctly assumed that the Turks would launch an offensive towards the Caucasus in the early spring after the initial winter thaw, and attempt to unite the peoples of Islam throughout the Caucasus, Afghanistan, Central Asia, and India. The continued violation of Persian neutrality by the British was discussed in consultation with Marling. It was conveyed to Persian authorities that any "withdrawal of British troops would expose the country to further violations of neutrality on the part of its enemies." The report outlined the confusing political and ethnic make-up of the Caucasus and stressed the importance of funding the Armenians and "the new volunteer army" made up of Georgians, Russians, Greeks, Armenians, and Assyrians: "Everything depends on our being able to supply funds to enable Major

Pike ... to keep the new army going until Dunsterville and his staff arrive to look after it. The importance of holding Trans-Caucasia can certainly not be exaggerated ... The Armenians, the nucleus of an army ... if organized and led, would certainly fight, as it is a question of life and death to them to resist a Turkish invasion ... Trans-Caucasia seems thus to be both the most promising and by far the most vital from the point of view of British interests." The report closes with the essential caveat that the Dunsterforce "enterprise, though of the first importance, and in certain respects very promising, is undoubtedly exposed to great risks of failure. It is a race against time ... General Dunsterville and his officers may arrive too late, indeed they may never be able to get there." In the meantime, the best course of action was to "finance Tiflis without delay" to springboard local military resources in aid of British strategic aims.[53]

Despite menacing weather, Dunsterville, still awaiting the majority of his force, decided to push on from Baghdad on 27 January with the limited resources he had at his disposal. He was well aware that numerous "unfavourable factors constituted a rather formidable list" on the six hundred–mile journey (from Baghdad to the port of Enzeli on the southern Caspian). His small force consisted of twelve officers, two clerks, and forty-one drivers for the Ford "touring cars" escorted by one armoured car. Dunsterville's assessment of adverse conditions included poor or non-existent roads, unforgiving weather, the violation of Persian neutrality, disease and illness,[54] hostility of locals including Kurds and the Jangalis of Gilan led by Kuchik Khan (who sought Persian democratic independence), a paucity of food and petrol amidst a biblical drought and famine in Persia, not to mention the inhospitable terrain during winter, which included mountain passes of seven to nine thousand feet.

Given these unknown parameters, on the 24 January (three days before his departure), a cautious Dunsterville sent Majors Sir Walter Bartelott, who had twice traversed the itinerary, and G.M. Goldsmith, an experienced intelligence officer, to scout the route as far as Hamadan, secure petrol supplies, and report on the attitudes of the local population. Goldsmith described a significant anti-British environment and relayed that numerous attempts had been made on their lives by hostile locals. He also reported punishing weather conditions, with heavy snowfall and accumulation through the Asadabad Pass on the approach to Hamadan, where the two officers arrived on 31 January. Dunsterville nevertheless proceeded to embark on what he dubbed "the great adventure!" He did have misgivings, however, remarking in his diary,

> I wonder if anyone will ever realize what a forlorn hope my mission is? I am proud and glad to have it and I think I can accomplish what I am told to, but that thought is based only on my optimism and not at all on calculation. If I were appreciating the situation for another man, I should say "It can't be done," but I can never say that for myself. I agree with Government that it is worth trying and the loss of a few lives etc., is a trifle compared with what may be gained. I am up against a hostile neutral, almost anarchical Persia and a possible hostile reception from our friends, the Russians. The Turks at Kifri are within 50 miles of my road at the start ... We will pass through 600 miles of barren, cold country, between 5000 and 7000 feet, and no sup-plies, and through Kurds all the time who are the same sort of independ-ent robbers that the Afridis [Pashtun peoples of Afghanistan, Pakistan, and northern Iran] are.[55]

On the morning of the twenty-seventh, the Dunsterforce advance party of forty-two vehicles and fifty-seven men of all ranks convoyed out of Baghdad on the first ninety-four-mile leg to Khanikin, which was reached "without excessive delay" in roughly eleven hours. Dunster-ville estimated that within *twelve days* he would be in Baku en route to Tiflis to take up his posting as commander of the British Military Mis-sion to the Caucasus – "if all went well." It would be a staggering seven months later that he would disembark at Baku.

The following day the party advanced to Pai-Taq, covering sixty-one miles in ten hours in the face of a gale of sleet and hail. On this leg of the journey the men got their first glimpse of the horror of drought and famine, aggravated by the destruction of three and a half years of war. "All the towns and villages ruined, burnt and demolished by the Turks and Russians," wrote Dunsterville. "Inhabitants very glad to meet peo-ple who do not burn, rape, or destroy ... everything devastated and the people dying of famine ... it is very depressing. What a vile thing is man."[56] Next morning, the party was to travel forty-one miles to Harun-abad. The deep snow and blustery winds, allied with steep inclines at the entrance of the western slope of the Zagros Mountain range, made for extremely slow progress. After having literally pushed, pulled, and ploughed the vehicles through snowdrifts upwards of twelve feet deep, the haggard party finally reached Harunabad five days later on 2 Feb-ruary. Here they were greeted by "a rosy-faced Hampshire lad sitting on the edge of a rock, a sentry from one of the last picquets that guarded the road for us. This war has produced many scenes of marvellous contrast, but I think the picture of that young soldier was among the most striking. There on the road from Persia to Babylon, the road trodden by the Medes and the Persians, on the rocky barren hillside of the Persian mountains sat a youngster from the kindly Hampshire downs."[57]

Dunsterville pushed on a further seventy miles, reaching Kermanshah on 3 February. Since leaving Baghdad, this was the first settlement of any considerable size, boasting roughly fifty thousand inhabitants, and was home to American missionary orders, a British post office and consulate, and a regional centre of the Imperial Bank of Persia. Here Dunsterville parlayed with Cossack commander Colonel Bicherakov for the first time. Together they shaped a plan to safeguard the advances to northern Persia from Kuchik Khan with a view to sailing to Baku via the northern Persian port of Enzeli. Of course, Bicherakov was reminded that he and his men would be handsomely paid, at an inflated price, for their services rendered to the Crown. While Dunsterville and his party were billeted in fashionable Persian homes, evidence of the famine turned their brief stay into what Savige dubbed a "melancholy fact." On the approach to the city, Savige recounted the locals eating grass and bark, and "every step in the city brought one face to face with a living skeleton." Major Donohoe recounted similar observations that he was now "face to face with the terrible reality, I understood for the first time its full significance. Men and women, shrivelled in huddled heaps of stricken humanity, lay dead in the public ways, their stiffened fingers still clutching a bunch of grass ... At other times a gaunt, haggard figure, bearing some resemblance to a human being would crawl on all fours across the roadway ... the country seemed destitute of life."[58]

The following morning, the party left for Hamadan. After a brutal blizzard enveloped the route through the Asadabad Pass, they reached their destination on 7 February. Hamadan, believed to be one of the oldest cities in the world dating back to 1,200 BCE, and built atop one of the capital cities of the Persian Empire, became the central headquarters for Dunsterforce. As small follow-on parties trickled in, Dunsterville was required to release penny-packet forces to guard the passage, en route stock stations, and a lengthening supply line, from Baghdad to Hamadan, and also the northern routes of Persia to Enzeli. General Marshall refused, or surreptitiously delayed, to release troops to perform these tasks. For example, the 115 miles of track from Kermanshah

6.3 A convoy of Dunsterforce Ford touring cars ready to depart Hamadan, June 1918
(Australian War Memorial).

to Hamadan was being held by a total of fourteen men and one armoured car. Dunsterville was also forced to erect numerous wireless signal stations along these routes in an attempt to ensure proper communications. As mentioned, the two main contingents of Dunsterforce arrived in Baghdad only on 19 and 28 March respectively, and General Marshall refused to release them until all roads were passable and the harsh winter thawed. Hamadan was not only headquarters, it also served as the release and rallying point for all of Dunsterville's smaller detachments and commands. Hamadan was a hive for all sorts. Armenian refugees fleeing the ethnic violence in the Caucasus and northern Persia streamed into Hamadan by the thousands. In conjunction with American missionaries and aid workers, the city became the epicentre of Dunsterforce's noteworthy famine relief.

The diaries of Dunsterforce members all detail the horrific plight of the Persian people. They allude to the piles of dead, the living too weak to perform the required and customary Islamic burial. Their first-hand accounts describe cannibalism, with their emotional distress evident in their prose. They all refer to one incident of a mother and daughter who killed the eight-year-old child of the latter and were apprehended while feasting on the flesh, after boiling the child in a cast-iron pot. "It was here, at this time, that I came across the only case, of any individual being 'stoned to death' in public, of which I have ever heard outside the Bible," wrote Colonel Rawlinson. "The crime was that of a mother eating her child!" Donohoe adds that the "half-cooked remains were removed in a basket ... their 'execution' – that of being stoned to death ... was a revolting spectacle ... yet on the following day there was the sequel to the case."[59]

To alleviate the conditions of famine, while also aiding the mission, the members of Dunsterforce initiated numerous famine-relief projects. The first was to arrest or alienate local politicians, clan leaders, and merchants who had made a fortune at the expense of others by withholding what food there was, or selling it piecemeal at exorbitant prices. The influx of British soldiers and currency also contributed to the supply and demand of foodstuffs, while inadvertently driving prices higher. In essence, members of Dunsterforce took control of every aspect of food production, storage, and distribution, setting reasonable standard local prices for all products. While this helped ease the famine slightly, they also set to work repairing farm equipment and aiding Persian farmers in their fields. Many of the Canadians and Australians had been farmers or ranchers in their former lives and welcomed the chance to engage in a civil pursuit away from the harsher realities of war. Local Persian men were hired to construct or repair roads and bridges on the routes used by Dunsterforce on the Baghdad-Hamadan-Enzeli corridor and offshoot tributaries. In addition, men who were, under the circumstances, deemed healthy, were formed into military units and began parade, drill, and rifle instruction, to act as roving patrols for Dunsterville's scattered elements. Food was provided, and they were also given a daily wage. Soup kitchens were erected for all locals, as the members of Dunsterforce unanimously agreed to go on three-quarter rations, so more food aid could be freed to the feed the starving multitudes, which increased daily as a constant flow of refugees trickled in. Hamadan's pre-war population of fifty thousand had swelled to over sixty-five thousand. If the locals originally harboured any resentment towards British occupation, these dissenters were quickly won over by the relief efforts. Many locals also provided valuable intelligence and maps.

The men of Dunsterforce were reasonably accustomed to their innumerable tasks, given their civilian jobs such as farmers, bankers, mechanics, cooks, engineers, construction workers, or teachers. They also marvelled at and recorded the historic sites in the region, with many quite knowledgeable about the history of the Persian Empire, its kings, and its fall under Darius III to Alexander the Great between 334 and 331 BCE at the battles of Issus (333 BCE) and Gaugamela (331 BCE). Colonel Rawlinson mentions, "The most striking part of this old country is the absence of any change or progress during the lapse of the 3,000 years ... in the Old Testament of our Bible. All the old characters of the Bible are here met in everyday life, exactly the same in every respect as their prototypes of ancient times."[60]

While the relief work carried out by the men of Dunsterforce from February through September 1918 was admirable, it was secondary to their assigned task of protecting the Caucasus oil. By mid-February Dunsterville had solidified his routes, supply lines, communications, and headquarters at Hamadan as well as could be expected, given the small size of his force and the reluctance of General Marshall to forward reinforcements and supplies. It was now time to advance on Baku, which could be reached by only one of two routes. The first required moving 280 miles north through Kasvin and Resht to the Caspian port of Enzeli. From here the force could traverse the remaining 225 miles north across the Caspian to Baku by whatever means of aquatic transportation could be bought, borrowed, or bartered. The second option was to proceed 350 arduous miles overland, impassable by motor vehicle, to the railhead at Tabriz for a 450-mile train passage to Tiflis, where Dunsterville intended to centre his command. Baku, although connected by a railway, lay some 325 miles to the east. Reconnaissance patrols were sent to scout the terrain and passable routes for both courses of action. Although the approaches to Enzeli were watched by Kuchik Khan and his four to five thousand Jangali fighters, and Enzeli itself was under control of a committee of Bolshevik sympathizers, Dunsterville decided on the first option. "Balancing the pros and cons, it did not seem in any way possible to attempt any movement by this road [in the second option] with any prospect of success."[61]

Led by an armoured car in the midst of a snowstorm, on 15 February Dunsterville, along with twelve officers, two clerks, and forty-one drivers, left Hamadan for Enzeli. The convoy averaged ten miles per hour on the hundred miles north to Kasvin, where the situation was bleak. Disgruntled Russians were leaving en masse, and the small detachment of British residents and entrepreneurs was sullen and terrified. After consulting with Sir Charles Marling, the British ambassador to Persia, who had driven from Tehran to update Dunsterville, the column pushed forward through terrible roads and blizzards the following morning, leaving the "filthy, filthy town" behind. After picking up prearranged fuel at Menjil from a friendly Russian road crew, they warily pressed on through Jangali territory. En route to Resht the column sporadically passed Khan's "fierce-looking and heavily-armed warriors ... soldiers [who] really looked as if they meant business," according to Dunsterville's personal account. The British, however, were allowed to pass through the narrow Menjil defiles unopposed. After a brief council with British residents, and British Consul Maclaren in Resht, and twenty more miles, the party reached Enzeli twenty-two days after leaving Baghdad. "Now," wrote Dunsterville, "we have to see how the Bolsheviks and other brands of Revolutionaries would receive us."[62]

Dunsterville was unaware that Major Goldsmith, whom he had sent ahead some weeks earlier with a Kurdish interpreter, had secured fuel and safe passage for the British through Jangali territory. He had also obtained passage for Dunsterforce from Enzeli to Baku after negotiating with the Bolshevik committee in Enzeli and handsomely greasing their palms. Goldsmith himself had already made passage to Baku when Dunsterville arrived in Enzeli, and proceeded to Tiflis where he took up intelligence duties for Dunsterville under Colonel Pike. Goldsmith had also received assurances from Stepan Shaumian, leader of the Baku Soviet, that the British would be welcomed in Baku in transit to Tiflis.

Enzeli was a typical bustling port city supporting the two main industries of fishing and caviar. It was controlled by a Bolshevik committee that was subordinate to its superior formation at Baku. The port was jointly administered by the Russians and the Persians, who from Enzeli controlled the southern reaches of the Caspian and its coastline. "The town is entirely Bolshevik," noted Dunsterville, "and they are a very good and orderly organization – but we were prisoners from the moment of our arrival." The British party was billeted in the care of the Belgian customs officers, with Bolshevik guards patrolling the streets: "They put sentries on all the ships to prevent my leaving and they have a gun-boat ready to sink us if we try – our home is guarded night and day and the situation is absurd."[63]

That night, Dunsterville was "cross examined" by the president and other members of the committee about his intentions (of which they had already been made aware by German intelligence). Dunsterville, fluent in Russian, informed them that he was to proceed to Tiflis to ascertain and report the situation on the Anatolian front, and whether the Turks had designs on advancing into the Caucasus, as "our position in Mesopotamia depends largely on the situation in the Caucasus." He repeated that neither he nor the British had any interest in

Russian politics and was ordered to proceed to Tiflis regardless of what party might be in power, "as the interior politics of Russia are not our concern." The president of the committee informed him that the constituents of the recently formed Trans-Caucasian federation "do not recognize the Bolshevik Government at Petrograd, and [are] therefore the enemy of the Bolsheviks. As the headquarters of the Union are at Tiflis, how could the Committee allow the English Mission to go to their enemies at Tiflis, where they would hear and be influenced by the views of the opposite party, and that the British Government had not yet recognized the Bolshevik Government." Dunsterville was then informed that the meeting would resume in the morning with more committee members present and that they would "wire details regarding us to their Committee at Baku. The latter, possibly after communicating with Petrograd, would send an answer as to whether the Mission is to be allowed to proceed further ... while studiously polite during these proceedings, it was obvious that they intended to do all in their power to prevent the Mission proceeding further."[64]

In the morning, the situation remained unchanged. Nevertheless, Dunsterville informed the twelve committee members that he intended to proceed to Tiflis and that he had sufficient arms to guarantee his passage. When the committee began to argue about a proper response, Dunsterville realized his bluff had failed and excused himself, expecting to be arrested. He reconvened with his party and local British spies, who informed him that although both the Russians and the Jangalis wanted them detained, neither group was actually willing to act, for fear of a larger British reprisal. He weighed his only three options: seize a vessel and force his way through the gunboats to Baku, where he might also be arrested; immediate withdrawal back to Hamadan as quickly as possible; or remain in Enzeli and continue negotiations. Dunsterville then held a private meeting with the president of the committee and somehow secured the freedom to return to Hamadan in his *fully fuelled* Ford vehicles. The following day, Red Guards arrived from Baku to detain the British party, which had already departed. Dunsterville arrived back in Hamadan without incident five days later, on 25 February. It appears that any promise given earlier to Goldsmith by Shaumian was a ruse to capture the British party and its commander to prevent further British forces from entering the region.[65]

As Dunsterville was engaged in his Enzeli escapades, the political situation surrounding his mission had come under scrutiny from Marshall, and from politicians and senior command in London.

On 6 February the War Cabinet requested that Marshall advise them on the materiel and military requirements to control the northwestern Persian corridor and Dunsterville's supply routes from Baghdad to Enzeli. Marshall replied that such an undertaking would require a full cavalry brigade, an infantry division augmented with artillery, service and support elements, and "practically all of the transport in Mesopotamia to maintain it." Marshall believed that any threat to the British in Persia from either the Turks or the Bolsheviks was exaggerated and refused to have any of his MEF troops siphoned to support Dunsterforce or any other "absurd adventure."[66]

Instead, Marshall proposed an offensive in strength on Mosul to capture the city and the surrounding oilfields, while driving Turkish and German forces north, back to the heartland of the shrinking Ottoman Empire. He also recommended that his northwest advance on Mosul be part of a pincer movement, carried out in unison with a northeast advance on Damascus by Allenby's EEF, which had recently captured Jerusalem. To support his grand design, he referenced intelligence reports that Armenian, Assyrian, and Georgian representatives believed that a move towards Mosul would have "more beneficial results in Southern Caucasus and Persia" than any smaller deployment to either region. The oilfields of Mosul province once captured, he reasoned, would be secure and could be immediately exploited, whereas those of the Caucasus would remain continuously threatened by numerous factions including the Bolsheviks, Turks, and Germans, and by Azerbaijani, Georgian, and Armenian independence movements. He also reiterated the widely known fact that the Caucasus was on the verge of intensified civil war, particularly in Baku, and that any force deployed to the region would be entering a maelstrom of ethnic violence.[67] Over the next three months, Marshall used all means necessary to handicap Dunsterforce to promote his own agenda and refused to release any additional resources.

While Dunsterforce was always seen as a secret stopgap or reconnaissance-in-force mission, it was also understood by those involved in the planning of the mission that Dunsterforce was to be the foundation for follow-on forces and a new strategic design in the Caucasus. The meagre force was never intended to be a stand-alone force. The inability of Dunsterville to enlarge his force, aggravated by Marshall, severely hampered its effectiveness. His situation was made worse by an overextended supply line, arduous terrain, hostile elements in northern Persia and Baku, poor communications (which would later cost him his reputation), ironically a lack of petrol for his vehicles, and confusion about the actual purpose of his mission in the upper echelons of the War Office. The overall situation of Dunsterforce was further worsened by the erratic political environment in the Caucasus.

Upon his return to Hamadan, Dunsterville dutifully submitted a situation report detailing his return trip to Enzeli and immediately asked for "one cavalry regiment, one Brigade infantry, one battery mountain artillery, one L.A.M.B. [Light Armoured Motor Battery] and aeroplanes." With these reinforcements he urged that "action could be taken at once to send British troops to occupy Enzeli" and "would be sufficient to accomplish my mission ... as unless supported by British troops [I] cannot remain in Persia."[68] After consulting with the War Office, Marshall replied, "It has been decided by the War Cabinet that you remain for present in Persia." He promised to send "cavalry and armoured cars as soon as the condition of the road allows ... and reinforcements arriving at Basrah will not proceed further till you send for them." On 12 March, the War Office relinquished direct command of Dunsterforce to Marshall with the instruction that Dunsterforce be tasked "to frustrate enemy penetration through North-West Persia ... [S]o long as he remains in Persia, General Dunsterville will remain under your orders, subject to your general instructions ... and he is at your disposal to place in command of any troops you may think it necessary to detach to him."[69]

The War Office instructed Dunsterville on his task, but also stressed that his only option of reaching Tiflis/Baku was via Tabriz, which they knew to be impossible, even in tepid weather. Dunsterville responded that the Tabriz route was impassable and pointless, and he pleaded for more men and materials in order to facilitate a second attempt at crossing from Enzeli to Baku. General Marshall, who was the middleman for messages to and from Dunsterville and the War Office, refused to acquiesce: "We realize the importance of gaining control of the Caspian and preventing the enemy penetrating into N.W. Persia, but troops will not be available beyond Hamadan for at least two months ... You should in due course submit your estimate of troops which you consider will be required by you to attain the objects mentioned."[70] As detailed earlier, Dunsterville's two main contingents from the Western Front were being held at Basra by Marshall who refused to send river transport to shuttle them to Baghdad, much to the bitterness of Colonel Warden and his comrades.

Dunsterville's confusion and disappointment are evident in the entries of his diary. On 19 February he wrote, "I foresaw this from the very start – the mission was two months too late and could only end in failure." His 26 February reads, "They want me to go by the Tabriz road – how little they understand of the situation ... I have implored Baghdad and London to send troops, but they take no notice." After his transfer to Marshall and his new orders, he concluded, "I am no longer on a mission to the Caucasus ... I am no longer independent. I am under Baghdad, and they are told to shove troops up here as soon as they can ... But Baghdad are very sticky and take a long time to get a move on ... they 'contemplate' sending them ... But it is vile being helpless without troops ... I have done my best, in sending fierce cables, and the War Office are at last awake to it, but Baghdad is very lethargic ... and no troops."[71]

In early April, the first reinforcement of fifty men of the Royal Hampshire Regiment arrived in Hamadan tasked by Marshall specifically to guard the northwest corridors of Persia in the Tabriz area, thus protecting the right flank of his MEF. Two weeks later, one squadron of the 14th Hussars arrived, in addition to a small advance party from the main Dunsterforce contingents now in Baghdad. Dunsterville toiled with his limited force by pushing a small unit of fifty-two men towards Tabriz, while sending Bicherakov's Cossacks to hold Kasvin. Transport and other materials, however, were withheld by Marshall, who at one point ordered that no member of Dunsterforce "was to be furnished with supplies from the military canteens" of the MEF.[72]

In mid-April, a frustrated Dunsterville shared a laugh with his intelligence officer, Major M.H. Donohoe, and senior officer Lieutenant-Colonel Alfred Rawlinson over a request for resources after these initial reinforcements arrived. In the words of Rawlinson,

> At this time a good deal of trouble and delay was caused to the Hush-Hush Army by the difficulty of obtaining stores, and assistance generally, from Headquarters at Baghdad ... One case occurs to me especially, as illustrative of this state of affairs. When steps were at first being taken to alleviate the famine at Hamadan we were called upon to produce bread and provide meat in entirely unforeseen quantities, and in the face of this urgent demand a telegram was sent to Baghdad asking that a "butcher" and a "baker" might be sent up at first opportunity ... when the reply eventually arrived our state of mind may be conceived when we read the following message: "It is not understood for what purpose the services of a butcher and baker are required"! ... There appeared to be only one possible answer that could meet the case, and I wrote it out and handed it in,

but I much fear it was never sent; it was: "A Butcher is required to Bake the Bread, and a Baker to cut up the Meat!" Perhaps it was a pity if it was never sent, as it would quite probably have produced the men at once, and relieved the somewhat strained relations.

Of this comic relief, Dunsterville wrote, "Baghdad beat their own record yesterday. As I have now some British troops I wired asking for a 'butcher and a baker.' They have replied 'For what purpose do you require a butcher and a baker?'!"[73]

While Dunsterforce sat in limbo in Persia, the same cannot be said of events in the Caucasus. During this time the situation had transformed immeasurably, and not for the better for the British. Nevertheless, securing the Caucasus oil was still a principal British war aim; however, this ambition was now shared by the Germans, Turks, and Bolsheviks as well. In the following months, the Caucasus would bear witness to mass ethnic cleansing and slaughter, pitched battles between supposed German and Turkish allies, convoluted political manoeuvrings, and invasion from all four fronts: the Germans from the northwest, the Turks from the southwest, the Bolsheviks from the northeast and, the British from the south. All were in pursuit of one prize – the precious oil of Baku.

Chapter Seven

The Battle for Baku

In late March and early April 1918, Essad Bey, a young Muslim stu-
dent at the unofficial and fledgling Baku State University, described
the scenes of horror on the boulevards of Baku: "The national hatred
that raged in the streets spared no one. The Armenians who were the
victors this time, took the bloodiest kind of revenge for 1905. Women,
children, and old men were killed in their homes. In the mosques,
where the inhabitants sought refuge, massacres took place."[1] In September, he would be writing about another massacre in Baku, although
in this instance the Armenians were the victims. Shortly after the Brest-
Litovsk Treaty was signed on 3 March, the sporadic ethnic fighting in
and around the environs of Baku, which had been escalating since the
beginning of 1918, flared into a full-scale massacre in late March.

In order to maintain power, the Bolshevik government under Armenian Stepan Shaumian formed a loose coalition with the Armenian
Dashnak Party and smaller social revolutionary parties to consolidate
his power in the region, while alienating the Muslim Musavat Party. By
February, "the Baku Soviet gerrymandered and invalidated the Musavat's electoral strength, excluding it from legitimate power-sharing
in the democratic community."[2] Having gained Armenian support,
Shaumian integrated the well-armed Armenian militia of six to eight
thousand men into his Bolshevik Guard of four thousand (creating
the Red Army of the Caucasus), knowing full well that this unification
"gave the civil war some of the character of a national bloodbath, but
this was unavoidable. We went forward conscious of this."[3]

On 29 March, members of the disbanded and predominantly Muslim Imperial Russian Caucasian Native Mountain Division, commonly
known as the "Savage Division," arrived in Baku to attend the funeral of

the son of oil tycoon and builder of the Baku Opera House Zeynalabdin Taghiyev. Following the procession, the Red Guard was ordered to disarm these men, regarding them as Turkish allies. This potential action caused outrage among their commanders and the local Muslim population now fearing full-scale ethnic cleansing. While politicians from all parties attempted to defuse the precarious situation, shots were fired on 30 March, igniting three days of slaughter. In retribution for past injustices, local Armenians joined the Bolshevik-Armenian troops in the mass killing of Muslims. In a letter home to his wife in London, William Lacey, manager of the Baku office of Cheleken Oil Limited, described "the bad time we had here for 3 days the end of March, when fighting took place in the town between the Bolsheviks and the Tartars ... and how it will end God only knows, though many thousands on both sides have lost their lives. Can it go on much longer one wonders? ... 'Tis the darkest hour before the dawn, and we can only pray better days are not far off."[4] Finally, on 1 April, only after the Musavat bowed to the authority of the Baku Soviet committee, did the killing cease, but not before as many as thirteen thousand Muslims had been killed and hundreds of others had fled the city in what has been historically labelled the "March Days."[5] Six months later, however, the Muslims would realize their revenge.

While Baku was engulfed in ethnic violence, the Ottoman Third Army under Vehib Pasha, comprising some fifty thousand well-rested and well-supplied men, broke the fragile Erzincan peace of December and invaded the Caucasus. The newly formed Transcaucasian Commissariat refused to acknowledge the broad territorial claims promised to Turkey at Brest-Litovsk, including the three *vilayets* of Ardahan, Kars, and Batum. Georgian politicians harboured extreme, if not unrealistic, national ambitions and inveigled the Armenian and Azerbaijani representatives to validate this fierce independence movement. At the same time, violence broke out between Georgia and the Muslims in Abkhazia, southern Ossetia, and Chechnya who were also vying for an independent Islamic state – disputes that would reignite with the collapse of the Soviet Union in 1991. For the Ottomans, "the importance of this retrocession of the three Vilayets lay not so much in the return to Turkey of the great fortress of Kars, but in the fact that Batum was the key port for the rich Baku petroleum." General Ludendorff remarked that, by initiating an invasion of the Caucasus, the Turks had not only broken the agreements of Brest-Litovsk, but also "seized the opportunity to fill the resulting political and military vacuum." It was, he admonished his fellow officers on the German General Staff, "the predestined moment for the realization of all their ambitious schemes in the direction of the Caucasus" and motivation for their pan-Turanian schemes of expansion, fuelled eastward into Central Asia by Baku's precious oil.[6] Following the "March Days" the Ottoman advance gained tempo, not only as self-proclaimed protectors of their Muslim brethren, but also with the realization that Germany also had designs on Batum and Baku. The alliance between the Germans and Ottomans on policy in the Middle East and the Caucasus was becoming increasingly fragile.

The Turks made rapid progress through eastern Anatolia, consistently forcing the retreat of local Armenian forces. Defending the Caucasus in the face of this Ottoman offensive were never more than sixteen thousand Armenians, already engaged with Muslim guerrillas, and ten thousand Georgians of questionable morale showing little inclination to fight. By 12 February the Turks had entered Erzurum, approaching the former Russian frontier. By late March, the Turks were poised on the Transcaucasian border while deliberations deteriorated at the Trebizond Conference. In early April both Sarikamish and Van fell to the Turks, who attacked Batum on 14 February, accepting surrender a few hours later. Kars followed, amid looting and pillaging.[7] Germany viewed the Ottoman offensive as a betrayal and outright threat to their own interests in the Caucasus. "There are political and economic reasons," wrote the Foreign Ministry, "for not wishing the Turks to establish themselves permanently in Batum and on the routes leading to the Transcaucasian oil and mineral fields."[8]

In the face of this rapid Ottoman advance, representatives of the Transcaucasian Republic agreed to Turkish demands for a new peace proposal to be negotiated at Batum. The conference opened on 11 May with the Turkish delegates presenting their demands and ultimatums. The most important was Ottoman control of all railways and oil facilities in the Caucasus. This would enable speedy advance into northern Persia and the conquest of Baku and beyond, via the Transcaucasian railway on the eastern shores of the Caspian: "The impending crisis brought about by the long-delayed but now complete collapse on the military front now also tore apart the short-lived Trans-Caucasian Commissariat."[9] Armenians blocked the Turkish route to northern Persia and Baku, while the Georgian railway from Batum to Baku was a vital possession. By war or through negotiation, these were the primary military objectives of Ottoman leaders, with the protection of the Mosul *vilayet* a distant secondary aim. Palestine and Syria had been all but abandoned. The Muslim populations of Azerbaijan, and the smaller enclaves in Abkhazia and Chechnya, viewed the Ottomans as potential liberators and abetted their advance by conducting guerrilla attacks in the rear of Georgian and Armenian positions. Muslims in Baku viewed the Ottomans as a medium to exact revenge for the March Days on Shaumian, his Armenians, and the Bolshevik oppressors. The Armenians, who had fought a valiant rearguard action against the Turks, were tired and demoralized and lacked the resources to continue their dogged defence. The Georgians, now isolated, entertained propositions from the German emissaries at Batum, General Otto von Lossow and Colonel Friedrich Kress von Kressenstein.

Fissures in the Ottoman-German alliance began to appear in late 1917 over the destination of troop deployments and allocation of resources. With the British capture of Baghdad in March 1917, followed by Jerusalem in December, the Germans viewed these theatres as pivotal to halting the British conquest of the Middle East. German policymakers preferred to strengthen Ottoman-German forces along these fronts to retake lost ground, while offering protection to Mosul and the heart of the Ottoman Empire. To facilitate these goals, the Germans initiated the creation of the Yildirim (lightning) Army or Heeresgruppe (Army Group) F. Cobbled together from German officers, veterans of the Eastern Front, and Turks withdrawn from Galicia, its initial mission was the recapture of Baghdad. After a thorough review of the Middle Eastern fronts, however, it was diverted to Palestine, which was viewed to be the most immediate threat. As it turned out, the "offensive potential of the Yilderim [sic] force was a chimera."[10] By this time, the war in Mesopotamia was at a stalemate as "the Turks were almost incapable of fighting for the time being, and the British lacked the transport facilities to reach them and strike a heavy blow."[11] Only two Turkish divisions of a promised nine joined the Yildirim, while Enver had assembled nine fully equipped divisions in the Caucasus, many of which had been resting for over a year.

It must also be remembered that the Germans were also planning an advance from the southern Ukraine and Crimea into the Caucasus to secure agricultural and mineral resources and although they were "aware that Turkish troops sent to Palestine tied down British forces, tried unsuccessfully to stop Turkey denuding their other fronts" to reinforce their Caucasian armies.[12] German appeals to the Ottoman senior staff that using Turkish troops in Mesopotamia and Palestine would have more effect, went unheeded by Enver and his inner circle.

Since the outbreak of war, they had set their sights on the Caucasus and the consummation of their pan-Turanian crusade. The official British history of the Mesopotamian campaign suggests, "The detachment of large Turkish forces to the Caucasus at a period when their Syrian and Mesopotamian fronts were in urgent need of reinforcement is difficult to understand from a purely military point of view. It can only be explained satisfactorily if it is regarded as an attempt to vindicate their national ideal by building up a new state which would include the ancient home of their race."[13]

As British intelligence revealed, the Turks had lost interest in Palestine, and "available men were dispatched to adventures in the Caucasus and in Persia, where the peace of Brest-Litovsk had opened wide fields for Pan-Turanian dreams of empire." German generals, including Falkenhayn, Liman von Sanders, and Kress, complained to higher command that the Turks were frittering away soldiers and supplies in their "Transcaucasian adventures," and that, not only did promised reinforcements never arrive, the Turks were actually transferring able-bodied soldiers from Palestine to the Caucasus. Kress complained that he was losing as many as four thousand Turkish soldiers per month from disease and desertion, while awaiting Allenby's offensive in "fragile tents with nothing to cheer their spirits." In fact, Turkish troops diverted to the Caucasus were promised (although they never received) increased pay and promotion: "The consequent drain on the Palestinian units became enormous, for only the sick and mortally exhausted could resist the lure of money and fame."[14] In addition, the professional working relationship between German and Ottoman senior officers was dysfunctional, as they had developed an acute personal dislike for one another. For example, Kress referred to Vehib Pasha, commander of the Third Army in the Caucasus, as "that animal." The Germans felt betrayed and handicapped by alliance warfare. As Churchill remarked to Roosevelt and Stalin at the Tehran Conference in November 1943, "There is at least one thing worse than fighting with allies – And that is to fight without them."[15] With Enver poised to take the Caucasus, German actions would rebuff Churchill's later statement.

The Germans were increasingly desperate for oil. The Allied blockade was finally beginning to strangle German imports, and the German war machine was quickly and literally grinding to a halt at the front and at home. Extreme rationing was introduced, and starvation gripped the German population – a condition even more pronounced within the Austro-Hungarian Empire. Facing a dire shortage of petrol, the Germans were forced to reduce U-boat flotillas in size and scope, allowing the Allies greater ease in materiel transport across the Atlantic. The last-gamble German Kaiserschlacht or Spring Offensive, beginning 21 March 1918, failed, in part as a result of German inability to resupply the forward "stormtrooper" units, which were unable to carry enough supplies to sustain themselves for more than a few days. Vehicle transport fleets sat idle on empty fuel tanks, with German troops advancing beyond viable railheads. Needing a continuous supply of feed and fodder, the horse-drawn transport units could not counter the lack of mechanical mobility and speed. A dearth of petroleum was rendering German forces impotent.

The setback on the Western Front in July 1918, however, did not weaken Germany's determination to expand eastwards, for as Ludendorff remarked, the shortage of oil made the possession of Baku "an ever more vital question."[16] Germany's *Drang nach Osten* route had changed its course, but as the chief of the Imperial General Staff Henry Wilson affirmed in February 1918, shortly after he replaced Robertson, the German "varies his methods but not his aims ... he still aims for the east."[17] In early March, Wilson submitted a report to the War Cabinet outlining the strategic position of the war in the Middle East and the Caucasus:

We must consider the effect of German access to Odessa, the possibility of the enemy transporting troops across the Black Sea from Odessa to Batoum and thence to Baku ... with the result that it is now easier for the Germans than it was to get a footing in Caucasia, while it is becoming hourly more difficult for us to do so ... Germany went into this war with the object of making herself a dominant world power ... She aimed at establishing complete control over Central Europe and the Near East with a view to expansion eastwards. It seems certain that Germany has not yet abandoned the attainment of these objectives but the course of the war has altered the methods of attainment ... If she succeeds in dominating Russia effectively she will have secured the northern flank of this line of advance and may even hope ultimately to develop a new "drang nach osten" which will place her eventually on the shores of the Pacific ... Our immediate answer therefore to the dangers which German access through Russia to the East open up are:– ... To stretch out from Baghdad into North-West Persia and on a foundation of organized military strength between Baghdad and the Caspian build up local organizations and work our way into the Caucasus with a firm intention of winning over Armenia, and making our influence predominate on

the eastern ports of the Black Sea ... I desire to press upon the War Cabinet
my conviction that unless immediate action on the above lines is taken we
run a grave risk of permitting the Germans to establish themselves in a position which will eventually lead to the downfall of our Eastern Empire.[18]

The Foreign Office agreed that the "rapid advance of the Germans
eastwards through the Ukraine serves to draw attention once again to
their evident designs upon the Caucasus."[19] The secure footing desired
by the Germans in the Caucasus was presented, gift-wrapped, by the
Georgians.

The Transcaucasian government realized its weak and inferior position while negotiations continued at Batum during a brief cessation of
hostilities. On 15 May, Georgia, having already been partially occupied
by the Turks, was in the weakest position and stalled negotiations with
the Turks, while appealing to Germany for protection: "The only possible way out of their predicament seemed to be the proclamation of
Georgia's independence and the dissolution of Transcaucasia as a federation. Once Georgia was independent, she could invite the Germans
to protect her against the Turks."[20] The Germans were eager to discuss
possible approaches, as keeping the covetous Turks from Baku was a
high priority. They also wanted Georgia's manganese, and control of
its railways, which would facilitate the movement of oil and troops
across the entire southern Caucasus. A significant number of former
German prisoners of war were drifting around the region and could be
mustered to aid Georgia, thus advancing German aims in the region.
Ludendorff reacted quickly to the offer, realizing the constraints on time
and the limited window of opportunity, stressing to his German delegates that "Germany's recognition and protection will at the same time
give Georgia security against the greedy Turks ... We should not postpone decisions ... If Georgia is our advanced base, it is to be hoped that
the Caucasian territory will be gradually pacified and that we should
be able to draw from there the raw materials we so urgently need ...
Also, Baku should not be ceded to the Turks ... It would be an act of
hostility towards us if the Turks were to occupy the Tiflis-Baku line and
Baku itself, an occupation which might lead to the destruction of the
local oil industry." Ludendorff was also being prodded by leaders of
German industry, who were clamouring for an opportunity to exploit
the vast resources of the Caucasus and the oilfields of Baku. Furthermore, the kaiser was convinced that Baku would be valuable brokering
leverage if, and when, peace negotiations commenced.[21]

On 25 May, a secret German-Georgian agreement was reached whereby Georgia would be incorporated "in the German Reich, either as a Federal state ruled by a German prince, or in a relationship like that of a British dominion under a German viceroy."[22] On the same day, Germany again appealed to the Turks to transfer their forces in the Caucasus to Mesopotamia and Palestine, warning, "If the Turkish government, in pursuit of political interests in other areas, neglects the defense of its own national territory and causes us trouble in the Caucasus ... it must not assume that we shall later recoup its own national territory at our expense."[23] A few hours later, in response, Ottoman forces captured the major rail line running north towards Tiflis.

The following day, Georgia announced its nominal independence, as an unofficial German protectorate, with its capital at Tiflis. Two days later, the independent republics of Armenia and Azerbaijan were declared and the short-lived Transcaucasian Republic ceased to exist, much to the frustration of Ottoman representatives, who now had to negotiate three individual treaties. On the 28 May, a preliminary agreement was ratified by Georgia and Germany, followed by three supplementary amendments. In summary, Germany received the rights to, and control over, Georgian ports inclusive of actual vessels and shipping, all mining and oil facilities, and railroads and stations, all of which were to be occupied by German troops. Economically, although these ventures were deemed Georgian-German enterprises under the provisions of the treaty, Georgia agreed to "channel all mineral exports to the Reich for the duration of the war."[24] Although the first two German battalions arrived at Poti on 3 June, Georgia, still in a weak military position, concluded a peace treaty with the Turks, as a cost for securing independence. Georgia relinquished two small districts east of the Russo-Turkish frontier of 1877 and allowed Turkey the use of its railways. However, a "clash between the Germans and the Turks in the Caucasus was thus imminent; Georgia had given full transit rights on the Caucasus railway to Turkey, but control of the railway to Germany."[25]

On 4 June, Armenia, lacking any powerful benefactor like that secured by Georgia, bowed to Ottoman demands, which were far more severe. The territory allotted to the infant independent republic amounted to roughly twelve thousand square miles, and its capital of Yerevan was easily within artillery range of the newly defined Turco-Armenian border. In addition, Armenia was forced to grant the Turks control of all railways crossing its terrain: "Under these circumstances, the fact that the Turks had at least acknowledged the existence of an 'independent'

Armenian state could hardly be very encouraging to most Armenians."
On the same day, the remaining treaty was signed with Azerbaijan but
was markedly different in scope. It reflected Enver's pan-Turanian
designs and his self-professed vision of the Ottomans as protectors of
Islam. While acknowledging the independence of Azerbaijan, the Turks
promised military and economic aid for the new state. In exchange,
Azerbaijan gave the Turks absolute control over all means of transportation in and through Azerbaijani territory "for an advance on Baku,
the implication being that the conquest of the oil city would be a joint
venture."[26] Following the suppression of the Musavat Party in early
April, Baku remained an isolated Bolshevik outpost, under a weak and
reeling Soviet committee. While potentially abetting an Ottoman invasion, the city was surrounded by hostile Muslims seeking revenge for
the March Days. These three fledgling republics would be swallowed
by the Soviet Union between 1919 and 1921, eventually regaining independence in 1991.

Meanwhile, after the agreement with Georgia, German troops occupied the Georgian Black Sea ports of Poti and Sukhum, solidified
control of Tiflis, and began to fan out across the Georgian railways.
They also occupied the north-south rail lines and roads from Aleksan-
dropol (Gumru) and Karakilise in northern Armenia to Tiflis, severely
restricting Turkish troop movements. Reinforcements arrived from the
Ukraine, from the Syrian front, and directly from Germany. These soldiers joined freed German prisoners of war to form the basis of a bud-
ding German Caucasian army, now five thousand strong. While it was
planned to raise a force of thirty-five thousand, the German presence
in the Caucasus never surpassed fifteen thousand men.[27] "I knew there
was a German occupation," described Captain Leslie R. Hulls, a British agent in Tiflis, "But I had no idea they would be in such numbers. I
met them in every street ... I felt that my freedom would not have been
worth much had they known of my presence ... I didn't dream of seeing the British in this part of the Caucasus for many months. As far as
I knew I was the only Englishman in Tiflis – certainly the only British
Officer. We had no Consul here, for he, together with the Consuls of
Italy and France and other allies, had left before the Germans arrived."
Hulls was captured by the Turks, only to escape after two months in
captivity. He worked his way east to Baku, being safe-housed in transit
by Armenian peasants.[28]

Between 7 and 9 June a series of gruff and imperious communications were sent by Ludendorff and Hindenburg to "that mad imperialist

7.1 German officers consult with local leaders in Tiflis, Georgia,
June 1918 (Imperial War Museum).

Enver." Ludendorff, above all else, stressed that the "Baku oil region
[must] be spared any disturbance by Turkish troops or Turkish-Tartar
irregular forces." In response, Enver, who replied with equal hauteur,
reiterated that he would not abandon his commitment to protect his
Muslim brethren across the Caucasus, including those at Baku who
had recently been "subject to sadism" at the hands of Armenians and
Bolsheviks.[29] British intelligence reported to the War Office, "Intense
ill-feeling continues between the Germans and the Turks and the latter
are apparently determined to prosecute their plans for the occupation
of Baku in defiance of Germany."[30] This political dissonance quickly
manifested itself on the actual battlefield.

On 2 June, the Ottoman Eastern Military Command issued an order
that all German arms in regions already seized by the Turks, and
those within the projected Turkish eastern sphere of influence, must
be seized. German soldiers were to be taken to a "collection camp"
at Kars. On 10 June, Vehib Pasha ordered his 9th Division to advance

on Tiflis. Moving north along the main road to Tiflis, forward Ottoman units came into contact with two German-Georgian companies
at Vorontsovka, marking the first instance of combat between the supposed allies. The Turks dominated the brief but violent skirmish and
took "a considerable number of prisoners." Not surprisingly, the Germans were irate, if not embarrassed, over this "scandalous incident"
and threatened to eliminate all German military and monetary support
if the Turks did not immediately release all German prisoners and halt
their advance on Baku.[31] Enver dutifully bowed to German demands,
but had by no means forsaken his eastern pan-Turanian thrust towards
Baku. Although in direct violation of Brest-Litovsk, he initiated a clever
plan to both placate the Germans (and Georgians) and continue his
push through the Caucasus by reorganizing his Eastern Army Group.

Enver placed his uncle, Halil Pasha, in command of the entire "Army
of the East" and reorganized the Ninth Army under Yakup Sevki Pasha
after recalling Vehib Pasha to Constantinople. Its mission, as Enver
reported to the Germans, was to counter British and Bolshevik penetration into northern Persia. As such, its axis-of-advance was reoriented
south towards northwest Persia to link up with Ottoman reconnaissance elements already advancing on Tabriz. After its capture, the combined Ottoman force would take a sharp turn, heading east through
northern Persia to form the southern wing of a pincer movement on
Baku. The northern or direct assault would be carried out by Enver's
newly established "Army of Islam," commanded by his half-brother
Nuri Pasha, also a pan-Turanian zealot. This force was composed of the
Ottoman 5th Division (six thousand men) and ten to twelve thousand
local Muslim irregulars and militia, predominantly from the defunct
Savage Division, with other members from Azerbaijan and Dagestan.
The vast majority of officers, however, were highly motivated and reli-
able Christian former tsarist commanders, seizing on the opportunity
to battle the Bolsheviks.

The 5th Division crossed through Armenian territory, thus bypass-
ing the main railway and also German positions (as did the Ninth
Army). It then linked up with the Muslim militias at their rendezvous
point at Giandzha/Ganja (Elisavetpol) along the Tiflis-Baku railway
deep inside Azerbaijan. By the end of June, the Army of Islam, relatively unopposed, was approaching striking distance of Baku. The oil
kingdom lay a mere two hundred miles to the east. Enver's Caucasian thrust also prompted the local Muslims in Abkhazia, Ossetia, and
Chechnya, who refused to recognize the validity of any outside claims

to their territories, to intensify their guerrilla campaigns. Grozny's oil-fields, which had been set alight in January, burned for months, with the flames visible for over eighty miles.[32]

For the Germans, a Turkish occupation of Baku would be accompanied by their failure in "administering the country and regulating petroleum production." The Germans also feared that if the Turks failed to control their Muslim irregulars and the "Tartars got into town, they would loot it and burn the oil-wells." Ludendorff had still not given up hope of beating the Turks to Baku and stressed the need for more German reinforcements while also raising additional Georgian formations. Neither was feasible. Germany and its peripheral theatres of war had been drained of all non-essential troops and resources to support the ongoing Spring Offensive on the Western Front. Georgia had attained independence and, already battling a Muslim insurgency in its northern provinces, hardly wanted to be swept up in what would appear to be an ethno-religious war. Nevertheless, Ludendorff concluded that the "oil question" warranted the dispatch of German soldiers to Baku "if necessary."[33] He was resolved that "it had become essential for us to show a strong hand in this district – not merely because we hoped to secure some military assistance from this quarter, but also in order to obtain raw materials. That we could not rely on Turkey in this matter had been once demonstrated by her conduct in Batum, where she claimed the right to retain all the stocks for herself. We could expect to get oil from Baku only if we helped ourselves." Simultaneously, Ludendorff channelled diplomatic efforts to Lenin, proposing that Germany would be entitled to exploit a portion of Baku's oil in return for "guaranteeing possession of Baku to the Russians." To this Lenin responded, "Of course, we will agree."[34]

When Lloyd George was made aware of the mushrooming Turco-German enmity and that the two had "fallen out over who should get to Baku first," he suggested to the War Cabinet that, given this "remarkable situation," Britain might secure a general peace with the Ottomans by promising them Baku. "The Turks," he reasoned, "were more anxious to acquire this rich country than to regain Mesopotamia or Palestine. Some peace arrangement might be arrived at with the Turkish Government by which Turanian territory might be given them." He contended that it would be better from a British standpoint if the Turks held Baku, rather than either the Germans or the Russians. It was vital to deny Germany its oil resources, and while it was improbable that the Turks "would ever be dangerous to our interests in the East, Russia if in the future regenerated, might be so." He added that Russia "was an ambitious military power, which, although friendly to us at the moment, is our historical world rival."[35] While the War Cabinet dismissed this overture as their prime minister's typical overstimulated opportunist speculation, these recent events in the Caucasus did alter the position and mission of Dunsterforce. "Unless we can get Dunsterville and his crowd through in the next few weeks," argued Wilson, "the German landing at Batum will have put themselves in possession of the whole of the Caucasus, and will have control of the Caspian as well and get through to Turkestan." Not only did Curzon agree, he was also contemplating the future consequences of a German-occupied Baku: "I believe 20 per cent of the production of petroleum in the world comes from ... oil wells at Baku and Grozny, and you can well conceive that if Germany possessed these resources, as she is on the verge of doing, she will be absolutely independent of the American supply for the future."[36]

As the political and military environs of the Caucasus underwent drastic realignment, Dunsterforce remained in a holding pattern. Throughout April and May, piecemeal elements continued to patrol the routes from Kermanshah to Hamadan, Hamadan to Tabriz, and from Hamadan to Kasvin, where Dunsterville arrived with his headquarters on 1 June. During this time, confusion about the future purpose of Dunsterforce puzzled the War Office, General Marshall, the India Office, and Dunsterville himself. An endless barrage of communications flowed between these offices and their personnel, to the exasperation of Marshall, who had also been denied his advance on Mosul. Although he ventured north and captured Kirkuk in early May, he soon abandoned these gains (much to the anxiety of the Kurds who had allied with his force), as maintaining and occupying this position two hundred miles beyond the Baghdad railhead with insufficient alternative transportation was simply "too much altogether." As for Dunsterforce and its "rotten policy," Marshall bluntly told General Wilson that he "hoped against hope for the cancellation of the project," comparing it to "Napoleon's Moscow campaign, hardly an unqualified success."[37]

Any and all parties with the slightest connection to Dunsterforce offered suggestions. They ranged from maintaining the status quo to capturing Enzeli and the Bolshevik Caspian fleet; sending a small covert party of five men to Baku to destroy the oil installations (which would have been a herculean task, given the size of Baku's oil infrastructure); reinforcing Dunsterforce for a full-scale assault on Baku;

and, finally, sending individual British attachés to Enzeli and Baku to gauge and report on the overall situation. Few realized the complexities of the region and the innumerable obstacles faced by Dunsterville, including Marshall's obstinate refusal to cooperate. The problems were many: the approaches from Kasvin to Enzeli had to be cleansed of the Jangali threat; naval vessels (feasibly the Caspian fleet) had to be obtained for passage to Baku; and, most importantly, both Enzeli and Baku were controlled by hostile Soviet committees who had previously denied Dunsterville access to either port city.

With confusion mounting, and telegrams getting crossed, arriving late, or not delivered at all, finally on 26 May Dunsterville received affirmation: "Latest news leads me to have another try at Baku ... join up with Bicherakov and his Cossacks at Kasvin and then make war on the Jangalis on the Enzeli road – if we are not delayed we may get to Baku in time to save the town and oil-wells from falling into the hands of the Turks and Germans, who are racing up from Tiflis to get them. Are we to be always too late? It's not my fault anyway as they refuse me all the troops and aeroplanes I need." On the twenty-eighth, his orders were rescinded with a "War Office wire absolutely forbidding me to go to the Caucasus at the present time, so the Germans will get the Baku oil, the Krasnovodsk cotton, the Astrakhan wheat and the Caspian Sea."[38] He was, however, authorized to take Enzeli and seize the Caspian fleet, and "if possible reach Baku." The War Office closed its directive to Dunsterville with the stipulation that "a permanent occupation of Baku is not in the question ... If we can get complete control of the Caspian shipping, destroy the Baku pumping plant, pipe line and oil reservoirs, we shall have attained our present objective." In Baghdad, Marshall was dumbfounded by these naive orders: "I had never seen Baku, but I did know that it contained some 200 oil wells, each about 500 feet deep and protected by ferro-concreate and asbestos coverings, and how many tons of high explosives would have been required to blow them all up is a question I did not enter into. The inhabitants of Baku may not have had much stomach to fight against the Turks, but one can hardly imagine that they would have looked on, with hands in their pockets, whilst a few British troops went about blowing their means of livelihood sky-high."[39] After questioning the War Office, Wilson responded to Marshall in a "note of asperity," cautioning him that "H.M. Government attach more importance to the success in that sphere and to securing temporary control of the Caspian than you appear to appreciate."[40]

7.2 A small portion of the oil installations at Baku, August 1918.
According to one Dunsterforce soldier, "The country around Baku is a mass of
oil wells – a regular forest of pumping towers and one gets completely lost
in them." (Imperial War Museum).

Despite Marshall's consternation, Dunsterville sent Colonel C.B.
Stokes under a flag of truce to negotiate with Kuchik Khan for safe pas-
sage to Enzeli. "It fell to my lot," he wrote, "to visit Kuchik Khan in his
jungle abode and to try to persuade him not to oppose the passage of
British and Russian troops on their way to Baku via Resht and Enzeli ...
On reaching the Jangali outpost found ourselves talking to a German
Officer who was working with the Jangalis. He was one of 20 German
Officers who had been sent out earlier in the war to travel across Persia
to Afghanistan ... After Kuchik Khan had consulted his colleagues he
informed us that he would give us a definite answer in five days."[41]
Events, however, moved faster. Dunsterville finally received his fre-
quently requested and long-awaited support in the form of five hundred Ford vans carrying a thousand soldiers of the Hampshires and
Gurkhas, the remainder of the 14th Hussar Regiment, eight armoured
cars, a battery of field artillery, and four Martinsyde airplanes, whose

appearance in the skies over Kasvin and Resht alone was sufficient to inspire awe and fear in the local populations.

On 12 June, hours after breaking off negotiations with Kuchik Khan, Stokes departed for Enzeli. Immediately, escorted by two aircraft, Bicherakov's twelve hundred Cossacks, two armoured cars, four horse-drawn artillery pieces, and a squadron of the 14th Hussars attacked Jangali positions along the Menjil Bridge gap sector. Bicherakov ordered a heavy combined-arms bombardment of Jangali positions, followed by a slow and methodical advance of his armoured cars, cavalry, and infantry, which reached the bridge without incident. Taken by surprise, and in the face of this superior firepower, the enemy had already scattered, leaving behind a large number of dead, wounded, and prisoners. Bicherakov claimed a decisive victory and had secured the choke-point at the bridge, rendering the road north to Enzeli safe for follow-on forces. On 18 June, a Jangali ambush on a British column near Resht was driven off, with the British suffering one killed and six wounded. As a result, larger and more numerous British patrols ran the route between Kasvin and Enzeli, where Bicherakov had arrived a few days earlier.

After routing the Jangalis, Bicherakov continued on to Enzeli, where he became an honorary Bolshevik, declaring, "I am neither a Bolshevik nor a Menshevik. But I love my homeland, I can fight a little, and I will come to the aid of the Baku soviet to defend the town of Baku from invasion by the Turks ... I don't understand anything about politics or socialism ... I'm a Cossack, I know a little something about combat and military matters, and that's all." Bolshevik newspapers quickly applauded the conversion of their new comrade. Immediately, he was given the rank of major-general and was placed in command of the Red Army of the Caucasus at Baku, at a time when his leadership and his loyal Cossacks were desperately needed. Between 16 June and 1 July, after an initial Red Army victory, the Army of Islam, buttressed by Ottoman reinforcements, scored a series of decisive triumphs over the Armenian and Bolshevik defenders of Baku, who were reeling from a crippling dysentery epidemic.[42]

After a quick reconnaissance of the situation in and around Baku, Bicherakov returned to Enzeli on 22 June to await Dunsterville, who entered Enzeli for the second time five days later. While sanctioning his move to Enzeli, Marshall bluntly reminded Dunsterville that he was not to proceed to Baku, that no reinforcements could be expected in the near future, and he scolded that the renegade "Bicherakhov is just trying to make money out of us." He explained, whether fact or fiction, that he was already having "extreme difficulty in supplying Dunsterforce with lubricants, petrol, ordnance stores, ammunition and spare parts and could not guarantee to maintain a larger force."[43] After consulting with Bicherakov and the Soviet Committee, Dunsterville decided to send Bicherakov and his force to Baku. Dunsterville insisted, as instructed by the War Office, that four British armoured cars (and a significant amount of money) in the care of Major Harold K. Newcombe, a banker in Canada before the war, and three fellow Canadians, accompany Bicherakov. For all intents and purposes, these Canadians became Bolshevik soldiers in Lenin's Red Army!

On 5 July, dressed in Red Army uniforms, to avoid any dissension with the Bolsheviks, Bicherakov's force arrived at Alyat forty miles south of Baku, where the railway from Ganja approaches the Baku peninsula before heading north to the oil city. While militarily this was a vital location to impede Turkish advances on Baku, Bicherakov also chose not to defend Baku directly in order to preserve the independence of his "British-Bolshevik force" from the numerous conflicting interests among the political parties in Baku. The Soviet committee in Baku was teetering on collapse, as the steady advance of the Army of Islam inched closer to securing its petroleum prize. Bicherakov was immediately engaged by vanguard Turkish forces. Outmanned and outgunned, his attached Red Army troops fled the field, leaving his small Dunsterforce detachment to fight a hard delaying action as they fell back towards Baku. On 25 July, the Turks occupied the Alyat heights and controlled the railway heading north to the heart of Baku, with its oil rigs and towers now clearly visible for the first time.

While the defenders of Baku faced a series of setbacks throughout July, Dunsterville travelled to both Tehran and Baghdad to press his case to deploy to Baku. He also continued to negotiate with the Soviet committee in Enzeli for safe passage. Dunsterville fortuitously arrived in Baghdad on 18 July to find General Marshall on leave in India. He presented his argument to the acting commander, Major-General Hew D. Fanshawe, who knew very little about the contentious mission. Following discussions with the War Office, it was concluded that although the information on Baku and the Caucasus was fragmentary, the War Office agreed to Fanshawe's recommendation to permit the dispatch of one or two battalions to Baku, to be followed by reinforcements and secondary support if the situation permitted. Dunsterville had finally circumvented Marshall's authority in his quest to reach Baku. Leaving

Baghdad on 20 July, Dunsterville travelled via Kermanshah, Hamadan, Kasvin, and Resht to Enzeli, in order to inspect the elements of Dunsterforce still patrolling these vital supply lanes. Three days later, while Dunsterville was in Kasvin, 2,500 Jangalis launched a determined assault against the 450-man British detachment at Resht. Over the next two days, aided by bombing runs from two airplanes and continuous strafing by armoured cars, the British drove the Jangalis back to their forest camps. Although Dunsterforce suffered one dead and fifty wounded, the corollaries of the battle were advantageous to its overall position. Realizing he could not negate nor match British firepower, after suffering detrimental losses each time he engaged them, Kuchik Khan immediately negotiated a ceasefire. A formal peace was declared between the two parties on 12 August. This in turn, freed more Dunsterforce troops and supplies for the defence of Baku, which was in the midst of a political coup to overthrow Shaumian and his Bolshevik committee.

Given the ethnic and political diversity of Baku, Shaumian's Bolsheviks maintained a tenuous government by aligning with the Armenian Dashnaks and smaller revolutionary parties, thus alienating the Musavat Party representing the large Muslim population. As the Turks inched closer to Baku, the Dashnaks and other political groups demanded that Shaumian secure Bolshevik reinforcements. For the Armenians, following the events of March, the defeat of the advancing Ottoman force was literally a matter of life and death. However, Moscow, to where Lenin had moved his government in early 1918, did not recognize the independence of the three infant republics. Bolshevik leaders challenged Georgia's claims to "non-Georgian territory" such as Abkhazia and Ossetia and nurtured national Muslim insurgencies in those regions: "National self-determination, the Bolsheviks showed, could be a two-edged sword."[44] The Bolshevik policy was to gain German acknowledgment that the "problems of Georgia, Armenia, and Azerbaijan were internal affairs of Russia." Logically, however, Stalin realized, "It is possible that we would have to give in to the Germans on the question of Georgia, but such a concession would be finally made only on condition that the Germans declare their non-interference in the affairs of Armenia and Azerbaijan."[45]

Shaumian desperately searched for any support he could muster. He refused to concede to the demands of the opposition parties to invite Dunsterville and the British to help defend Baku. On 25 July, he presented a resolution to deny the British access to Baku, which failed to garner a majority. His Bolshevik vote was not weighty enough to counter those of the other now-allied political parties, which were resolute to secure British relief. Shaumian argued that the British could not bring more than a few thousand soldiers to bear against the Turks, and he promised to obtain reinforcements and supplies with "extraordinary measures of mobilization." He wired Lenin directly to update him on the situation, while asking for a large Red Army contingent. Lenin accepted that he did not have the means to reinforce the Bolshevik position at Baku, telling Shaumian, "We will take measures to send you forces, however, we cannot give a definite promise." Stalin added that any thought of inviting the British would be a direct violation of "the will of Russia for the sake of ... the Anglo-French imperialists," and in iconic Bolshevik rhetoric implored Baku to initiate a "determined struggle against the agents of foreign capital."[46] Lenin and Stalin both agreed that, if the worst happened and Baku was to be temporarily occupied by a foreign power, they would rather dislodge the inferior Turks from Baku than the more experienced British. Two days later, Shaumian's promised reinforcements arrived from Astrakhan – nine hundred poorly trained and equipped men. Armenian leaders had previously sent emissaries to Enzeli to keep Dunsterville abreast of the quickly evolving events in Baku. Perceiving an imminent coup, and having already been given permission by his superiors to send a force to Baku, Dunsterville traded a desperate Shaumian ten Ford cars for fifty thousand pounds of invaluable petrol, knowing full well that these vehicles would soon be back in his possession.[47] These meagre reinforcements did nothing to bolster Soviet power within the combative political arenas of Baku. In fact, Shaumian's efforts produced quite the opposite effect.

By 30 July, the Turks were in sight of Baku, and Shaumian's detractors urged him once gain to invite the British. He would not surrender his position and reiterated his view (and that of Lenin and Stalin) that, given the choice between the British or the Turks, he would choose the latter. Rather than create an atmosphere of outright hostilities or be imprisoned, Shaumian dissolved the Soviet committee and officially resigned as president. The following day, seventeen ships of the Caspian fleet were loaded with munitions, stores, and soldiers loyal to the Bolshevik cause with the realization that the city would soon fall to the Turks. "As long as the proletariat continues to be deceived, preferring the British to Soviet Russia," he declared in his final words to the assembly, "as long as there are not enough forces to repel both the Turko-Germans and the English beasts of prey, the Soviet cannot stay in Baku."[48] The Soviet was replaced by the Centro-Caspian Dictatorship, a coalition dominated by the Russian Social Revolutionary and Armenian Dashnak parties, led by five supreme members. The Caspian Fleet immediately defected, and with the aid of heavily armed patrol boats sent by the new government, the Bolshevik transports returned to Baku, whereupon their valuable cargo was seized and their passengers imprisoned. While the coup against Shaumian had been a glorified and bloodless success, it also robbed Baku of three to four thousand Bolshevik defenders who were incarcerated, fled the region, or simply refused to fight.

In addition, while securing the Caspian Fleet, many of its senior officers remained loyal Bolsheviks and refused to sail under the new regime. It is interesting that this was not an issue that would hinder the new government or Dunsterville. On 27 July, when the War Office finally granted Dunsterville permission to temporarily occupy Baku, a naval mission was sent from Baghdad that same day. As mentioned, seizing the Caspian Fleet was a primary goal of the mission in the eyes of the War Office, and, quite perceptively, it had authorized a naval mission to proceed to Enzeli led by Commodore David T. Norris. On 27 July, a party of six officers and eighty-six seamen with a cargo of twelve naval guns, mountings, and ammunition left via the overland route from Baghdad to the Caspian, preceded by a smaller party of sixty-eight sailors, hauling one four-inch and two twelve-pounder guns. Accomplishing the seemingly impossible, especially given General Marshall's gripes about road conditions, Norris and his advance party of twenty-three men transporting three naval guns arrived at their destination of Enzeli on 2 August after traversing nearly six hundred miles of inhospitable terrain – an incredible feat of perseverance and raw grit.[49]

The Centro-Caspian Dictatorship immediately signalled their representatives in Enzeli to invite Dunsterforce to organize the defence of Baku. Dunsterville promptly had the Enzeli Soviet leaders arrested after substantial documented proof incriminated them for cooperating with the Jangalis. "To have arrested the Committee merely as Bolsheviks would have been taking a false step and would have put the whole of Baku against us," Dunsterville wrote. "The only safe grounds on which we could attack the Enzeli committee were on a charge of complicity with our declared enemies, the Jangalis."[50] Dunsterville's path to Baku was finally unchecked.

On 4 August, the first small administrative detachment of Dunsterforce arrived in Baku under the command of Colonel Stokes. As he professed on the voyage from Enzeli to Baku,

At various times in my life I have had to think very hard as to the best course to pursue. But I do not think I have ever done harder thinking than I did on this short journey. The problem as I saw it was this: firstly it was important almost at any cost to deny to the enemy the oil supplies of Baku. He was short of oil and possession of Baku would be of great value to him ... if the Turks took Baku there would inevitably be a terrible massacre of Armenians – if only in revenge for the Armenian massacre of Tartars in the previous March. Of the great importance of denying the enemy the oil supplies, I was in no doubt, for the War Office had bombarded us with telegrams demanding the destruction of the oil fields if there was no other way of attaining that object. It always seemed to me that someone in the War Office had a picture in his mind of an officer landing secretly from a boat with a box of matches and setting fire to the oil fields in several places and hastily rowing away leaving them in flames. As it happens the oil fields cover several square miles and gave employment to 120,000 men, all of whom had rifles and none of whom was likely to stand by and watch a foreigner deprive him of his means of livelihood.[51]

Stokes and his small force of seventy men liaised with the new government officials and quickly began reorganizing the local militias and defensive positions "to keep out the Turks who at any rate had no business in Baku."[52] On this same day, as the first British contingent arrived, Bicherakov and his Cossacks quit Baku, marching north 150 miles along the Caspian to Derbend in Dagestan. Here, they fought alongside General Anton Denikin's White Army, desperately attempting to stall the Bolshevik offensive in the northern Caucasus. The four "brevet Canadian Bolsheviks" attached to Bicherakov arrived back in Baku with their armoured cars on 14 August. Bicherakov and his Cossacks, however, never returned, robbing Baku's garrison of an additional twelve hundred experienced defenders.

Aware of Bicherakov's flight, the Turks were quick to seize the opportunity, launching the first assault on the city the following day. Baku's outnumbered defenders, primarily Armenian, held firm, outflanking the Turks now in a full retreat, having sustained almost 2,500 casualties to the Armenian 655. "This sudden retreat just when they had got into the outskirts of Baku astonished all of us," a stunned Stokes reported. "It soon became evident that the whole Turkish line was in retreat. This retreat remained a mystery to me until after the Armistice when I heard from the Turks what had happened. It seemed that the German and Turkish Staffs at Tiflis had disagreed and the Germans had stopped the Turkish ammunition supplies so that the Turks who attacked Baku on August 5th had fired their last cartridge and then had to retire. This they did to a ridge of hills some 3 to 4 miles from the town."[53] In addition, the dysentery epidemic that had plagued the Armenians had recently struck the Army of Islam, which was already suffering from severe bouts of cholera caused by a dire lack of potable water. As a result, the potency of the Ottoman force was drastically reduced, and only 7,500 soldiers were available on the day of the attack. After suffering heavy losses, and with dwindling provisions (and impressed with the stout resistance of the Armenians), Nuri called off the general attack and awaited reinforcements, allowing Dunsterville to move the bulk of his forces into the city while repositioning and strengthening his defensive lines. During the remainder of August, the Turks remained inactive, aside from probing attacks on British outposts, as Ottoman reinforcements were slow to arrive.

Until additional resources appeared, the Ottoman situation at Baku was untenable. Unknown to Nuri's forces laying siege to Baku, German, Bolshevik, and British personnel and agencies were cooperating to stymie their advance: "The official opposition both from London and Moscow, however, did not stop their local representatives considering such cooperation and establishing some contacts." With all four entries competing in the race for Baku's petroleum, and with the Turks on the brink to realizing this goal, cooperation, however unlikely, occurred among the three trailing contestants, so long as it suited a common interest and while the Turks maintained the lead. Bolsheviks, Germans, and Armenians burned bridges and raided Turkish supply columns in Georgia and northern Armenia, while Bolshevik and British troops mirrored these actions in northern Persia. According to an intelligence report from Goldsmith, the Georgian military road and vital rail stations en route to Baku "were controlled by a combined team of the British and Bolsheviks against the German and Turkish agents."[54]

The entire region was awash with modern weaponry, as all four belligerents buttressed proxy wars to serve their own means of securing Baku's petroleum. The Germans armed the Georgians, while the Bolsheviks countered by arming Muslims in Abkhazia, Chechnya, and Ossetia to invalidate Georgian territorial claims. The British equipped the Armenians to withstand the Turks, while the Turks funnelled weaponry to the Muslims of Azerbaijan to eradicate the Armenians. In light of these actions, the Turkish-German rancour intensified. In fact, "the maps of the Ottoman Third Army in August 1918 identified the German sentry posts along Georgia's railroads as 'enemy positions,' and there are numerous other indications that Germanophobia was rapidly spreading in the Turkish officer corps because of the Transcaucasian quarrel."[55] Within this tumultuous atmosphere of shifting allegiances, Dunsterville acknowledged that at any given moment it was hard to distinguish "friend from foe."

In late August, unbeknownst to the British, the remaining loyal Bolsheviks in Baku smuggled in German intelligence officers and a cohort of petroleum engineers. Although the 1918 German Spring Offensive on the Western Front ended in disaster, and the Allied counter-attack at Amiens was one of the finest military achievements of the war, the Germans had not yet given up on their cherished vision of *Drang nach Osten*. German planners still clung to the hope that Baku's oil could turn the tide on the Western Front, or at least be used to counter Allied demands during the peace.

At Amiens on 8 August, with the Canadian and Australian Corps acting as spearhead formations, the British Fourth Army under General Henry Rawlinson struck a demoralizing blow in what Ludendorff called the "black day of the German Army in the history of the war." Ludendorff went on the reveal in his memoirs,

> Mainly with Australian and Canadian divisions ... in no great superiority ... The Divisions in the line at that point allowed themselves to be completely overwhelmed. The losses through the battle had been so heavy that we were forced to break up about ten divisions and use their infantry as reserves for others ... in so doing be obliged to bury many hopes ... and while still occupied with these thoughts the blow of August 8 fell upon me [and] put the decline of our fighting power beyond all doubt ... The fate of the German people was to me too high a stake.

By late September he was finally resolved that "the war must be ended."[56] On 8 August alone, the Canadian Corps advanced eight miles, captured over six thousand prisoners, 161 guns, and other war materials, including two complete divisional headquarters. The effect of the Battle of Amiens on German morale was so great that it compelled the kaiser to make an immediate offer of peace through the medium of the Queen of Netherlands on 14 August.[57]

Nevertheless, German high command, infused with new optimism with the stalled Turkish offensive in the Caucasus, was still resolved that Baku and its precious oil must be secured. An intercepted German transmission revealed the full extent of Germany's petroleum shortage. The report ascertained that fuel supplies for aircraft, motor vehicles, industry, and shipping could hold out only one to two more months, "then they will be completely immobilized [and] machines will be brought to a standstill."[58]

Following Nuri's failed assault on Baku, Ludendorff delivered a message to Enver: "Unless the advance on Baku is halted at once and the troops are withdrawn to their original positions, I shall have to propose to His Majesty the recall of German officers in the Turkish High Command. I cannot tolerate that the threat of a new war with Greater Russia is conjured up by the patently treaty-violating conduct of responsible Turkish authorities."[59] Although Enver appealed to Ludendorff for joint Turkish-German collaboration in taking Baku, noting the growing presence of Dunsterforce in the city, Ludendorff dismissed the invitation. Instead, he set about securing a covenant with the Bolsheviks, who publicly stated that they would rather see the British stay in Baku than have the Turks gain possession.

On 27 August, a lengthy Russo-German supplement to Brest-Litovsk was finalized in Berlin. This amendment settled the question of the Baltics, financial arrangements, and a mutual petroleum policy in the Caucasus. In return for Russia's recognition of Georgian independence, Germany vowed not to militarily assist any third party (other than Georgia) within the Caucasus, and promised to do "all that she could not to admit the Turks to Baku [and] that German troops might be used to expel the British from the oil city if the Bolsheviks should not be able to do the job themselves." More importantly, it was agreed that although Baku would remain in Russian hands, Germany would receive either a quarter of all petroleum, or a certain monthly minimum quota based on actual production to be determined later: "Presumably these assurances were connected with the allocation of the produce of the Baku oil-fields," the War Office noted. "And control of the pipeline to Batum ... Russia, on her side, has undertaken to place a portion of the produce of the wells at the disposal of Germany." Immediately, Ludendorff, in an attempt to keep the Army of Islam immobilized, ordered General Kress "to assemble as quickly as possible a German task force [of five thousand troops] for use in the Baku area."[60] Since he had only roughly seven thousand troops at his disposal, with the majority needed to maintain security in Georgia and to safeguard the approaches to Baku, the assembly of the German expeditionary force to Baku took several weeks to materialize. This proved to be much too long.

By mid-August, all available British troops had embarked at Baku, with Dunsterville himself arriving to take field command on 17 August. Of his voyage on the *Kruger* he wrote, "A British General on the Caspian, the only sea un-ploughed before by British keels, on board a ship named after a South African Dutch president and whilom enemy, sailing from a Persian port, under the Serbian flag [an imperial Russian flag turned sideways], to relieve from the Turks a body of Armenians in a revolutionary town. Let the reader pick his way through that delirious tangle, and envy us our task who will!"[61] The task at hand was much more problematic than he expected.

Local troops were far fewer and more disorganized than estimated. Numerous reports, diaries, and memoirs chastise the Armenian defenders as cowards and thieves, with the writers at odds with the Armenian refusal to take seriously the Turkish threat to not only Baku itself, but to their personal safety and that of their families. Colonel Warden, never one to mince words, wrote on 31 August that the Armenians "are rotters. The men I mean. I do not blame the Turks for killing them off. They are worse than the Jews or Bolsheviks. They will not fight nor defend their women folks or children (who are very pretty). They are cowards but they will get controal [*sic*] & fleece one & all out of every cent one has even while the Turks are drawing their knives at the door to cut their throats."[62] It was well recorded that the Armenian defenders were frequently absent, refused to advance, or fled at the first instance of shelling or rifle fire, while a few even sold their munitions to the Turks. Rawlinson reported, "It is hard to describe the Caucasian Armenian's attitude towards fighting, as he seems incapable of grasping the possibility of himself actually fighting, even in defence of his life. On being asked the reason why they should *not* advance to that particular spot, they replied, with hysterical laughter: 'Of course we couldn't go *there*. Why, that is the very place to which the enemy is advancing!' What kind of fight can be expected from soldiers (?) of this quality?"[63]

Dunsterforce officers tried with unwavering effort and patience to institute a semblance of order. Of the ten thousand locals supposedly manning the line, only two thousand were relatively reliable. The British never accounted for more than: twelve hundred men, supported by one machine-gun company, 120 artillery pieces made in Russia, Britain, France, and Germany of various calibres and in various states of efficiency, four airplanes (two British and two Russian), and six armoured cars. This combined force was divided into twenty battalions of 200 to 250 men each, with each battalion containing a unit of British soldiers/

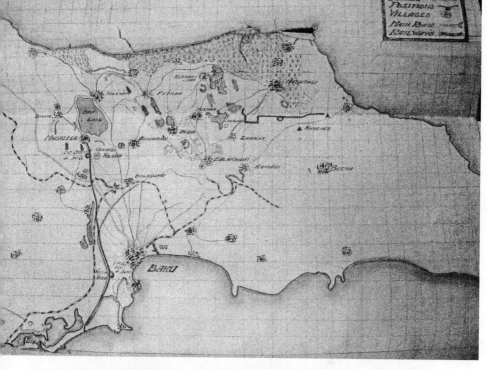

7.3 Major-General Lionel Dunsterville's original map of the defences at Baku, 17 August 1918 (National Archives, UK).

advisors to the bulk of the Armenian defenders. A refitted defensive position was occupied by these newly created battalions, which rotated in and out of the front line. This defensive position contained gaps in the line of up to three to four hundred metres between entrenchments. Warden commented, "This is the most disorganized show I have ever been on. Gen. Dunsterville has not the vaguest idea of organization, & most of his Staff is worse. I am sure that unless G.H.Q. Baghdad takes a hold of us, we shall be in a mess this winter ... I do not mind fighting if I have a chance, but I object to being forced into committing suside [*sic*]. This is the biggest game of Bluff I ever saw played."[64] The opposing Turkish fighting strength, including Azeri irregulars, fluctuated between six and eight thousand from a total force of roughly fourteen thousand.

7.4 Major-General Lionel Dunsterville inspecting his Armenian
defenders of Baku, August 1918 (Australian War Memorial).

The Turks launched successful attacks on 26 and 31 August, driving the defenders back to the extreme outskirts of the city. As predicted, the men of Dunsterforce shouldered the weight of the fighting (and casualties), as the majority of their alleged Armenian and Russian allies abandoned their forward positions at the first sight of the attacking forces. Realizing his precarious position, Dunsterville telegraphed Marshall and the War Office on the thirty-first that any further effort to defend Baku would be a "waste of time and life ... doubtful if it would be possible to save Baku" if he did not receive reinforcements immediately. On the same day he received replies from both the War Office and Marshall that in light of the circumstances, and with no reinforcements forthcoming, he was to secure the Caspian Fleet, destroy all oil installations, and evacuate Baku. After all, Dunsterville was reminded by his superiors, permanent occupation of Baku was never the objective nor his direct orders, and it was he who had pushed so hard for the deployment to Baku.

Dunsterville's response would discredit him for the remainder of his life: "This expedition should never have been ordered if it was simply to result in placing a handful of British troops in the firing line where they remain without relief and if not supported faces the prospect of certain annihilation." He then singled out and slandered his superior officer, Marshall, directly: "The responsibility for the present situation therefore rests entirely with you and it is inconceivable that while there remains a good chance of saving it [oil] and the town you should propose the abandonment of all work at the outset. The contrast between the loyalty and Chivalry of Bicherakov and this attitude will utterly discredit the British Army in the eyes of all Russians." Upon receipt of this message, Wilson personally wired Marshall, bluntly stating, "The attitude of recrimination which he now adopts adds to our former misgivings and should you deem it advisable you are at full liberty as soon as the situation permits to relieve General Dunsterville from his command."[65]

Still on the 31 August, Dunsterville disseminated orders "in case an evacuation of Baku becomes necessary ... before the occasion arises to carry them out." On 5 September he issued an order cancelling the evacuation plan, as "there is every hope of saving the town if the next attack can be beaten off. British troops must therefore hold on to their positions at all costs."[66] By disobeying direct orders and cancelling his planned evacuation, Dunsterville was gambling that his men could withstand the Turks' final assault and save the oil, the town, and his

7.5 A British-Armenian signalling station above Baku and its harbour,
September 1918 (Australian War Memorial).

reputation. Given the circumstances, he should have realized that it was a wager he could not win. His hopes of success, however, were boosted when a Turkish officer defected to the British on 12 September, revealing that the Turks would attack in strength two days later on the morning of 14 September.

The attack came as planned, and although the men of Dunsterforce fought an extremely well-coordinated and brave defence, by noon the preliminary orders to evacuate were passed down the chain of command. Dunsterforce fought a brilliant delaying action to allow the ships to be loaded, secured, and made ready for sea. The final evacuation order was given at 4:00 that afternoon. Although the Caspian Dictatorship forbade Dunsterville from evacuating, regarding it as treachery and imperial deceit, the process continued in spite of their threats of firing on the ships. After thirteen hours of fighting, the exhausted men of Dunsterforce, stores of munitions, and a handful of civilians embarked on four transports bound for Enzeli. Over eight thousand scared and helpless Armenian civilians, including the dictators, commandeered and clambered aboard all and any seaworthy vessels amidst utter chaos, as the Turks continued to shell the town and wharf. These refugees eventually made their way to Astrakhan or Krasnovodsk, depending on their political affiliation. At roughly midnight, upon dimming all lights, and with British service revolvers pointed at the heads of the Russian crews and captains, the convoy departed and successfully ran the gantlet of shellfire and blocking vessels ordered to intervene by Baku's dictators. Dunsterforce disembarked at Enzeli the following morning on 15 September, abandoning Baku to its fate.

Upon receiving news that the British had absconded, Nuri claimed Baku in the name of the Republic of Azerbaijani, although his Turkish regulars did not enter the city. Instead, the Azeri militia was allowed to claim this right, and their revenge. The massacre that ensued over the next two days is best described by eyewitness Essad Bey:

The English packed quickly and confiscated steamers. In the evening not a single English soldier was left in the city. I have heard that this good general was later court-martialed for endangering British prestige. The Azerbaijanian [sic] troops who had fought together with the Turks demanded the observance of the age-old oriental custom of abandoning the captured city to pillage. They were remembering too the last massacre ... The Turkish soldiers stayed outside the city during this time. The native troops entered ... The Great Vengeance began ... Again blood flowed in the streets of the oil-city, this time Armenian blood. Men and women were killed mercilessly. The victors cut open the bodies of their victims, smashed their skulls and laid themselves on the corpses, howling in the delirium of victory, literally bathing in blood. They tore their bodies into shreds, bit through their throats, drank their blood. Several hundred Armenians were not put to death immediately but taken to the large city square and there guarded by soldiers. Every Mohammedan – child, woman, or old man – might come and kill as many Armenians as mortal vengeance required ... Bloody shreds of Armenians flesh became the symbol of those three days ... As the third day drew to an end, the government announced by cannon-shots that peace and order had again been restored ... Anyone who robbed, murdered, or stole after the cannon-shots was promptly hanged ... Hundreds were hanged and swung on gallows for days. Each corpse was decorated with a sign describing his crime: "Hanged for stealing a pound of nuts" or something similar.[67]

Estimates of the carnage vary between six thousand and thirty thousand dead. Given that as many as eight thousand Armenians escaped across the Caspian, recent figures conclude that between nine and twelve thousand Armenians were killed. In contrast, during the defence of Baku, the British suffered 180 casualties, including 95 dead. Upon reaching Enzeli, Dunsterville wrote that the attempt to hold Baku had "cost the British nothing." In reality, it cost him his job and his reputation.

On 16 September, Dunsterville received a "wire telling me to return to Baghdad. I am not offended. I have done excellent work under trying conditions, and produced very good results out of nothing in spite of apathy and misunderstanding of the War Office and Baghdad. But after my telegrams they had no course but to relieve me and to try me, I suppose by Court Martial." The historical legacy of Dunsterforce, and of its success or failure, occupies opposite ends of the spectrum. No one, neither participants nor revisionist historians, has taken the middle ground. Many members of Dunsterforce outwardly criticized their commander and the mission. Colonel Warden, who by now was calling the mission "Dunsterfarce," summed up his opinion upon arriving in Enzeli: "I never expected to witness such chaos among British military, especially regulars. They did not appear to have the vaguest idea of what to do or how to do it or when, where & etc. Baku could have been held by good sound management & organization but Gen. Dunsterville was not capable of doing either & his staff was far worse ... Mjr Gen. Dunsterville should be made a full Gen. & knighted & kicked out as they do everyone who makes a mess of his job."[68] His view was shared by many of his fellow soldiers, and also by General Marshall, who dubbed Dunsterville an incompetent "Don Quixote." Numerous commentators conclude that Dunsterforce was a fiasco and that the only success of the entire mission was the skilfully managed retreat and evacuation. Although he failed to carry out his order to damage the oil installations, this was never a feasible course of action, noted even by General Marshall. It was an unrealistic order given in haste by members of the War Office far removed from the situation with little knowledge of Baku's immense oil industry.

Keeping in mind that a permanent occupation of Baku was never the objective of the mission, many others, including Lloyd George, believed that Dunsterforce kept the Turks and Germans from acquiring much-needed oil for six crucial weeks in August and September while the war with Germany was decided on the Western Front, and victory over Turkey was secured in Mesopotamia, Palestine, and on the

Salonika/Bulgarian front. In this light then, the mission was a success. In actuality, what prevented Baku from falling to the Turks earlier was not Dunsterforce; rather, it was the Turkish belief that British reinforcements would arrive in large numbers. Nuri attacked the city only after he realized these supplementary defences would never materialize. Perhaps then, the game of bluff alluded to by Warden was also a success. Neither the Turks nor the Germans were ever able to make much use of Baku's prized oil.

Dunsterforce also carried out noble humanitarian famine relief efforts in Persia and built roads and hospitals, many of which are still in use today. Armchair strategists continue to argue about the validity and result of the mission. British special agent Captain Reginald Teague-Jones, one of the greatest spies of the entire war, accurately summed up Dunsterforce, which he aided with intelligence throughout its mission: "That the Dunsterforce venture ended militarily in failure in no way reflects discredit ... However feasible the original objective of the operation may have appeared ... in practice the venture was doomed to failure because of two main factors (among many others): the force was too small for the task assigned to it, and it arrived much too late ... To anyone who knew the complexity of the local situation and could appreciate the magnitude of the odds against our troops, the Dunsterforce venture was a magnificent effort."[69]

Although he was never court-martialled for disobeying orders and slandering a superior officer, Dunsterville was made the scapegoat for what was deemed a failed mission. He was much maligned in the press and became a pariah in the social and military circles of the British Army. He was relieved of duty, replaced by Major-General William Thomson, and summarily dispatched to India to serve out his remaining years in obscurity as a brigade commander until his retirement in 1920 (only after a favour was called in by his influential friend Rudyard Kipling). He spent the remainder of his life supplementing his meagre army pension by writing his memoirs, giving paid speeches (also done in an attempt to save his reputation), organizing the Kipling Society, and attempting to "cash in on his reminiscences of Rudyard Kipling." For a time, he worked as a motorcycle salesman for the British Small Arms Company before settling down in southern England, living quietly until his death in 1946. In a letter to Colonel Stokes (who would soon become the senior British diplomat in Tiflis) in October 1918, Dunsterville acknowledged, "They will never forgive me for my spiteful telegrams and I agree that they contained matter rather contrary to

discipline – so I have no pause and I shall be quite gay in retirement."
It appeared as though Dunsterville had come to terms with his post-
Dunsterforce reality, although his proud diary entries suggest otherwise.[70] Dunsterforce itself was disbanded, although many members
joined Thomson's larger North-Persian Force (Noperforce) initially
composed of sixteen hundred men, which reoccupied Baku and the
greater Caucasus in November 1918. Others reenlisted for service in
Siberia, another futile Allied sideshow during intervention in the Russian Civil War.

The contest for Baku, however, was not over. Following the Ottoman
occupation, after tireless bargaining, on 23 September the Germans
secured the right to "administer" the oil industry at Baku, the pipeline
from Baku to Batum, and the railroad running parallel to the pipeline,
in exchange for a large sum of money. This monetary payout added to
the total of $800,000 ($80 billion today) already supplied to the Turks in
resources and cash by Germany.[71] Ludendorff immediately ordered the
dispatch of German troops and petroleum experts to start the export of
Baku oil to the Reich. Upon arriving in Baku, although they were welcomed by local civilians, the Azeri politicians and oil magnates refused
to cooperate with German enterprises, viewing their obvious aim of
exploiting local resources as "yet another imperialist venture." As of
24 October, Kress reported that the German "delegation in Baku had
made no progress whatsoever … Nuri hides behind [the government
of] Azerbaijan and the latter behind him." Germany reminded Ottoman
leaders that "the Baku oil was urgently needed for the German war
effort." In response, on 30 October, the Ottomans granted Germany full
access to Baku, to the oil reserves at Batum, while stating that Nuri had
been recalled. The message closed by stressing that "any further inquir-
ies about the Baku oil should henceforth be directed to the Azerbaijani
government."[72] On this same day, Ottoman representatives signed the
Armistice of Mudros with Britain.

Enver's Caucasian fantasies, to the impairment of his other fronts, had
cost him dearly. On 25 September, Allenby's forces thrashed the Turks
at Megiddo and took Damascus on 1 October, quickly followed by Beirut and Aleppo. Correspondingly, Marshall began his hasty advance
on Mosul on 23 October, recapturing Kirkuk two days later, followed
by Sharqat, halfway between Tikrit and Mosul, on the twenty-eighth.
To make matters worse, the collapse of Bulgaria on 28 September, followed by its capitulation to the Allies two days later, left Constantinople completely exposed. The British-French-Greek force of half a million

at Salonika now had an unimpeded invasion route through Thrace to the Ottoman capital. On 8 October the triumvirate resigned, with Enver, Talaat, and Djemal fleeing their separate ways. All three would be slain – Talaat and Djemal were both assassinated in 1921 in Berlin and Tiflis respectively, while Enver was killed in combat the following year in Turkestan, still clinging to his pan-Turanian dream. Following their resignation, Turkey was left without a functioning government until 14 October, when Sultan Mehmed VI, who had succeeded his father only in July, appointed a new cabinet.

The new Turkish administration, appreciating that their war was lost and that Germany was merely denying and delaying the same inevitable fate, immediately opened truce talks with the British, who deliberately excluded the French: "It did not take much to rouse French suspicion that Britain was planning to exclude them from the Middle East altogether. The postwar outlook was stormy."[73] With negotiations moving quickly, British representatives stalled the signing of the armistice for as long as possible. Members of the War Cabinet were concerned that the war would end before Marshall could conquer the Mosul *vilayet*. He was immediately ordered to "occupy as large a portion of the oil-bearing regions as possible." The armistice specified that all hostilities would cease at noon on the 31 October. At that moment, British troops had just taken Quaiyara. Marshall, who had received news of the armistice only on 1 November, parlayed with the Turkish commander of the Mosul garrison, who politely refused to vacate the city but guaranteed that he would not fire on British troops. Marshall informed him that he had orders to take Mosul. Between 2 and 4 November, British troops secured Mosul and the surrounding region and were greeted by a Turkish band playing "God Save the King" as they entered the city.[74] This perfidious occupation of Mosul would become a major point of contention among the British, French, and Turks during formalities of the peace, as they all pursued possession of its rich oilfields.

With the signing of the armistice on 30 October, the Ottomans were forced to concede to British demands, which now included control of oil regions as a first-class peace aim: "The bill for Enver's Caspian gambit was high indeed: the Turks were forced to abandon all recent gains, from Baku and Batumi to Ardahan and Sarikamis, going all the way back to the 1914 borders. Worst of all, the British fleet now sailed unopposed through the Dardanelles, achieving in one afternoon what the combined Allied forces at Gallipoli had failed to do all through 1915."[75] As a result, and with Denikin's White Army stalling the Bolshevik southern advance into the Caucasus, General Thomson's Noperforce, including many former Dunsterforce members, reoccupied Baku on 17 November 1918. According to Baku resident Essad Bey, the British "acted as though they were doing us a favor by sojourning in the richest oil-land in Asia."[76] Thomson announced himself governor and declared that "Baku and its oilfields would be occupied, while the rest of the country would remain under the control of the Azerbaijani Government and its troops." The official position of the British Government mirrored that of Herbert Allen, chairman of the Bibi Eibat Oil Company, who declared in London in early December, "Never in the history of these islands was there such an opportunity for the peaceful penetration of the British influence and British trade, for the creation of a second India or a second Egypt ... The oil industry of Russia liberally financed and properly organized under British auspices would in itself be a valuable asset to the Empire ... A golden opportunity offers itself to the British government to exercise a powerful influence upon the immense production of the Grosni, Baku, and Transcaspia fields."[77] The problem with this appraisal, however, was that the Bolsheviks also wanted Baku and its vital oil as part of their expanding Soviet Empire. While the first Battle of Baku was over, the second battle, this time between British and Bolshevik, had just begun.

In September 1919, upon leaving Baku for his home in England, Sergeant A.J. Foster, a wounded veteran of East Africa, Mesopotamia, Dunsterforce, and Noperforce, eloquently scribbled his thoughts and recollections of the war in his diary with obvious indications of "shell shock" or post-traumatic stress disorder (PTSD):

I look at my photo taken in camp. It seems hardly credible that that round-faced boy – can be me; my mirror shows me a long thin face, brown and lined like a middle-aged man. Years of poor living, hardship, and wounds and sickness have undoubtedly made a man of me ... I am filled with a great disgust – disgust at man's knowledge which has crept insidiously upon me; disgust at the mature wisdom forced on me by circumstances before, as I know now, my mind was ready to use it – disgust at my vanquished youth. Much have I acquired – more especially comprehension of the basic emotions – much have I lost. How the balance will stand in years to come I cannot easily picture. I have absorbed so much of cruelty, lawlessness, disregard for human life and other people's property; recklessness bred of the trenches that it stands to reason some portions of these things are going to remain as part of me? Particularly my outlook on life.

Intimacy with death has taught me to value life more than cheaply ... Why worry over Death? Yet if when I go home and in a temper I kill someone I shall be hung. Why? I have been expertly trained in dealing out Death. The whole strata of humanity seems to have a core of rottenness I believe, though, that the stress of War has uncovered streaks which normally would lie dormant. I can imagine some of us living placid life in peace.[78]

The decades following the Paris Peace Conference and the Treaty of Versailles – the peace to end all wars – would be anything but peaceful.

Chapter Eight

Peace and Petroleum

By the time the Paris Peace Conference officially concluded with entrenchment of the Treaty of Versailles on 21 January 1920, the map of the world had been entirely redrawn with enduring consequences. The decisions made in Paris, beginning 18 January 1919, defined the modern world and set in motion a chain of historical events and extended warfare that have yet to run their course. "The world has never seen anything quite like it, and never will again," acknowledges Margaret MacMillan, author of *Paris 1919* (2001).[1] The peace treaty premeditated every aspect of war and diplomacy in the eras that followed, and we are still spectators to the post-Versailles age. Its legacy and influence, although waning, have yet to be eclipsed. We still live among the war-torn shadows of the First World War and its peace. According to Hew Strachan, "The reality was that, given the enormity of the task that confronted the victors, they drew up a settlement which promised far more than it proved able to deliver in practice ... The programme was ambitious, and in the long view of the twentieth century it failed."[2]

On 6 October 1918, David Lloyd George was in Paris meeting with his French counterpart Georges Clemenceau trying to configure the armistice terms that would be offered to their enemies and how the Allies would proceed in "the cutting up of Turkey." He mused that the Ottomans had reduced the "cradle of civilization" into "a blighted desert." In summary, he argued, "The Turks must never be allowed to misgovern these great lands in the future." The questions surrounding the post-war Middle East were complex, made more uncertain by the ongoing Russian Civil War, the Greco-Turkish War or Turkish War of Independence (1919–23), the final disintegration of the Ottoman Empire, the imperial contest among the victors, and prior arrangements, most notably the 1916 Sykes-Picot Agreement. Lloyd George had previously denounced this agreement, arguing that since Russia was no longer a viable partner to the tenets, the entire pact was forfeit. In his opinion, the deal was "quite inapplicable to the present circumstances, and ... altogether a most undesirable agreement from the British point of view."[3] More specifically, Mosul, which was in the French sphere of influence under the arrangement, but had been occupied by British forces in early November, was the centrepiece of contention and diplomacy. In fact, Sykes had informed Picot as early as March 1918 that the terms of the agreement "do not appear suitable to present conditions."[4] According to Maurice Hankey, who had championed British oil interests during the last year of the war, the prime minister "wanted to go back on the Sykes-Picot agreement, so as to get Palestine for us and to bring Mosul into the British zone ... to obtain the undisputed control of the greatest amount of Petroleum that we can."[5] Britain, however, was vying with France, America, and Turkey for this increasingly valuable commodity. Now, Middle Eastern oil was a first-class British peace aim. British oil designs, however, were not confined to this region alone.

At a meeting of the Eastern Committee on 2 December, the chair, Lord Curzon, opened the session with the most pressing issue – control of the Caucasus. "The whole experience of the war," he began,

has taught us the supreme importance of this region, with a view to the countries further east, over which it is essential, in the interests of India and our Empire, that we should exercise some measure of political control ... which would involve the holding of the Batum, Tiflis, and Baku, the policing of the line, the control of railways, telegraphs, and so on ... I am seriously afraid that the great Power from whom we have the most to fear in the future is France, and I almost shudder at the possibility of putting France in such a position. She is powerful in almost all parts of the world, even around India. Are we to place her in a position to control this railway from Batum to Baku?

South African General Jan Smuts agreed, quickly espousing his francophobia:

France was a very bad neighbor to us in the past ... I am afraid her arrogant diplomacy may be revived by the great change which has come over her fortunes. She has always been very ambitious, is militant and imperialist in temperament, and her policies leave generally a nasty trail of finance and concession-hunting behind them. I fear we shall find her a difficult if not an intolerable neighbor ... and in the Sykes-Picot agreement ... I see the seeds of future trouble for Europe, and I think no effort should be left untried to get out of this hopeless blunder in policy.[6]

Above all else, the resounding agreement among the Eastern Committee delegates was that France should not obtain the precious oil resources of Baku (or Mosul) in any form.

For the British, the situation in the Caucasus was capricious at best, with a small British force defending strategic oil interests in the midst of the Russian Civil War. Red Army forces were penetrating south to also secure this much-needed black gold and were increasingly getting the better of General Denikin's White Army forces in the region. In addition, the fledging independent nations of Georgia, Armenia, and Azerbaijan all sought to bolster autonomy and be rid of all imperialist interference. The Muslim enclaves of Dagestan, Abkhazia, and Chechnya in the northern Caucasus were immersed in a firestorm of insurrection against all trespassers as they attempted to create a state centred on the firmest interpretation of sharia law. These conflicts were left seething and continue to plague the region. In northern Persia, the Islamic Shia revolution of Kuchik Khan, so apparent in the Dunsterforce backstory, was spreading into southern Azerbaijan in order to facilitate the creation of his Socialist Republic of Gilan.

Concurrent widespread Muslim uprisings were taking place in Egypt, Libya, Algeria, Turkey, Somalia, Morocco, Afghanistan, Turkmenistan, Tajikistan, Kyrgyzstan, India, and Mesopotamia. Although, this laundry list of names invokes images of the Arab Spring launched in late 2010, this antecedent was a struggle for independence from successive *colonial* rule. In the immediate post-war years, the Middle East and the Caucasus became a heavily armed society and "with a deeply ingrained tradition of resistance was acquiring a political agenda, and political leadership. The result was explosive." The War Office joked, "In the quest for arms the Arab showed qualities of courage, cunning and perseverance which, if turned to a better cause would have ensured success in any walk of life."[7] The dissident leaders of these well-armed Islamic proto-Marxist revolutions were studied and esteemed by leftist guerrilla thinkers and sovereigns of later generations, including Ho Chi Minh, Mao Zedong, Ernesto "Che" Guevara, and the Ayatollah Ruhollah Khomeini. Many are still venerated by their modern nation states.

Contemporary radical Islamist groups have evolved from these leaders and their organizations, most notably Egyptian Sayyid Qutb, future leader of the Muslim Brotherhood, who was reaching political consciousness during this intense and violent Muslim renaissance: "Qutb's ideas underlie most modern Islamist extremist movements, including al-Qaeda ... If the modern world faced a series of simultaneous wars like this, we would have no hesitation in speaking grimly of a global jihad, with a scope and appeal far beyond anything ever achieved by al-Qaeda." Exiled Indian Muslims, disenchanted with British rule as their attempts to form sharia societies were repeatedly vanquished, fled infidel rule to seek their fortunes in their only option left – Afghanistan. Their descendants joined the Soviet-era mujahideen and eventually the upper echelons of the Taliban between 1979 and 2001.[8] Nevertheless, despite this tumultuous environment, the Caucasus oil remained a first class British peace aim.

Prior to the opening of the Paris Peace Conference on 18 January 1919, the victors, specifically France and Britain, were already squabbling about the territorial spoils of war. Allied leaders were busy in the months prior to the conference, hustling back-door transactions. They attempted to solidify mutually beneficial strategies and claims heading into the discussions and negotiations, in order to present a unified front, or fronts, when dealing with other nations, specifically what were regarded to be the scrutinizing and self-righteous Americans. For example, on 1 December French leader Georges Clemenceau arrived in London to "discuss tactics ahead of the peace conference." Preceding his arrival, he had been warned that British backing for the French recovery of Alsace-Lorraine (France's core objective in the peace), lost to Germany in 1871 as a result of the Franco-Prussian War, was by no means a guarantee. This region, including the Ruhr, contained 75 per cent of Germany's iron ore, 68 per cent of its zinc ore, and 26 per cent of its coal.[9] Given these resources, Lloyd George was leveraging this territory to secure Mosul and Palestine.

Upon his arrival, Clemenceau bluntly sighed, "Well? What are we to discuss?"
　　Lloyd George wasted no time: "Mesopotamia and Palestine."
　　The French leader responded, "Tell me what you want."
　　Lloyd George: "I want Mosul."
　　Clemenceau: "You shall have it. Anything else?"
　　Lloyd George: "Yes, I want Jerusalem too."
　　Clemenceau: "You shall have it."

He then warned his British counterpart that his advisors and other French politicians and diplomats would "make difficulties about Mosul."[10]

Although Clemenceau personally was not interested in the Middle East, and prior to 1918 had castigated "oil adventurism," his views were not shared by the majority of French senior politicians and military personnel. In return for Mesopotamia, including Mosul, and Palestine, Lloyd George promised Clemenceau British support of France, including against the sanctimonious President Woodrow Wilson and the Americans, over territorial claims on the Lebanese coast and in Syria, and a share of any oil extracted from the Mosul province. Clemenceau believed that he had also secured British support for French demands to territory along the Rhine River, specifically Saarland and Alsace-Lorraine: "Lloyd George does not mention that part of the deal in his memoirs. Were the French wrong or the British being perfidious (again)? Unfortunately there was no official record of the conversation. It was an ill-omened start for an issue that was to poison French-British relations during the Peace Conference and for many years after."[11]

The Paris Peace Conference formally opened on 18 January 1919. This date was deliberately chosen by the French to humiliate Germany by having the conference commence on the anniversary of the Unification of Germany, which had been proclaimed at Versailles forty-eight years earlier. More than thirty-seven nation states officially participated in the conference, although other nationalities or ethnicities sent representatives. The proceedings, however, were dominated by the four "Great Powers": the United Kingdom (David Lloyd George), France (Georges Clemenceau), the United States of America (Woodrow Wilson), and, to a much lesser extent, Italy (Vittorio Orlando). Orlando, in a fit of rage over Wilson's refusal to grant Italy portions of the Dalmatian Coast, including Fiume (which had been promised by the Allies), left Paris on 23 April. He resigned on 19 June, nine days before the actual signing of the Treaty of Versailles. The victorious nations of Europe sidelined and snubbed their Japanese ally. This dishonour and ignominy was not forgotten and was left seething until the next war. Russian political factions, including the Russian Socialist Federative Soviet Republic, were excluded after the Prinkipo Proposal, initiated by Canadian Prime Minister Sir Robert Borden, failed to gain support. Germany and its former allies were also barred from attending.

On the opening day, historian and intelligence officer Arnold Toynbee, an advisor to the British delegation, gained insight into his prime minister's

8.1 David Lloyd George, Vittorio Orlando, Georges Clemenceau, and Woodrow Wilson, May 1919 (Library of Congress).

strategy on the Middle East: "Lloyd George, to my delight, had forgotten my presence and had begun to think aloud. 'Mesopotamia ... yes ... oil ... irrigation ... we must have Mesopotamia; Palestine ... yes ... the Holy Land ... Zionism ... we must have Palestine; Syria ... h'm ... what is there in Syria? Let the French have that.'" Although the November 1917 Balfour Declaration promised the Jews a homeland in Palestine, the real motivation behind this guarantee was that Palestine, as Curzon noted, "was the military gate to Egypt and the Suez Canal." Margaret MacMillan summed up the approach and desires of her great-grandfather David Lloyd George, who was

intoxicated by the possibilities of the Middle East: a restored Hellenic
world in Asia Minor; a new Jewish civilization in Palestine; Suez and all
the links to India safe from threat; loyal and obedient Arab states along
the Fertile Crescent and the valleys of the Tigris and Euphrates; protection of British oil supplies from Persia and the possibility of new sources
under direct British control; the Americans obligingly taking mandates
here and there; the French doing what they were told ... He wanted to
exclude France as much as possible from the Middle East, even at the cost
of breaking previous promises. And that meant above all Sykes-Picot,
'that unfortunate agreement,' as Curzon put it, 'which has being hanging
like a millstone round our necks ever since.'[12]

During a conference so rife with rancour and contrasting political
and moral ideologies, Mesopotamia had been given little mention,
except as a possible mandate, which everyone assumed would be British. The British single-handedly (discounting Russia, as was the thinking at the time) defeated the Turks, and had done the lion's share of
fighting in the Middle East for over four years – so to the victors go
the spoils, was the British consensus. Lloyd George candidly reminded
Clemenceau, "Except for Britain no one had contributed anything more
than a handful of black troops to the expedition in Palestine ... The
British had now some 500,000 men on Turkish soil. The British had
captured three or four Turkish armies and had incurred hundreds of
thousands of casualties in a war with Turkey. The other governments
had only put in a few nigger policemen to see that we did not steal the
Holy Sepulchre! When, however, it came to signing the armistice, all
this fuss was made."[13] After all, General Maude had taken Baghdad in
March 1917 and General Marshall occupied Mosul in early November
1918. Furthermore, the British still had sizeable occupation forces in
the region. Nobody seemed concerned about, or wanted to question,
British suzerainty over Mesopotamia, including Mosul. At this point,
the British, realizing the strategic value of the ethnic Kurds in northern Mesopotamia, made overtures: "Southern Kurdistan, though the
inhabitants are of different nationality from those of Mesopotamia, and
should therefore be allowed, as is here proposed, to constitute, if possible, a political unit, is bound up with Mesopotamia geographically
and economically ... therefore recommended that the mandate given
by the Conference to the Power opted for in Mesopotamia should ...
be extended to Southern Kurdistan."[14] Well aware of the possibility of
the Mosul oilfields extending north, the British sought to include these

lands in their yet uncontested Mesopotamian mandate, under the guise of self-determination for the Kurds – a principle that, however posturing and shallow, was agreeable to the United States and was in concert with President Wilson's Fourteen Points. "A state did not materialize, however, because of resistance by Turkey, British determination to retain the oil of Mosul province for Iraq, and lingering tribal divisions among the Kurds. The Kurdish people were instead divided among Turkey, Iran, Syria, and Iraq, comprising 20 percent of the population of Iraq."[15] Nevertheless, British suzerainty over the Mesopotamian mandate and oil concessions did not last.

Discussions concerning Mesopotamia took a drastic shift on 21 May, when Clemenceau and Lloyd George engaged in a ferociously heated debate over the former Ottoman Empire. The core issue was Britain's assertion that the Palmyra oasis, situated halfway between Damascus and the Euphrates, was part of Mesopotamia, not Syria. Lloyd George had been instructed by his oil experts that this location would be a vital station along any pipeline or railway running from Mosul to the Mediterranean ports of export. To Clemenceau this was a treacherous repudiation of their gentleman's agreement made in December. "From the very day after the Armistice I found you an enemy of France," barked Clemenceau, to which his British counterpart volleyed, "Well, was it not always our traditional policy?" Not amused, Clemenceau threatened to default on his offer of Mosul while bellowing, "I won't budge. I won't give way on anything more." He accused Lloyd George of being "a cheat" and that he had turned him "into a Syrian."[16] Rumour has it that he even challenged Lloyd George to a duel, extending a choice of swords or pistols. The whole Mesopotamia question, which to British relief had thus far been skirted, was now put before the larger arena. France had until this session "apparently given up any claim. Clemenceau spoke in anger but he may have also begun to realize just what he had given up so blithely: oil."[17]

Representatives of the Admiralty, Sir Percy Cox, and other politicians bluntly reminded Lloyd George (based on Admiral Sir Edmund Slade's July 1918 report detailed in chapter 4) that Mesopotamia would produce the greatest oil yields in the world, and it would be folly to allow the French any rights to territory or petroleum concessions. The "maintenance of our present position in Mesopotamia is a factor of enormous importance to our general interests in the Middle East and India. From an economic point of view I think it is common knowledge that the possibilities of Mesopotamia in oil, cotton and wheat make it a country of great importance ... Oil is, of course ... of very large concerns."[18] The Petroleum Committee reiterated, "The lack of adequate stocks of oil caused great anxiety during the war and ... oil in this country is a vital necessity."[19] To secure transportation of this oil, it was deemed necessary to acquire by whatever means all German railways (the completed portions of the Berlin to Baghdad Railway and other secondary lines). It also called into question "the need for a permanent Petroleum Department" separate from any other ministerial oversight: "The need for a clearly defined and settled oil policy is daily becoming more apparent, and this is recognized by the French, who have recently constituted a separate Ministry of Petroleum under the charge of a Senator [Bérenger], and are taking up a very decided attitude on petroleum questions at the Peace Conference ... and this country, to which petroleum is even more vital, should not be allowed to be at a disadvantage through lack of a similar organization."[20] This was done on 20 November with the establishment of the independent Department of the Petroleum Executive headed by Lieutenant-Colonel Sir Hamar Greenwood.[21] Discussions between the French and British over Mosul, Mesopotamia, and Syria, however, would not resume until the summer of 1919. During this interlude, Royal Dutch Shell made it apparent that it would not consider becoming "British" until an agreement had been reached with the French on the boundaries of Mosul and the Middle East at large (although this was never wholly fulfilled).[22]

Redrawing the post-war map of the world was not a casual charge, and it is easy in hindsight to cast blame on the "peacemakers" for creating the majority of future war. They attempted to broker a peace to end all wars, and unwittingly, and quite ignorantly, prepared a peace to end all peace. This, however, was never the desired end state, which is precisely why Britain and France, and even America, blithely ignored Hitler's overtures of war from 1933 to 1939. It was the failure to persistently foist the treaty, not the tenets of the treaty itself, that helped provoke Germany's revenge war. Certainly, the terms and aftermath of Germany's unconditional surrender in 1945 was a much more humiliating trial of victor's justice than that of 1919. As Adrian Gregory notes, however,

> Few condemn that peace, mainly because no one has been able to construct a false causality by which it was blamed for starting another war. The causality by which Versailles is held responsible for Hitler's war is phoney ... Versailles was harsh, but it was nowhere near as vindictive as subsequent

legend suggests ... Bodged treaty as it was, Versailles could have guaranteed European security. It was the failure to defend and enforce Versailles that led directly to the Second World War. Responsibility for that war rests less with those who imposed the treaty than with those who passively accepted and even connived in its rejection.[23]

The course of history that these peacemakers had written in 1919 was still unpublished, and they quite innocently believed that the world would never choose to suffer a similar fate, or as it happened between 1939 and 1945, become even more shattering. "The Europe of Versailles was less stable than that of 1914," concedes Raymond Aron. "Territorial partition had not put an end to international quarrels, it had replaced the old quarrels by new ones ... Speculation on what might have been the outcome of a different policy is a waste of time. Yet the principal causes of the Second World War resulted from prolongation of the first war and, above all, of the Russian Revolution and the Fascist reaction to it in Italy and Germany ... Since 1914, Europe has been shaken by wars in 'chain reaction.'"[24]

In reality, four of President Woodrow Wilson's Fourteen Points alluded, in some manner, to the interests and self-determination (a term borrowed and altered from Lenin's "national self-determination") of indigenous or local populations, as America transparently showed no territorial colonial aspirations. The Americans were concerned primarily with expanding markets for U.S. economic enterprises. Given that the United States had neither colonies in the Middle East nor considerable commerce in the region, during his Mount Vernon Address on 4 July 1918 President Wilson furtively spoke directly to Britain and France. He championed the policy that any mandates or settlements should not rest "upon the basis of the material interest or advantage of any other nation or people which may desire a different settlement for the sake of its own exterior influence or mastery."[25] This ideal was met with rancour by European powers interested in imperial gains at the expense of Germany and Turkey; after all, the Americans had fought for only six months and had made a fortune in the previous three and a half years as an arms dealer to the British and French body count. Without this American monetary and material assistance, however, the outcome of the war might have been very different, an aspect not lost on Wilson or his politicians.

Nevertheless, during negotiations Wilson and American diplomats were seemingly marginalized, as Wilson's utopic post-war designs were as far as could be from those of the victorious European powers. He was adamantly opposed to the notion of "victor's justice" or "the guilt clause" and attempted at every turn to hinder imperialistic proposals. To Clemenceau and Lloyd George the verdict of Germany's war guilt was unambiguous and irrefutable. Germany had violated Belgian neutrality. Germany had invaded France. Germany had first declared war on Russia. France, Belgium, and Russia were the primary arenas of the war that left cities, economies, infrastructure, and agricultural pastures in tatters, not to mention the toll on the civilian populations. It is no wonder then, why the victors would argue for and demand just recompense. It is easy to steer judgment with the knowledge that, whatever Germany's culpability and financial obligations, punishment is a poor footing for future friendship. This, however, was not the mindset or the reasoning at the time. And how could it be after over four years of appalling war?

Within this paradigm of peace, Wilson was consistently the odd man out. "Talk to Wilson?," an angry Clemenceau barked at Lloyd George while broaching the Saar Basin. "How can I talk to a fellow who thinks himself the first man for two thousand years who has known anything about peace on earth? Wilson imagines he is the second Messiah!"[26] On Wilson's Fourteen Points, Clemenceau groused that "God himself was content with ten commandments. Wilson ... inflicted ... on us fourteen commandments of the most empty theory."[27] In fact, following the Treaty of Versailles Wilson preached that "at last the world knows America as the savior of the world!"[28] While Wilson did possess some clout, he was constantly fighting an uphill battle. A brooding twenty-six-year-old Mao Zedong compared Wilson's posture in Paris to an "ant in a hot skillet." He just "didn't know what to do when surrounded by thieves," such as Lloyd George and Clemenceau.[29]

The First World War was America's first true measure in global power-politics, as the Spanish-American War (1898) was brief and relatively isolated, and did not disquiet the great powers of the world. The central conflicted notion and binding thread of Wilsonianism was "the folly of the Old World and the virtue of the New World." Wilson, however, was swimming in unchartered waters, as none of his forerunners, aside from perhaps Theodore Roosevelt, had held such a position of international power and prestige. He was the first American head of state to leave the Western Hemisphere while in office, and the first to be directly encompassed in a European war (the War of 1812 notwithstanding): "Lacking adequate guidance from the American diplomatic tradition, he internationalized the heritage of his country."[30]

On 25 January, the delegates did agree to the establishment in some form of Wilson's proposed League of Nations, which was officially ratified by forty-four nations in Part I of the Treaty of Versailles on 28 June 1919. But in the end the U.S. Senate refused to ratify the treaty, boycotted the League of Nations, and refused a mandate to govern Armenia. The idea of mandates was being discussed prior to the sanctioning of the League of Nations. Questions arose over German colonies, demarcation lines between newly created nations, and the expansion or reduction of existing states. Encompassed within these broad themes were the issues of Russian borders, the fragmentation and boundaries of the former Ottoman Empire, and the demands of ethnic interest groups and lobbyists.

Out of the ashes, the borders of Europe were significantly altered, and nine new countries, including Yugoslavia, Poland, and Czechoslovakia, were created or revived, at the territorial expense of Germany, Russia, and the Ottoman and Austro-Hungarian Empires, which ceased to exist. German colonies in the Pacific and Africa were divided as mandates among the major Entente powers, as well as New Zealand, South Africa, and Australia. After rearranging demarcation lines, Africa was divided into possessions and spheres of influence among Britain, France, Portugal, Spain, Belgium, Italy, and South Africa. The arrangement in China and the Pacific mirrored that of Africa, with Britain, France, Japan, the Netherlands, the United States, Portugal, Australia, and New Zealand enduring, or newly announced, as colonial constituents. Eventually, in the Middle East five new states were "created on putatively national lines – Syria, Lebanon, Iraq, Palestine and Transjordan ... were even more artificial and they existed only within a new imperial framework, imposed by Britain and France."[31]

Eventually, after years of squabbling, mandates were given out in the ominously reinvented Middle East, although it was not without international rumblings. Any promises made during the war, including Arab independence or Sykes-Picot, were fraudulent checks and callous covenants. The partitioning of the Middle East was wrought with enormous complications, as both Russia and Turkey remained at war against Allied-sponsored forces, in the form of the White Army and Greece respectively, making concrete boundaries seemingly untenable until these wars and the fate of these regions were decided. Oil, however, remained omnipresent in demands and during negotiations concerning Mesopotamia, Persia, and the Caucasus.

The Red Army was driving south towards the Caucasus and the Persian border, pressing the White Army under General Denikin on all southern fronts. In addition, the Allies were backing Greece and Armenia in the Turkish War. Turkey, under the brilliant leadership of Mustafa Kemal (Ataturk) – the hero of Gallipoli – was fighting to remove Allied occupation forces, to cleanse Turkey of Greeks and Armenians and to maintain some semblance of a Turkish homeland. Kemal was adamant that northern Mesopotamia, including Mosul, and northern Syria should remain part of Turkey, as they had been for millennia. In short, British oil interests were threatened in all three spheres, and still no agreement had been reached at the Peace Conference concerning Middle Eastern mandates.

With the protracted Bolshevik southern offensive and the parsimonious tactics of the Great Powers in Paris, Curzon, now acting foreign secretary, was determined to protect Persia's "great assets in the shape of oil fields ... which give us a commanding interest in that part of the world without assuming direct control over Persian administration." Curzon stressed that Persia would not "be converted in any sense into a British Protectorate," rather an autonomous entity under advisory British counsel, and he superficially paid homage to this credence to assuage the rhetoric of self-determination espoused by the American camp. This posturing was a mere "nod to the principle of self-determination and a smokescreen to shroud imperial ambitions."[32] Curzon was also well aware of the U.S. State Department instruction to American diplomats and analysts to "give special attention to helping American interests in obtaining oil properties abroad." The great oil boom in the western states of Texas, Oklahoma, California, Wyoming, and Colorado did not occur until the mid-to-late 1920s, and America, in fear of depleting domestic oil, now entered the contest for foreign petroleum possessions. "The most conspicuous interests asserted by the United States were those of American oil companies," stresses Fromkin. "It was these that brought the United States and Britain into collision."[33] Standard Oil, the dominant American oil magnate, warned Congress that domestic production would be exhausted within two decades at best and nine years at worst, and that "Great Britain sought to control the world's most promising sources of oil."[34] An assessment conducted by the United States Geological Survey in 1919 reported that U.S. oil reserves would be exhausted within ten years, and urged policymakers to exploit foreign sources, listing the Middle East and South America as its top two priorities.

Behind the scenes, American delegates at the Peace Conference were trying to ascertain if any agreement had been reached on Mosul,

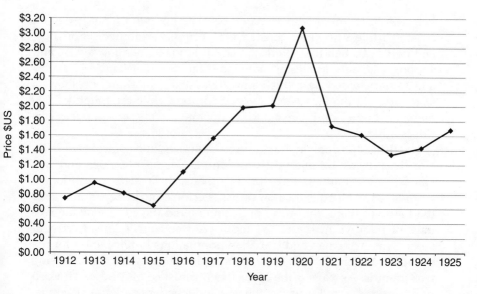

8.2 Crude oil average annual price per barrel, 1912–1925 ($US).

explaining to their French and British colleagues that it would be "very desirable if you give us some idea of the negotiations [so that] American interests are not excluded from participation."[35] The Americans viewed the so-called mandate classification as purely political in design, involving no economic preferential treatment. Wilson argued that mandates were granted by the League of Nations; therefore, any territory bestowed as a mandate belonged to the world at large, not the individual state proprietor.[36] The price of oil had risen dramatically since 1915, reaching its zenith of this era in 1920 at a price per barrel of $3.07. This exaggerated increase was driven partially by propaganda promulgated by oil companies and the government sensationalizing what they opportunely perceived to be a paucity of oil supplies, reserves, and future fields. It is not surprising then that during the peace negotiations at Paris, and the more specific subsequent treaties and agreements ratified in the early 1920s, that oil concessions became a prized and fiercely contested commodity.

With American overtures and the continued disputation over Mosul and Baku, in addition to the uncertainty surrounding the Russian Civil War, Curzon sought to secure British oil fields and facilities, and APOC interests in Persia. The British still maintained a sizeable contingent in

Persia in the form of Noperforce. It consisted of two rifle brigades, an inflated artillery brigade, Dunsterforce's original armoured car brigade, and two and a half RAF flights, in addition to augmenting service and support elements. Malleson's mission (Malmiss) of 950 mixed infantry and cavalry, aided by a fluctuating 1,000–2,000 local anti-Bolsheviks, also patrolled the far eastern Persian cordon, while the roughly 7,600 members of the South Persian Rifles operated in the southwestern corridors of Persia.[37]

The British position in the southern Caucasus, and control over Baku and the railway through Tiflis to Batum, was also tenuous and was allied to the situation, and Curzon's plans, in Persia. As mentioned, following the hasty extraction of Dunsterforce on 14 September after the Battle of Baku, the Army of Islam entered the city following two days of punitive massacres by local Azeri and other Muslim irregulars on the Armenian and Christian populations in retribution for the events in March. Turkish soldiers occupied the city for the following two months. As part of the 30 October armistice of Mudros, Turkish troops were ordered to vacate the now independent nations of Georgia, Armenia, and Azerbaijan and withdraw to eastern Anatolia. The question that dominated Eastern Committee discussions was how to proceed in order to protect British oil interests in the Caucasus in the face of objections from France and the United States, and the last remaining military threat from the advancing Red Army.

Prior to the Peace Conference, although still nebulous, British intentions in the Caucasus focused on three main objectives. According to the peace delegation, the first was safeguarding Baku oil, and the railways in the Caucasus, primarily the line from Baku to Batum, the principle port of oil export. The second, in conjunction, was the ever-present need to protect the route to India via the Caucasus and Persia. Lastly, it was deemed desirable to keep the French out of any lands north of Syria, including the Caucasus.[38] On 9 December 1918, Balfour bluntly told Curzon that anything but French occupation was desirable. "Of course the Caucasus would be much better governed under our aegis than it would be under the French aegis. But why should it not be misgoverned?" Curzon sarcastically answered, "That is the other alternative – let them cut each other's throats." To which Balfour replied, "I am in favour of that." Given that France was most likely to gain Syria, the addition of the Caucasus "would be setting up France as a great Power occupying a huge bloc of territory and excising political influence from the eastern corner of the Levant right up to the Caucasus … If you have a friendly France there is no danger, but if you have, as one day you may, a hostile France, why add to her power of offence?"[39] To this he added, "Nor would her appearance on the northern frontier of Persia be likely to improve our position in that country."[40] Concerning the Middle East and the Caucasus, in October Lloyd George bluntly told the War Cabinet that "Britain had won the war in the Middle East and there was no reason why France should profit from it."[41]

As mentioned, on 17 November 1918, Noperforce under General Thomson occupied Baku, along with the Royal Navy Caspian Flotilla commanded by Commodore David Norris. At this time the naval force consisted of ten coastal freighters with upgraded armaments, twelve coastal motor/torpedo boats, and four tankers, in addition to an RAF detachment of forty aircraft. Naval personnel totalled 1,110 British sailors and 307 Russian crew members.[42] By January 1919 three more infantry divisions, detached from the Salonika Army, had been deposited into the Caucasus to safeguard Batum and the vital railway link to Baku. By this time, the British presence in the Caucasus totalled 40,000, the largest of all British intervention contingents in Russia. The Bolshevik threat, however, still loomed over the Caucasus and Persia.

Curzon viewed possession of the Caucasus as a barrier between Bolshevism and British possessions across the Middle East and Central Asia and sought to amalgamate the oil-producing realm of Baku into British Persia. The biggest fear was that the Bolsheviks would ally with Turkey, threatening British hegemony in the region, while dragging out Allied interventions against both belligerents.[43] For once, Curzon and Balfour agreed that while a concrete Caucasus policy was being discussed it was vital to hold Baku and the rail link through Tiflis to Batum to secure the export of oil. As for the fate of the local inhabitants, Balfour reiterated, "If they want to cut their own throats why do we not let them do it ... as I understand it we do let the tribes of the North-West Frontier [of India], outside our own frontier, cut each other's throats in moderation ... We do not try to introduce good order there ... that is the way I should be inclined to treat these nations. I should say we are not going to spend all our money and men civilizing a few people who do not want to be civilized."[44]

British policy and future intentions in the Caucasus were anything but clear or unanimous in the circles of Whitehall. On 17 December 1918, the India Office bluntly stated, "As far as the defence of India is concerned it does not seem necessary for us to give a thought to the Caucasus ... I have not forgotten the Baku oil-fields and the allegation

that they are of international interest ... Even though we have troops
there at present, I do not think we should accept the task of safeguarding the oil fields alone ... retention of troops in the Caucasus ... appears
unwarranted on either political or strategic grounds."[45] Lloyd George,
Balfour, and Wilson all agreed that "the Caucasus is neither the corridor
to India nor a part of the glacis of the Indian fortress."[46] In stark con-
tradiction, in a rebuttal three days later, the political and intelligence
branches in the Caucasus prepared a lengthy and detailed memorandum highlighting the benefits of securing the region. Above all else it
stressed the immense natural resources present, including cotton, manganese, coal, copper, and of course oil. The report, however, did not
confine oil interests to Baku alone, but stressed the potential of the fields
at Maikop and Grozny as vital to British securities. Lastly, the report
emphasized that the need for control of the pipelines, rail networks,
and shipping lanes on the Caspian and Black Seas would confer British economic dominance in the Middle East and Central Asia, smartly
paying specific attention to Mesopotamia, Persia, and India. In order
to execute control of the region, it was estimated that a British force of
"20,000 would be sufficient to guard the railway and that portion of
the Trans-Caucasus which it is proposed the British should police."[47]
Curzon, ever championing British oil imperialism, was adamant that
with the appropriation of Baku's oil by the British, the petroleum crisis
would be solved and the Admiralty would have a vast supply of secure
fuel. This Caucasus oil would augment Persian and Mesopotamian
output, thereby reducing dependence on American imports.

   While no concrete policy was sanctioned, the Admiralty was ordered
to submit a paper outlining the potential of Baku oil. The report, prepared by Admiral R.E. Wemyss, concluded that without Caucasus oil,
or a drastic increase in production from Persia, as Mesopotamian fields
remained unknown, "we must therefore continue for a long time to
come to look to the United States."[48] In conjunction, Hamar Greenwood of the newly minted Petroleum Department submitted a thorough report on the obvious "advantages which would accrue if export
of oil from South Russia could be arranged for. In the interests of South
Russia and Trans-Caucasia it is vitally important that exports should be
restarted from those areas ... as the 'Shell' group are prepared to take
up the business and no question of any cost being thrown upon H.M.
Government is involved ... as regards the Baku field." The report also
stressed the potential of Maikop and Grozny as increasingly viable British oil markets.[49]

It was reasoned that "a strong foreign protectorate was desirable" for Azerbaijan, or at the least to place all "oil-fields under some kind of direct international control," as the Caucasus campaign of the Red Army threatened international oil assets. British officials realized that securing the oilfields under any system would be a monumental challenge as Baku was plagued by racial strife. It was also recognized that both Dagestan and Chechnya were "a conglomeration of wild Muslim tribes, and with no cohesion, which took the Russians nearly a century to conquer ... but they can hardly be left to themselves, since the railway from Baku to Russia runs through their territory, and the oilfields of Baku and Grozhny in which there is important British interests would be exposed to their raids. Grozhny has in fact been beset by them for many months since the revolution ... The task of establishing law and order will be a thankless one, and possibly formidable, from the military point of view."[50] This Chechen-Russian War, and its conflict over oil, railways, and pipelines, continues a century later, as Chechnya seeks independence from Russia, control over its petroleum resources, and international recognition.

During the winter and spring of 1919 discussions surrounding the fate of the Caucasus continued, with British oil control shadowing all possible solutions: "Special steps may require to be taken for the due safeguarding of interests in the oil and oil-fields of Baku ... reluctantly if pressed to do so, might Great Britain provisionally accept the task."[51] It was agreed that "a cordon should at least be left on the line Baku–Batum until the Peace Conference should appoint a mandatory Power to take charge of the area."[52] However, there were numerous considerations to the "Caucasus question."

The first was that the War Office unwaveringly stressed that British resources were already severely overstretched with occupation forces scattered across Germany, Mesopotamia, Persia, Egypt, Turkey, Vladivostok, Murmansk, Archangel, throughout Africa, and already in the Caucasus – *in a war that was already won*. The twenty thousand men thought needed to secure the Caucasus were not possible. It was deemed that a further five thousand to supplement the force already present would even be a stretch. In addition, the British were facing anarchy and revolution in Ireland, which also drained potential resources. Lloyd George candidly pointed out that Caucasus policy "might involve a protracted occupation ... How did the War Office propose to find the troops?" To this, the chief of the Imperial General Staff, Henry Wilson, curtly replied, "The sooner we get out of the Caucasus the better." This withdrawal, according to Curzon, would reopen the Persian frontier to the Bolsheviks and threaten the British position on the Caspian Sea.[53]

The second dilemma was who would fill the vacuum if the British were to evacuate the Caucasus. President Wilson and the American camp, although championing Armenian independence with lip service, remained steadfast on the principle that there is "nothing the people of the United States would be less inclined to accept than military responsibility in Asia."[54] Although the British repeatedly reminded the pro-Armenian Americans that without an occupying power, Armenian independence would be doomed and the Armenians themselves would again face wholesale slaughter. The Americans, however, refused to budge. With France considered "most undesirable," the British turned to the Italians. After unrelenting pressure, in April the Italians who also wanted oil resources agreed to send a force to replace the British in the Caucasus but delayed deployment. With "the Italians taking over the occupation of Trans-Caucasia," General Thomson, commander of Noperforce, mused, "the height of absurdity was reached" in negotiations surrounding the Caucasus.[55] Following Orlando's fall from power on 19 June 1919, the new Italian administration immediately cancelled the expedition to the Caucasus, causing Balfour to retort, "As usual it is the Italians who have got us into this mess."[56] The British, however, were also rethinking this policy, as the reaction of the local population to the substitution of British forces by Italians "was received with bitter disappointment ... and generally speaking, has created a situation verging on panic ... saying that even the Portuguese would have been preferable by them." In reality, it was the British who forced the Italians to default on their commitment, after a report had been released on not only the value of oil but also the potential of the Caucasus as an emerging market for British exports. To save face, however, the British publicly castigated the Italians for reneging on their promise.[57]

Finally, another pressing concern was the protracted fighting between the Bolsheviks and the Allied-sponsored White Army, not only in the Caucasus but also in Siberia and northern Russia. British presence in the Caucasus was only one element within the muddled Allied policy of intervention in the Russian Civil War. In the Caucasus, without amplified British support, General Denikin could not forestall the Bolshevik offensive indefinitely. Furthermore, Lieutenant-General George Milne, commander of the British Army of the Black Sea (Caucasus), stressed that without British reinforcements his limited force was extremely vulnerable to high casualties should Denikin's line crumble.[58] Wilson, in light of reports from Milne and Major-General H.C. Holman, the commander of the British Military Mission South Russia, indicated that fifty thousand soldiers were needed to secure the British military position and economic oil goals in the region. Curzon, touting this increased British presence, stressed to the Cabinet that there were significant problems with "the retreat of General Denikin and the consequent threat to the Caucasus and the Caspian ... the Caspian Sea was the pivot of our whole strategical position in the East. Its capture by the Bolsheviks would bring about the final downfall of Denikin, turn the frontier of the Caucasus, expose Northern Persia to attack, and immensely increase the resources of the Bolsheviks by gaining them control of the oil and other produce of those regions."[59] Milne, the senior commander in the Caucasus, saw no reason for the British to commit to such an onerous responsibility and cared little about the ramifications of a British evacuation. "I am fully aware that the withdrawal of the British troops would probably lead to anarchy," he wrote to the War Cabinet. "But I cannot see that the world would lose much if the whole inhabitants of the country cut each other's throats. They are certainly not worth the life of one British soldier."[60]

Given these issues surrounding intercession in the Caucasus and other Russian fronts, and what Lloyd George deemed to be an increasing economic drain, and with growing public opinion for withdrawal to avoid pointless British lives being lost, a decision (at least on paper) was made in June 1919 to extract all British forces from Russia, including the Caucasus. Furthermore, Lloyd George reiterated, "It was quite clear that the operation should not be undertaken ... for the troops do not exist."[61] It is important to note, however, that it was also at this time that preliminary negotiations reopened between Britain and France over Middle Eastern mandates. For the British, Mesopotamian oil concessions could easily supplant the loss of Caucasus oil, while shrinking global British military and economic commitments, allowing for a concentration of political and economic focus on the development of Persian and Mesopotamian oil resources. "The economic aims in Britain's post war negations with France over the Middle East," acknowledges Marian Kent, "concerned the desire to secure Britain's future oil supplies."[62]

In short, the Allies' publicly unpopular intervention in the Russian Civil War was nearing its end. The populations of the major contributing nations of Britain, America, and Canada were war weary and wanted an end to this continuation of the war. For example, Canadian Prime Minister Sir Robert Borden maintained that all Canadian soldiers within Allied intervention were under Canadian, not British, control. Furthermore, Borden arranged for the evacuation of Canadian soldiers from these Russian theatres prior to the British withdrawal, even though the imperial force in Vladivostok was under Canadian, not British, command. Dominion support for the perpetuation of the war, including the Chanak Crisis and intervention in Russia, which by this time was essential for political and military clout within the facade of empire, was fleeting, save for New Zealand.

It was planned, although by still no means concrete, that British troops would begin their extradition from Russia in mid-August, to be completed by mid-October. Balfour prophetically recognized, however, that "from the Caucasus evidence is reaching us from every quarter that the withdrawal of the British troops will be followed by the most appalling massacre of the Armenians and general bloodshed throughout the Caucasus." He went on to admit, however, "I am entirely in favour of the policy of withdrawal. In fact I think it is essential from every point of view. But I confess that I do not like to look forward to the day when it will be said that while they had the fullest warning beforehand, the British precipitated a massacre of Armenians by deliberately withdrawing their troops in the face of the advice of all local authorities as to the probable consequences. Coming on top of the withdrawal from Archangel [northern Russia] I do not think it will make a very pretty story." Although Balfour conceded that the "only one way out is that America should take charge" of Armenia, as a realist he knew that America was not prepared to militarily support its moral ideology, nor the wishes of the large Armenian diaspora of the United States, and that "our intention of leaving was made known to the '4' [Great Powers] as far back as March and April."[63] As Curzon reasoned, unless the Americans took up the British mantle in the Caucasus (to which he was diametrically opposed), the region would be left to the Bolsheviks, "who know no restraint and are resolved to destroy all law."[64] Frustrated with his own political comrades and with the dawdling process of the peace, the unabashedly arrogant and sweepingly determined Curzon took matters into his own hands.

The Treaty of Versailles with Germany was signed on 28 June 1919, but by no means was it an all-encompassing document. Negotiations over mandates, oil concessions, and peace with other Central Powers, chiefly the Ottoman Empire, continued in Paris until January 1920. After the exodus of Allied leaders from Paris, individual nations, most notably the United States, Britain, and France, forwarded their own agendas through individual agreements. Certain arrangements were made by a coalition of these state actors, principally an Anglo-Franco alliance to exclude the United States, while others were furtively made in isolation. Agreeing countries, such as Persia and Turkey, frequently made similar agreements with these three nations respectively and used the Anglo-American-French rivalry as leverage to their advantage.

By this time, as Fiona Venn points out, all four ingredients of the oil war had been assembled: concern over potential shortages of both domestic and foreign oil; acquisition of additional concessions and sources wherever possible; aggressive government policy abetting national oil companies; and an escalating vitriolic relationship between Britain and the United States, and to a lesser extent France.[65] While the Treaty of Versailles concluded the First World War, the First World Oil War raged on into the inter-war years, as Britain and America fought for global oil hegemony within the new Great Game.

As we approach the centennials within the four years of the First World War it becomes unmistakable that these events remain in the shadows of all that has come to pass. The First World War and its "peace to end all peace" is directly responsible, or fostered the environment, for every conflict since: "Ultimately the meaning of the War would depend on the persistence of the Peace."[66] The Paris Peace Conference and the Treaty of Versailles, as Fromkin notes, "does not belong entirely or even mostly to the past; it is at the very heart of current wars, conflicts, and politics in the Middle East ... being contested by force of arms, year after year, in the ruined streets of Beirut, along the banks of the slow-moving Tigris-Euphrates, and by the waters of Biblical Jordan."[67] History, it seems, has a strange way of repeating itself.

Chapter Nine

Oil and the New Great Game

While staying in Paris during the Peace Conference, President Wilson and his wife Edith were housed in the luxury Hôtel du prince Murat, which was witness to many American political assemblies and conferences. One morning Edith entered the grand salon to find her husband and his entourage of advisors on their hands and knees, poring over huge maps of Europe and the Middle East sprawled across Napoleon-era rugs. "You look like a lot of little boys playing a game," she giggled. The president looked up somberly above his spectacles, "Alas, it is the most serious game ever undertaken, for on the result of it hangs, in my estimation, the future peace of the world."[1] Wilson's estimation included the oil concessions of the Middle East, and a thinly disguised altruism did not hide his primary motive of promoting American economic prospects. Never had the post–Peace of Westphalia (1648) map of the world been redrawn so radically, and Wilson's near-fanatical insistence on the "Open Door" policy envisioned American companies flourishing within these new boundaries however and wherever they were drawn. Not surprisingly, the British harboured similar machinations.

With questions surrounding Mesopotamia and the Caucasus festering in political indecision, Curzon sought alternative avenues to safeguard Persia and its burgeoning oil resources. On 9 August 1919, Curzon proudly announced his Anglo-Persian Agreement, which was prepared outside the parameters of the formal peace. "A great triumph," he wrote, "I have done it all alone."[2] The agreement was formally arranged in Tehran between Sir Percy Cox and Persian Prime Minister Vosuq and two of his senior cabinet ministers, who demanded and received £131,000 before endorsement. Under the terms of the agreement Britain pledged "to respect absolutely the independence and integrity of Persia." Britain was also to supply munitions and equipment for an army trained and led by Britain. Persia received a £2 million loan at 7 per cent interest, and Britain agreed to a revision of customs, duties, and tariffs. Lastly, British engineers would conduct surveys to facilitate the building of rail and roads (ostensibly to ease the exportation of Persian oil). In two subsequent clauses, Britain relinquished the cost of maintaining troops in Persia, and no claims of compensation could be made for damages caused by their presence. Lastly, "the rectification of the frontier of Persia at points where it is agreed upon by the parties to be justifiable."[3]

The Persian and international response was resoundingly negative. All twenty-six Persian newspapers, aside from the government-sponsored *Raad*, denounced the agreement and scorned the prime minister and his cronies for accepting personal bribes. In addition, the Majlis (Persian parliament) refused to ratify the agreement, doubting Britain's sincerity. The Bolsheviks decried the agreement. France and America accused Britain of hegemonic treachery "to gain economic control of Persia." The French declared, "If these various stipulations don't constitute a protectorate, in the fullest sense of the words, words no longer have any meaning." In Paris, Balfour successfully blocked the Persian delegation coming before the Council of Foreign Ministers on three separate occasions, infuriating the Americans, who believed that "there was a growing feeling, particularly among American oil interests that there was some design to discriminate against them in the Near East." In private, Curzon agreed that "that was the sordid side of the situation," but outwardly appealed to the Americans that it would be a misfortune if Persia "were given for the suspicions of the Great Powers ... and were thrown back into the vortex of international jealousy and competition from which it has suffered so sorely in the past.[4] According to David Fromkin, "Curzon made no provision for the possibility that oil-conscious allies – France and the United States – might react against the apparent grant to Britain of a political monopoly."[5] To Curzon the reality of the British oil position was clear: "I view the situation with considerable alarm, for it seems to me that we are running a serious risk of coming more and more under the control of the United States for our supplies of both petrol and fuel oil."[6] British politicians deliberated on the negative consequences of the Persian Agreement. In light of stiff American objections, Sir Edward Grey, the ambassador to the United States, bluntly conveyed his opinion in a letter to Curzon: "We shall in effect drift into an extension of our frontier from Himalayas to Caucasus. We shall have no friend to help us, for our Persian policy will have permanently alienated all other Powers, as the Anglo-Persian Agreement has temporarily, through a misunderstanding, alienated the United States already." Curzon did not reply.[7]

On 17 May 1920, President Wilson weighed in on what appeared to him to be a British policy to

> bring about the exclusion of aliens from the control of the petroleum sup-plies of the Empire, and to endeavour to secure some measure of control over oil properties in foreign countries. This policy appears to be develop-ing along the following lines, which are directly or indirectly restrictive on citizens of the United States:–
>
> 1 By debarring foreigners and foreign nationals from owning or operating oil-producing properties in the British Isles, colonies, and protectorates.
> 2 By direct participation in ownership and control of petroleum properties.
> 3 By arrangements to prevent British oil companies from selling their prop-erties to foreign-owned or controlled companies.
> 4 By Orders ain Council that prohibit the transfer of shares in British oil companies to other than British subjects or nationals.[8]

Within Great Power politics, acrimony surrounded Curzon's Anglo-Persian Agreement. To make matters worse for the British, the Soviets also acted to undermine British hegemony in Persia.

The Soviet government forfeited all economic titles belonging to Russia or Russians in Persia, annulled Persian debts, cancelled all Rus-sian concessions, and surrendered all Russian property and territorial claims in Persia. "Of course it could be pointed out that the Soviet gov-ernment was surrendering claims it was too weak to enforce; in that sense, it was giving away nothing."[9] The Soviets were also in no mili-tary position to make war with Persia in any sense and viewed this as a sign of good faith, while also placing Curzon's agreement in stark con-trast. Nevertheless, despite international condemnation, or whether by fair or foul means, for the time being Britain had secured a monopoly on Persian oil. Britain already controlled the southern Persian oilfields via the APOC and was now given rights to the five northern provinces formerly under the Russian sphere of influence. These were quickly secured by two British battalions. Major-General William E. Dickson was dispatched as the senior military advisor, and Hermitage Smith headed the new economic portfolio and financial administration.[10]

In 1923, Churchill, who a decade earlier had orchestrated the ascent of the government-sponsored APOC, reported a government profit of £26 million.[11]

While Curzon seemingly secured and expanded British oil interests in Persia, evacuation of the Caucasus began in mid-August. The British exodus commenced in Baku and progressed westward along the railway to Batum. The last British forces left Baku on 24 August, and a vast array of military stores, RAF aircraft, and the Royal Navy Caspian Flotilla were officially handed over to Denikin's White Russians on 2 September.[12] Denikin's "Caucasus Group" of 25,000 men was tasked, as he put it, "to liberate the North Caucasus, break through and establish contact with the English at Enzeli [Caspian port in northern Persia], and cut off Soviet Russia from the Baku and Groznyi oilfields." Facing Denikin's inadequate numbers, however, was a Bolshevik Red Army force of over 80,000 men reconstituted as the Eleventh and Twelfth Red Armies, and a Caspian fleet of thirty-six vessels, including eight destroyers, five armed freighters, a mine layer, and three submarines.[13] Stalin, however, also realized, as he told *Pravda*, "the important meaning of the Caucasus for the revolution is determined not only by the fact that it is a source of raw materials, fuel, and food supplies but by its position between Europe and Asia and in particular between Russia and Turkey and the presence of the most important economic and strategic roads."[14] Lenin also appreciated the fact that possession of the Baku oilfields was vital and declared that "his new revolutionary state could not survive without Baku's oil."[15] While the Bolsheviks took control of the oilfields at Maikop and Grozny, upon retreating Denikin's Cossacks had blown up the oil installations: nine out of the ten million puds of stocked oil had also literally gone up in smoke. The oil wells burned for four months and could be seen over eighty miles away.[16] Baku's oil was now even more precious to the Bolshevik cause.

While the withdrawal of British troops from the Caucasus continued, Denikin's forces were repeatedly defeated under the tide of growing Red Army commitments to the Caucasus front. Only in January 1920, when the inevitable collapse of the White Army was at hand, did the British recognize the independence of Azerbaijan, Armenia, and Georgia. The War Office, in a gesture of goodwill, sent the fledgling Georgian army a surplus stock of the faulty and extremely problematic Canadian-made Ross Rifle, which had been removed from service on the Western Front in 1916 because it jammed constantly under modern war conditions.[17]

9.1 The oilfields at Grozny in flames, March 1918
(Oil Museum of Canada).

On 27 April 1920, Bolshevik forces entered Azerbaijan, causing General Milne to lament to the War Office that the "Soviet system has been adopted by Azerbaijan. Russian Red troops have arrived and communication between Baku and Tiflis is cut ... Oil pumping ceased ... No useful military purpose being served by retention of Batoum ... evacuation must be carried out *en bloc.*"[18] The Soviets arrived in Baku on the twenty-eighth, but not before the British had transported twenty thousand tons of oil to the home islands via Batum. The British also refused to pay their debt of over £100,000 to the Georgians for supplies, use of railways, and other materials as promised. In addition, the British pocketed a further £49,000 in taxes collected from Georgian ports for the export of their oil![19] After all, the cost of the British fiasco in southern Russia exceeded £94 million, although half of this amount was measured to be "non-marketable military stores" – unusable surplus following peace in Europe. The last British soldiers left the Caucasus in July 1920, and the single remaining British attaché, Lieutenant-Colonel C.B. Stokes, departed Batum in early March 1921 with his Russian war bride. His departure signalled the anticlimactic end of British Caucasian oil adventures (for the time being), and, as we will see, had dire consequences for Persia, just as Curzon had predicted.[20]

The Bolsheviks seized power in Baku in early May, and in August nationalized the oilfields and installations, before occupying the rest of Azerbaijan. Armenia, swollen with over half a million starving refugees, fell to the Bolsheviks in December. Georgia was next. The Red Army captured Tiflis on 25 February 1921, followed by western Georgia and Batum on 17–18 March, where Soviet and Turkish forces met. On 21 March 1921, the Treaty of Moscow was signed between Russia and Turkey, drawing the borders of present-day Armenia and Georgia, which were declared Soviet republics. By October 1921, the entire Caucasus had been pacified and came under Soviet rule, solidified by the 11 September 1922 Treaty of Kars, the successor to the Moscow treaty. "In the end," writes Charles King, "not a single territorial issue in the Caucasus was resolved by the Paris negotiations. They were all settled by force."[21]

In December 1919, four months after Curzon's bold initiatives in Persia, an agreement was finally reached between France and Britain on Mosul and Middle Eastern mandates. Sir John Cadman had been part of Churchill's quest to "find the oil" since 1913. He had traversed Persia and Mesopotamia seeking fertile fields and working behind the scenes to secure concessions, wherever they could be bought or bribed. By December 1918, Cadman, the former professor of mining at Birmingham University turned savvy businessman, was directing the British Petroleum Executive. While negotiations over Mosul were in flux, Cadman advised Lloyd George, "It is urged that British control should be secured at least over the whole of the Vilayet of Mosul ... and that any territorial adjustments in Syria or elsewhere wayleaves for pipelines etc from Mesopotamia and from Persia to the Mediterranean should be secured for British interests."[22] He also stressed that Britain must disavow itself from dependence on American oil and thrive at all costs to develop Mesopotamian fields: "The war has brought into relief the extent to which we are at present dependent on Foreign sources for supply of petroleum, and especially upon America, from which we were compelled to draw 80 per cent of our war requirements. A continuance

of this situation is clearly most undesirable ... The French are as determined as ourselves to reduce their dependence on foreign-controlled
supplies of oil ... The French are inexperienced in petroleum matters,
and if they do not link up with us are certain to turn to the United States
for assistance."[23] He did not, however, believe that American oil was
reaching a breaking point. "I don't expect that you or any other oil man
·in America," he wrote to his U.S. counterpart, "really believes that your
supplies are going to be exhausted in the next 20 or 30 years."[24] Securing alternative oil resources was also dominant in British intelligence
circles, which believed that the security of Britain and her empire was
"dependent on oil ... fuel oil is now essential to the maintenance of British sea power ... our power to control the world's shipping in time of
war is likely in the future to be measured largely by the proportion of
the world's oil supply that we shall command."[25]

Senator Henry Bérenger, the chief French negotiator, acknowledged
to Sir Hamar Greenwood that the British were vying to create a "petroleum interest extending from Egypt to Burmah and from Circassia to
the Persian Gulf which is intended to be an offset to the great American
petroleum interests." He described the policy as "justified," adding that
France would agree to the terms in exchange for "a legitimate share
in oil enterprises."[26] In his interminable torrent of communications
to Clemenceau during the peace conference, Bérenger was relentless
in pursuing French oil interests: "He who owns the oil will own the
world, for he will rule the sea by means of the heavy oils, the air by
means of the ultra refined oils, and the land by means of petrol and the
illuminating oils. And in addition to these he will rule his fellow men in
an economic sense, by reason of the fantastic wealth he will derive from
oil – the wonderful substance which is more sought after and more precious today then gold itself."[27]

Finally, after over a year of bickering, an agreement was reached
on 6 December 1919. Britain was granted the mandates for Palestine
(upholding the 1917 Balfour Declaration) and Mesopotamia, which
included Mosul. France received Syria. These commitments were officially ratified by the League of Nations in 1922. Under the terms, France
was given what had been the 25 per cent German Deutsche Bank share
of the Turkish Petroleum Company, which essentially meant 25 per cent
of all oil produced in Mesopotamia. The French quickly created the subsidiary Compagnie française des petroles (CFP), headed by Berneger,
to develop its newly acquired Mesopotamian interests. This agreement
was endorsed by the British (and the French) for no other reason other

than to keep the Americans out of this oil sphere. While France was given 25 per cent of the oil, the British retained 75 per cent, and the settlement included the clause that in the future "any company developing oil in Mesopotamia should be under permanent British control."

The war, and U.S. oil production dominance, had shown the British and French that the United States was gaining political, economic, and military prowess and leverage at their expense. Keeping this upstart world power in check was a high priority, whether dealing with oil or the larger implications and musings of the Peace Conference. The American foreign trade advisor had presaged to Wilson that the British were "leaving no stone unturned to gain control of all oil properties on the surface of the earth, and I am quite certain that if Palestine is to fall under the sphere of British influence the Standard Oil Company will encounter serious difficulties ... emphasize to the British authorities that they may expect a scrap if they attempt any freezing out process of American interests in Palestine hereafter."[28] To satisfy the Americans and remove a minor source of tension, the British split the trivial oil concessions of Palestine between Standard Oil NJ and the APOC, although few oil benefits were ever actually realized. As Golda Meir, the Israeli prime minister from 1969 to 1974, once ruefully joked, "Let me tell you something that we Israelis have against Moses. He took us 40 years through the desert in order to bring us to the one spot in the Middle East that has no oil."[29]

In return for France's 25 per cent acquisition in Mesopotamia, Britain also attained generous rights to construct pipelines, refineries, ports, and other facilities, with mutual exemption from paying transit fees, tariffs, or export duties when traversing each other's mandated territories. The French agreed to give up any claim on Mosul, and essentially Britain was given free territorial and economic privilege to construct pipelines from the oilfields of greater Mesopotamia to ports on Syria's Mediterranean coast. Britain also secured equal rights to concessions in French-colonial Algeria. According to the agreement, all German holdings in Romanian oil were divided equally between Britain and France, purposefully excluding the Americans.[30] When the Americans condemned the British, claiming they were scheming "desperately to control the oil supply of the world, to the detriment of the United States," the British responded with stereotypical deadpan British rhetoric: "So strongly entrenched is the United States in the great world reservoir of oil, that it would be well-nigh impossible to take the lead away from her."[31]

In light of this Anglo-French understanding, the Admiralty urged "that the development of the potential oilfields within the sphere of British influence or British control, such as that now in Mesopotamia, should be pushed forward with all possible speed."[32] On 24 April 1920, at San Remo, Italy, without American participation, these provisions were solidified, and put into writing with the Treaty of Sevres on 10 August 1920. The Turks, however, refused to acknowledge the treaties and the peace terms dictated upon them. Turkey, still at war with the Allied-Greek coalition on three incongruent but major fronts, objected to the inclusion of Mosul, arguing that it had been occupied by the British after the formal Armistice of Mudros was signed on 30 October 1918.[33]

The Americans viewed the San Remo agreement as a direct threat to American oil companies, but also to national security and American military interests. "The Anglo-French combination is determined to keep American companies out of the new oil fields of the Near East," grumbled Hugh C. Wallace, the U.S. ambassador to France.[34] American politicians protested to Curzon, who reminded them in reply that America controlled over 80 per cent of the world's oil resources and excluded non-American companies from these global oil interests and concessions, while Britain (including Persia) controlled a paltry 4.5 per cent by comparison. "The predominance of the United States in regard to oil production is assured for many years to come," wrote Curzon to the U.S. Ambassador John W. Davis. "There is, in any case, no justification for supposing that Great Britain, whose present oil resources are altogether insignificant in comparison, can seriously threaten American supremacy, and any prophecies as to the oil-bearing resources of countries at present unexplored and quite undeveloped must be accepted with reserve." Curzon then elaborated: "The nervousness of American opinion concerning the alleged grasping activities of British oil interests appears singularly unintelligible in view of these facts, and yet it is notable that the United States, notwithstanding their assured supremacy, have taken powers to reserve for American interests the right to drill for oil … In the absence of particulars, which the United States Government were requested to furnish, I can only express my regret at being unable to prove positively that the reports quoted by you are based on misapprehension."[35]

In Congress, Senator Kenneth McKeller of Tennessee, who in January 1921 tabled the Oil Export Embargo Bill, retorted, "I admire her attempts to obtain control of the oil supply of the world. But I do not think we will be good Americans if we can stand idly by and let her gobble up the oil supply of the world if we can prevent it, and we can

Table 9.1 Main sources of global oil production, 1913–1920 (tons)

Country	1913	1914	1915	1916	1917	1918	1919	1920
Australia	5,435	16,016	4,952	5,576	10,121	10,366	10,000	8,000
Canada (including Newfoundland)	32,583	30,868	30,781	28,303	30,547	43,534	34,352	28,134
Egypt	12,618	103,605	34,961	54,800	134,700	272,494	232,148	155,578
India	1,110,211	1,037,371	1,148,374	1,188,759	1,131,038	1,146,340	1,222,607	1,000,000
New Zealand	444	412	556	560	600	600	500	400
Sarawak (Borneo/ Malaysia)	19,953	45,039	55,460	90,570	76,738	71,366	85,143	148,633
Trinidad	70,506	90,092	147,015	129,903	224,324	291,489	257,746	297,588
United Kingdom	289,684	285,464	263,083	247,472	249,598	242,501	213,886	234,000
British Empire (Total)	1,541,434	1,608,867	1,685,182	1,745,943	1,857,666	2,078,690	2,056,382	1,872,333
Argentina	18,970	40,073	74,650	118,755	166,193	180,790	172,169	207,031
Dutch East Indies	1,509,566	1,543,998	1,617,032	1,702,374	1,660,272	1,679,246	2,125,017	2,250,000
France							47,226	55,000
Galicia	1,095,506	645,077	666,063	912,535	887,415	667,733	818,333	752,528
Germany	142,252	142,252	142,252	142,252	142,252	186,000	32,775	30,000
Italy	6,466	5,453	6,007	6,922	5,577	4,828	4,773	5,400
Japan (including Formosa/Taiwan)	273,522	371,628	412,808	417,645	403,371	342,814	285,000	280,000
Mexico	3,670,899	3,747,915	4,701,501	5,792,245	7,898,967	9,118,332	12,439,000	22,280,000
Persia	243,621	381,890	474,553	587,502	937,902	1,131,489	1,194,000	1,712,267
Peru	271,709	248,605	357,325	357,670	341,514	329,618	343,000	360,000
Romania	1,845,927	1,755,276	1,646,255	1,224,099	56,567	1,194,705	905,064	1,017,382
Russia	8,976,337	9,574,360	9,792,580	10,400,159	8,362,903	3,143,960	3,642,571	3,483,143
United States	35,492,319	37,966,076	42,966,737	47,902,229	50,848,817	53,959,857	53,959,857	63,343,143
Venezuela					17,962	49,895	63,589	67,429

Source: Kent, *Oil and Empire*, appendix 8, 202–3.
Notice the huge decrease in German oil production in 1919 and 1920. This is due to the stipulations of the Treaty of Versailles and the transfer of German lands in Pomerania, Prussia, and Galicia to Poland and the lands of Alsace-Lorraine and the Saar to France. Also, notice the drastic decrease in Romanian output from 1916 to 1917, due to the work of Norton-Griffiths and his team destroying Romanian oil installations in November–December 1916. Newfoundland was independent until it joined Canadian Confederation in 1949.

Table 9.2 American and British percentage of global oil production, 1913–1920

Country	1913	1914	1915	1916	1917	1918	1919	1920
United States as % of global total	64.4	65.4	66.5	67.2	69.1	72.9	69.1	81.5
British Empire as % of global total, excluding Persia	2.8	2.8	2.6	2.4	2.5	2.8	2.6	2.4
British Empire as % of global total, including Persia	3.2	3.4	3.3	3.3	3.8	4.3	4.2	4.6

Source: Kent, *Oil and Empire*, appendix 8, 202–3.

easily prevent it."[36] The oil war-of-words was in full swing. "For six years Britain waged an exhausting war, with the main object of ruining German shipping for ever," wrote French economist Francis Delaisi in 1920. "Yet now, from the very war which destroyed that competitor, a new one has arisen, twice as formidable as the old, for, in addition to a superiority in tonnage, it enjoys the practical monopoly of a fuel which Britain has none. The burning of American oil in the boiler-rooms of the great liners may be the downfall of the British Empire!"[37]

In order to dominate oil, European imperial powers created the borders of Mesopotamia (Iraq) arbitrarily. "In 1919 there was no Iraqi people." Contends Margaret MacMillan, "History, religion, geography pulled the people apart, not together. Basra looked south, toward India and the Gulf; Baghdad had strong links with Persia; and Mosul had closer ties with Turkey and Syria. Putting together these three Ottoman provinces and expecting to create a nation was, in European terms, like hoping to have Bosnian Muslims, Croats, and Serbs make one country. As in the Balkans, the clash of empires and civilizations had left deep fissures."[38] Daniel Yergin reiterates this point: "Securing new supplies became a strategic objective. That is one of the major reasons that, after World War I, the three easternmost oil-prospective provinces of the now-defunct Ottoman Turkish Empire – one Kurdish [Mosul], one Sunni Arab [Baghdad], and one Shia Arab [Basra] – were cobbled together to create the new state of Iraq."[39] The Iraqi population was about half Shia Muslim and a quarter Sunni, with other minorities from Jews to Christians. Ethnic divisions also ran across religious divides, as half of the inhabitants were Arab, and the rest were Kurds, Persians, or Assyrians. Nevertheless, Britain was given the mandate for this newly created religiously and ethnically diverse nation of Iraq. The northern borders with Turkey, however, were yet to be defined.

The Turks remained in fierce opposition to the Treaty of Sevres. In the face of Turkish objection, Curzon bluntly stated, "It is both a novel and startling pretension that a Power that has been vanquished in war should dictate to the victors the manner in which they are to dispose of the territories which they have wrested from the former ... That the Mosul Vilayet, with its little minority of Turkomans and its enormous majority of non-Turks [primarily Kurds with an Arab minority], is to be taken away from the victors in the great war and returned to the vanquished."[40] While the Turks and British remained at odds, France and Turkey signed the Treaty of Ankara on 20 October 1921. Turkey acknowledged the French mandate in Syria, the northern boundary between Turkey and Syria was established, and all fighting on this Cilician front ceased. The war, however, dragged on in eastern Thrace and eastern Anatolia.

Shortly after the San Remo Conference, rebellion broke out across Mesopotamia in July 1920. With continued cuts to the armed forces in men, materiel, and funding following the peace in Europe, Britain was understaffed in Mesopotamia. In November 1918, the British Empire had 3.5 million subjects in service worldwide, a figure that fell to 800,000 a year later. By November 1920, the number of imperial soldiers available was 370,000.[41] At this time the British army of occupation in Mesopotamia consisted of 60,000 British and Indian troops scattered across isolated garrisons to protect oil interests, two RAF squadrons, and eight Royal Navy gunboats. To make matters worse, Britain was engaged in a war in Afghanistan, the third full-scale conflict to date, and was also attempting to suppress a rebellion of dissident Muslims in Waziristan, a Pashtu region of unremitting violence and turmoil and a headache for the British administration of India. Waziristan is now the southern end of Pakistan's Federally Administered Tribal Areas bordering eastern Afghanistan, home to the Taliban and frequent American drone strikes. Concurrently, the British were fighting the Islamist forces of Mohammed Abdullah Hassan, whom the British dubbed the "Mad Mullah" in another familiar theatre of war – Somalia. The British also faced signs of opposition in Palestine, as insulted Muslims under al-Husayni organized mob assaults on Jews in Jerusalem.[42] British chief of the Imperial General Staff, Sir Henry Wilson, fumed, "We have between 20 and 30 wars raging in different parts of the world ... [We are] totally unfit and unable to govern."[43]

The insurgence in Mesopotamia could not have come at a worse time, both militarily and politically. Militarily the British were already spread thin. Britain was also still struggling to solidify and substantiate its Mesopotamian mandate. This rebellion might convince the League of Nations, and the Americans, that British lordship over the region was against domestic wishes. The uprising could also be painted as evidence that British control over its so-called sphere of influence was anything but, and that Britain was merely a paper tiger. Britain's hold over her post-war world, and her oil-bearing regions, was unconvincing at best. The forceful British response to the rebellion would prove otherwise. Churchill adamantly argued, "In Mesopotamia, or especially in the Mosul Vilayet, is the one potential asset which has come to use from the war. It is surely worth some sacrifice in the present to reap its unbounded possibilities in the future." Prime Minister David Lloyd George agreed that Mesopotamia "is a country with great possibilities. It has rich oil deposits."[44]

To protect oil interests, the British launched a harsh retribution on the people of Mesopotamia using modern air assaults on villages and cities and new gas weaponry. According to an officer of the RAF, having chosen the "the most prominent tribe which it is desired to punish, the attack with bombs and machine guns must be unrelenting and unremitting and carried out continuously by day and night, on houses, inhabitants, crops and cattle." The RAF's manual, *Notes on the Method of Employment of the Air Arm in Iraq*, confirmed that "within 45 minutes a full-sized village ... can be practically wiped out and a third of the inhabitants killed and injured by four or five planes." To the British the revolt was not about nationalism; rather, it was a lethal combination of "anarchy plus fanaticism."[45] As Robert Fisk concedes,

> All the precedents were there. For Kufa 1920, read Kufa 2004. For Najaf 1920, read Najaf 2004. For Yazdi in 1920, read Grand Ayatolla Ali al-Sistani in 2004. For Badr in 1920, read Muqtada al-Sadr in 2004. For "anarchy and fanaticism" in 1920, read "Saddam remnants" and al-Qaeda in 2004 ... By this stage, British officials in Baghdad were blaming the violence on "local political agitation, originated outside Iraq," suggesting that Syria [with French and Turkish backing] might be involved. For Syria 1920, read America's claim that Syria [with Russian and Iranian backing] was supporting the insurrection in 2004.[46]

The British claimed in 1920 that a policy of conciliation to extremists would be a dangerous position, and that men and money must be pumped into Mesopotamia, as it was recognized that the shift to

9.2 The Royal Air Force patrolling the skies above Mosul, May 1932
(Imperial War Museum).

constitutional and democratic institutions takes time and patience.
Now read Bush, Blair, Rumsfeld, and Rice in 2004.

The British campaign in Mesopotamia was grisly in kind and casualties. General Aylmer Haldane, the senior commander of British Mesopotamian Forces from 1920 to 1922, recorded in his diary that it was
necessary to "teach the insurgents the price thay [sic] had to pay for
throwing down the gauntlet to the British Empire. The punishment had
of necessity to be exemplary."[47] Indeed it was, and as usual, civilians
bore the brunt of the conflict with at least 10,000 killed, while the British losses numbered 426. Many of these were the same Arabs who had
fought alongside T.E. Lawrence and Sherif Hussein of Mecca in the 1916,
rebelling against Ottoman occupation with promises of independence

from the British, provoking Lawrence to remark to the *Times*, "The Arabs rebelled against the Turks during the war not because the Turk Government was notably bad, but because they wanted independence. They did not risk their lives in battle to change masters, to become British subjects ... but to win a show of their own. Whether they are fit for independence or not remains to be tried. Merit is no qualification for freedom." In August 1920, Lawrence spoke to the *London Sunday Times* more candidly about his opinion of British policy in Mesopotamia with words that could have just as easily been directed at Prime Minister Tony Blair or President George W. Bush eighty-four years later:

> The people of England have been led in Mesopotamia into a trap from which it will be hard to escape with dignity and honour. They have been tricked into it by a steady withholding of information. The Baghdad communiques are belated, insincere, incomplete. Things have been far worse than we have been told, our administration more bloody and inefficient than the public knows ... We are to-day not far from disaster ... Our unfortunate troops ... under hard conditions of climate and supply, are policing an immense area, paying dearly every day in lives for the willfully wrong policy of the civil administration.[48]

The financial toll in Mesopotamia for 1920 alone was £32 million, more than the total U.K. health budget, but the prospect of oil was a convincing motivator to stay the course and led to imperial interests across the region. "If we leave," Lloyd George told his Cabinet, "we may find a year or two after we have departed that we have handed over to the French and the Americans some of the richest oilfields in the world."[49] To this end, Walter Hume Long, now First Lord of the Admiralty, advocated to his political colleagues, "If we secure the supplies of oil now available in the world we can do what we like."[50] Consequently, the new Great Game in Mesopotamia continued.

On 12 March 1921, relevant British political and military leaders, summoned by Churchill, who was now the colonial secretary, met in Cairo to discuss British policy in the Middle East. It was agreed that the French should maintain their possession of Syria and Lebanon (the latter carved out of the former for political expediency), and that the British maintain jurisdiction over Palestine (while upholding the Balfour Declaration) and Mesopotamia, while inaugurating the region of Transjordan, as an adjunct of Palestine. It was decided, however, to mollify Arab nationalism through indirect British rule. In theory, British mandates would be ruled by a British-appointed Arab monarch based on a common law presided over by an elected assembly. Sherif Hussein's sons Faisal and Abdullah were chosen to rule the new kingdoms of Mesopotamia and Transjordan respectively. Although essentially one mandate, the British ruled over the lands west of the Jordan River and Abdullah the lands to the east. Faisal, who had previously been proclaimed king of Syria, was exiled to Britain after the French took ownership of their mandate. He was subsequently chosen to rule Iraq, although he was not Iraqi and, as a Sunni, was not a member of Iraq's Shia majority. After bribing local tribal elders and chiefs, the British conducted a referendum to install Faisal to the throne, who received a laughable 96 per cent of the vote. After all, there was no other candidate, as the British had quietly deported all likely challengers.

In August 1921, much to the indignation of the French, Faisal became king of Iraq, even though the new name was not officially adopted until 1929. By 1925, a general assembly resembling parliament had been established, and the Anglo-Iraqi Treaty was signed guaranteeing the British special international and financial interests. Prior to the inauguration of the assembly and the actual treaty, however, Britain had secured oil concessions in Iraq through the TPC, which would remain entirely owned and operated by Britain and British nationals: "Thus modern Iraq was born out of the dictates of a foreign government, with oil playing a central role."[51]

Shortly before the outbreak of the 1920 insurrection in Mesopotamia, British oil hegemony in Persia was also irreversibly challenged. The Americans were hell-bent on acquiring concessions in Persia for Standard Oil, which was busy buying mass "editorial columns" in every major American newspaper, which in turn published articulate posts from alleged "concerned citizens" smearing British policy in the Middle East.[52] The American government was lobbying Persian authorities for concessions in the northern provinces and had secretly dispatched geologists to prospect for petroleum. It was agreed in Washington that the interests of the "United States in Persia and Mesopotamia was confined to the question of oil."[53] In April 1920, Curzon, in a letter to the British minister for Persia, Sir Percy Cox, recounted his recent meeting with John W. Davis, the American ambassador. After a lengthy appeal for potential American economic programs in Persia, "incidentally at the end of his explanation he dropped in the word oil. I at once realized that he was referring to the American Standard Oil Company, and that that omnivorous organization was endeavouring to secure a foothold on Persian soil ... I warned him very strongly against any attempt to introduce the Standard Oil Company in Persia, assuring him that this would mean a competition which would be a source of certain trouble in the future and which the British Government could not be expected to regard with any favour."[54] With negotiations at a standstill, Standard Oil would have to find another way into Persia and, with the clandestine aid of the U.S. government, it did just that.

On 21 February 1921, coinciding with Soviet control of the Caucasus, Persian nationalists led by Seyid Zia al-Tabatabai and Colonel Reza Khan, having secured covert American backing, orchestrated a coup d'état and overthrew the discredited Persian government. The new government denounced the Anglo-Persian Treaty of 1919 and quickly signed a Treaty of Friendship with Soviet Russia establishing the border, equal maritime rights on the Caspian, and trade agreements. More importantly, the new Majlis (parliament) awarded Standard Oil NJ the petroleum concessions for the five northern provinces of Persia: "Standard Oil later used this concession to gain entry into the oil negotiations surrounding Mesopotamia. What began as an idea to control the world's untapped oil reserves ultimately evolved into a Middle East oil cartel in which British, American, and French oil companies shared."[55] In a fruitless effort to halt American oil infiltration in Persia, in April 1921 Curzon berated the British ambassador in Washington that under no circumstances "were oil concessions to be awarded to American companies in the British Middle East."[56] It was too late, and the situation had metastasized beyond the spin-doctoring genius of the obstinate Curzon. The U.S. "Open Door" economic policy championed by Wilson, despite pleas from advisors to withdraw from the "whole disgusting scramble" for Middle Eastern oil, was partially realized, and Persia was only the beginning of American penetration into Middle Eastern oil markets. The *Times* reported that the War Office was also tiring of the whole Mesopotamian fiasco. "We can only surmise," wrote the *Times*, "that somewhere in the background there are traces of the influence of oil ... the hidden hand ... behind the scenes."[57]

At this time both the Americans and British also sought to secure oil concessions in Baku during negotiations with Soviet Russia. Diplomats from both nations forwarded a joint stance on behalf of the rights of private property and business, including oil facilities, seized by the Bolshevik government. Not all negotiations, however, were this transparent. In July 1920, in a strictly paper-deal, Standard Oil NJ bought out all of Nobel's Russian oil interests (roughly 35 per cent of the Russian

total). The Nobel brothers feared that the Bolsheviks would nationalize Russian oil, which materialized a month later, and were content to
receive $11.5 million for their stake. To disguise ownership, the sale and
fiscal exchange was carried out by a Swiss-based company contracted
by Standard Oil.[58] In 1921, Sir Henry Deterding, of British-owned Royal
Dutch Shell, had been sanctioned by Churchill's Colonial Office to
enter negotiations with the Soviets concerning Baku oil rights. Deterding had even formed the Anglo-Caucasian Oil Company in anticipa-
tion of securing these concessions in the Caucasus. Concurrently, Lloyd
George signed the Anglo-Russian Trade Agreement and encouraged
the purchase of crude oil from Russian fields.

Correspondingly, however, Harry Sinclair, of the American Sinclair Petroleum Company, was also courting the Soviets for Baku's oil
resources and the Persians for concessions in the north straddling the
border with the southern Caucasus. In conjunction with the secretary
of the interior, Albert Fall, and the company's vice-president, Archibald
Roosevelt (son of Theodore), Sinclair obtained a concession to develop
Baku oilfields, to develop oil deposits on Sakhalin Island, and to form a
50:50 joint venture company with the Soviet government. Sinclair per-
suaded President Warren Harding to offer a $115 million loan to the
venture, essentially recognizing Soviet legitimacy.

On the eve of Harding's announcement of economic and trade ties
with the Soviets, the Teapot Dome scandal rocked his administration.
The affair, covertly uncovered in part by Deterding, implicated Fall,
Sinclair, and Harding in secret corrupt contacts for oil development
on government lands at Teapot Dome, Wyoming, and two other locations in California. On 14 April 1922, the *Wall Street Journal* ran a cover
piece implicating these men, including the president, in the illegal venture, detailing their wealth accumulated by these unlawful contracts:
"Within a year, Harding himself was dead, the death surrounded by
strange circumstances. The Coolidge presidency dropped Sinclair, the
Baku project with it, and any plans to recognize Russia. There was
more than a little suspicion that the skillful hand of British Secret Intelligence was active in blocking this American bid to dominate Russian
oil development."[59]

By 1922, petroleum production in Baku was half that of pre-
revolutionary output, and one-quarter of the 1903 yield, as nationalization had deported foreign expertize, modern equipment, and funding.
Soviet industry and economics were paralyzed. Lenin, in a comical
speciousness of Marxism and his scorn for the West, sought foreign

knowledge and capital to reinvigorate the Russian economy, including oil earnings. Although Lenin offered concessions to foreign companies, they were not nearly as lucrative as pre-revolutionary financial agreements, and collectively American, French, and British companies instigated a boycott of Russian oil. After Stalin took power in 1922, these sanctions began to crumble as the seven major companies bought Russian oil below market rates to retail at a profit to undercut their sister rivals. This capitalist petroleum rivalry was planned and perfectly executed by Stalin himself by "luring one company after another and setting them against each other, and making nonsense of any legalistic or ideological stand."[60] Soon foreign companies returned on shaky concession arrangements and Baku's oil industry once again boomed.

Also in April–May of 1922, the Genoa Conference was convened with thirty-four countries represented to discuss global economic concerns and approaches to rebuilding war-torn Europe. The focus, however, was the economic relationship between the capitalist West and the Bolshevik Marxism of the emergent Soviet Union. The conference was the honeypot for oil tycoons wishing to bid on Russian oil contracts. Negotiations continued that June at The Hague Conference. Recognizing the intrinsic value of oil as leverage in the geopolitical game and vital to the burgeoning military-industrial complex, Stalin poured money into domestic training and modern facilities, and by 1928 Baku oil production again reached its turn-of-the-century apex. As domestic capital and expertize increased, the need for outside aid diminished, and Russian oil rights were realigned under full Soviet control. On the eve of the Second World War, the Soviet Union trailed only America in crude output.[61] At the onset of the Second World War, the Caucasus provided 93.5 per cent of all Soviet oil from the three main fields of Baku, Grozny, and Maikop.[62] Baku's oil would remain in the Soviet sphere, stagnating in both output and industrial improvement, until 1991.

As the Teapot Dome scandal was dominating headlines in America, the Armistice of Mudanya was signed on 11 October 1922, ending the Turkish War in the aftermath of the Chanak Crisis. Allied leaders met with Turkish officials at Lausanne, Switzerland, to negotiate the terms of the peace. The Americans were again sidelined. They had no formal reason to be represented, as they were never at war with the Ottoman Empire. Although this military epilogue to the Great War was a victory for Turkey, which secured a much larger land base than had been given in 1920 under the Treaty of Sevres, this peripheral war had displaced or killed hundreds of thousands of Greeks, Armenians, and Muslims.

Neither belligerent had a monopoly on carnage and pogroms. As usual, estimates vary, but roughly 1.5 million Greeks and 400,000 Muslims were relocated, fled in mass exodus, or were exchanged after the cessation of hostilities. In addition, roughly 35,000 Turkish, 250,000 Greek, and 150,000 Armenian civilians were brutally killed during the war. The Treaty of Lausanne, which led to international recognition of the Republic of Turkey, was signed by the participants between August 1923 and its official acknowledgment one year later.[63]

In short, the modern boundaries of Turkey and its adjoining neighbours were established, save for Iraq. That border was settled through arbitration by the League of Nations in December 1925 by establishing the "Brussels Line" – the border we have today. The Turks, however, still refused to recognize the decision. They were secretly being goaded by the Americans to militarily retake Mosul, an act that would ensure U.S. oil rights in the region, because thus far the Americans had been unable to secure oil privileges in Mesopotamia. The British Petroleum Department was well aware that "neither the United States nor France would be sorry to see the Turks back in Mosul and in a position to give to their nationals oil concessions which are at present claimed by His Majesty's Government ... The United States government may still intend to maintain their opposition to the draft of 'A' mandates until the question of this concession is cleared up."[64] Turkey also signed treaties of friendship with the French, Russians, Americans, and Italians in an attempt to alienate the British. Finally, in 1926, under the Mosul Agreement, the Turks agreed to the border and the British mandate over Mesopotamia in exchange for 10 per cent of Iraqi oil revenues. In the end, the new Turkish administration, in dire fiscal distress, settled for a one-time lump-sum payment of £500,000:[65] "In the Treaty of Lausanne the Turkish nationalists managed to reverse the humiliating concessions imposed in the Treaty of Sevres and fully restored Turkish sovereignty over Anatolia and Istanbul. They had also beaten back Russian demands for control of the [Dardanelles/Bosphorus] Straits. Buttressed by these accomplishments and exhausted by the decades of war, Mustafa Kemal decided that it would be imprudent to fight the British over Mosul. Moreover, following a wise policy of seeking friendship with all neighbors, including the Greeks, Kemal realized that British friendship and support would be an important asset in the postwar period."[66]

In an interesting twist, during the Lausanne negotiations, Turkey offered a separate concession of oil and rail rights in Mesopotamia to an

American conglomerate led by retired U.S. admiral Colby M. Chester. What became known as the Chester Concession ultimately failed, as the U.S. Senate refused to ratify the agreement, viewing it as fraudulent, similar to its refusal to endorse the Treaty of Versailles. To save face, the Turkish government also annulled the concession in December 1923. It did, however, create the "Open Door" policy so longed for by American business, whereby an American oil consortium, led by Standard Oil, entered into negotiations with the British-French-controlled Turkish Petroleum Company. As it stood, Britain had 75 per cent holdings through the APOC and British Shell, while the French via the San Remo Agreement possessed the remaining 25 per cent, causing Churchill to quip that "so long as the Americans are excluded from Iraq oil, we shall never see an end of our difficulties in the Middle East."[67] According to Fromkin, "At the same time the Foreign Office was advised that the prospects – if they did materialize – were so vast that Britain lacked the capital resources to develop them by herself and would have to invite American participation."[68] Negotiations therefore began in March 1922 between Sir John Cadman and representatives of Standard Oil. While dialogue continued, President Calvin Coolidge created the Federal Oil Conservation Board in 1924, an organization that associated the future of oil within the strategic framework of national security. Coolidge was adamant "that the supremacy of nations may be determined by the possession of available petroleum and its products."[69] Churchill had recognized this paradigm and acted on this principle ten years earlier, shortly before the outbreak of war, by securing 51 per cent of the APOC for the Crown.

In order to secure American recognition of the Mesopotamia/Iraq (which would also nullify any Turkish claim), inclusive of oil concessions, the British discussed the possibility of offering Standard Oil 25 per cent of the British share:

> Such a proposal presupposes that the Standard Oil company might be willing to entertain and accept the idea of participation: that, as a consequence, the United States Government would no longer dispute the validity of the claim: that their objection to the monopolistic nature of the rights ... would be weakened, if not entirely waived; and that the claim would be recognized ... Such a situation appears actually to have arisen in connection with the recent negotiations now satisfactorily concluded, between the Anglo-Persian Oil Company and the Standard Oil Company in connection with the North Persia Oil concessions ... in the course of which a tentative offer

of co-operation with the Anglo-Persian Oil Company in Iraq was made by the Standard Oil Company. Sir John Cadman and 2 Directors of the Standard Oil Company will shortly be arriving in this country from America, and it is not improbable that conversations will shortly be initiated by the Standard Oil Company which, in view of the favourable atmosphere of co-operation created by the recent North-Persia Agreement, will make it possible for the Anglo-Persian Oil Company to negotiate a preliminary agreement with the Standard Oil Company, which while satisfying the latter Company's aspirations in Iraq, will provide for the maintenance of a majority holding by the Anglo-Persian Oil Company ... and will ensure that the latter will remain a predominantly British concern ... We asked only to agree to the admission of American Oil interests to participation in the development of the Iraq oil resources by means of a minority holding.[70]

On 14 October 1927, oil was at last struck by the Turkish Petroleum Company in northern Iraq at Baba Gurgur, ten miles northwest of Kirkuk. With this discovery negotiations intensified, and on 31 July 1928 a contract was signed in Ostend, Belgium, and American denigration of the British Mesopotamian mandate mystically evaporated. Royal Dutch Shell, the APOC, Compagnie française des petroles (renamed Total in 1985), and the American Near East Development Corporation fronted by Standard Oil (which gradually bought out the three other members to secure control by the 1930s)[71] each received 23.75 per cent of the Turkish Petroleum Company/Mesopotamian oil rights. The TPC was renamed the Iraq Petroleum Company (IPC) in 1929. Calouste Gulbenkian, who had established the TPC before the war, smilingly retained his 5 per cent, earning him the immortal nickname "Mr Five Per Cent."[72] To celebrate his millions, Gulbenkian set off on a Mediterranean cruise with his daughter Rita. While on voyage he glimpsed a large strange-shaped ship he had never seen before. As Rita explained, this was his first encounter with an oil tanker.[73]

According to legend, oil representatives of Britain, America, and France, in the presence of Gulbenkian, who obviously had no objection, drew a thick red line around a tactfully enlarged former Ottoman Empire: from the Black Sea in the north, to the Suez Canal and Red Sea in the west, south to the Arabian Sea, turning northward through the Oman and Persian Gulfs, following the Iraqi-Persian border to the perimeter of the western Caucasus, before heading west to its beginning at the Black Sea. "That was the old Ottoman Empire which I knew in 1914," Gulbenkian explained. "And I ought to know, I was born in it, lived in it, and served in it."[74] Gulbenkian distrusted oil outsiders, but the agreement solidified his place and profit within a secure and powerful petroleum union. He was happy to oblige, as he believed that most "oil men are like cats; you can never tell from the sound of them whether they are fighting or making love." He sardonically added that contrary to the "Open Door" policy so mulishly promoted by U.S. officials, "never was that open door so hermetically sealed."[75] Clearly, the U.S. Open Door policy authorized American entrance only. This "Red Line Agreement" eventually included all major oil-producing fields in the Middle East, save for those in Persia (Iran) and Kuwait, excluding the Soviet-Russian controlled, and nationalized, Caucasus. An American oil baron commented that the Red Line Agreement "is an outstanding example of a restrictive combination for the control of a large portion of the world's supply by a group of companies which together dominate the world market for this commodity." The French participants vaunted that the agreement "marked the beginning of a long-term plan for the world control and distribution of oil in the Near East [operated] to avoid any publicity which might jeopardize the long-term plan of the private interests of the group."[76]

In September 1928, as a supplement to the Red Line Agreement, Walter C. Teagle, representing Standard Oil NJ, and Sir John Cadman, representing the APOC, met at Achnacarry Castle, Scotland, the home of Shell President Sir Henri Deterding. Together they hashed out the "As Is Agreement of 1928" or the "Achnacarry Agreement," which was not fully unveiled until 1952. In summary, the tenets set out the acceptance and maintenance of the status quo "as is" market shares for each member. It was also stipulated that construction of new facilities must be approved by all members, and secured the preservation of financial advantage for each producing area by ensuring that surplus from one given area did not undermine commercial gains in another, essentially a quota for each respective region. This covenant was followed by three further agreements defining in greater detail the specifics for local geographical cartels: Memorandum for European Markets (1930), Heads of Agreement for Distribution (1932), and Memorandum of Principles (1934). The main measures concerned fixing quotas and prices, under-over trading and surplus, and the exclusion and dialogue with outside overtures for admittance. It was agreed that two independent "export associations" would supervise quota limits. In fact, the term *Seven Sisters* was coined in 1957 by Enrico Mattei, president of the Italian state-owned oil company Eni, after he was denied membership.[77] Although

Persia and Kuwait were outside the red line, their concessions were owned by members of this expanding cartel. Within the Red Line Agreement, it was also "recognized that it is desirable to convert uncontrolled outlets into the controlled class; in view of this, the purchase by the 'as is' members ... to improve the stability of the markets."[78]

In summary, the "sinews of an Anglo-American Special Relationship had been definitively formed around control of oil ... The oil wars which had shaken the world for more than a decade, were finally resolved in a 'ceasefire,' which resulted in creation of the enormously powerful Anglo-American oil cartel."[79] The core capitalist underpinning of this cartel was controlled by the Americans, as the fixed price of oil was dictated by domestic American production and value *at its Gulf of Mexico ports*, whence most U.S. oil was exported. Under this "Gulf-Plus Pricing System" the price of oil per unit was to be the same at every global distribution depot, as it was at American ports dotting the Gulf of Mexico, *plus* the standard freight charges. The final cost at the port of delivery varied according to its distance from the Gulf of Mexico. Accordingly, the U.S. dollar became the cartel's common international currency.[80] In a brazen act of duplicitous economic bigotry, however strategic, this system still exists today. It was designed to keep oil prices high as American oil was becoming more expensive, and cheaper oil from South and Central America (and to a lesser extent the Middle East) threatened to drive down prices. It allows the United States to dictate oil prices for strategic economic and political purposes. The "As Is Agreement" and its augmentations was "not so much a list of rules, as a constitution, or a declaration of intent." Aside from the "Big Three," which were its principle architects, it was also approved by fifteen other American companies, including the other four sisters – Gulf, Standard Oil CA, Standard Oil NY, and Texaco.[81] The Anglo-American entrenchment, founded in the aftermath of the Great War, remains just as economically, politically, and militarily powerful, and motivated, today (as does the American pricing and policing of global oil).

Persia, as mentioned, was still controlled by Standard Oil in the north and the APOC in the south. After the outright cancellation of the APOC's concessions in 1932 by Shah Reza Pahlavi (in 1926 Reza Khan took the name Pahlavi as his dynastic title),[82] subsequent heated negotiations were directed by an enduring but exasperated Cadman on behalf of the Crown's 51 per cent share of the APOC. Finally, in 1933 the APOC's concessions, although undergoing "Persianization," were reinstated until the extended date of 1993. They did, however, become less lucrative as Persia was guaranteed 20 per cent profit (up from 16 per cent), a fixed royalty to protect against fluctuating prices, and an annual payment of £750,000. Nevertheless, the company's crude oil production rose from 7.1 million tons in 1933 to 10.2 million in 1937. This increase was also met with loftier royalty and tax payments to the Iranian government under the new terms, as payments increased from £1.34 million to £3.55 million during these same years.[83]

Iran's flirtation with democracy between 1951 and 1953 under Mohammed Mossadeq, and his attempt to nationalize all foreign oil companies, was met with an Anglo-American (MI6/CIA) backed coup (organized by Kermit Roosevelt, chief CIA operative in Iran and the grandson of President Theodore Roosevelt), that restored the Pahlavi dynasty (1925–79) and secured Anglo-American oil interests. Both America and Britain feared that Mossadeq and Iran could set a precedent to tempt other independent movements across the oil world, leading to "an epidemic of nationalization and expropriation." The coup (dubbed Operation Boot [UK]/Operation Ajax [US]), was first and foremost about oil, but it was also about using Iran and the shah as a Western puppet regime in the region, and to act as a bastion against southern Soviet expansion. By 1975, Iran was the leading purchaser of U.S. armaments in the world, and between 1972 and 1977 military sales to Iran topped $16 billion. To this end, over 11,000 Iranian military personnel were trained by the Pentagon, including the Iranian special paramilitary security force SAVAK, who was responsible for cleansing Iran of "anti-shah elements" and ensuring the safe passage of oil. The Standard/APOC oil monopoly in Persia/Iran, while somewhat economically constrained, was nevertheless preserved until the 1979 Iranian Revolution under Ayatollah Khomeini, which overthrew the British- and American-backed Pahlavi dynasty, and with it, all oil concessions. Between the coup and the revolution, however, 24 billion barrels of oil were drained from Iranian soil by the Anglo-American petroleum conglomerate.[84]

In neighbouring Iraq, Anglo-American oil concessions were secure under the puppet regime of King Faisal, crowned in 1921. Upon his death in 1933, Ghazi, his only son, took up his mantle. He was a staunch pan-Arab nationalist and was known to harbour Nazi sympathies. He supported the military coup led by General Bakr Sidqi that replaced the elected assembly with a military junta. Sidqi was assassinated in 1937, in a plot commonly thought to be sponsored by the British. Two years later Ghazi followed him, dying in a mysterious sports car accident, and the throne passed to his only son, Faisal II. In 1941, as the first elements of General Erwin Rommel's Afrika Korps arrived in Libya, a pro-Nazi coup d'état led by the "Golden Square" of senior Iraqi military officers attempted to seize power. Like the kaiser before him, Hitler declared, "The *Arab liberation movement* in the Middle East is our natural ally against England." Although this time the British had secured Iraq prior to the outbreak of war, they "reinvaded" Iraq for a second time, fighting off Luftwaffe attacks staged from Vichy France and Lebanon. Five of the coups inner circle were hanged, while hundreds of others were imprisoned, including Khairallah Tulfa, the uncle of a four-year-old Iraqi boy named Saddam Hussein. A second Nazi-sponsored jihad against British rule proved futile.[85]

In July 1958, Iraqi forces under General Abdul-Karim Qassim stormed the royal palace, killing King Faisal III and his entourage, the regent, the prime minister, and members of the royal family, putting an end to the Iraqi monarchy and Hashemite dynastic rule. Now in power, Qassim cancelled the Anti-Soviet Baghdad Pact and threatened to invade Kuwait, which, in his opinion, historically belonged to Iraq. Enraged by these actions and his regime's threat to American oil interests, the CIA subsidized a Baathist Party coup in 1963. According to a 1975 Congressional Select Committee on Intelligence, a young Saddam Hussein was "among party members colluding with the CIA in 1962 and 1963." Qassim was executed after he was tracked down by a group of Baathists, including a wounded Hussein, who emerged as the party's vice-chairman, following yet another American-backed Baathist coup in 1968.[86] He remained in this position, nominally second-in-command of the country, until 1979, when President Ahmed Hassan al-Bakr, Saddam's cousin, retired. Saddam held a dinner for Baath Party leaders at the presidential palace, and one by one invited them to denounce themselves. The following day, one by one the execution of his Baathist colleagues began. Saddam had consolidated his tyrannical rule of Iraq.[87]

Saddam would be responsible for the countless deaths of Kurds, Shia, Iranians, and even those of his own Sunni minority. He dragged Iraq into the merciless Iran-Iraq War (1980–8), with 1.2 million casualties, including untold numbers of civilians, followed by his foolhardy invasion of Kuwait in August 1990. Its petroleum resources would have made Iraq the world's foremost oil power, resulting in a jarring shift in the balance of international authority and leverage. These wars led America (and other Western powers) farther down the Middle Eastern rabbit hole in order to protect oil interests, with disastrous and enduring consequences. While Saddam's reign of terror ended with his capture by U.S. forces in 2003 and his subsequent execution in 2006, the state of affairs and oil concerns in Iraq remain precarious, as protracted civil war rages on. After the final withdrawal of U.S. combat forces from Iraq in late 2011/early 2012, the tempo and ferocity of the civil war has amplified, and the rogue terrorist organization, Islamic State of Iraq and the Levant (ISIL), or simply the Islamic State (IS), even too extreme for al-Qaeda, which is at odds with its basic ideologies, has continued to gain ground. Their ultimate goal, one that al-Qaeda fervently disavows, is to create an Islamic Sunni state in the Middle East in order to wage war on all infidels including the Western world (and regional oil installations), and all other religious denominations, including non-Sunni Muslims.

Like Persia/Iran and Mesopotamia/Iraq, the majority of the Persian Gulf's sheikdoms relinquished relative sovereignty to Britain, beginning with the Trucial States or the "Pirate Coast" in 1820 (a group of seven British-allied/protectorate sheikdoms that merged in 1971–2 to become the United Arab Emirates), followed by Bahrain in 1880 and Kuwait in 1899. These tiny Gulf states agreed not to grant foreigners oil concessions without British approval. In return, Britain supplied military protection, infrastructure projects, and financial support, including handsome payouts to the ruling families. This arrangement lasted until the 1973 oil crisis, although it could be argued it is still in place, given the 1990–1 Gulf War to liberate Kuwait from Saddam's Iraqi forces.[88] In the mid-1920s Kuwait's economic mainstay of pearl-diving was devastated by the Japanese introduction of farm-cultured pearls, and another resource was needed to offset this unexpected financial forfeiture. As a result, in 1928, after the frontiers between Kuwait and Saudi Arabia were successfully negotiated with Saudi ruler Abdul Aziz Ibn Saud, potential Kuwaiti and Bahraini oilfields were awarded to the APOC and the American-owned Gulf Oil Company (and later Chevron and Texaco), which hastily and unwisely transferred its holdings to a Canadian subsidiary under Standard Oil (California) for a measly $50,000. Oil was struck in Bahrain in 1932 and in Kuwait six years later. These companies then created a joint venture in the subsidiary form of the Kuwait Petroleum Company in 1933. Synchronously, in 1932 Britain formally recognized Iraqi "independence" it although retained rights to airbases and other military installations and, of course, to all oil assets. Two years later in 1934, the Americans followed suit by signing a mirroring agreement of commerce with Iraq. At the same time, the APOC obtained concessions in Qatar,

Oman, Yemen, and the Trucial States, while the APOC, Shell, Texaco, and Standard Oil NJ agreed to carve up Sweden's emergent oil industry at 25 per cent respectively.[89]

Concurrently, the largest concession in Canada, along the Mackenzie and Athabasca River basins in the Northwest Territories and Alberta, was awarded to the Imperial Oil Company, the Canadian arm of Standard Oil. This is now Canada's largest oil-producing region centred at the boom-town of Fort McMurray, Alberta, and home to Canada's misconstrued and maligned oil sands. The choice to award this concession to an American company signalled an emerging Canadian trend that had evolved gradu-ally since the First World War. Canada's wartime prime minister Sir Robert Borden broadcast to the Imperial War Cabinet in August 1918 his opin-ion that the British Empire was "unwieldy." Borden elaborated, "If our Empire is to continue as a world-wide commonwealth of Nations, it must rely not only upon its self-governing Dominions [Canada, Australia, New Zealand, South Africa, and Newfoundland], but upon the cooperation and support of the United States of America, with whom the closest and most intimate relation should be maintained."[90] Acutely aware of America's growing military-industrial power and post-war place in the arenas of the global Great Game politics, Canada was strategically courting the United States as a replacement for the Mother Country as its primary partner and friend for both defence and trade: "The course of the war to that point had demonstrated to a great many Canadians that their security depended on the good will and power of their southern neighbour rather than Britain … The angles of the North Atlantic Triangle were becoming much less symmetrical, and the balance was slipping southward."[91]

By 1921, the United States had replaced Britain as the largest foreign investor in Canada and became Canada's primary export destination for a lengthy list of raw natural resources, including oil. Currently, within this mutually beneficial marriage, 75 per cent of Canadian exports, led by oil and natural gas, head south across the longest inter-national border in the world, spanning an astounding 5,525 miles (with 350,000 people crossing per day). Likewise, 60 per cent of Canadian imports arrive from its southern neighbour, producing an annual trade in 2013 of roughly $610 billion. Between 1997 and 2001, there was a tidal wave of U.S. takeovers of Canadian oil firms, with an American buying spree that topped $40 billion.[92] By 2002, Canada had overtaken Saudi Arabia to become America's leading foreign oil supplier. In post–First World War economics, the United States was encroaching on Brit-ish traditional territory, in empire and beyond.

In Saudi Arabia, the British were wary of aligning with the Sunni Wahhabi fundamentalist Ibn Saud. Circumstances, however, out-weighed the morality of befriending the rogue Machiavellian Muslim chieftain. With his own fanatical military order dubbed the *Ikhwan* (Brothers), Ibn Saud was quickly expanding his power and land base by any means necessary. As Jenkins notes sardonically, "After all, what danger could Wahhabi Islam ever pose to the all-powerful West?"[93] In 1915, therefore, given the parameters of the war and the desire to crip-ple the Ottoman Empire, the British and Ibn Saud ratified the Treaty of Darin, declaring Saudi Arabia a British protectorate and ally. Between 1927 and 1929, with British military backing, Ibn Saud ruthlessly con-quered his rivals, including Sherif Hussein of Mecca (ruler of Hejaz and self-proclaimed caliph, whose sons would rule Iraq and Jordan), and suppressed numerous revolts, including that of his own *Ikhwan*.

Following his ruthless military and political consolidation of modern-day Saudi Arabia (and the Saud family dynasty) by 1932, Ibn Saud granted the first Saudi oil concessions to Standard Oil CA in 1933, after being rebuffed by Texaco, Standard Oil NJ, and Gulf. A sudden drop in the number of Muslims making the pilgrimage to the holy cities of Mecca and Medina had drastically reduced the ruler's coffers and forced him to find alternative sources of income, even if it meant seeking out Western infidels. By granting the concessions to an American company, it was also speculated that Ibn Saud was trying to distance Saudi Arabia from Britain and his earlier Treaty of Darin. American diplomats were convinced that "the oil of Saudi Arabia con-stitutes one of the world's greatest prizes ... [but] a covert contest ... [of] unpleasant proportions is prevailing upon the Middle East."[94] The trophy was oil. By 1935, Saudi oil accounted for 14 per cent of Amer-ica's total petroleum production. Consequently, with backing from the State Department, Standard gained further concessions under its subsidiary Arabian-American Oil Company or Aramco (which was 100 per cent U.S. owned until 1973, at which time the Saudis gained 25 per cent of the company). By 1947, the American consortium in Saudi Arabia came to include the predecessors to Chevron, Texaco, Exxon, and Mobil.[95] By this time, there was a growing realization in the State Department that "the US goals of security and access could be realised through the private operations of the major oil companies [and] the United States should focus on maintaining an international environment in which US oil companies could operate with security and profit."[96]

Throughout the 1950s, 1960s, and 1970s, Washington and London pursued the "twin pillar" strategy in the Persian Gulf, using Iran and Saudi Arabia as mediums through which the Anglo-American cartel could exercise hegemony across the region under the security blanket of American-supplied military hardware. It was in the 1970s, however, that Saudi Arabia would "gain its role as both a global energy powerhouse and a base for militant Islamic politics. But the foundations were laid during and right after the Great War."[97] The Al Saud family has maintained power through a "double Faustian pact." The West has provided security in exchange for oil concessions. Wahhabi clerics offer religious legitimacy in return for the state's sanction to enforce and promulgate their intolerant brand of Islam.

For Saudi-born Osama bin Laden, Saudi betrayal of Wahhabism, Islamic code, and its people began with Ibn Saud and his 1933 Standard Oil agreement. As bin Laden argued in 1997,

The regime started under the flag of applying Islamic law and under this banner all the people of Saudi Arabia came to help the Saudi family take power. But Abdul Aziz did not apply Islamic law; the country was set up for his family. Then after the discovery of petroleum, the Saudi regime found another support ... America ... and the money to make people rich ... The Americans must leave Saudi Arabia, must leave the Gulf. The "evils" of the Middle East arose from America's attempt to take over the region ... I [also] give this advice to the Government of Britain. The Americans came for oil ... Brezhnev wanted to reach the Hormuz Strait across Afghanistan for this same reason, but by the grace of Allah and the jihad he was not only defeated in Afghanistan but was finished here ... The American invasion [Operation Desert Storm, 1990–1] [was] ... to obtain oil at attractive prices ... For them to claim they are protecting Arabia from Iraq is untrue – the whole issue of Saddam is a trick.[98]

As bin Laden sat in his mountain-concealed Tora Bora complex in eastern Afghanistan giving this interview, the Union Oil Company of California Asian Oil Pipeline Project (UNOCAL), aided by the State Department, was in negotiations with the Taliban to secure rights for a pipeline to carry oil from Turkmenistan to Pakistan through Afghanistan. One of UNOCAL's leading Afghan employees/negotiators was Zalmay Khalilzad, who five years later would be selected President George W. Bush's special personal envoy to "liberated Afghanistan."

Another was a Pashtu leader named Hamid Karzai, who served as Afghanistan's president from December 2001 to September 2014.[99]

Bin Laden was also right on another reference now called Dutch Disease, after the discovery of natural gas in the Netherlands in the 1960s brought a sudden infusion of quick wealth concentrated in the hands of few, driving up domestic prices and eroding the purchasing power of those outside the natural gas–based economy. In the vast majority of nations where the Anglo-American oil cartel set roots, Dutch Disease spread. The populations of these countries saw little socio-economic benefits from their single oil-driven economies, with the derived wealth often confined to the pockets of despotic rulers, monarchies, or foreigners. The unbalanced location of oil resources in the Middle East has created a dreadful dichotomy between the exorbitantly rich and the dreadfully poor, that has no equivalent in the oil-producing nations in Central America or sub-Saharan Africa, such as Gabon and Nigeria, which still retain low per-capita GNPs compared with the Arab Gulf states.

The economic disparity in these oil sheikdoms is exacerbated by a laundry list of variously defined authoritarian political systems. "Is it any wonder that the unemployed, badly housed urban masses, despairing of their own secular advancement, are attracted to religious leaders or 'strongmen' appealing to Islamic pride, a sense of identity, and resistance to foreign powers and their local lackeys?," asks Paul Kennedy. "More than any other developing region, the future of the Middle East and North Africa is affected by issues of war and conflict. The area probably contains more soldiers, aircraft, missiles, and other weaponry than anywhere else in the world, with billions of dollars of armaments being supplied by Western, Soviet [Russian], and Chinese producers during the past few decades." Along these lines, Kennedy argues that the "possession of vast oil reserves could be a disadvantage, since it reduces the incentive to rely upon skills and quality of the people, as occurs in countries (Japan, Switzerland) with few natural resources. Such discouraging circumstances may also explain why so many educated and entrepreneurial Arabs, who passionately wanted their societies to borrow from the West, have emigrated."[100]

Historically, prior to Martin Luther's 1517 Reformation, which gave rise to the European Renaissance and the Age of Enlightenment, it was the Muslim world that drove academic advancement. The Islamic domain had long held sway in the progression of mathematics, art, medicine, cartography, navigation, and most other aspects of science and technology. This was accomplished, in part, through time-honoured and deeply rooted universities, observatories, and unrivalled libraries containing unbiased collections from antiquity and diverse regions. The efficacious rise of European technology and imperial expansionism following Luther's *Ninety-Five Theses* produced a cultural earthquake across the Muslim world, in magnitude even greater than the contentious seventh-century sectarian split between Shi'ite and Sunni. Tremors began with Europeans sailing

> along the Arab littoral, assisting in the demise of the Mughal Empire, penetrating strategic points with railways, canals, and ports, steadily moving into North Africa, the Nile Valley, the Persian Gulf, the Levant, and then Arabia itself, dividing the Middle East along unnatural boundaries as part of post–World War I diplomatic bargain, developing American power to buttress and then replace European influences, inserting an Israeli state in the midst of Arab peoples, instigating coups against local popular leaders, and usually indicating that this part of the globe was important only for its oil, the West may have played more of a role in turning the Muslim world into what it is today than outside commentators are willing to recognize.[101]

Having shrugged of the yoke of European political domination to gain independence in the decades following the Great War, the contemporary antiphon of the Muslim world can be generally categorized into two camps. The first is marked by an internal rejection of authoritarian regimes and corresponding economic frameworks, while seeking closer ties to Western economic and political principles, as witnessed by the recent Arab Springs. The other is an external expression of anger against Western ideals and economic occupation, and the espousing of sharia law and Islamic statehood. This polarization is evidenced by the rise of al-Qaeda and the Islamic State, the ongoing conflicts in Iraq/Syria and Israel/Palestine, the Boko Harem kidnappings and terror in Nigeria, and the al-Shabaab in Somalia, to list but a few currently active fanatical Islamic militant movements or terror organizations.

Al-Qaeda and its Taliban para-state have their recent roots planted within the mujahideen led and funded by Osama bin Laden during the Soviet occupation of a war-torn Afghanistan, or within the power vacuum created by Soviet withdrawal in 1989. Their ideological conception, however, date to the First World War and harken back to oil. In 1914, Achmed Abdullah, an educated Afghani mullah, foreshadowed an insurgent Islamic world. He warned Western powers that their occupation of Muslim lands, decadence, and greed for natural resources would incite "a coming struggle between Asia, all Asia, against Europe and America. You are heaping up material for a Jihad, a Pan-Islam, a Pan-Asia Holy War, a gigantic day of reckoning, an invasion of a new Attila and Tamerlane who will use rifles and bullets, instead of lances and spears. You are deaf to the voice of reason and fairness, and so you must be taught with the whirring swish of the sword when it is red." Bin Laden certainly viewed himself as the catalyst for this day of reckoning or Armageddon. In the post-war world, it was the reincarnation of Islamic (and pan-Arab) movements and a search for innovative foundations of authority following the collapse of the caliphate, conceived as a counter to Western imperialism and oil cartels, that created the modern Middle East, and by extension, the modern world: "The war made all things possible, and the world is still dealing with the consequences."[102] This encompassed Anglo-American oil domination in the Middle East and beyond.

The cartelizing nations of America and Britain (and France to a much lesser extent) vowed not to engage in oil operations or ventures within the red line except in collaboration with other members of the Turkish Petroleum Company. The advent of the 1928 "Red Line Agreement" set the "framework for future Middle Eastern oil development. It also became the focus for decades of bitter conflict."[103] Although the epicentre of the oil war was the Middle East, it spilled over into Latin America and soon became global. As the rest of the world was becoming acutely aware of the value of oil, companies representing America and Britain had already secured the bulk of oil concessions in South and Central America, producing quantifiable results, especially in Mexico and Venezuela.

The British were the first to exploit Mexican oil, but it soon became a contentious issue between the governments of the United States and the United Kingdom, and yet another front of the Anglo-American oil war. In 1889, a company founded by Weetman Pearson (Lord Cowdray, as of 1910) was contracted by the government of Porfirio Díaz to build the Gran Canal in Mexico City. This was followed by contracts for harbours, railways, electricity, mining, roads, and transport. Pearson quickly bought up landholdings throughout Mexico and began his quest for oil with terms mirroring the D'Arcy concession in Persia. Although minor private American business had been extracting small quantities of oil since 1901, Pearson hit the first major strike in 1908 and quickly founded the Mexican Eagle Oil Company. In 1910, on the coast of the Gulf of Mexico between Veracruz and Tampico, Mexican Eagle hit one of the largest known fields in the world. Pipelines, refineries, a shipping company, and a distribution corporation in the United Kingdom were soon added to the inventory of Mexican Eagle, which also secured more concessions throughout the country. As a result, Mexico became the epicentre of the oil rush, and by 1914 was the third-largest petroleum producer in the world after the United States and Russia. Shortly after Pearson's Tampico success, American companies flocked into the Mexican oil market. Standard Oil (NJ and NY) quickly bought up the trifling original American-owned companies and were quickly joined by Standard Oil CA, Gulf, and Texaco. By 1917, 92 per cent of Mexican oil was owned and produced by rival American or British companies.[104]

In 1911, however, the corrupt dictatorship of Díaz that had favoured Pearson was overthrown, instigating political uncertainty, revolution, and finally civil war, which lasted until 1920, immortalizing the renegade José Doroteo Arango Arámbula, commonly known as Pancho Villa. Between 1911 and 1916, Lord Cowdray declined offers from Texaco, Royal Dutch Shell, and Standard Oil NJ to sell his lucrative business. However, with the revolution in Mexico gaining momentum, and facing an uncertain economic future, by late 1916 Cowdray was ready to sell. Although he offered the British government 50 per cent of Mexican Eagle, its response was to impose legal economic restrictions forbidding any sale during wartime. Britain needed Mexican Eagle oil, and the fear of its purchase by an American company drove the government to drastic wartime measures. Finally in April 1919, Mexican Eagle was bought by Royal Dutch Shell. By this time Mexico was the second-largest oil producer in the world (albeit a distant second to the United States), as the Civil War in Russia had severely hampered its output.

During the war years, the consensus of the Wilson administration was "Europe first." America abstained from outright intervention in Mexico's civil conflict, aside from General John Pershing's fruitless punitive expedition to capture Pancho Villa after his raid on Columbus, New Mexico, in March 1916, despite pleas from U.S. oil companies for military and economic patronage. The Zimmerman Telegram of January 1917, intercepted by the British and quickly forwarded to the Americans, was an affront to the American Monroe Doctrine (1823) and was another act of German aggression pushing America closer to war. The telegram from German Foreign Secretary Arthur Zimmerman to the German ambassador to Mexico, Heinrich von Eckardt, proposed

a Mexican invasion of the American border-states in return for the
land surrendered by the Treaty of Guadalupe-Hidalgo concluding the
Mexican-American War (1846–8) following a general German victory in
Europe – essentially the western third of the United States. With Mexico
already in a state of chaos and civil war, and fearing German covert
and propagandist actions in the region, the United States dispatched
warships to patrol the Gulf Coast and "protect vital oil installations"
if required. In any event, America entered the war three months later,
and the oil situation in Mexico would be drastically altered that same
year.[105]

The conflict in Mexico strained relations between governments and
oil companies, which came to a head with the passing of Article 27 of
the 1917 Mexican Constitution. This clause nationalized ownership of
Mexican "subsoil," which included oil and other minerals, and required
all foreign companies to renegotiate concessions, which now had a
fifty-year maximum tenure. This decree was followed by increased
regulations and tax hikes in order to pay off foreign loans, most notably
its debt to the United States. American bankers were keen to finally see
Mexican balances making progress, paid by oil revenues and taxes, and
took Mexico's side in the oil war. Oil companies saw Mexico as a risky
investment, and a slow decline in capital and infrastructure plagued
output. By the late 1920s, as the American oil glut boomed, Mexican
output began to plummet, and it ceased to be a leading world producer.
In contrast, the British still viewed Mexican oil as potentially important,
especially during times of hostilities. John Balfour, head of the American department at the Foreign Office, stressed that, "unlike the United
States, the British rely on [other] countries for oil supplies vital to their
national defence and it is for this reason if for no other, that it has been
considered necessary to pursue firm action." He optimistically but
naively added, "The position which British oil companies have built up
affords the only basis on which the Empire can hope to have any assurances of securing the large supplies needed. As long as foreign governments are not directly concerned in the oil business they are much less
likely to interfere with the companies in the export of oil."[106] The fate of
Mexican oil, however, and the war between governments and oil corporations was sealed in 1938. In a backlash against "Yankee imperialism,"
President Lázaro Cárdenas nationalized Mexico's petroleum reserves
and industries, expropriating the funds, equipment, and all holdings
of foreign oil companies, including Standard Oil NJ and Royal Dutch
Shell, the two leading producers. Nazi Germany soon became Mexico's

Table 9.3 Sources of British oil, 1937 (%)

Country	% of total
Venezuela	40.0
Iran	19.4
United States	13.0
Mexico	5.2
Romania	5.0
Trinidad	4.8
Iraq	3.8
Others	8.8

Source: Kent, *Moguls and Mandarins*, 148.

best customer, followed by Fascist Italy. Japan was also a valued customer, and Japanese companies were exploring possible oilfields and were negotiating the construction of a pipeline to the Pacific.[107] For the next seventy-five years, the state-run Petróleos Mexicanos (Pemex) ran the entire commandeered oil industry – until very recently.

In December 2013, President Enrique Peña Nieto passed legislation ending the seventy-five-year barrier against foreign investment in Mexican oil to reverse three decades of slumping output and infuse much-needed capital into crumbling, archaic infrastructure and technology. The Big Four, ExxonMobil, Chevron, Shell, and BP, have entered a joint proposal to tap what they deem to be $15 to $20 trillion worth of reserves, promising to double Mexican production by 2020 with state-of-the-art drilling and piping systems. Mexico City has now become the new Baku, as foreign investors rush to secure one of the biggest crude resources in the world in what has been described by media as an "oil frenzy" in the new "Black Gold Boomtown."

Aside from Mexico, the Anglo-American cartel penetrated deep into the Latin American market. Shortly before the outbreak of war, and partly in response to Pearson's Mexican discovery, American and British firms were awarded concessions and acquired land in Bolivia, Ecuador, Panama, Costa Rica, Columbia, Guatemala, Chile, Brazil, Peru, Argentina, across the islands and archipelagos, and also in Venezuela. The governments of both the United States and Britain were extremely active in political lobbying to secure concessions for their national companies. Costa Rica, Guatemala, and Venezuela became key fronts of the Anglo-American oil war in the region. After legal wrangling and back-room hustling, by the early 1920s Britain was resigned to the fact that American companies would dominate Latin American oil, exclusive of Mexico.

The honeypot of Venezuela, however, was the only significant departure from this pattern. In 1919, there were more than thirty companies engaged in Venezuelan oil, primarily American (although output was trivial at 19,000 barrels/day). Production growth coincided with a rapid concentration of ownership. In 1939, on the eve of the Second World War, three companies controlled all of Venezuelan oil: Standard Oil NJ (52 per cent), Royal Dutch Shell (40 per cent), and Gulf (8 per cent). Oil output had also increased to 779,000 barrels/day, making Venezuela the third-largest producer in the world (10 per cent of the global total), behind the United States and the Soviet Union; however, the nation was the largest global exporter of petroleum. These three companies, in varying percentages and locations, dominated the Latin American oil market by 1939, as war once again threatened Anglo-American oil interests.[108] In the early 1970s successive Venezuelan administrations took steps to nationalize its oil industry, which officially occurred in 1976. By this time, nationalization had already been introduced in numerous other Latin American countries, although none came close to rivalling the output and potential of Venezuela. Similar to Mexico, after nationalization, all of these countries saw a spiralling deterioration in production and modernization, including Venezuela. Nevertheless, currently Venezuela is the tenth-largest oil-producing country, fifth in exports (65 per cent to the United States), and second in heavy crude reserves behind Canada.

Anglo-American control over the world's oil has been hegemonic, with few exceptions. By 1932, the seven major British and American oil companies – Esso, Mobil, Gulf, Texaco, Chevron, Royal Dutch Shell, and the APOC/British Petroleum (BP) – shrewdly monopolized global oil, save for fields within the Soviet sphere. These would eventually capitulate to Red Line investors in 1991 with the dismantling of the Soviet Union, escorting in a new contemporary era of oil wars within the new Great Game in the Caucasus, the Balkans, and the Middle East.[109] Many Russians believed "that the United States had deliberately orchestrated the collapse of the Soviet Union for the specific purpose of getting its hands on Caspian oil."[110] While resurrected petroleum concessions were certainly a corollary benefit to the dismantling of the Soviet empire, oil also played a key role in facilitating its demise.

Ironically, it was the very scourge of communist ideology that Karl Marx labelled "sucking vampire-like capitalism," through the medium of oil, that hastened the ruin of the Soviet Union and its satellite Eastern Bloc. While this disintegration had many causes, none was as straightforward as the plunge in the price of oil, which fell by two-thirds in real terms between 1980 and 1986. With this dramatic and sudden loss of revenue from its main export, the Soviet economic system was in a shambles. The far-reaching consequence was that the Soviet military machine, weapons technology, and research and development could not sustain the Cold War pace alongside prolific American output and cutting-edge innovation. President Ronald Reagan vigorously denounced the Soviet Union as an "evil empire" and started the largest military build-up in U.S. history, including long-range bombers and missiles, and a proposed Strategic Defence Initiative to develop a space-based weapon system (Star Wars) to intercept and destroy enemy missiles. While Reagan declared that "freedom and democracy will leave Marxism and Leninism on the ash heap of history," it was capitalism that was the kindling ember.

When Mikhail Gorbachev assumed power in 1985, he was forced by dismal internal economic conditions, wrought by sinking oil prices, to reform the Soviet Union's political system (glasnost) and reinvigorate and modernize its economy (perestroika). Gorbachev somewhat reluctantly conceded that these necessary reforms required significant reductions in military spending. Reagan was ready to negotiate, and they held a series of talks on arms control, which concluded agreements to reduce nuclear weapons stockpiles, and in 1988 Gorbachev started withdrawal of Soviet troops from Afghanistan. Reagan, despite starting his presidency as a Cold Warrior, left office repudiating his earlier, militant anti-Soviet stance. It was, however, a collapse in the price of oil that paved the way for perestroika and the eventual downfall of Lenin's failed communist experiment.

As will be detailed in the epilogue, the drastic bottoming-out of oil prices in the fall of 2014 might also signal the demise of Vladimir Putin and his quest to reincarnate the old Soviet-bloc sphere of influence. His administration has used blatant aggression in former Soviet provinces, such as Georgia and the Ukraine, while bidding economic leverage brokered behind Russian oil-exporting dominance to Europe. Like the Soviet Union, oil may also abruptly vanquish Putin's quest for a new Russian imperialist order.

In the late 1980s, as the Soviet Union was teetering on collapse and reconstituted as fifteen diverse independent nations, including Georgia, Armenia, and Azerbaijan, which flirted with independence in 1918, the Americans looked to the Caspian Basin with great interest. It was deduced that aside from Saudi Arabia, Canada, and the United States, this region, specifically the former Russian provinces of Kazakhstan and Azerbaijan, was "an area of vast resource potential thought to have more ultimately recoverable conventional oil resources" than anywhere else in the world. Caucasus oil once again entered the strategic sphere of the new Great Game, and this new oil boom would dwarf its nineteenth-century predecessor. As Yergin remarks, the Caspian was at the centre of the "greatest sale in the history of the world," as oilmen from America, Britain, Italy, France, China, Japan, and Russia sprinted to secure lucrative deals: "It echoed the era immediately preceding the First World War, when American and European industrial titans struggled for power and raw economic dominance ... Western nations relished the prospect of becoming less dependent on Persian Gulf energy suppliers, whom Washington and London increasingly mistrusted."[111] The Caspian oil war entered mainstream media as the backdrop for the 1999 James Bond movie *The World Is Not Enough* and the 2005 political thriller *Syriana*.

As oilmen and other nefarious characters spilled into the region, so too did the CIA, KGB, and surreptitious operators, furtively spying and moving pieces behind the scenes to benefit the bids of their national companies, reminiscent of *Greenmantle* and the covert activities of British, Russian, and German agents of the First World War era in the Middle East and the Caucasus: "And so 'pipeline politics' became a modern-day version of the nineteenth centuries Great Game, in which Britain and Russia had employed cunning and bluff to gain supremacy over the lands of the Caucasus and Central Asia ... At the dawn of the twenty-first century, the game was played once again across the harsh environs of the Caspian Sea."[112] Baku emerged from the ashes of Soviet-era neglect and once again became a boomtown on the model of a century earlier, with swank hotels, restaurants, casinos, and all the trappings of Western lavishness. In the years following the end of Soviet control, "one could not enter a bar or restaurant in Baku without finding a contingent of Texas oilmen and their nouveau riche Azerbaijani counterparts."[113]

The Kazakhstani offshore Kashagan field in the Caspian is the largest find since the 1960s, and is now the fifth-largest field in the world and the largest outside of the Middle East, while its Tengiz field ranks within the top ten. The Caucasus is currently responsible for 5 per cent of global oil production, which is expected to grow substantially in the coming years, as yields from offshore drilling in the Kazakhstani Caspian alone are projected to be twenty-five to thirty billion barrels.[114] In

1991, the oil infrastructure of the Caucasus pointed north to Moscow, designed to fuel the requirements of the greater Soviet empire. As the Iron Curtain rusted and crumbled away, and the last vestiges of communism in Europe were swept into Trotsky's "dustbin of history," the United States increasingly vied to swing the compass of this oil infrastructure west, boycotting Russia altogether, towards American transportation routes in the Middle East and Europe. In 1998, Dick Cheney, the CEO of Halliburton (with oil ownings and operations in eighty countries) and future vice-president, announced to a group of potential oil investors, "I can't think of a time when we've had a region emerge as suddenly to become as strategically significant as the Caspian."[115] As a result, Georgia, Azerbaijan, Armenia, and Kazakhstan became the largest per capita recipients of U.S. development aid in the world, with an opening lump sum of over $800 million to jump-start what was dubbed the Millennium Challenge Account.

With regional state backing, in return for financial aid, infrastructure projects, trade agreements, and military support and training, construction on a pipeline project was initiated. Beginning at the Azeri capital of Baku, the pipeline passed through the Georgian capital of Tbilisi (Tiflis), southwest through NATO-allied Turkey, to its terminus at the Mediterranean port of Ceyhan. The first crude oil pumped through the 1,100-mile-long underground Baku-Tbilisi-Ceyhan (BTC) pipeline reached its terminus in May 2006. The $4 billion pipeline was hailed as "the first great engineering project of the twenty-first century."[116] Correspondingly, in that same month, the south Caucasus gas pipeline opened from Baku through Tbilisi to Erzurum (BTE Pipeline) in Turkey, running parallel to the BTC line. Both lines are owned and operated by an Anglo-American consortium led by BP. Prior to either the BTC or its BTE cohort, a pipeline was built (and repaired, as it was forged during the Soviet era) solely by BP from Baku to the Black Sea port of Supsa in Georgia, which began shipping oil in 1999. All three lines skirt Armenia, even though geographically it would provide the shortest route. As output from the Kashagan field increases, planners want to reroute the Caspian Consortium Pipeline (CPC) to join the BTC at Baku. As an alternative, pipeline construction from Atyrau on the Caspian shore, and the closest port to the Tengiz field, to Baku to feed into the BTC, is seriously being considered. Although all three existing or potential pipelines are economically divided among international corporations, Chevron, ExxonMobil, Royal Dutch Shell, and BP are all major players in Caspian oil and provide what President George W. Bush described as "multiple pipelines that will ensure delivery of Caspian energy to world markets, unfettered by monopolies or constrained by geographic chokepoints."[117] As Michael Klare argues, the region is

> now the cockpit for a twenty-first-century energy version of the imperial "Great Game" of the nineteenth century ... a dangerous vortex of competitive pressures ... Right now, the United States, Russia and China are competing for the energy riches of the (Caspian Sea). All three powers have a vital stake in the global flow of oil ... of control over the political dynamics of the most important oil-producing regions. All three have deployed combat forces in these areas or established military ties with friendly local governments ... We can expect all three to bolster their strategic positions and to try to curb the influence of their rivals.[118]

While these powers and others play the new Great Game for control of Caspian oil, it has not been devoid of violence: "If the Soviet Union and its satellite states could be called an empire, it is fair to say that no empire in the twentieth century – the Austro-Hungarian, Russian, Ottoman, or even the British – unmade itself in so civil a fashion. The Caucasus was a major exception. Virtually all the armed conflicts associated with the end of Soviet power occurred there, including the territorial wars over Nagorno-Karabakh in Azerbaijan, over South Ossetia and Abkhazia in Georgia, and over Chechnya in Russia."[119] Since the initiation of hostilities in the Caucasus in the early 1990s, almost 2 million people have been uprooted and displaced, while 220,000 to 250,000 have been killed.[120] Curzon was deadly accurate when he described the Caucasus in 1918 as "a theatre either of actual war or of probable war. That alone indicates the world-character of the problem with which we are confronted."[121]

The oil imperialism engulfing the Caucasus since 1991 has created unstable and disputed borders and independence movements in the northern spheres, and resurrected racial divisions, all of which were so evident during the First World War. Since the partitioning of the Soviet Union and the contest to secure the region's precious resources, including oil, conflict has plagued the region. Chechnya and Russia have fought two wars as the Muslim Chechen "rebels" seek political independence from Russia and economic control of the Grozny oilfields, pipelines, and the largest refinery in the former Soviet Union, all of which Russia is loath to relinquish. In addition, the threat of Chechnya "leading the Northern Caucasus out of Russia and thus cutting it off from the 'warm waters' of the Caspian and Black seas is the recurring nightmare of Russian geo-strategists."[122]

Recent Russian aggression in the Crimea province of the Ukraine, cloaked in a similar veil, is a repercussion of this dilemma and can be directly attributed to the intricate web of oil diplomacy. As a safety measure in the event of a geographical or ethnic independence domino effect in the northern Caucasus (Ossetia, Circassia, and Abkhazia to the west of Chechnya, and Dagestan to its east), the Crimea preserves Russian access to the Black Sea for oil exportation to Europe, which is unreservedly reliant on Russian oil. Offshore oilfields also surround the Crimea in the Black and Azov Seas. In addition, the Dnieper-Donets Basin oilfield bestrides the six most eastern provinces of the Ukraine, where pro-Russian elements, supported by the Putin regime, have declared a motion to join Russia. These provinces also contain the entry points for eight Russian pipelines leading to Europe, the Ukraine's larg- est coal mines, the country's steel- and coke-making facilities, one of its largest power stations, and vital rail links crucial to transport.

The first Chechen-Russian War lasted from 1994 to 1996, while the second started in 1999 and continues, with protracted sporadic vio- lence. On the morning of 1 January 2005, the Russian assault on Grozny marked the first instance of heavy aerial bombardment of a European city since the Second World War. During this indiscriminate airstrike, and the follow-on ground campaign against Grozny, it is estimated that 60,000 people were killed, the vast majority civilians. Throughout the protracted conflict, Russian military losses paralleled those of its ten-year quagmire in Afghanistan, approaching 15 per cent casualty rates for any substantial operation. It is estimated that 10 per cent (roughly 100,000 to 130,000) of Chechnya's original population of 1.3 million have been killed, while 20 per cent (roughly 260,000) have fled. The region quickly became saturated with opportunists, Chechen mafia, radical religious movements, and smuggling rings for weapons, humans, and drugs. While foreign Muslim radicals, many veterans of the mujahi-deen who had fought the Soviets to a standstill in Afghanistan, viewed Chechnya as the next proxy war in their global jihad, Charles King asserts that while the Islamic dimensions of the struggle did manifest quickly, the "foreign Islamist presence was never as large in Chechnya as often claimed, nor did Arabs and other imported fighters become a unified group. ... But their arrival did change the social and politi-cal calculus."[123] They did, however, disseminate new terror tactics into the Chechen catalogue, such as hijacking, bombing of Russian civilian targets, and hostage-taking. Thousands of Russians have been killed by Chechen terror attacks, which have targeted shopping malls, apartment complexes, airports, subways, trains, schools, the infamous downtown Moscow Dubrovka Theatre, and the Sochi Olympics (and even perhaps a connection to the Boston Marathon bombings of 2013). Since 9/11, the Russians continue to assert that the conflict in Chechnya is just another front in the global war on terror.

The conflict in Chechnya spread to neighbouring provinces and nations. Russia and Georgia have fought two wars over South Ossetia, a northern Georgian province mirroring the Russian province of North Ossetia. In 1991, South Ossetian militia groups, backed by Russian forces and North Ossetian and Chechen supporters, fought Georgian troops to establish an independent nation. The war also engulfed Abkhazia, Georgia's larger separatist region – the western panhandle of Georgia cushioned between Russia and the Black Sea, another prospective outlet for Russian oil destined for European markets. In 1992, the Sochi Agreement was signed, demarcating the region into spheres of influence monitored by a joint Georgian-Russian-Ossetian peacekeeping force. Chechen separatists used this conflict, and the interim peace, to further their own independence agenda with the Beslan School hostage crisis of 2004 in Beslan, South Ossetia. The attack took place on 1 September, the traditional Russian first day of school. Two days later, the entrance to the school by Russian special forces ended the siege, which resulted in over 380 deaths, including 334 hostages, of which 186 were children.

The larger fragile peace and confusing "ceasefire" lasted until 2008, when tensions escalated again, leading to the Russo-Georgian War. After a week of armed conflict, Nicolas Sarkozy, president of the European Union, brokered a peace, and Russia pulled its forces out of Georgia proper. Russian troops, however, remain in South Ossetia and Abkhazia. This intervention is viewed by Georgia and its allies – primarily the United States as Georgia hosts part of the BTC pipeline – as a flagrant illegal occupation and flouting of international law and convention. Despite numerous peace negotiations and an official "ceasefire," the conflict remains unresolved and is still witness to sporadic armed incidents. Keeping the Caucasus region in turmoil also serves Russia by undermining security to the detriment of American and British oil interests in Azerbaijan and Georgia. For example, during the 2008 fighting, all three pipelines traversing Georgia were shut down by BP for "safety reasons." This same pattern can also be applied to Syria.

This disorder has also spread to landlocked Armenia lying south of Georgia, west of Azerbaijan, north of Iran, and east of Turkey. The Nagorno-Karabakh province of western Azerbaijan bordering Armenia has been witness to a protracted ethnic and economic war since 1988, if not carried over from the First World War. In 1988, when the region was still part of the Soviet Union, both the majority Armenians and minority Azeri began campaigns of ethnic cleansing. The main fighting took place between 1992 and 1994, when a tenuous ceasefire "froze" the conflict. The Azeri military and civilian freelance militia were backed by Russian money and military resources as of 1992, while Armenia and its militant civilian cadre secured funding and hardware from Russia prior to 1992, and thereafter from the West, most notably the Americans. Since then the conflict remains a "festering wound," and little to no progress has been made towards an official resolution. While sporadic fighting continues, the area has become home to displaced refugees, smugglers, and organized crime, and a haven for extremists. Before the war, Nagorno-Karabakh had a population of roughly two hundred thousand, of which 75 per cent were Armenian. It is estimated that twenty thousand people have been killed, while another million have been forced to flee the province, but also the borderlands of both Armenia and Azerbaijan. It is estimated that only forty to fifty thousand people remain in Nagorno-Karabakh.[124] In essence the region has become a black hole and a poverty-ridden wasteland, as this conflict prevented the building of oil pipelines through the region. "And the game is not finished yet. The conflict in Chechnya, the spread of violence to Russia's other north Caucasus territories, and a series of unresolved border disputes in the south Caucasus may eventually lead to even more changes."[125]

Conclusion

The overriding goal of Anglo-American foreign policy, in conjunction with "Big Oil," remains to protect and promote domestic prosperity. To achieve this end, the primary strategic objective has long been to prevent competition to this dominant position: "In order to ensure that its hegemonic position in the global order remains unchallenged and that the flow of oil onto the international markets is stabilized, the United States [and Britain] has long deployed military force across strategic regions of the global South." This geo-political position is characterized by four themes: the role of oil in the maintenance of American power; the role of American hard power in securing oil flow and fixed pricing to benefit the U.S. (and the U.K.) economies; the parallel between oil and American soft power such as trade agreements, military support, and coercive economic leverage; and the decisions surrounding the imperial logistics of when and where to use soft or hard power to achieve this strategic end.[1] While Afghanistan and Iraq are recent examples within this paradigm, these are only a few examples of American, or Western, intervention in the oil-rich Southern Hemisphere. The Caucasus, West Africa (Nigeria), North Africa (Libya and the Arab Spring states), East Africa (Sudan and South Sudan), and Latin America (Mexico, Venezuela, and Columbia) have all been recent recipients of this intense oleaginous foreign policy. This same game is being played out for the future supremacy of oil and its transportation through the Northwest Passage in Arctic waters as well. In 2010, the oil-based economy was worth an estimated $90 trillion, which is set to rise to $140 trillion by 2030.

By 2030, energy consumption is expected to rise 40 per cent from what it is today. As of 2010 the United States consumes 21 per cent of global oil, representing 40 per cent of all energy used in America. In any given day the United States consumes 24 per cent of global oil used, equal to the consumption of all European Union states *and* Japan *combined*, and with a population roughly double that of the United States. In 2006, 60 per cent of U.S. oil was imported. Left unchecked, this would rise to 75 per cent by 2030. On an environmental scale, one American represents twice the environmental damage of a Swede, Brit, or Canadian, 3 times that of an Italian or Spaniard, 13 times that of a Brazilian or Mexican, 35 times that of an Indian, and 280 times that of a Haitian, Afghani, or Congolese, among others![2]

Recently, American politicians have pledged to curb petroleum imports and ensure that North America becomes self-sufficient in energy. With expanding domestic drilling permits in North and South Dakota, Colorado, Montana, and Wyoming, and with an inexhaustible flow from Canada, and now increasingly Mexico, America can likely achieve this end. This does not, however, mitigate the carbon footprint or rising consumption. The latest assessments for the Bakken oilfield alone (predominantly in North Dakota, Montana, and southern Saskatchewan) place reserves at 24 billion barrels, with 7.5 billion immediately recoverable. However, environmental and green lobby groups in the United States have blocked American initiatives to reduce imports. The Obama administration's rejection of the Keystone XL pipeline from Canada and the "fracking" backlash are two recent high-profile examples of their political clout and relatively successful petitioning campaigns.

Like the United States, the vast majority of wealthy and/or industrial nations in the global order, save for Russia and Canada, require, or rely on, large amounts of imported oil. China, India, and Brazil import over half of their oil requirements, a figure that will increase in tandem with ever-growing industrial economies. At its current growth rate, by 2030, China's oil imports will quadruple. The European Union and Japan are almost wholly reliant on foreign oil, primarily Russian oil. In addition, in reaction to the March 2011 nuclear disaster at the Fukushima Daiichi complex in Japan, many countries, including France and Germany, have blacklisted a relatively clean and inexpensive energy source and have vowed to close all nuclear power plants within the next ten to twenty years: "It is in this context that Washington's political and military dominance over oil-rich political economies generate enormous structural power for the American state ... Not only does America benefit economically from the relatively low costs of Middle

Eastern oil, but America's security role in the region gives it indirect but politically critical leverage on the European and Asian economies that are also dependent on energy exports from the region."[3] The Middle East contains 61 per cent of all proven reserves in the world, and currently produces 30 per cent of global oil.

In the 1990s, the importance of oil declined following the Gulf War and the stabilization of Russian and Caucasus production and markets. In the late 1990s, however, emerging markets in Asia, and also Brazil and Russia, overheated, leading to financial chaos, bankruptcies, and debt defaults. Industrialization in these incipient nations stagnated, resulting in a substantial decrease in the demand for oil. Petroleum inventory quickly outpaced storage facilities, and oil prices plummeted to ten dollars per barrel. For those countries with a single petroleum-based economy, flirting with the Dutch Disease, it was a catastrophic setback. For the importing industrialized nations, and for many developing countries, it was equivalent to an immediate and lucrative tax cut – a stimulus package for industrial and economic growth, curbing inflation. In adjusted terms, prices at American gas pumps were at the lowest level ever, kindling the environmentally challenged, fuel-inefficient SUV and light-truck fashion trend.

Conversely, the diminution in growth and revenue for oil and gas companies led to large-scale restructuring, white-collar layoffs, and mergers, all designed to increase efficiency and decrease costs. Companies were quite aware that new sources of oil, especially deeper offshore drilling and encrusted shale deposits, would require a huge increase in financial expenditure, with some "mega-projects" costing upwards of fifteen to twenty billion dollars. During this oil rescission, as a cost-saving measure, the remaining seven sisters (as Gulf had already merged with Chevron [SOCAL] in 1984) forged new partnerships. BP swallowed Amoco (Standard Oil Indiana) in 1998, and ARCO (Atlantic Richfield Company/Sinclair) in 2000, emerging as a much larger entity. In 1999, Exxon (SO of NJ) and Mobil (SO of NY) merged to become the petroleum powerhouse ExxonMobil. In 2001, Texaco joined Chevron. Smaller companies followed suit, as Phillips combined with Conoco to become ConocoPhillips. In France, Total amalgamated its French and Belgian competitors. Only Royal Dutch Shell remained unaffected, although it did increase its holdings by incorporating substantially smaller companies in yet relatively untapped regions. And so the Seven Sisters became four: BP, Royal Dutch Shell, Chevron, and ExxonMobil.[4]

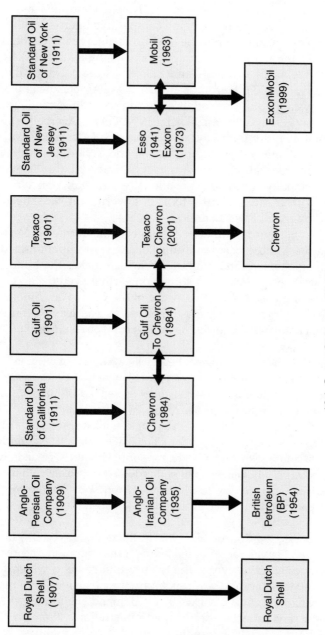

10.1 Seven Sisters to the Big Four

During this period other, predominantly state-controlled and nationalized petroleum companies became competitive international players in the new Great Game. A new Seven Sisters emerged to challenge the monopoly of the Big Four: Saudi Aramco, China National Petroleum Corporation (CNPC), Gazprom and Rosneft (Russia), National Iranian Oil Company (NIOC), Petrobras Brazil, PDVSA Venezuela, and Petronas Malaysia. In addition, other state-run companies made inroads, such as KazMunayGas (Kazakhstan), SOCAR (Azerbaijan), LNG (Qatar), StatoilHydro (Norway), and Sonatrach (Algeria). Private corporations also emerged, including Lukoil and TNK-BP of Russia. The landscape of international (or Anglo-American) oil was irreversibly altered. Nationally controlled or nationally influenced oil syndicates, such as Gazprom, are powerful tools of government-led statecraft, as evidenced by recent Russian antics.

However, the crucial difference between the former colonial territories in the Middle East, and other orphans of imperialism dotted around the globe, was and remains oil, which makes the Middle East the most strategic geo-political sphere on earth. Given the accelerated importance of oil since the failed peace of the Great War, America and Britain could not just simply close their doors and leave, even if they wanted to. History has recorded what has transpired since:

> Four wars between the Arabs and the Israelis; a ten-year civil war in Lebanon and a twenty-year one in Yemen; the slaughter of ethnic minorities in Syria and Iraq; four decades of state-sponsored terrorism; convulsions of religious extremism; four major American military interventions and a host of smaller ones; and for the Arab people, until very recently, a virtually unbroken string of cruel and/or kleptocratic dictatorships stretching from Tunisia to Iraq that left the great majority impoverished and disenfranchised. Certainly, blame for all of this doesn't rest solely with the terrible decisions that were made at the end of World War I, but it was then that one particularly toxic seed was planted [and that was oil].[5]

In the revised edition of his 1992 Pulitzer Prize-winning oil treatise, *The Prize*, Daniel Yergin equates this transformation to three decisive dynamics at the dawn of the twenty-first century, which form a tripartite relationship and are not mutually exclusive: 11 September 2001, globalization, and a surge in oil demand. Following the 9/11 al-Qaeda-inspired attacks, the Bush administration's "War on Terror" shook the foundations of international diplomacy, geopolitics, war, and petroleum economics. The American-led invasions of Afghanistan and Iraq unleashed a torrent of violence across the Middle East and North Africa – from civil war in Iraq, Syria, Nigeria, and the Sudans to list but a few – to the protests and domestic strife across the boundaries of the Arab Spring(s). Not surprisingly, the most extreme forms of unrest engulfed oil-producing nations.

These "springs" were not spontaneous; in fact, they were quite the opposite. They were the phoenix rising from the ashes of an unfulfilled British promise of Arab independence made through Lawrence in 1916. For the first time since 1918, Arabs are now choosing their own destiny through civic participation, albeit violent at times, and demanding personal freedoms by unleashing their anger inward on authoritarian regimes, rather than outward against a perceived external Western threat, which for the past sixty years has been puppeteered, promulgated, and propagandized by their corrupt dictators and despotic rulers.

This resurgent, diffusing, and expanding political and economic unrest was made possible in large part by globalization, inclusive of the Internet and social media, which are now omnipresent and inescapably invade every aspect of our global village. The world economy tripled in size between 1990 and 2009, and increasingly the percentage of the world's GDP was generated in the so-called developing world at the expense of G8 nations, which were reeling from the 2008 economic crash. With these emerging market economies, wages, and socioeconomic ladders within the nations, most notably China, India, and Brazil, oil again was in ever-increasing demand. Global consumption rose 30 per cent between 1991 and 2008. Given the poor pecuniary prospects of playing Western stock exchanges and markets, financial investors became increasingly involved in oil and other commodities, as "oil came to be seen as an asset class that provided an alternative to stocks, bonds, and real estate for pension funds, university endowments, and other investors seeking higher returns. At the same time, traditional commodity investors, speculators, and traders also put more money on the table."[6]

The public and the petroleum magnates were caught off-guard by this seemingly sudden demand for oil. During the decade of the 1990s oil recession, slow growth in demand created low levels of investment, research and development, and oil exploration. In the years surrounding the turn of the century, the balance sheet between petroleum supply and demand progressively tilted to demand. This movement was exacerbated by politics in its various forms, but most notably war, which brings us full circle back to 9/11. The offensive campaigns of the U.S.-managed Western coalitions in the "War on Terror" and corresponding economic sanctions produced reverberations across the globe that dramatically reduced the flow of international oil, whether from Venezuela, Nigeria, Libya, Iraq, Iran, the Sudans, Russia, the Ukraine, or a multitude of other petroleum producing nations: "All of these factors – supply and demand, geopolitics, costs, financial markets, expectations, and speculation – came together to carry oil prices from $30 at the beginning of the Iraq War through $100 and $120 and then over $145 a barrel in 2008 ... But it was only when global oil demand declined – in response to high prices, a financial crisis worse than any since the Great Depression, and a world recession – that the price collapsed."[7]

The simple replacement of oil with another cleaner, less-damaging fuel source could already likely be done. A replacement could also be found to substitute for petroleum by-products such as plastics, fabrics, and other oil-based materials. The international dynamics of oil, however, are not that simple and do not revolve solely around global gas pumps. Oil is the epicentre of the global economy and the balance that provides homeostasis to world finance, economic markets, and war. Oil is the brokering leverage of international geopolitics. Oil drives the military industrial complex, which fuels war within Churchill's vicious military-economic cycle. If oil is removed, something equivalent to its current (and growing) influence, stimulus, and sweeping importance would need to fill the vacuum. Here lies the dilemma. Currently, the developed world consumes fourteen barrels of oil per person per year. In the developing world this figure is three, but is increasing quickly. Today, one billion vehicles travel global transportation routes (which are also made from oil), and by 2030, this number will double. In this light, so long as the status quo remains and oil continues to nurture its importance, the dilemma becomes clearer, deepens its roots, and becomes more taxing, but also less approachable.

Oil, the "central factor in world politics and the global economy, in the global calculus of power, and in how people live their lives," is still consistently coupled to war, not deviating from the course of history it created a century ago.[8] And so pipeline politics endure, cloaked in disguises, but at its centre lives the Anglo-American petroleum cartel. Created during the First World War and in the wake of its fraudulent peace, it has shaped all facets of history, and all that has come to pass and will pass, until alternative energy sources unseat oil's monopoly of power-politics: "The quest for oil, which began here so long ago, still goes on. Petroleum continues to be a highly prized commodity. We do everything with it. We eat food packaged in it and wear clothing made from it. We drive cars filled with parts manufactured from it and fuelled by it. We drive on streets and walk on sidewalks constructed from it. Our houses are built from and filled with materials and furniture produced from it. Our lives, our good health, our very being, depend on its capture distilling, and conversion."[9] Since 1914, we have gone to war for it.

Epilogue

In November 2014, shortly before this manuscript was completed and submitted for the customary university press peer review and editing, the oil world was turned on its head. The bottom of the barrel fell out of crude oil prices.[1] In January 2013, the Brent Crude price per barrel hovered around $120. Three years later the price had plummeted to $30. This marked the first time crude prices have fallen below $57 since October 2008, when the world was reeling in the worst economic crisis since the Great Depression. Even more telling, in the two months from November 2014 to January 2015, the price per barrel dropped from roughly $100 to $45, accounting for two-thirds of the overall two-year decline. The reasons are many but quite simple. These causes, however, are all economically, militarily, and politically intertwined.

The first catalyst is the oilmen of North Dakota and Texas, and the staggering increase in American production since 2010. As prices hovered around $110 to $120 per barrel (until recently), oil extraction from shale formations, previously economically unviable, skyrocketed. In the four years between 2010 and 2014, as many as twenty-five thousand new wells have been sunk in the United States, ten times more than in Saudi Arabia. This has boosted American oil production by nearly 35 per cent from 5.4 million barrels per day to 8.5 million – a mere 800,000 barrels per day short of Saudi Arabia (for comparison and contrast, world output for 2014 was roughly 91 million barrels per day). At the same time, war-torn Libya increased production by over 40 per cent in one month from August to September 2014, and the Saudis boosted output to protect their market share in the face of this American escalation, while also trying to stymie new shale investments and Canadian and American development of Arctic resources. OPEC reiterated on numerous occasions that it would not attempt to shore up oil prices by reducing production or individual export quotas.

The plummet of oil prices was further aggrieved by hedge and mutual fund investors dumping oil from their customary economic portfolios after realizing their expectations were wrong that prices would continue to rise. Investors who purchased shares in oil, specifically in Canadian and American ventures, with the confidence of a gradual rise or a stable market share between $90 and $110 have also experienced a severe setback, as experts predict that prices will remain low for the foreseeable future. More than one-quarter of the world's "undiscovered" oil and gas lies in Arctic waters. But with the collapse of the oil market, leading oil firms are bailing on their Arctic ventures. Partners Gazprom (Russia) and Statoil (Norway) pulled the plug on their development of the Shtokman field in the Barents Sea (one of the largest in the world). Representatives of Total (French) and BP recently chided that energy exploration in the Arctic was "a licence to lose money." In short, with the current glut of oil, the Arctic fields still remain economically untenable.

Analysts suggest that over the next two years (as I write in April 2016) oil prices will rise to hover between $45 and $65 per barrel, due to a prevaricating economic recovery in Europe and a decrease in industrial output from China, the world's second-largest consumer of oil. If, however, prices settle at the current market ($35 to $45), the bill for energy consumers, most of all those importing nations such as China, India, and Brazil with rapidly expanding economies, will be reduced by $2.1 trillion per year. For China, the world's second-largest net importer of petroleum, based on 2013 figures, every $1 reduction in the price of oil saves the nation an annual $2.2 billion. On a more palatable level, if prices remain fixed, the average American motorist would save $1,500 per year, equivalent to a 2.4 per cent pay raise. Furthermore, the average new car uses 25 per cent less gasoline per kilometre than ten years ago. The immediate influence on the United States will be mixed, as America is simultaneously the world's largest consumer, importer, and soon to be, *if not already*, producer of oil. With the oil war and competition between American shalemen (and their Canadian sandman allies) and Arab sheikhs, the oil world has swiftly gone from shortage to surplus.

On the surface, cheaper oil benefits the vast majority of nations through increasingly economically efficient industries, travel and tourism, agriculture, and by extension, their peoples and workforce.

Table 11.1 Top twelve global producers, 2013

Country	2013 oil production (millions barrels/day)
Saudi Arabia	9.3
United States	8.5
Russia	7.8
China	4.2
Canada	4.1
United Arab Emirates	3.2
Iran	3.1
Iraq	3.0
Mexico	2.9
Venezuela	2.9
Kuwait	2.9
Brazil	2.8
Total: Top 12	54.7
Total: Rest of world	36.3

Source: *Economist*, 25 October 2014, 63.

However, a handful of seemingly hand-picked nations will suffer from the decline of oil prices, primarily the "axis of diesel," which appears to have been purposefully marginalized and targeted through clandestine dealings of international political and economic discourse (Somali pirates, the Islamic State, and other terror/extremist organizations that endow insurgencies with black-market oil revenues such as those in Yemen, Nigeria, Sudan, Chechnya, Abkhazia, and increasingly those of Indonesia and South/Central America will also be derailed by sinking oil prices). Increased American output has had its desired short-term effect and end-state, and has been successfully deployed as a precision economic weapon system against those who challenge American global hegemony – specifically Russia, Iran, and Venezuela. The Anglo-American oil cartel has gone on the offensive, using oil as a weapon to reclaim its monopoly from upstart nationalized oil states. The Oil War that began over a century ago has come full circle.

For governments like Russia, Iran, and Venezuela who have recently used their windfall of oil revenues from higher prices to drive aggressive – if not outwardly belligerent, in Putin's case – foreign policies and internal nationalist rhetoric, the future looks undeniably bleak. Not surprisingly, all three are also among the top ten oil-producing nations, under nationalized oil economies and infrastructure. Venezuela was already in financial trouble prior to the recent oil crash due to President Hugo Chavez's anti-American Bolivarian Revolution, and his reckless spending. Given that Venezuelan oil has been nationalized since 1976, a state-run fund intended to accumulate oil profits to be dispersed in times of decreased oil revenue and economic depression was cancelled by Chavez, and its deposits frittered away. Venezuela accumulated tens of billions of dollars in debt (which is coming due and likely to default) during his tenure, and inflation is rampant. The country's fiscal deficit for 2013 was a staggering 17 per cent of GDP. In response, the government printed additional currency, driving inflation even higher. The untenable blueprint, as promulgated by Chavez, for Venezuela's current budget (excluding rising debt and interest payments) is based on a *minimum* price per barrel of $120. The citizens of Venezuela are feeling the aftershocks of Chavez's failed economic and diplomatic experiments, as the standard of living has tumbled and increasing shortages of everyday goods such as flour, paper, and toiletries are becoming more prevalent. Likewise, Nigeria, with its continuing ethnic and religious war, subsidized by control of oil revenues, faces the same future as Venezuela. Both are teetering on defaulting on their debts and need an influx of foreign (read Anglo-American) investment to shore up their precarious economies. The Big Four oil companies – BP, Shell, ExxonMobil, and Chevron – are no doubt waiting for Caracas to denationalize its oil and to be invited to revamp at least this portion of its shattered economy. Iran, however, is even more vulnerable than Venezuela.

For Iran, having already endured decades of Western sanctions designed to curb its nuclear program, the repercussions are more immediate and pronounced. Unlike Venezuela, these sanctions also mean that it cannot borrow its way out of economic stagnation. Furthermore, to circumvent these protracted sanctions, in 2013, Iran spent $100 billion on consumer subsidies – an astounding 25 per cent of GDP. To balance its current profligate budget, buttressed with the prodigious spending schemes of its former president, Mahmoud Ahmadinejad, Iran needs oil to increase to $130 to $140 per barrel, which is highly implausible. Perhaps, given the recent meetings between U.S. President Barack Obama and Saudi King Abdullah bin Abdulaziz, Sunni Saudi Arabia is conspiring with America to use oil as an economic weapon to put pressure on its Shia rival of Iran to conform to Western demands. So far, it appears as if the furtive ultimatum is having the desired effect. Iran has been increasingly diplomatic and cordial to Western solicitations and has even done the inconceivable by collaborating with the United States, and its allies, in military planning and airstrikes against the Islamic State in Iraq and Syria.

Russia, however, is the primary target of recent American economic oil policy. The West is wary of putting boots on the ground in the Ukraine, or in the Caucasus (Georgia, Ossetia, Abkhazia, Armenia) six years before, to halt unabashed Russian militaristic imperialism unquestionably driven by Caucasus petroleum revenue and corresponding pipelines and shipping lanes. Alternatively, the Obama administration has opted for victorious suffocation by means of a prolonged economic oil war. After all, the successful sharp-spear of Anglo-American oil diplomacy, and continuation of action, was previously driven by President George W. Bush and British Prime Minister Tony Blair in the greater Middle East beginning in 2001, or, in reality, by President George H.W. Bush in 1990–1, as the Soviet superpower imploded.

Currently, nearly two-thirds of Russian exports come from energy, as well as half of the federal budget. In the past ten years, as Putin witnessed the threat of the rise in American petroleum output to the detriment of his new "Soviet empire," he has sought ways to aid a floundering Russian economy. He has appealed to nationalist rhetoric, which has taken him only so far. He has invaded sovereign nations such as Georgia and the Ukraine to further Russian energy outlets. He has manipulated Russian politics to promote his own power. Yet he is closer now to crisis than he could have realized. His oil-backed consumption-led economy saw an unprecedented fifteen years of growth, if not for a brief stumble in 2008–9. This revenue fed his appetite for energy outlets in Georgia and the Ukraine, which were met by sanctions from the Western world. His foreign adventurism has not served him well, and the fall in oil prices jeopardizes what should have been years of capital gains. He sought, as did Argentina in 1982 by starting the unwinnable Falklands War, to shore up support in the midst of an economic downturn and hyperinflation by appealing to jingoism. This patriotic fervour, however, can no longer boost living standards in a state fraught with an economic reality that Putin would either rather avoid or pretend does not exist.

Russia's central bank raised interest rates six times in 2014, reaching an astounding 17 per cent (going from 10.5 to 17 per cent in one day!). The $80 billion spent from its reserves, which are projected to last no more than a maximum of two years (as of April 2016), failed to halt a 53 per cent loss of value of the Russian rouble in 2014 – the world's worst-performing currency of 2014, and its worst slide since 1998. To make matters worse, 2014 saw the Russian GDP shrink for the first time since 2009. The draft budget for the Russian economy is

Table 11.2 Break-even oil prices per barrel, 2015 ($US)

Country	2015 projected break-even oil budgets (per barrel)
Iran (OPEC)	135
Bahrain	134
Ecuador (OPEC)	122
Venezuela (OPEC)	120
Algeria (OPEC)	119
Nigeria (OPEC)	118
Iraq (OPEC)	115
Libya (OPEC)	109
Russia	100
Angola (OPEC)	94
Saudi Arabia (OPEC)	92
Oman	85
Kuwait (OPEC)	71
Qatar (OPEC)	70
UAE (OPEC)	69
Canada	64
United States	60

Source: *Economist*, 25 October 2014, 63. $60/barrel is the magic number.

calculated on oil at $100 per barrel. Russia and its kleptocratic leader can probably weather the storm for another year to two, but reserves and money will eventually dry up. The military spending of the Putin regime, which has absorbed nearly 22 per cent of public spending over the past decade, now appears to be a fruitless extravagance. Projected oil prices and a decreased standard of living in Russia will render his military ventures foolhardy and a terrible mistake. Any partial block or increased sanctions by a coalition of the willing would immediately cripple the already reeling Russian economy, as they did Iran's. Correspondingly, increasing Russian foreign forays would incite more sanctions, and the nationalist card so long held by Putin and his cronies will be unplayable.

The increasing output of the United States and that of its staunch allies (Canada, Saudi Arabia, UAE, Kuwait, Brazil, and now recently Iraq and Mexico) has rendered the "axis of diesel" impotent, including Russia, which is on the brink of disaster, and has reincarnated the Anglo-American oil monopoly (the only outliers in the Top 12 are Russia, China, Iran, and Venezuela). This trump card, as witnessed, can outweigh military potency as an instrument of war if used with thoughtful strategic diplomacy:

So the economics of oil have changed. The market will still be subject to political shocks: war in the Middle East or the overdue implosion of Vladimir Putin's kleptocracy would send the price soaring. But, absent such an event, the oil price should be less vulnerable to shocks or manipulation. Even if the 3m extra b/d that the United States now pumps out is a tiny fraction of the 90m the world consumes, America's shale is a genuine rival to Saudi Arabia as the world's marginal producer. That should reduce the volatility not just of the oil price but also of the world economy. Oil and finance have proved themselves the only two industries able to tip the world into recession. At least one of them should in the future be a bit more stable.[2]

And with this statement comes stability in the global order created during and in the immediate years of the First World War. Oil continues to dominate the global economic balance of power, reasserted by the Anglo-American cartel through unrivalled potential U.S. output, and can be safely added to the arsenal of war-winning weapons within the First World Oil War.

Appendix

Petroleum Situation in the British Empire

Admiral Sir Edmond J.W. Slade, 29 July 1918

the national archives

Col. Dally Jones.

202

PETROLEUM SITUATION IN THE BRITISH EMPIRE.

12

Admiralty Memorandum for the Imperial War Cabinet.

T.5267

        The Admiralty desire to bring to the notice of
the Imperial War Cabinet the attached important and
instructive paper written by Admiral Sir Edmund Slade,
and in doing so they wish to endorse in the strongest
manner possible, the general principles and general
conclusions set forth therein.

        There are certain statements in this document
which are irrefutable and which the Admiralty look upon
as questions of primary policy and strategy. It cannot
be too emphatically stated that the holding in our hands
of the motive power of sea-borne traffic - coal - has
been one of the weapons which, for many a long year, has
proved of inestimable value in that Maintenance of sea
power on which the whole edifice of the Empire rests.
Never has this been more strikingly demonstrated than
during the last four years of War.

        The gradual substitution of Oil for Coal will
in the future, if the question is not immediately faced,
wrest from our grasp one of the principal factors on
which the maintenance of our Naval position depends.
The case as stated in the paper is sufficiently
alarming to make the question one for immediate decision
else we may find ourselves out-manoeuvred not only by
the enemy but by neutrals or even by our present Allies.

        It is understood that a discussion will shortly
take place on War Aims which must include the retention
or otherwise of Mesopotamia, and it is hoped that in
reviewing this question the extreme importance of that
country in regard to the Petroleum situation will not
be lost sight of.

                            (signed) R.E. WEMYSS.

30th July 1918.

Forwarded.

    (signed) ERIC GEDDES.

PAPER BY ADMIRAL SIR EDMOND SLADE ON THE
PETROLEUM SITUATION IN THE BRITISH EMPIRE.

There are two main points of view from which the study
of the Petroleum situation in the British Empire must be considered.
The first and most important is the strategic and the second is
that of supply. The two are to a great extent interdependent, but
the question of sufficiency of supply may be satisfied without the
strategic position, for which we ought to strive, being obtained.

During the war we have been able to maintain our control
of the shipping of the world through our control of bunker fuel
and whether bunker fuel of the future is to be oil or coal, it is
essential that we retain the command of it. If we lose it, half
our sea power is gone and our position may become a most precarious
one. It is no exaggeration to say that our life as an Empire is
largely dependent upon our ability to maintain the control of
bunker fuel.. As improved methods of using bunker fuel are adopted
and vessels are able to travel further for a given weight of fuel,
the problem becomes more difficult and it becomes more important to
us to find a solution that will enable us to retain the control.

Oil fuel used as a means of raising steam is about twice
as economical as coal and, used in an internal combustion engine,
about four times. Oil must therefore gradually take the place of
coal for all marine purposes and it is consequently of paramount
importance to us to obtain the undisputed control of the greatest
amount of Petroleum that we can. This control must be absolute
and there must be no foreign interests involved in it of any sort
or kind, otherwise we shall find these interests using every means
at their disposal, honestly or dishonestly, openly or secretly, to
hamper the development of British interests.

Also they might and probably would be guided in their
policy of development of oil territories by their private interests
and not by what is best in the national interest. For instance,
assuming they hold large producing wells (which means cheap
production) in say Mexico, they would neglect development of oil
fields in say Trinidad, Canada or Nigeria, if the wells in those
fields were of smaller calibre. It is quite conceivable that they
would adopt this policy even though the latter wells could be
worked remuneratively, although not at such a high rate of profit
as the former and notwithstanding it was in the national interest
that they should be developed.

It must be remembered that vast sums of money are involved.
At the present moment foreign interests are taking between 20 and
25 million sterling a year from this country out of the profits of
the oil business and they are not going to give up any part of
this large profit without a very determined struggle. If the
British Government can obtain the control of any source or sources
of supply that will provide a material proportion of the Petroleum
requirements of the Empire, then it is obvious that the predominence
now enjoyed by foreign oil corporations will be a thing of the past
and we shall be masters in our own house in all matters relating
to oil, which is not the case at present. Then and then only will
the strategic position be secured and we shall be able to look
forward with confidence to maintaining our hold over the sea
communications of the world in the event of another war breaking out.

The main sources of supply of the <u>United Kingdom</u> before
the war were :-

The United States	68.3%
Roumania	11.6%
Russia	7.7%
Netherlands Colonies	7.7%
Mexico	4.1%
Other Countries	6.5%

8.   204

Taking other parts of the Empire, India is mainly
supplied from Burmah, the Dutch East Indies, Persia and to a
minor extent from the United States. Australasia draws its
requirements from the United States and the Dutch East Indies.
Canada from her own fields and the United States. South Africa
from the United States and the Dutch East Indies.

In these remarks it is not proposed to consider individual products, but to confine them to the broad question of
Petroleum generally and the prospects of the fields being able
to continue the necessary supplies and to indicate where future
development should be sought for.

When we endeavour to estimate the capacity of the
various fields to supply our wants, it is of no use to take the
output of each country and conclude, if it is large, that we can
draw ample supplies from it. The figure we have to consider is
the exportable surplus, which is a totally different one and
which is in many cases an extremely disappointing one.

During the years immediately preceding the war, The
United States exported approximately 20% of its output. Roumania
50%, Russia 6%, Mexico 50% - the remainder being consumed in the
local markets, but only a small proportion of this exportable
surplus was delivered to the United Kingdom and the rest of the
British Empire. The following table shows the amounts in round
figures in tons for 1913.

	Total output	Exportable surplus.	Amount received by U.K.		
A.	33,150,000	7,120,000	16% of total or	1,100,000
ania	1,880,000	940,000	19%	-do-	330,000
ia	6,370,000	670,000	19%	-do-	130,000
co	3,400,000	1,740,000	4%	-do-	70,000
h	1,560,000		8%	-do-	125,000
dies.					

Canada takes approximately 9% and the remainder of the
British Empire about 5% of the United States total exportable
surplus. This is approximately a total of 3,100,000.

The effect of the war has been to change very consider-
ably the sources of supply, because both Russia and Roumania have
been cut off and, owing to enemy action, it has become necessary
to supply the Western Area from the United States and the Eastern
Area and most of the Mediterranean from the Dutch East Indies,
Burmah and Persia, thus dislocating existing arrangements for the
distribution of American and other oils.

This dislocation will probably cease to be so acute
soon after the war comes to an end and the causes which have
brought it about cease to operate. There are, however, other
conditions of a far more radical kind, which will not come to an
end with the war and which it is necessary to consider in order
to form some sort of an estimate of the Petroleum position of the
future.

The first and most important factor is the life of the
United States fields. The situation is causing a great deal of
anxiety in the States and the President of the Standard Oil Company
has made some very pessimistic statements on the subject. The
United States Senate ordered an enquiry into the Gasolene (motor
spirit) question and at the beginning of 1916 the Secretary of the
Interior presented his report in which it is stated that most of the
fields have reached and passed their prime and are now on the
downward grade. That this is so is shown by the statistics of
production which, notwithstanding the constant development which
is going on, shows a steady decline in some of the older fields.
He estimates that the reserves lie between 7,000 and 10,000
million barrels (42 American gallons) (900,000,000 and

205

3.

1,300,000,000 tons). Other estimates place the reserves between
10,000 and 25,000 million barrels (1,300,000,000 and 3,300,000,000
tons). The present consumption is at the rate of about 360
million barrels (50,000,000) a year including export, so that the
estimated reserves at the lowest figure will only last 20 to 25 years
and, as the yearly consumption rises, it will be proportionately
less. Exports are at the rate of 60,000,000 barrels (over 8,000,000
tons) a year and it is to be expected that these will be curtailed
as soon as conditions become serious. As is at present,
notwithstanding that the United States are eking out their
reserves by importing Mexican crude at the rate of 4 million tons
a year, the consumption is greater than the production and stocks
are being reduced. It is therefore safe to assume the United
States authorities will not sit still and see the Petroleum
resources of their country endangered, but that within a
measurable period, say 10 years, the amount of the Petroleum that
we shall be able to draw from the United States will be greatly
diminished if not entirely stopped. The following tables gives
the important figures

Estimated amount of exhaustion and reserves still available in

the United States oil fields.

Taken from the report to the Senate of the
Secretary of the Interior in 1916.

Field.	Estimated percentage of exhaustion.	Reserve in millions of barrels.
Appalachian	74	481
Lime-Indiana	93	31
Illinois	60	244
Mid Continent	50	1,874
North Texas	41	484
North West Louisiana	47	124
Gulf Coast	79	1,500
Colorado	79	6
Wyoming	5	540
California	34	2,345

The Russian fields are capable of further development,
but it is not to be expected that they will show a large increase
in the future. The production is not rising and in any
circumstances it is probable that the whole of the output will,
with the increase of industrial development in Russia, continue
to be absorbed in that country. It is also evident that the
efforts of the Central Empires must be to divert to their own
needs whatever exportable surplus there may be available in order
to make up for the loss of Petroleum from the failing Galician
fields.

The Roumanian fields have also apparently reached their
prime and the rate of production, even before the war, was
showing signs of diminution. Here Germany has imposed onerous
terms which they hope will secure the bulk of Roumanian Petroleum
for the German Empire. Whether the policy of the Central Empires
will be maintained or not, the claims of the local markets will
inevitably draw more and more Roumanian products to themselves
and decrease the surplus available for export over sea. No
increase of supply can therefore be expected from Roumania, quite
apart from any question of political control.

206

4.

In Mexico there is a very large field yet untouched.
American geologists estimate the Mexican Petroleum Company and its
subsidiary the Huastocs Petroleum Company have an undeveloped
supply in Tampico of 750,000,000 tons, the Mexican Eagle Company
430,000,000 tons, the Shell Company 130,000,000 tons, the other
Companies about 67,000,000. This represents a probable reserve of
between 2,000 and 3,000 million tons.

It is however highly probable that the greater part of
this supply will be taken   by the United States. At the present
moment she absorbs 75% of the exportable surplus and as Stocks in
the United States decrease and consumption increases, it is
almost certain she will take more. In considering Mexican figures
it must be remembered that a great part of the crude is of a very
low grade and only yields 60% of usable oil and therefore a
considerable reduction must be made on the gross figures.

The export of the Dutch East Indies to this country is
only 8% of their total production, the remainder being absorbed in
local markets and markets nearer the source of production. It is
therefore improbable that we can expect to obtain much relief
from there. The total production also is not large enough even if
the whole of it could be taken to provide more than a very small
proportion of all we want.

The Burmah fields are not capable of great expansion and in
any case Indian markets will probably absorb the greater part of
their production.

The present imports of Petroleum into the United Kingdom
is approximately 6,000,000 tons a year namely -

Fuel Oil	4,300,000 tons
Motor Spirit	750,000 "
Kerosine	600,000 "
Lubricating Oil	350,000 "
	6,000,000 tons

The consumption of Petroleum products in the United
Kingdom after the war may be estimated at very little less than our
present war requirements. Motor traction will far more general
than it used to be for two reasons :-

1. The large reduction in the number of horses available both for
   road and agricultural purposes.

2. The large number of motor vehicles of all kinds that will be
   put on the market by the State when the Army is demobilised.
   These will be sold at low prices and will be bought up by
   anybody who has need of transport, either for business or
   pleasure.

The consumption of fuel oil will be largely increased from
what it was before the war, owing to the number of vessels that
are being converted to burn oil in place of coal. The economy
of this fuel, when once it is experienced, will induce those
Companies who have been forced to adopt it now, to retain it after
the war if possible. The Naval demand will be greatly decreased,
but the saving on this account will be to a certain extent absorbed
by the requirements of the Mercantile Marine. Therefore we may
estimate the demand to be somewhere in the neighbourhood of 3/2
million tons a year which, with a million tons for building up
stocks of Naval fuel and 1/2 million tons for other products, will
give a total of 6 million tons a year to be provided in
round figures for the United Kingdom and for bunkers in the
Western area.

6.

In addition to this there are the requirements of the Dominions, Colonies and India. The latter, including Railways and bunkers may be placed at 1,500,000 tons to be provided from Burmah, Persia and Borneo. Australia, New Zealand, Ceylon, South and East Africa 2,000,000 tons including bunkers. Hong Kong, including bunkers 500,000 tons. This gives a total of 4,000,000 tons or a grand total for the Empire of 10,000,000 tons a year and in five to ten years time this may be expected to be largely increased.

It is obvious that the sources of supply from which we drew our requirements before the war will not be sufficient to give us this enormously increased amount and we must look to other sources from which it can be drawn.

It is here necessary to remark that we must also consider what other countries will require and what effect their competition for the limited available supplies will have on our policy.

The United States are building up a very large shipping trade: their demands for Fuel Oil and other Petroleum products will be much higher than it was and will increase the already enormous consumption in that country and hasten the time when exports will be seriously curtailed.

Germany is building a large mercantile marine and intends to compete with the Allies for the control of the carrying trade of the world. Motor traction in the interior will also largely increase for the same reasons as it will in the United Kingdom. The exportable surplus from Russia, Roumania and Galicia and the produce of her own wells are not sufficient to supply her demands and she must therefore compete for the exportable surplus of other countries.

Germany also realises from bitter experience the effect of our control of coal and she will hesitate at nothing that will prevent the control of liquid fuel from passing into our hands and will endeavour by every means in-her power to secure it for herself. She has already established a huge State monopoly Company by which the Government is to control the whole of the Petroleum policy of the Empire. What this policy will be need not be expatiated upon, but it will be followed ruthlessly and with the whole of the resources of the State behind it. The procedure may be expected to be much the same as that followed by the German Government in pressing and supporting German interests in their endeavour before the war to wrest the control of the freight market from Britain shipping firms.

In France, Italy and the rest of Europe the demands will be greater than they were before the war and except in Russia and Roumania, they have to be not almost entirely from outside sources.

It is therefore clear that competition will be most severe and that everything possible must be done to secure our position if we are not to be left behind in the struggle.

The undeveloped oil fields of the world which promise to give large supplies, so far as is at present known, lie in Persia, Mesopotamia, Venezuela, Colombia and Central America.

The Venezuela field is mainly held by the Royal Dutch and they state that it is going to be a very large one. So far it has only been partially proved, but there is no reason to doubt that it will be of considerable importance, but in peace time the oil produced from it would, for geographical reasons, be very largely absorbed in the United States and Central and South America.

6.

The Columbian and Central American fields are falling into the hands of American Companies and it may be considered that the whole of their resources will also be called upon to make good the deficit in the United States. In any case the exportable surplus from those fields and from Venezuela will not be large enough for some years to come and it is only reasonable to expect that it will be absorbed by neighbouring markets in Central and South America and in the United States and will not be available to any great extent for our requirements.

In Persia and Mesopotamia lie the largest undeveloped resources at present known in the world. An area has been proved and is now developed in Persia which will, at the end of this year or so soon as the necessary plant will have been delivered, be capable of supplying more than the whole of the Roumanian and Galician fields put together. There is besides another proved area on the borders of Persia and Mesopotamia which promises to be a very large field. Between these two areas are numerous fields and there is every reason to expect that the yield from them will be very large. There are also many known deposits of oil in other parts of Persia and Mesopotamia which will form reserves for the future, when they are once developed so as to bring them into bearing.

It is not too much to estimate that the oil lands of Persia and Mesopotamia which will extend over an area of 360,000 square miles, or more than twice the size of the oil lands of Russia, should not in the future provide a supply equal to that now given by the United States.

If this estimate is anywhere near the truth, then it is evident that the Power that controls the oil lands of Persia and Mesopotamia will control the source of supply of the majority of the liquid fuel of the future. If this control is combined with that of coal, then that Power will hold the control of bunker fuel and will be in a position to dictate its own terms to all shipping in case of war. We now hold that control through coal and it is absolutely essential for the national safety that we do not part with it nor share it with any foreign Power whatsoever. We must therefore at all costs retain our hold on the Persian and Mesopotamian oil fields and any other fields which may exist in the British Empire and we must not allow the intrusion in any form of any foreign interests, however much disguised they may be. We shall then be in a position of paramount control of the majority of all bunker fuel for many years to come and enjoy all the advantages that this will give us if we find ourselves forced into another war. These advantages are very great and we cannot expect to enjoy them without making some sacrifices for them and we must be prepared to defend our claim against everybody. Conventions and Treaties are only paper and can be torn up and are not sufficient safeguard. We must have absolute security in this matter. It we admit foreign interests at all, those interests even if apparently in a small and unimportant proportion now, will always be working against us and will in the future, when the lessons of this war are forgotten, gradually absorb the controlling situation because the chief end and aim of the foreign oil interests is World Monopoly. We have the object lesson of German penetration into the shipping and other commercial interests and we must not allow it to be repeated.

The monopoly in Germany previously referred to has been granted to a very powerful Petroleum Syndicate which has been formed under the auspices of the Deutsches Bank and the leadership of von Riedermann, Ballin and Stinnes. It has acquired the undertaking of the so called German American Petroleum Company and the recently acquired German interests in the Roumanian oil fields. The creation of this powerful Syndicate at the present time shows clearly that Germany recognises the great strategic importance of

7.

securing a dominating position in the control of oil supplies and that we must take prompt action if our oil position is to be safeguarded.

The interest that is most inimical to British control at the present time is the Royal Dutch Company which holds a controlling interest in one of the most important of the so called British Companies. This Company is in intimate relations with and trading with Germany so far as it can without danger of being black-listed and it will almost certainly re-open with the new Syndicate the negotiations, which were in progress before the war and which have since been suspended, for securing closer relations with German oil interests. One of the stipulations put forward by the Germans in connection with these negotiations was that the German Government should be given the right to nominate a director of the Royal Dutch Company with certain powers of control. German oil interests are now centered in the new Syndicate which is in effect a German Government monopoly and it is quite obvious that if Germany cannot obtain the coveted control directly as the result of a victorious war, she will endeavour to obtain it through peaceful penetration.

So far as the conduct of the war is concerned, the retention and development of the Persian oil lands is absolutely essential to the carrying on of the Mesopotamian expedition.

If they are interfered with in any way, the British Forces in the Middle East will have to retreat. The effect of such a contingency on our ... position in the East would nothing short of disastrous and might well lead to most serious complications in India. Besides this the whole of our oil policy would be destroyed and our control of the bunker fuel of the future would be rendered impossible. The present fuel position in the Mediterranean and Italy would be seriously jeopardised and industry in India would be greatly crippled.

Of other minor fields that are not yet developed, there is the Papuan, which promises to be able to supply a certain proportion of the Australian requirements. This must also be kept out of the hands of foreign interests.

The Nigerian and Gold Coast fields do not show any signs of being important producing areas at present, but the development should be pushed on as fast as possible by British interests.

New Brunswick is now being examined, but it is too early to give an opinion on it. The oil shale in this area may prove to be worth development for the supply of local markets.

The Argentine field is a promising one and is being steadily developed, but it is falling into the hands of German and Dutch interests who are said to have secured considerable rights in it.

The production in Japan is steadily increasing and is now in the neighbourhood of half a million tons a year. The Japanese have unfortunately secured an option on the oil lands in British North Borneo and they are busily engaged in prospecting in that region. It was a most injudicious action to have ever allowed them to come in. If there is a large reserve of oil there, it should have been retained for British requirements. If there is not, the Japanese will use the concession as a stepping stone to further undesirable action.

There is said to be oil in Portuguese West Africa, Timour, Madagascar, Algeria and a few other places, but so far as is at present known none of these deposits are likely to give large outputs.

210

8.

In conclusion the policy I would urge upon the
Admiralty is :-

1.　　　To press the Government to take the most energetic
measures to prevent the enemy in any way from endangering the oil
fields and works in Persia. This is indispensable to the success
of the war.

2.　　　To push forward as soon as possible the further
development of the oil lands of Persia and those in Mesopotamia
by purely British interests.

3.　　　To push forward the exploration and development of all
possible oil lands in the British Empire by purely British
interests.

4.　　　To encourage and assist British Companies to obtain control
of as much oil lands in foreign countries as possible, with the
stipulation (to prevent control being obtained by foreign interests)
that the oil produced shall only be sold to or through British oil
distributing Companies. These oil lands can be developed to assist
to provide our requirements in peace whilst our own resources in
British territory can be conserved for war.

5.　　　To exclude from participation in British Petroleum
business all foreign interests in any shape or form, such
participation being only a stepping stone to ultimate control and
a very great danger in any future war.

                    (signed) E. J. W. SLADE.

                              29.7.18.

211

PRODUCTION OF PETROLEUM FROM THE PRINCIPAL COUNTRIES SINCE 1900.
TONS

	ROUMANIA.	UNITED STATES.	RUSSIA.	GALICIA.	DUTCH E. INDIES.	MEXICO.
1900	217,000	8,475,000	10,105,000	311,000	300,000	73,000
1901	223,000	9,245,000	10,155,000	435,000	554,000	48,000
1902	274,000	11,810,000	10,750,000	549,000	631,800	
1903	362,500	12,880,000	10,420,000	698,000	725,000	166,000
1904	480,000	15,280,000		733,000	968,000	200,000
1905	589,000	17,970,000	7,560,000	718,000	1,046,000	257,000
1906	850,000	18,250,000	8,200,000	1,125,000	1,090,000	573,000
1907	1,080,000	23,160,000	8,720,000	790,000	1,371,000	504,000
1908	1,100,000	24,410,000	8,775,000	665,000	1,473,000	
1909	1,242,000	25,640,000	9,075,000	684,000	1,470,000	2,105,000
1910	1,294,000	27,940,000	8,830,000	1,404,000	1,620,000	
1911	1,435,000	29,700,000	8,378,000	1,041,000	1,448,000	3,512,000
1912	1,730,000	33,126,000	8,110,000	672,000	1,800,000	3,810,000
1913	1,808,000	35,280,000	9,160,000	554,000	1,646,000	
1914	1,710,000	37,380,000		863,000	1,651,000	4,936,000
1915	1,648,000	41,000,000			1,766,000	6,645,000
1916	1,571,000					

212

UNITED STATES PRODUCTION IN TONS
BASED ON RETURNS OF THE UNITED STATES GEOLOGICAL SURVEY.
UNLESS TAKEN 1 BARREL = 42 GALLONS AMERICAN CRUDE 300 AMERICA GALLONS = 1 TON
7.5 = 1 TON REFINED PRODUCTS 315

YEAR	PRODUCTION	CRUDE IMPORT	CRUDE EXPORT	NETT EXPORTS	CRUDE STOCK ON 31. DEC.	ESTIMATED THROUGHPUT	LOSS ON REFINING	EXPORT OF REFINED PRODUCTS	ESTIMATED CONSUMPTION IN U.S.
1.	2.	3.	4.	5.	6.	7.	8.	9.	
1905	17,970,000	16,000	538,000	572,000	18,300,000				
1906	16,860,000	822,000	630,000	187,000	16,390,000				
1907	22,580,000	787,000	620,000	167,000	18,320,000				
1908	23,410,000		400,000		18,820,000				
1909	24,410,000								
1910	27,640,000								
1911	28,400,000					31,786,000	3,179,000	5,341,000	25,266,000
1912	29,700,000					35,955,000	3,595,000	8,145,000	33,873,000
1913	33,128,000	3,556,000	526,000	3,156,000	25,746,000	35,748,000	3,274,000	8,270,000	34,819,000
1914	35,450,000	3,380,000	573,000	2,161,000	35,200,000	33,743,000	3,613,000	8,838,000	21,416,000
1915	37,480,000	3,043,000	571,000	2,442,000	30,260,000	43,462,000	4,613,000	7,738,000	23,323,000
1916	40,100,000	4,400,000		3,829,000		52,226,000	5,223,000	7,900,000	33,192,000
1917	45,557,000								

The estimated throughput is computed from columns 3, 4, 5, and 6.

The estimated internal consumption is computed from columns 7, 8, and 9.

@ The fall in consumption is probably due to some manipulation of the stocks, the explanation of which is not evident on the face of the returns.

Notes

Introduction

1 J.R.R. Tolkien, *The Lord of the Rings* (New York: HarperCollins, 1995), 614.

2 See, Neil Hanson, *Unknown Soldiers: The Story of the Missing of the First World War* (New York: Vintage, 2007).

3 Karen Armstrong, *Fields of Blood: Religion and the History of Violence* (New York: Alfred A. Knopf, 2014), 300–1.

4 Both the French and Germans used non-lethal and relatively benign tear-gas agents as early as October 1914.

5 See Charles Harington, *Plumer of Messines* (London: J. Murray, 1935).

6 Niall Ferguson, *The Pity of War: Explaining World War I* (London: Penguin, 1998), 260; Daniel Yergin, *The Prize: The Epic Quest for Oil, Money and Power* (New York: Free Press, 2008), 155–6; Gerd Hardach, *The First World War 1914–1918* (New York: Penguin Books, 1987), 87. The Germans produced only twenty tanks (the bulky thirty-three-ton A7V with a crew of eighteen), and by the end of the war only had 23,000 operational transport vehicles and 2,270 aircraft. The French entered the war with 110 trucks and 132 airplanes. The Americans brought over 105,000 trucks and 4,000 planes.

7 Hew Strachan, *The First World War* (Oxford: Oxford University Press, 2001), 1:1087–8.

8 Martin Van Creveld, *The Transformation of War* (New York: Free Press, 1991), 101.

9 Ibid., 101–6.

10 F. William Engdahl, *A Century of War: Anglo-American Oil Politics and the New World Order* (Wiesbaden: edition.engdahl, 2011), 47.

11 National Archives, UK (hereafter NA), ADM 1/8537/240, "Oil Situation, 1916."

12 Valerie Marcel, *Oil Titans: National Oil Companies in the Middle East* (London: Chatham House, 2006), 16.

13 Eugene Rogan, *The Fall of the Ottomans: The Great War in the Middle East* (New York: Basic, 2015), xvii.

14 Helmut Mejcher, "British Middle East Policy 1917–1921: The Inter-Departmental Level," *Journal of Contemporary History* 8, no. 4 (1973): 81; V.H. Rothwell, "Mesopotamia in British War Aims, 1914–1918," *Historical Journal* 13, no. 2 (1970): 275.

15 Peter L. Hahn, *Missions Accomplished?: The United States and Iraq since World War I* (Oxford: Oxford University Press, 2011), 14.

16 Armstrong, *Fields of Blood*, 306–7.

17 Sean McMeekin, *The Berlin-Baghdad Express: The Ottoman Empire and Germany's Bid for World Power* (Toronto: Penguin, 2011), 6.

18 Philip Jenkins, *The Great and Holy War: How World War I Became a Religious Crusade* (New York: HarperCollins, 2014), 25.

19 Sarah Shields, "Mosul Questions: Economy, Identity, and Annexation," in Simon and Tejirian, *Creation of Iraq*, 54.

20 S.A. Cohen, "The Genesis of the British Campaign in Mesopotamia, 1914," *Middle Eastern Studies* 12, no. 2 (1976): 119–32; F.J. Moberly, *The Campaign in Mesopotamia, 1914–1918* (London: HMSO, 1927), 4:ii.

21 Priya Satia, *Spies in Arabia: The Great War and the Cultural Foundations of Britain's Covert Empire in the Middle East* (Oxford: Oxford University Press, 2008), 14.

22 Peter Hopkirk, *On Secret Service East of Constantinople: The Plot to Bring Down the British Empire* (London: John Murray, 1994), 6.

23 Ibid., 6–7.

24 Engdahl, *Century of War*.

25 Brock Millman, "A Counsel of Despair: British Strategy and War Aims, 1917–1918," *Journal of Contemporary History* 36, no. 2 (2001): 242.

26 Artin H. Arslanian, "Britain and the Transcaucasian Nationalities during the Russian Civil War," *Kennan Institute for Advanced Russian Studies Occasional Paper*, Wilson Center, 1980), 7.

27 David Fromkin, *A Peace to End All Peace: The Fall of the Ottoman Empire and the Creation of the Middle East* (New York: Henry Holt, 1989), 257.

28 Fiona Venn, "Oleaginous Diplomacy: Oil, Anglo-American Relations and the Lausanne Conference, 1922–1923," *Diplomacy & Statecraft* 2 (2009): 414.

29 Francis Delaisi, *Oil: Its Influence on Politics* (London: George Allen & Unwin, 1920), 3, 17.

30 John Keegan, *The First World War* (Toronto: Vintage, 2000), 308.

31 Richard Overy, *Why the Allies Won* (New York: W.W. Norton, 1996), 231.

32 Ibid., 231–4. While occupying Maikop, the Germans gained a mere seventy barrels of oil a day.

33 Daniel Yergin, *The Quest: Energy, Security, and the Remaking of the Modern World* (New York: Penguin, 2011), 51, 231; Overy, *Why the Allies Won*, 228–33.

34 Arnold Krammer, "Fueling the Third Reich," *Technology & Culture* 19, no. 3 (1978): 394–422.

35 Overy, *Why the Allies Won*, 233.

36 Ibid., 232–4.

37 See Lutz Kleveman, *The New Great Game: Blood and Oil in Central Asia* (New York: Atlantic Monthly, 2003); Elkhan Nuriyev, *The South Caucasus at the Crossroads: Conflicts, Caspian Oil and Great Power Politics* (Berlin: Lit Verlag, 2007).

38 Michael Eisenstadt and Eric Mathewson, *U.S. Policy in Post-Saddam Iraq: Lessons from the British Experience* (Washington DC: Washington Institute for Near East Policy, 2003), 90.

39 Rogan, *Fall of the Ottomans*, 325.

40 Robert Fisk, *The Great War for Civilization: The Conquest of the Middle East* (New York: Harper, 2006), 175–6.

41 The forum for Arctic discussion is the Arctic Council made up of three tiers –Member voting nations: Canada, Denmark, Finland, Iceland, Norway, Sweden, Russia, and the United States; observer non-voting nations: China, France, Germany, India, Italy, Japan, Netherlands, Poland, Singapore, Spain, South Korea, and the United Kingdom; permanent non-voting participants: Arctic Athabaskan Council, Aleut International Association, Gwich'in Council International, Inuit Circumpolar Council, Russian Association of Indigenous Peoples of the North, and the Saami Council.

42 Fromkin, *Peace to End All Peace*, 262.

43 David Reynolds, *The Long Shadow: The Legacies of the Great War in the Twentieth Century* (New York: W.W. Norton, 2014), xviii.

44 The common figure of 620,000 dead during the Civil War is outdated. Recent estimates place the fatalities between 750,000 and 800,000. Of these deaths, roughly 65 per cent were caused by disease rather than combat.

45 Moberly, *History of the Great War*, 4:i, 331.

46 Raymond Aron, *The Century of Total War* (Boston: Beacon, 1955), 72.

47 James W. Blinn, *The Aardvark Is Ready for War: A Novel* (San Diego: San Diego State University Press, 1995).

48 The eight nuclear-weapons-states are: the United States, France, the United Kingdom, China, Russia, India, Pakistan, and Israel. North Korea remains an unknown, although they conducted nuclear testing as early as 2006.

1 Oil and the Great Game

1 Hopkirk, *On Secret Service East of Constantinople*, 22.
2 Ibid., 23.
3 McMeekin, *Berlin-Baghdad Express*, 13–14.
4 Ibid., 15–16.
5 Hew Strachan, *The First World War* (New York: Viking, 2004), 99, 104; Jenkins, *Great and Holy War*, 336.
6 McMeekin, *Berlin-Baghdad Express*, 16.
7 On Wilhelm's life, personality, and relationship with George and Nicholas, see Miranda Carter, *George, Nicholas and Wilhelm: Three Royal Cousins and the Road to World War I* (New York: Vintage, 2011). George and Wilhelm were Queen Victoria's grandchildren, and Nicholas was her grandchild-in-law. George's father was Edward VII (Victoria's son), and Wilhelm II was Princess Victoria's son (Queen Victoria's daughter who married the German emperor). George was first cousins with both Wilhelm and Nicholas, but Wilhelm and Nicholas were not first cousins with each other. Wilhelm was first cousins with the wife of Tsar Nicholas.
8 Hopkirk, *On Secret Service East of Constantinople*, 17.
9 Fromkin, *Peace to End All Peace*, 27. In 1841 in Bukhara, an Uzbek emir, cast Conolly for two months into a well filled with reptiles and insects. What was left of him was brought up and beheaded.
10 R.W. Ferrier, *The History of the British Petroleum Company* (Cambridge: Cambridge University Press, 1982), 2:22, 25.
11 Hahn, *Missions Accomplished?*, 17.
12 John A. DeNovo, *American Interests and Policies in the Middle East, 1900–1939* (Minneapolis: University of Minnesota Press, 1963), 38–9.
13 Evidence in both China and India date the earliest sedentary, agrarian cultures between 5,000 and 3,000 BCE. The rise of dynastic Egypt occurred in approximately 3,200 BCE, while Proto-Inca in Peru, known as the Norte Chico civilization, established interconnecting settlements at roughly the same time.
14 Firuz Kazemzadeh, *The Struggle for Transcaucasia, 1917–1921* (Oxford: George Ronald, 1951), 4–5.
15 See Patrick Balfour Kinross, *The Ottoman Centuries: The Rise and Fall of the Turkish Empire* (New York: Harper, 1979); Caroline Finkel, *Osman's*

Dream: The History of the Ottoman Empire (New York: Basic Books, 2007); Donald Quataert, *The Ottoman Empire 1700–1922* (Cambridge: Cambridge University Press, 2000).

16 The argument dates back to the death in 632 of Islam's founder, the Prophet Muhammad. Those who followed him were split over who should inherit what was both a political and a religious office. The majority, who became Sunnis, and today make up 80 per cent of Muslims, backed Abu Bakr, the father of Muhammad's wife Aisha. Others thought Muhammad's kin were the rightful successors. They claimed Muhammad had chosen Ali, his cousin and son-in-law. This group became the Shi'ites or Shia. The split in the sects of Islam was cemented in 680 when Ali's son Hussein was killed by Sunni zealots. Sunni rulers continued to dominate political and religious arenas. Over time the religious beliefs of the two groups started to diverge.

17 Fromkin, *Peace to End All Peace*, 34–5.

18 Margaret MacMillan, *The War That Ended Peace: The Road to 1914* (New York: Random House, 2013), 43, 165.

19 See Justin McCarthy, *Death and Exile: The Ethnic Cleansing of Ottoman Muslims, 1821–1922* (Princeton: Darwin, 1996); Cathie Carmichael, *Ethnic Cleansing in the Balkans: Nationalism and the Destruction of Tradition* (New York: Routledge, 2002); Misha Glenny, *The Balkans: Nationalism, War and the Great Powers, 1804–1999* (London: Granta Books, 1999).

20 See Feroz Ahmed, *Young Turks: The Committee of Union and Progress in Turkish Politics, 1908–1914* (London: Hurst, 2009); M. Şükrü Hanioğlu, *Preparation for a Revolution: The Young Turks, 1902–1908* (Oxford: Oxford University Press, 2001); Erik J. Zurcher, *The Young Turk Legacy and Nation Building: From the Ottoman Empire to Ataturk's Turkey* (London: I.B. Taurus, 2010).

21 Muzaffer Erendil, "The Ottoman Empire in World War I: The Home Front and Military Affairs," in *War and Society in Central Europe*, ed. Bela K. Kiraly and Nandor F. Dreisziger (New York: Columbia University Press, 1985), 19:369–370.

22 Fromkin, *Peace to End All Peace*, 35.

23 Donald M. McKale, "Germany and the Arab Question before World War I," *Historian* 59, no. 2 (1997): 311–13.

24 "Press Article," 4 December 1914, *British Documents on Foreign Affairs*, pt 2, series H, *The First World War, 1914–1918* (New York: University Publications of America, 1985), 4:417.

25 Joseph Heller, *British Policy towards the Ottoman Empire, 1908–1914* (London: Frank Cass, 1983), 91.

26 Hopkirk, *On Secret Service East of Constantinople*, 27.
27 McMeekin, *Berlin-Baghdad Express*, 42.
28 Fromkin, *Peace to End All Peace*, 25.
29 Heller, *British Policy towards the Ottoman Empire*, 90.
30 *British Documents on Foreign Affairs: Reports and papers from the Foreign Office Confidential Print*, part 1, series B (New York: University Publications of America, 1985), 17:215–427.
31 For the intricacies of the construction of the Berlin-Baghdad Railway, see McMeekin, *Berlin-Baghdad Express*, chap. 2.
32 Engdahl, *Century of War*, 49.
33 Relative in the sense the Crimean War (1853–6), the Franco-Prussian War (1870–1) and the Balkan Wars (1812–13) never became general European wars.
34 Tim Cook, *At the Sharp End: Canadians Fighting the Great War* (Toronto: Penguin, 2007), 1:10.
35 D.C.M. Platt, "Economic Factors in British Policy during the "New Imperialism,'" *Past & Present* 39 (1968): 127–8.
36 See Wm Roger Louis, *Great Britain and Germany's Lost Colonies, 1914–1919* (Oxford: Clarendon, 1967).
37 Hopkirk, *On Secret Service East of Constantinople*, 12.
38 Fromkin, *Peace to End All Peace*, 30.
39 McMeekin, *Berlin-Baghdad Express*, 36.
40 Fromkin, *Peace to End All Peace*, 31.
41 This arrangement was made official under the 1915 Constantinople Agreement, whereby Russia agreed to recognize British authority in Persia in exchange for sole jurisdiction over the Dardanelles, the Bosporus, and Constantinople in the event of victory. Obviously, the Russian Revolution unhinged this agreement.
42 MacMillan, *War That Ended Peace*, 48.
43 McKale, "Germany and the Arab Question before World War I," 316.
44 Italy joined the alliance in 1882 but was always viewed with suspicion by all European powers, including Germany. When war broke out, Italy refused to go to war, claiming the alliance was defensive in nature and that Germany was the aggressor. After a period of waffling, indecision, and negotiations, Italy joined the Allies in May 1915.
45 Strachan, *First World War*, 103.
46 Fromkin, *Peace to End All Peace*, 49.
47 For a detailed account of the Ottoman quest for an ally and entry into the war see Strachan, *First World War*, vol. 1: *To Arms*, chap. 8.
48 Fromkin, *Peace to End All Peace*, 48.

49 Ibid., 54–76.

50 In addition, the Bank of England had refunded the Ottoman down payment on these ships on 7 August, and promised delivery after the war, while paying for any repairs or in the event of loss full value, in addition to weekly "loan installments" from the date of seizure! Of course, this was all censored from the Turkish public and press.

52 Charles King, *The Ghosts of Freedom: A History of the Caucasus* (Oxford: Oxford University Press, 2008), 3, 8–9.

53 Michael Occleshaw, *Dances in Deep Shadows: The Clandestine War in Russia, 1917–1920* (New York: Carroll & Graf, 2006), 253.

54 Hopkirk, *On Secret Service East of Constantinople*, 259.

55 Strachan, *First World War*, 1:713–14.

56 King, *Ghosts of Freedom*, 6.

57 Yergin, *Quest*, 44.

58 King, *Ghosts of Freedom*, 3, 7–13.

59 Ibid., 19.

60 Alan Clark, *The Donkeys: A History of the British Expeditionary Force in 1915* (London: Hutchinson, 1961).

61 David Lloyd George, *War Memoirs* (London: Ivor Nicholson & Watson, 1936), 6:3197. Keep in mind that Lloyd George (and Churchill) portrayed themselves in their post-war writings as hostages to stubborn and unimaginable generals who did not see that there was a cheaper way of winning the war by knocking away Germany's props (allies) rather than a series of futile frontal assaults against the Germans in France and Flanders with devastating casualties.

62 Library and Archives Canada (LAC), MG30, E192, LCol J.W. Warden File-Diary 1918–1919.

63 Edmund Candler, *The Long Road to Baghdad* (London: Cassell, 1919), 2:286.

64 These refer to ethnic groups that were at this time seldom associated with an actual country of the same name. They were part of the Ottoman or Russian Empires or undefined border regions within the Middle East.

65 Roy MacLaren, *Canadian in Russia, 1918–1919* (Toronto: Maclean Hunter, 1976), 14–24; Michael Kettle, *The Road to Intervention; March–November 1918* (London: Routledge, 1988), 205, 217, 296–9; John Silverlight, *The Victor's Dilemma: Allied Intervention in the Russian Civil War* (London: Barrie & Jenkins, 1970), 95–9. The Germans had secretly negotiated contracts with local representatives for cotton, manganese, and oil. General Erich von Ludendorff flatly stated on 9 June 1918 that any attempt by the Turks to occupy Baku would be regarded as an act of open hostility.

66 Lloyd George, *War Memoirs*, 6:1908–9.

67 Alan Bodger, "Russia and the End of the Ottoman Empire," in *The Great Powers and the End of the Ottoman Empire*, ed. Marian Kent (London: Allen & Unwin, 1984), 83–4.
68 Alex Marshall, *The Caucasus under Soviet Rule* (London: Routledge, 2010), 91.
69 Lloyd George, *War Memoirs*, 2:1888.
70 Strachan, *First World War*, 101.
71 Fritz Fischer, *Germany's Aims in the First World War* (New York: W.W. Norton, 1967), 126.
72 John Buchan, *Greenmantle* (New York: Penguin Classic Reprint, 2008), 7, 9.
73 David French, *British Strategy & War Aims 1914–1916* (London: Allen & Unwin, 1986), 33.
74 John Fisher, *Curzon and British Imperialism in the Middle East, 1916–1919* (London: Frank Cass, 1999), 276.

2 Petroleum and Pipeline Politics

1 Charles Townshend, *When God Made Hell: The British Invasion of Mesopotamia and the Creation of Iraq, 1914–1921* (London: Faber and Faber, 2011), 9–10. Young became a political officer in Mesopotamia during the war, winning the Distinguished Service Order (DSO) in 1918. In 1932, he was appointed the first minister of Baghdad. He went on to become the governor of Nyasaland/Malawi, Northern Rhodesia, and Trinidad and Tobago. He was knighted in 1934. He wrote of his experiences in a travelogue/book, *The Independent Arab*.
2 The Anglo-Persian Oil Company began as the First Exploration Company in 1903, adopting the name Anglo-Persian in 1909, which became the Anglo-Iranian Oil Company in 1935, which in 1954 became the British Petroleum Company or BP. BP is the third-largest energy company and the fourth-largest overall in the world measured by revenues. It has operations in over eighty countries.
3 Geoffrey Jones, *The State and the Emergence of the British Oil Industry* (London: Macmillan, 1981), 12.
4 Winston Churchill, *The World Crisis, 1911–1918* (New York: First Free Press, 2005), 75–6. Further support for the conversion to oil was Welsh coal-mining strikes and labour unrest.
5 Although friends, by 1912 Fisher's relationship with Churchill had soured. Fisher resigned as First Sea Lord in May 1915 amidst bitter arguments with Churchill over the Gallipoli campaign, to which Fisher was adamantly opposed.

6 Matthew S. Seligmann, *The Royal Navy and the German Threat 1901–1914: Admiralty Plans to Protect British Trade in a War against Germany* (Oxford: Oxford University Press, 2012), 4–6.

7 MacMillan, *War That Ended Peace*, 119.

8 Fromkin, *Peace to End All Peace*, 54–61.

9 Ferguson, *Pity of War*, 106.

10 Engdahl, *Century of War*, 17–18. In 1882 German agriculture had some twenty thousand machines.

11 Briton Cooper Busch, *Britain and the Persian Gulf, 1894–1914* (Berkeley: University of California Press, 1967), appendix G.

12 Marian Kent, *Moguls and Mandarins: Oil, Imperialism and the Middle East in British Foreign Policy, 1900–1940* (London: Frank Cass, 1993), 11–13.

13 MacMillan, *War That Ended Peace*, 113–14. After the war, Childers joined the Irish rebels and was executed by firing squad. His son became president of Ireland in 1973.

14 Nicholas A. Lambert, *Planning Armageddon: British Economic Warfare and the First World War* (Cambridge, MA: Harvard University Press, 2012), 21–2.

15 Jones, *State and the Emergence of the British Oil Industry*, 27.

16 David Jablonsky, *Churchill, the Great Game and Total War* (London: Frank Cass, 1991), 46.

17 Christopher M. Bell, *Churchill and Sea Power* (Oxford: Oxford University Press, 2012), 1–2, 11–12.

18 Fiona Venn, *Oil Diplomacy in the Twentieth Century* (New York: St Martin's, 1986), 3.

19 Jones, *State and the Emergence of the British Oil Industry*, 4.

20 The *Nevada* was hit six times at Pearl Harbour, with 60 killed and 109 wounded. After drastic refurbishment the ship participated in the Aleutian Islands campaign in May 1943, and then during the D-Day Normandy landings it fired at targets on the Cherbourg Peninsula. After supporting the landing in southern France, the *Nevada* was transferred to the Pacific theatre and took part in the battles of Iwo Jima and Okinawa. She was decommissioned in 1946 and was used for target practice and sunk at Pearl Harbour in 1948.

21 Jon Tetsuro Sumida, *In Defence of Naval Supremacy: Finance, Technology and British Naval Policy, 1889–1914* (Boston: Unwin Hyman, 1989), 260–1.

22 Yergin, *Prize*, 139–40. Also see Anton Mohr, *The Oil War* (New York: Harcourt Brace, 1926).

23 The *Queen Elizabeth* was launched at Portsmouth in October 1913 and became the flagship during the Gallipoli campaign, and also for Sir Ian Hamilton, commander of the British Mediterranean Expeditionary Force.

24 Marian Jack, "The Purchase of the British Government's Shares in the British Petroleum Company 1912–1914," *Past & Present* 39 (1968): 147–9.

25 Matthew S. Seligmann, *Spies in Uniform: British Military and Naval Intelligence on the Eve of the First World War* (Oxford: Oxford University Press, 2006), 132.

26 Sumida, *In Defence of Naval Supremacy*, 260–1.

27 NA, CAB/24/59, Petroleum Situation in the British Empire, 29 July 1918; Mohr, *Oil War*, 121.

28 Jablonsky, *Churchill, the Great Game and Total War*, 47.

29 Charles van der Leeuw, *Oil and Gas in the Caucasus & Caspian: A History* (New York: St Martin's, 2000), 27–8; Gary May, *Hard Oiler!: The Story of Canadians" Quest for Oil at Home and Abroad* (Toronto: Dundurn, 1998), 18–19. Petroleum is derived from the Latin/Greek words *petra* ("rock") and *oleum* ("oil").

30 Between 1862 and 1892, various types and improvements were made to the internal combustion engine by men with now familiar last names: Daimler, Benz, and Diesel.

31 The Supreme Court also ordered the American Tobacco Company to dissolve on the same day that it ordered the dissolution of Standard Oil.

32 May, *Hard Oiler!*, 30–5. Also see Ida Minerva Tarbell, *The History of the Standard Oil Company*, originally published in 1904, listed as no. 5 in a 1999 list by New York University of the top 100 works of twentieth-century American journalism.

33 Christopher Clark, *The Sleepwalkers: How Europe Went to War in 1914* (New York: HarperCollins, 2013), 316.

34 Maurice Pearton, *Oil and the Romanian State* (Oxford: Clarendon, 1971), 30, 36.

35 Townshend, *When God Made Hell*, 4–6.

36 NA, CAB/24/59, Petroleum Situation in the British Empire, 29 July 1918; R.W. Ferrier, *The History of the British Petroleum Company* (Cambridge: Cambridge University Press, 1982), 1:18–19.

37 Van der Leeuw, *Oil and Gas in the Caucasus & Caspian*, 34.

38 The Treaty of Gulistan confirmed inclusion of modern-day Azerbaijan, including Baku, Dagestan, and Eastern Georgia into the Russian Empire.

39 One or two men would be lowered into these narrow pits, between twenty-five and fifty feet deep, to fill buckets with oil that was raised by primitive pulley systems.

40 Pearton, *Oil and the Romanian State*, 8.

41 John P. McKay, "Baku Oil and Transcaucasian Pipelines, 1883–1891: A Study in Tsarist Economic Policy," *Slavic Review* 43, no. 4 (1984): 606–7. A second pipeline was completed by the Russian government in 1906.

42 Thomas de Waal, *The Caucasus: An Introduction* (Oxford: Oxford Univeristy Press, 2010), 49.

43 Yergin, *Prize*, 41–6.

44 Van der Leeuw, *Oil and Gas in the Caucasus & Caspian*, 17–18; Nuriyev, *South Caucasus at the Crossroads*, 32–4.

45 King, *Ghosts of Freedom*, 150–2.

46 *British Documents on Foreign Affairs, Part II, Series B,* "Memorandum: Transcaucasia," 24 December 1919, 1:355–63; "Report on the Grozny Crude Oil Industry," 7 November 1918, 1:409–412; Strachan, *First World War*, 1:714.

47 Yergin, *Quest*, 50–1.

48 Kent, *Moguls and Mandarins*, 89. The bank limped on during the interwar period, finally closing its doors in 1931.

49 Jack, "Purchase of the British Government's Shares," 153–7.

50 Ibid, 153–7.

51 Ferrier, *History of the British Petroleum Company*, 177.

52 Anthony Sampson, *The Seven Sisters: The Great Oil Companies and the World They Made* (London: Hodder and Stoughton, 1975), 43.

53 Churchill as quoted in NA, CAB/24/59, Petroleum Situation in the British Empire, 29 July 1918.

54 Aron, *Century of Total War*, 59.

55 Peter Sluglett, *Britain in Iraq, 1914–1932* (London: Ithaca, 1976), 104–5.

56 *British Documents on Foreign Affairs, Part II, Series H, The First World War, 1914–1918,* "Turkish Petroleum Concessions," 19 March 1914, 3:379–80.

57 Clark, *Sleepwalkers*, 338.

58 Jack, "Purchase of the British Government's Shares," 145, 154, 160–6. Payment of rebates began in 1918. For 1918–19 the rebate was 3s. 6d. per ton, and by 1920–1921 rose to the set maximum of 10s. per ton (one-third of the set price).

59 Leonardo Maugeri, *The Age of Oil: The Mythology, History, and the Future of the World's Most Controversial Resource* (London: Praeger, 2006), 24.

60 Ferrier, *History of the British Petroleum Company*, 201.

61 Cohen, "Genesis of the British Campaign in Mesopotamia, 1914," 122; Townshend, *When God Made Hell*, 37–8.

62 Roger Ford, *Eden to Armageddon: World War I in the Middle East* (London: Weidenfeld and Nicolson, 2009), 23–4. At the outbreak of war, there were only 17,000 Turkish soldiers in all of Mesopotamia. During the opening battles of the campaign, the British consistently over-estimated Turkish strengths.

63 A.J. Barker, *The First Iraq War, 1914–1918: Britain's Mesopotamian Campaign* (New York: Enigma Books, 2009), xi, 21. This book was originally

released in 1967 in the United States as *The Bastard War: The Mesopotamian Campaign of 1914–1918*, and in the United Kingdom as *The Neglected War: Mesopotamia, 1914–1918*.

64 Cohen, "Genesis of the British Campaign in Mesopotamia, 1914," 122–3.

65 Townshend, *When God Made Hell*, 33.

66 Rogan, *Fall of the Ottomans*, 86.

67 Ford, *Eden to Armageddon*, 28.

68 Townshend, *When God Made Hell*, 93.

69 Ibid., 37–8. Cox had been the British political resident in Persia from 1904 to 1914. Cox, a tireless worker, was extremely familiar with the history and people of Persia, and provided valuable British influence in the area during his tenure.

70 Hahn, *Missions Accomplished?*, 11.

71 *British Documents on Foreign Affairs, Part II, Series H, The First World War, 1914–1918*, "Memorandum Respecting Oil Concessions in Mesopotamia," 27 April 1918, 3:373–81.

72 Strachan, *First World War*, 1:718.

73 Edmund Candler, *On the Edge of the World* (London: Cassell, 1919), 192–4.

74 May, *Hard Oilers!*, 175.

75 Donald M. McKale, *War by Revolution: Germany and Great Britain in the Middle East in the Era of World War I* (Kent, OH: Kent State University Press, 1998), 82–5, 131–3.

76 Fromkin, *Peace to End All Peace*, 351.

3 The Last Crusade in the Middle East

1 Keegan, *First World War*, 257.

2 Erich Maria Remarque, *All Quiet on the Western Front* (New York: Fawcett Crest, 1982), 134–5.

3 Philip J. Haythornthwaite, *The World War One Source Book* (London: Brockhampton, 1992), 107.

4 Denis Winter, *Haig's Command: A Reassessment* (London: Penguin Books, 1999), 214–15. Although the Americans had two Armies totalling over a million men in Europe under General John Pershing by the summer of 1918, unlike their allies, they had not had the benefit of almost four years of experience and learning in trench warfare.

5 LAC, MG30E100, vol. 38, file 170, Ludendorff: Captured Document, 4 August 1918.

6 Millman, "Counsel of Despair," 247.

7 The net gain of the *Westheer* between November 1917 and March 1918 has been the subject of much debate. See John Hussey, "Debate: The

Movement of German Divisions to the Western Front, Winter 1917–1918,"
War in History 4, no. 2 (1997): 213–20; Tim Travers, "Debate: Reply to John
Hussey: The Movement of German Divisions to the Western Front, Winter
1917–1918," *War in History* 5, no. 3 (1998): 367–70; Giordan Fong, "Debate:
The Movement of German Divisions to the Western Front, Winter 1917–.
1918," *War in History* 7, no. 2 (2000): 225–35.

8 Jenkins, *Great and Holy War*, 279.

9 Z.A.B. Zeman, ed., *Germany and the Revolution in Russia, 1915–1918:
Documents from the Archives of the German Foreign Ministry* (London: Oxford
University Press, 1958), 128–9, 133.

10 Fisher, *Curzon and British Imperialism in the Middle East*, 159.

11 LAC, RG9IIIA3, vol. 358, file 39, American HQ, Intelligence Summaries;
Lloyd George, *War Memoirs*, 6:3155–7; Leon Trotsky, *The Trotsky Papers,
1917–1922* (The Hague: Mouton, 1964), 1:10–25, 50–5; Erich Von
Ludendorff, *My War Memories, 1914–1918* (London: Hutchison, 1919),
2:511, 544–50. Petrograd is modern-day St Petersburg. The Germans had
12,000 troops in the Baltic provinces and an additional 33,000 in Finland
under General Rudiger von der Goltz. He was also commanding some
50,000 Finns. The Bolsheviks were also receiving aid from Sweden in
the form of 123,000 rifles, 9,000,000 Swedish crowns, and the passage of
German weapons through its land.

12 Trotsky, *Trotsky Papers*, 1:10–25, 50–5; Ludendorff, *My War Memories*,
2:511, 544–50; Richard Luckett, *The White Generals* (London: Longman
Group, 1971), 109–12; C.E.W. Bean, *Official History of Australia in the War of
1914–1918* (Sydney: Angus and Robertson, 1937), 5:735–8.

13 See Edmund Ironside, *The Diaries of Major-General Sir Edmund Ironside
1920–1922* (London: Leo Cooper, 1972); Charles Maynard, *The Murmansk
Adventure* (London: Hodder & Stoughton, 1969); Andrew Soutar, *With
Ironside in North Russia* (London: Anchor, 1940). One hundred and
thirty British Royal Marines landed in Murmansk ("Syren") on 6 March
1918. The Allies landed at Archangel ("Elope") on 2 August 1918. By
December 1918, the Allies had 14,475 personnel at Murmansk and 15,996
at Archangel. The combined force of Murmansk and Archangel never
exceeded 35,000. The contributing nations were Britain, Canada, France,
United States, Italy, Poland, Serbia, Finland, and White Russia. The Allies
began landing at Vladivostock in Siberia in April 1918. The contributing
nations were Japan (70,000), United States (10,000), Poland (12,000),
Britain/Canada (6,000), Serbia and Romania (4,000 each), France (2,000),
and Italy (2,000), in addition to the Czech-Slovak Legion (70,000) fighting
the Bolsheviks along the Trans-Siberian Railway. Murmansk, Archangel,

and Vladivostock all had large quantities of Allied military and civil stores that had been provided on credit to the tsarist regime. The main objectives of these forces were (1) to reconstruct Russian or Allied forces in the area to oppose Germany, (2) to prevent access to the sea through Archangel, Murmansk, and Vladivostock, should the Germans continue their advance into Russia, and (3) to support the White Russians and prevent supplies from falling into Bolshevik or German hands. Major-General Frederick Poole was assigned command of the overall forces in northern Russia (March–September 1918) but was replaced by Major-General Edmund Ironside (September 1918–October 1919). Brigadier-General R.G. Finlayson commanded the Archangel force, while Major-General Sir Charles Maynard commanded the force at Murmansk. General Henry (Lord) Rawlinson, who had commanded the Fourth Army on the Western Front, was chosen to orchestrate the evacuations of the British forces from northern Russia in September–October 1919. Japanese General Kikuzo Otani, appointed on 18 August 1918, was Allied commander-in-chief in Siberia.

14 MacLaren, *Canadians in Russia*, 2.

15 Aleksandr V. Kolchak, *The Testimony of Kolchak and Other Siberian Materials* (Stanford: Stanford University Press, 1935), 102. On 18 November 1918, Admiral Kolchak executed a successful coup d'etat against the Socialists and assumed dictatorship over Siberia under the title of supreme ruler. He was recognized by the Allies to represent the provisional Russian government in Siberia. He was captured and shot by the Bolsheviks in 1920.

16 Lloyd George, *War Memoirs*, 6:3157–8.

17 Aron, *Century of Total War*, 27.

18 Manganese ore is an essential requirement in the production of steel.

19 Yergin, *Quest*, 25.

20 LAC, RG9IIIA3, vol. 362, file A3SEF115, Notes: Brigadier-General James H. Elmsley, Military Intervention in Siberia.

21 Strachan, *First World War*, 247; Keegan, *First World War*, 329.

22 Casualty totals for these battles, most notably those of Passchendaele, are contested, and as Keegan argues, "statistical disputes make the argument profitless" when omitting German casualty figures for Passchendaele in his work. I have given what I believe to be the most accurate figures based on a variety of sources. German casualties were as follows: Arras: 125,000; Nivelle: 163,000; Passchendaele: 250,000.

23 Italian casualties for the Tenth and Eleventh Battles of the Isonzo (12 May–6 June and 18 August–12 September) totalled 160,000 and 166,000 respectively.

24 See Alan Palmer, *The Gardeners of Salonika: The Macedonian Campaign, 1915–1918* (London: Faber, 2011).

25 Jenkins, *Great and Holy War*, 178–80; Rogan, *Fall of the Ottomans*, 351–3.

26 Matthew Hughes, *Allenby and British Strategy in the Middle East, 1917–1919* (London: Frank Cass, 1999), 26–7.

27 F.G. Marsh, "Experiences in the Caucasus and North Persia, 1914–1918," *Royal United Service Institution Journal* 70 (1925): 718, 723. In March 1917, Army Order No. 1 was issued by the Soviet, or Council of Soldiers and Workmen, which essentially informed Russian soldiers that they possessed political and social rights equal to their officers and need no longer salute them, creating a breakdown in any semblance of command and control.

28 Efraim and Inari Karsh, *Empires of the Sand: The Struggle for Mastery in the Middle East, 1789–1923* (Cambridge, MA: Harvard University Press, 1999), 118–23.

29 Muzaffer Erendil, "The Ottoman Empire in World War I: The Home Front and Military Affairs," in *War and Society in East Central Europe*, ed. Bela K. Kiraly and Nandor F. Dreisziger (New York: Columbia University Press, 1985), 19:371.

30 F. William Engdahl, "Oil and the Origins of the "War to Make the World Safe for Democracy," *Geopolitics-Geoeconomics* (2007): 9.

31 Reynolds, *Shattering Empires*, 120.

32 Staniforth Smith, *Australian Campaigns in the Great War* (Melbourne: Macmillan, 1919), 11. The Turks suffered roughly 800 dead with another 3,000 wounded or taken prisoner. British losses were 50 killed and 150 wounded. Liman von Sanders was in command of all Turkish and German forces in the southern sector, including Gallipoli. He had been appointed the head of the German military mission in Turkey in 1913, and began training Turkish forces. He commanded the Fifth Turkish Army at Gallipoli and then was transferred to Palestine in 1917.

33 Between December 1915 and May 1916, British diplomat Sir Mark Sykes and M. Georges Picot, a French diplomat, drew up an agreement, which was accepted by their respective governments, and also by the Russian government. The Sykes-Picot agreement set out the mandates for these three countries and divided the Middle East into spheres of power or influence among these three countries. Arab independence was given only lip-service in order to acquire Arab support for the war effort. Nevertheless, Hussein led the successful Arab Revolt in June 1916, with the help of T.E. Lawrence, against the Turks in Palestine and Arabia.

34 Rogan, *Fall of the Ottomans*, 285.

35 Reynolds, *Long Shadow*, 95.

36 David French, *British Economic and Strategic Planning 1905–1915* (London: George Allen & Unwin, 1982), 103–6. In fact, between July 1914 and July 1917 retail food prices increased by 104 per cent.

37 Lambert, *Planning Armageddon*, 335.

38 Seligmann, *Royal Navy and the German Threat*, 132–3.

39 French, *British Strategy & War Aims*, xii–xiii, 7.

40 Ibid., 83.

41 Ibid., 79.

42 Smith, *Australian Campaigns in the Great War*, 14–41. Two British battleships and one French battleship were sunk by mines. Another French battleship ran ashore and was captured, and a British cruiser was disabled beyond repair. Four other ships were also damaged. Hamilton was replaced by Lieutenant-General Charles Munro in September 1915. He immediately recommended evacuation of the Dardanelles. His evacuation operation is credited with saving a bulk of Allied soldiers. Hamilton had estimated 50 per cent casualties for his evacuation plan. Munro evacuated all soldiers with relatively few casualties.

43 Keegan, *First World War*, 237–43. ANZAC stands for Australian New Zealand Army Corps. In all, 500,000 troops were deployed by the Allies. Roughly 265,000 became casualties. The Turkish losses numbered 300,000. It was at Gallipoli that Mustapha Kemal made a name for himself while commanding the 19th Turkish Division. He was one of the earliest Young Turks and would rise to power in Turkey after the war as Ataturk. He had a profound impact on modernizing Turkey and bringing it into the "Western fold."

44 Richard H. Ullman, *Anglo-Soviet Relations, 1917–1921* (Princeton: Princeton University Press, 1968), 2:68–70.

45 French, *British Strategy & War Aims*, 146.

46 Mohammed Gholi Majd, *The Great Famine and Genocide in Persia, 1917–1919* (Toronto: University Press of America, 2003), 3–8; M.H. Donohoe, *With the Persian Expedition* (London: Edward Arnold, 1919), 88–9, 117–31; Alfred Rawlinson, *Adventures in the Near East, 1918–1922* (London: Andrew Melrose, 1923), 41–62; Lionel Dunsterville, *The Adventures of Dunsterforce* (London: Edward Arnold, 1920), 102.

47 Rogan, *Fall of the Ottomans*, 290–1.

48 Ullman, *Anglo-Soviet Relations*, 1:303; John Swettenham, *The Allied Intervention in Russia 1918–1919: And the Part Played by Canada* (Toronto: Ryerson, 1967), 41; Smith, *Australian Campaigns in the Great War*, 2–4. Britain and France arrived at an agreement in 1904 to divide the Middle East into regions and promote the idea of "splendid isolation" in the region.

49 Keegan, *First World War*, 414–15; *Bible*, Book of Revelation 16:12–16; Lloyd George, *War Memoirs*, 6:3224–5. Allenby had been a commander on the Western Front and had a credible reputation. He had been the BEF cavalry commander and the commander of the Third Army.

50 Dunsterville, *Adventures of Dunsterforce*, 4–8; G.W.L. Nicholson, *Canadian Expeditionary Force, 1914–1919: Official History of the Canadian Army in the First World War* (Ottawa: Queen's Printer, 1962), 460–72. In 1916, British and Canadian engineers were sent to build bridges in Palestine in support of General Allenby's campaign. From 1915 onwards, 4,000 Canadians (mostly from British Columbia) operated barges in the Middle East along the Tigris and Euphrates Rivers. (They helped transport Dunsterforce.)

51 Jenkins, *Great and Holy War*, 236–8, 247, 253.

52 Keegan, *First World War*, 414–15; T.E. Lawrence, *Seven Pillars of Wisdom* (Toronto: J. Cape, 1935).

53 Silverlight, *Victor's Dilemma*, 93–5; Dunsterville, *Adventures of Dunsterforce*, 1–7.

54 A.H. Burne, *Mesopotamia: The Last Phase* (London: Gale & Polden, 1936), 6–10.

55 McMeekin, *Berlin-Baghdad Express*, 330.

56 NA, CAB/24/144, Eastern Report 28, 9 August 1917.

57 NA, CAB/24/144, Eastern Report 44, 29 November 1917.

58 NA, CAB/24/25, War Cabinet Memorandum Panturanian Movement, 7 August 1917; CAB, /24/143, Eastern Report 13, 26 April 1917.

59 Thomas L. Hughes, "The German Mission to Afghanistan, 1915–1916," *German Studies Review* 25, no. 3 (2002): 446–8.

60 McMeekin, *Berlin-Baghdad Express*, 221.

61 Peter Hopkirk, *On Secret Service East of Constantinople*, 158–9.

62 McMeekin, *Berlin-Baghdad Express*, 227–8.

63 Ibid., 228.

64 Hans-Ulrich Seidt, "From Palestine to the Causasus: Oskar Niedermayer and Germany's Middle Eastern Strategy in 1918," *German Studies Review* 24, no. 1 (2001): 7.

65 Hughes, "German Mission to Afghanistan," 465–71.

66 McMeekin, *Berlin-Baghdad Express*, 290.

67 Seidt, "From Palestine to the Caucasus," 4–8.

68 Hughes, "German Mission to Afghanistan," 446–8.

69 Swettenham, *Allied Intervention in Russia*, 41.

70 There were "sideshows" all over the world encompassing Africa, northern Russia, Siberia, the Balkans, South/Central America, China, New Guinea, and, for the importance of this context, in the Middle East, the Caucasus, and Central Asia.

4 The Black Blood of Victory

1 Yergin, *Prize*, 167.
2 Ludendorff, *My War Memories, 1914–1918*, 2:340.
3 Yergin, *Prize*, 164.
4 Pearton, *Oil and the Romanian State*, 80–3.
5 NA, CAB/24/59, "Petroleum Situation in the British Empire," 29 July 1918.
6 Yergin, *Prize*, 164–6.
7 See Alison Fleig Frank, *Oil Empire: Visions of Prosperity in Austrian Galicia* (Cambridge, MA: Harvard University Press, 2005).
8 Hughes, *Allenby and British Strategy in the Middle East*, 120.
9 Strachan, *First World War*, 216.
10 French, *British Economic and Strategic Planning*, 113–14.
11 Lambert, *Planning Armageddon*, 407.
12 Jones, *State and the Emergence of the British Oil Industry*, 180–1.
13 French, *British Economic and Strategic Planning*, 116.
14 Lambert, *Planning Armageddon*, 250.
15 Donald E. Schmidt, *The Folly of War: American Foreign Policy, 1898–2005* (New York: Algora, 2005), 72.
16 Lloyd George, *War Memoirs*, 2:1473.
17 George E. Gruen, "The Oil Resources of Iraq: Their Role in the Policies of the Great Powers," in Simon and Tejirian, *Creation of Iraq*, 114.
18 NA, CAB/24/144, War Cabinet Eastern Report, 17 January 1918.
19 NA, CAB 27/7, WP 70, British Military Policy 1918–1919: Situation of the Military Forces of the British Empire, 25 July 1918.
20 McMeekin, *Berlin-Baghdad Express*, 317.
21 David French, *The Strategy of the Lloyd George Coalition 1916–1918* (Oxford: Clarendon, 1995), 176–7.
22 Rothwell, "Mesopotamia in British War Aims," 286n80.
23 Fromkin, *Peace to End All Peace*, 199–20. Also see Ulrich Trumpener, "Liman von Sanders and the German-Ottoman Alliance," *Journal of Contemporary History* 1, no. 4 (1966): 179–92; Trumpener, *Germany and the Ottoman Empire, 1914–1918* (Princeton: Princeton University Press, 1968).
24 Reynolds, *Shattering Empires*, 126.
25 *British Documents on Foreign Affairs, Part II, Series H, The First World War, 1914–1918*, 4:420.
26 Ford, *Eden to Armageddon*, 127.
27 Rogan, *Fall of the Ottomans*, 106.
28 For a thorough account of the battle, see Edward J. Erickson, *Ordered to Die: A History of the Ottoman Army in the First World War* (London: Greenwood, 2001), 52–65.

29 Strachan, *First World War*, 1:722–3.
30 As usual there is some discrepancy on actual Turkish casualty rates, although it is acknowledged that more died from starvation and the extreme climate than from Russian armaments. Fromkin (*Peace to End All Peace*, 121): "Of the perhaps 100,000 men who took part in the attack, 86% were lost." Hopkirk (*On Secret Service*, 76): 90,000 committed, 15,000 survived (84 per cent losses). Trumpener (*Germany and the Ottoman Empire*, 79): "Perhaps 10 to 20% of the Third Army survived the campaign." Keegan (*First World War*, 223): 18,000 of 95,000 survived (81 per cent casualties). McMeekin (*Berlin-Baghdad Express*, 189) argues that most numbers are grossly inflated and that the casualty rate was roughly 50 per cent, or 50,000 of 100,000. His note on page 389 offers an explanation and details the history of the raw data used. However, seeing as the Porte went to extreme measures to conceal casualty figures and the devastating military setback, casualty rates were seemingly very high and quite troublesome to Turkish command. Erickson (*Ordered to Die*, 59–60) also offers an explanation of casualty figures and discrepancies. W.E.D. Allen and Paul Muratoff (*Caucasian Battlefields: A History of the Wars in the Turco-Caucasian Border 1828–1921* [Nashville: Battery, 1999], 284–5) take a middle line, suggesting 75,000 casualties (or 67 per cent). Hew Strachan also takes a middle stance (*First World War*, 111): "Casualties were at least 75,000 men, and some estimates rise as high as 90,000." Russian losses ranged from 28,000 to 32,000. While there were roughly 120,000 Russians serving on the Caucus and Persian (mainly at Tabriz) fronts, it is estimated that only 60,000 to 75,000 served in this particular campaign.
31 Fromkin, *Peace to End All Peace*, 121.
32 Strachan, *First World War*, 1:728; Erickson, *Ordered to Die*, 61–2. Erickson compares Sarikamish to Union General Joseph Hooker's Chancellorsville campaign of May 1863 during the American Civil War. Essentially, both Enver and Hooker were defeated by a "trap within a trap."
33 Bodger, "Russia and the End of the Ottoman Empire," 98–9.
34 Hopkirk, *On Secret Service East of Constantinople*, 72.
35 Lloyd George, *War Memoirs*, 2:1070.
36 NA, CAB 24/51/4564, Memorandum Long, 15 May 1917; NA, CAB/24/16, Memorandum Long, 11 June 1917.
37 Marian Kent, *Oil and Empire: British Policy and Mesopotamian Oil, 1900–1920* (London: Macmillan, 1976), 134.
38 NA, CAB/24/23, Memorandum Long, 16 August 1917; Rothwell, "Mesopotamia in British War Aims," 287–8.
39 NA, CAB/24/23, Memorandum Long, 16 August 1917.
40 Yergin, *Prize*, 160.

41 NA, CAB/24/59, Petroleum Executive Memorandum, 31 July 1918.
42 Ibid.
43 French, *Strategy of the Lloyd George Coalition 1916–1918*, 151.
44 Sumida, *In Defence of Naval Supremacy*, 265.
45 Gruen, "The Oil Resources of Iraq," 116. The primary source for this legendary quote, however, remains a mystery.
46 Mohr, *Oil War*, 148–9.
47 NA, CAB/24/66, Memorandum Walter Hume Long, 5 October 1918.
48 Yergin, *Quest*, 230.
49 NA, CAB/24/59, "Petroleum Situation in the British Empire," 29 July 1918.
50 NA, CAB/24/22, Secret Memorandum: The Present Situation in Russia and the Near East, 7 March 1918; NA, CAB/24/59, "Petroleum Situation in the British Empire," 29 July 1918.
51 NA, CAB/24/22, Secret Memorandum.
52 Helmut Mejcher, "Oil and British Policy towards Mesopotamia, 1914–1918," *Middle Eastern Studies* 8, no. 3 (1972): 383.
53 NA, CAB/24/59, "Petroleum Situation in the British Empire."
54 Ibid.
55 Ian Rutledge, *Addicted to Oil: America's Relentless Drive for Energy Security* (New York: I.B. Tauris, 2005), 13–15; Maugeri, *Age of Oil*, 22.
56 Gerald D. Nash, *United States Oil Policy, 1890–1964* (Westport, CT: Greenwood, 1968), 6.
57 NA CAB/24/59. "Petroleum Situation in the British Empire."
58 Ibid.
59 Yergin, *Quest*, 230.
60 NA CAB/24/59. "Petroleum Situation in the British Empire."
61 NA CAB/24/64. Geddes to War Cabinet, 17 September 1918.
62 NA CAB/21/119. Hankey to Geddes, 30 July 1918.
63 NA CAB/21/119. Hankey to Balfour, 1 August 1918.
64 NA, CAB/21/119, Hankey to Lloyd George, 1 August 1918.
65 NA, CAB/21/119, Hankey to Wemyss, 1 August 1918.
66 NA, CAB/24/60, Admiralty Memorandum on the Reported Oil Fields of Mesopotamia and Part of Persia, 2 August 1918.
67 NA, CAB/24/60, Petroleum Situation in the British Empire: Notes by the Chief of Air Staff, 9 August 1918.
68 NA, CAB 21/119, Hankey to Balfour, 12 August 1918.
69 NA, CAB 23/43, Imperial War Cabinet Minutes, 13 August 1918.
70 Hughes, *Allenby and British Strategy in the Middle East*, 122.
71 Satia, *Spies in Arabia*, 14.

72 NA, CAB 23/43, Imperial War Cabinet Minutes, 13 August 1918.

73 Lloyd George, *War Memoirs*, 2:1544.

74 Yergin, *Prize*, 166.

75 Moberly, *Official History*, 4:259.

76 *British Documents on Foreign Affairs, Part II, Series H*, "The Economic Situation in Germany in December 1917, Being the Forty-First Month of the War," January 1918, 12:58–9.

77 Lloyd George, *War Memoirs*, 2:1888–91.

78 Percy Sykes, Major Poole, and L.C. Dunsterville, "From Baghdad to the Caspian in 1918: Discussion," *Geographical Journal* 57, no. 3 (1921): 164–5.

79 Percy Sykes, "The British Flag on the Caspian: A Side-Show of the Great War," *Foreign Affairs* 2, no. 2 (1923): 283.

80 Christopher Paul, Colin P. Clarke, and Beth Grill, *Victory Has a Thousand Fathers: Sources of Success in Counterinsurgency* (Santa Monica, CA: RAND, 2010), 1.

81 Buchan, *Greenmantle*, 8–11. Hannay is purportedly based on General Sir Edmund Ironside, a spy during the Second Anglo-Boer War, commander of Allied forces in northern Russia (1918–19) during the Russian Civil War, and commander of British and Persian forces in Persia in 1921.

5 The Deployment of Dunsterforce

1 Diary of Sgt Crofford Campbell, 28 January 1918. Private Collection.

2 Assyrians are also known as Syriacs or Chaldeans.

3 For an eye-witness account of the Azeri-Armenian War of 1905–6 see Mammad Said Ordubadi, *Years of Blood: A History of the Armenian-Muslim Clashes in the Caucasus, 1905–1906* (Reading, UK: Ithaca, 2011); Glenny, *Balkans*, 249–306. During the violence of 1894–6, roughly 60,000 Armenians perished.

4 Jenkins, *Great and Holy War*, 287.

5 Erickson, *Ordered to Die*, 104.

6 Vahakn N. Dadrian, *The History of the Armenian Genocide: Ethnic Conflict from the Balkans to Anatolia to the Caucasus* (Oxford: Berghahn Books, 1995), 350–1.

7 Daniel Allen Butler, *Shadow of the Sultan's Realm: The Destruction of the Ottoman Empire and the Creation of the Modern Middle East* (Washington, DC: Potomac Books, 2011), 156. Morgenthau's massive archive of records and reports would become the basis for Armenian evidential claims of a systematic genocide.

8 James Bryce, *The Treatment of the Armenians in the Ottoman Empire 1915–16: Documents Presented to Viscount Grey of Fallodon, Secretary of State Foreign Affairs,*

ed. Arnold J. Toynbee (London: His Majesty's Stationary Office / Causton and Sons, 1916). The document concludes with an excellent appendix, "A Summary of Armenian History up to and Including the Year 1915." The book includes eyewitness accounts from United States consular and missionary sources, as well as the testimony of German, Italian, Danish, Swedish, Norwegian, Greek, Kurdish, and Armenian witnesses.

9 Jenkins, *Great and Holy War*, 191–3.
10 Reynolds, *Shattering Empires*, 46.
11 Bryce, *Treatment of the Armenians in the Ottoman Empire*, 152.
12 Hopkirk, *On Secret Service East of Constantinople*, 131.
13 Armstrong, *Fields of Blood*, 318.
14 Butler, *Shadow of the Sultan's Realm*, 152; Karsh, *Empires of the Sand*, 156.
15 Reynolds, *Shattering Empires*, 145–6.
16 Erickson, *Ordered to Die*, 99–103.
17 Ford, *Eden to Armageddon*, 144.
18 Karsh, *Empires of the Sand*, 154–5.
19 Butler, *Shadow of the Sultan's Realm*, 151.
20 Jenkins, *Great and Holy War*, 299.
21 Fuat Dundar, *Crime of Numbers: The Role of Statistics in the Armenian Question, 1878–1918* (New Brunswick, NJ: Transaction Publishers, 2010), 150–2; Butler, *Shadow of the Sultan's Realm*, 155; Reynolds, *Shattering Empires*, 155; Karsh, *Empires of the Sand*, 156–7; King, *Ghosts of Freedom*, 158; Donald Bloxham, *The Great Game of Genocide: Imperialism, Nationalism, and the Destruction of the Ottoman Armenians* (Oxford: Oxford University Press, 2005).
22 David Gaunt, *Massacres, Resistance, Protectors: Muslim-Christian Relations in Eastern Anatolia during World War I* (Piscataway, NY: Gorgias, 2006), 300–2; Karsh, *Empires of the Sand*, 160.
23 Jenkins, *Great and Holy War*, 312–14.
24 Reynolds, *Shattering Empires*, 154–5.
25 King, *Ghosts of Freedom*, 158.
26 McMeekin, *Berlin-Baghdad Express*, 252–3.
27 Bloxham, *Great Game of Genocide*, 144.
28 Ibid., 144; Artin H. Arslanian, "British Wartime Pledges, 1917–1918: The Armenian Case," *Journal of Contemporary History* 13, no. 3 (1978): 520.
29 NA, CAB/24/29/GT2347, Robertson to War Cabinet, 20 October 1917.
30 NA, CAB/24/144, Eastern Committee Report XLV, 6 December 1917.
31 NA, CAB24/4, German and Turkish Territories Captured in the War: Their Future, 5 December 1917.
32 Arslanian, "British Wartime Pledges," 520.
33 Occleshaw, *Dances in Deep Shadows*, 43.

34 NA, CAB/24/36/GT3068, Organization of Military Forces in South Russia and on the Persian Frontier, 21 December 1917.

35 Occleshaw, *Dances in Deep Shadows*, 44–5.

36 Lloyd George, *War Memoirs*, 6:3193–4.

37 NA, CAB/24/144, Eastern Report No. LI, 17 January 1918.

38 Fisher, *Curzon and British Imperialism in the Middle East*, 158–60.

39 NA, CAB 23/43, Imperial War Cabinet, 25 June 1918.

40 NA, CAB/24/144, Eastern Report No. LVII, 28 February 1918.

41 Michael Sargent, *British Involvement in Transcaspia (1918–1919)* (London: Defence Academy of the United Kingdom, Conflict Studies Research Centre, 2004), 6.

42 For an excellent primary account of this mission, see C.H. Ellis, *The British "Intervention" in Transcaspia, 1918–1919* (Berkeley: University of California Press, 1963). Also see Sargent, *British Involvement in Transcaspia*. Malleson had served as director of intelligence for the Indian Army of the British Raj from 1904 to 1914. He was a brigade commander from 1915 to 1916 in the East Africa campaign. He was chosen to lead this mission on the basis of his knowledge of the "Middle Asian area," although from diaries and primary accounts his personality was less than inspiring, and he was overly cautious to the point of becoming a financial and administrative burden and nightmare to the War Office.

43 For two intriguing primary accounts of this mission, see Latham V.S. Blacker, *On a Secret Patrol in High Asia* (London: John Murray, 1922); F.M. Bailey, *Mission to Tashkent* (London: Cape, 1946). Macartney's mission consisted of himself and sixteen others. The soldiers were all cavalry guides with unique skills and were selected for linguistic prowess in the languages and dialects of the region. Blacker was part of this mission, as he acted as a guide in the Afghan area throughout the war. Macartney was the British consul-general in Kashgar and was near retirement when ordered to lead this mission. In fact, his successor, Colonel Etherton, had already arrived in Kashgar to conduct the administrative handover.

44 Strachan, *First World War*, 1:713–14.

45 King, *Ghosts of Freedom*, 98.

46 Burne, *Mesopotamia*. 88.

47 Robert H. McDowell, "Russian Revolution and the Civil War in the Caucasus," *Russian Review* 27, no. 4 (1968): 456–7. McDowell, the son of American missionary parents, was U.S.-born, but brought up in Van in eastern Anatolia. He was fluent in German, Russian, French, Turkish, Armenian, and Syriac. He also acquired five years" U.S. university education.

48 Dunsterville, *Adventures of Dunsterforce*, 9.
49 Lionel Dunsterville, *Stalky's Reminiscences* (London: Jonathan Cape, 1928), 68, 178.
50 Rudyard Kipling, *Stalky & Co.* (London: Macmillan, 1899).
51 Dunsterville, *Stalky's Reminiscences*, 25.
52 Artin H. Arslanian, "Dunsterville's Adventures: A Reappraisal," *International Journal of Middle East Studies* 12, no. 2 (1980): 200.
53 Dunsterville, *Stalky's Reminiscences*, 220–69.
54 Dunsterville, *Adventures of Dunsterforce*, 11.
55 LAC, RG24, vol. 1840, file GAQ 10–28, "The Dunsterforce" (Baghdad Mission): Mesopotamian Expeditionary Force, 1918.
56 King, *Ghosts of Freedom*, 144–5.
57 Hopkirk, *On Secret Service East of Constantinople*, 259.
58 Swettenham, *Allied Intervention in Russia*, 43–4.
59 R.P. Serle, "John Joseph Byron," *Australian Dictionary of Biography*, http://adb.anu.edu.au/biography/byron-john-joseph-5459.
60 AWM224, MSS576, Dunsterforce File, War Office to Dominion contingent commanders, 3 January 1918.
61 LAC, RG24, vol. 1840, file GAQ 10-28, "The Dunsterforce" (Baghdad Mission): Mesopotamian Expeditionary Force, 1918.
62 LAC, RG24, vol. 1840, file GAQ 10-28, "The Dunsterforce" (Baghdad Mission): Mesopotamian Expeditionary Force, 1918.
63 LAC, RG9III, vol. 3096, file 0-11-36, Canadians in Dunsterforce Narrative: Captain R. Harrison, 20 May 1919.
64 Donohoe, *With the Persian Expedition*, 5.
65 LAC, MG30, E192, LCol. J.W. Warden File – Diary 1918–1919. Entry: 8 January 1918.
66 LAC, RG24, vol. 1840, file GAQ 10-28, "The Dunsterforce" (Baghdad Mission): Mesopotamian Expeditionary Force, 1918; MacLaren, *Canadians in Russia, 1918–1919*, 9–10. The Ministry of Overseas Military Forces was established in November 1916 to administer Canadian forces in the United Kingdom, especially in the training of reinforcements, and to act as the communications channel between the Militia Department, the British War Office, and the Canadian Corps in France. Prime Minister Borden created the ministry to alienate and curtail the activities of the Minister of Militia Sir Sam Hughes (who was fired by Borden in November 1916). Borden also used the ministry to attain greater autonomy for Canadian forces within the BEF. By this time Borden and other dominion leaders were tiring of their lack of inclusion in the strategic arenas of the war.
67 S.G. Savige, *Stalky's Forlorn Hope* (Melbourne: McCubbin, 1919), 24.

68 W.S. Austin, *The Official History of the New Zealand Rifle Brigade* (Wellington: L.T. Watkins, 1924), 536–7.

69 Donohoe, *With the Persian Expedition*, 3–4. Of the Canadians, all had won at least one commendation for bravery. Also, ten of the fifteen officers and eight of the twenty-six NCOs had been wounded in fighting on the Western Front.

70 Dunsterville, *Adventures of Dunsterforce*, 9.

71 Dunsterville, *Stalky's Reminiscences*, 275; Dunsterville, *Adventures of Dunsterforce*, 11. Dunsterville has contradicting dates. In the former he claims to have reached Baghdad on 6 January. In the latter, 18 January is given as the date of arrival, which is correct.

72 Lionel C. Dunsterville, "The Diaries of General Lionel Dunsterville, 1911–1922," 12–19 January 1918. http://www.gwpda.org/Dunsterville/Dunsterville_main.html.

73 William Marshall, *Memories of Four Fronts* (London: Ernest Benn, 1929), 282.

74 Ibid, 282–7.

75 LAC, RG24, vol. 1840, file GAQ 10-28. "The Dunsterforce" (Baghdad Mission): Mesopotamian Expeditionary Force, 1918; Bean, *Official History of Australia in the War of 1914–1918*, 5:730–1. In total, 297 men were gathered: 93 officers and 204 NCOs. The figures of nationality are conflicting and incomplete. However, these numbers are correct: Canada: 15 officers, 29 NCOs; Australia: 20 officers and 20 NCOs; New Zealand: 11 officers, 23 NCOs; South Africa: 12 officers; Britain (Scotland and Ireland): 20 officers (some were to serve as staff officers); Russia: 14 officers; Persia: 1 officer.

76 Standard issue heavy wool greatcoat.

77 LAC, RG24, vol. 1840, file GAQ 10-28. "The Dunsterforce" (Baghdad Mission): Mesopotamian Expeditionary Force, 1918.

78 Savige, *Stalky's Forlorn Hope*, 24.

79 The majority of Irish-Australians and French-Canadians were opposed to the war, and rioted against conscription measures.

80 MacLaren, *Canadians in Russia*, 11.

81 LAC, RG24, vol. 1840, file GAQ 10-28. "The Dunsterforce" (Baghdad Mission): Mesopotamian Expeditionary Force, 1918; Savige, *Stalky's Forlorn Hope*, 24.

82 LAC, MG30, E192, LCol J.W. Warden File-Diary 1918–1919.

83 NA, CAB/27/34/GT3145, The Present Military Situation, 29 December 1917. On Robertson's views, see Brock Millman, "The Problem with Generals: Military Observers and the Origins of the Intervention in Russia and Persia, 1917–1918," *Journal of Contemporary History* 33, no. 2 (1998): 291–320.

84 French, *Strategy of the Lloyd George Coalition*, 51, 133.

85 LAC, MG30, E192, LCol J.W. Warden File-Diary 1918–1919, Diary Entry
    28 January 1918; Murray, "Canadians in Dunsterforce" 211–12.
86 LAC, RG9III, vol. 3096, file 0-11-36, Canadians in Dunsterforce Narrative:
    Captain R. Harrison, 20 May 1919.
87 Savige, *Stalky's Forlorn Hope*, 24.
88 LAC, RG24, vol. 1840, file GAQ 10-28, "The Dunsterforce" (Baghdad
    Mission): Mesopotamian Expeditionary Force, 1918.
89 Alan Stewart, *Persian Expedition: The Australians in Dunsterforce 1918*
    (Loftus, NSW: Australian Military History Publications, 2006), 33.
90 LAC, RG9III, vol. 3096, file 0-11-36, Canadians in Dunsterforce Narrative:
    Captain R. Harrison, 20 May 1919. Turner was awarded the Victoria Cross on
    29 November 1900 for bravery during actions at Leliefontein on 7 November,
    while serving as a lieutenant with the Royal Canadian Dragoons. At the
    outbreak of the First World War Turner commanded the 3rd Brigade, and
    although his performance at 2nd Ypres (April 1915) was questioned, he
    was promoted to command the 2nd Division, against strong objections.
    Following his disaster at St Eloi in March/April 1916, he was buried in
    various administrative positions and never again commanded a combat unit.
91 Savige, *Stalky's Forlorn Hope*, 25.
92 LAC, MG30, E192, LCol J.W. Warden File – Diary 1918–1919.
93 Stewart, *Persian Expedition*, 34.
94 Savige, *Stalky's Forlorn Hope*, 25.
95 LAC, MG30, E192, LCol J.W. Warden File – Diary 1918–1919, Diary Entry
    11 February 1918.
96 LAC, MG30, E192, LCol J.W. Warden File – Diary 1918–1919, Diary
    Entries 1, 6, 10 February 1918.
97 Of the eighty-seven Allied ships sunk by U-boats in January 1918,
    fifty-three (61 per cent) occurred in either the English Channel or the
    Mediterranean.
98 LAC, MG30, E192, LCol J.W. Warden File – Diary 1918–1919, Diary Entry
    10 February 1918.
99 Savige, *Stalky's Forlorn Hope*, 27.
100 Donohoe, *With the Persian Expedition*, 10.
101 See Percy Sykes, *A History of Persia* (London: Macmillan, 1921); F.J.
    Moberly, *Operations in Persia, 1914–1919* (London: Her Majesty's
    Stationery Office, 1929).
102 Sykes, "British Flag on the Caspian," 283.
103 LAC, MG30, E192, LCol J.W. Warden File – Diary 1918–1919, Diary Entry
    16 February 1918.
104 Bean, *Official History*, 731.

105 Donohoe, *With the Persian Expedition*, 11.
106 Ibid., 12.
107 LAC, MG30, E192, LCol J.W. Warden File – Diary 1918–1919, Diary Entries 17, 22 February, 1–2 March 1918; Sgt Crofford Campbell, Diary Entries 17, 21 February 1918 (Private Collection).
108 Donohoe, *With the Persian Expedition*, 15.
109 LAC, MG30, E192, LCol J.W. Warden File – Diary 1918–1919.
110 LAC RG9III, vol. 3096, file 0-11-36, Canadians in Dunsterforce Narrative: Captain R. Harrison, 20 May 1919; Savige, *Stalky's Forlorn Hope*, 27.
111 Donohoe, *With the Persian Expedition*, 19.
112 LAC MG30 E192, LCol J.W. Warden File-Diary 1918–1919. Diary Entry 2 March 1918.
113 Savige, *Stalky's Forlorn Hope*, 27.
114 Dunsterville, Diary Entries, 19, 24 January 1918.

6 Basra to Baghdad to Baku

1 Dunsterville, Diary Entry 14 January 1918.
2 Townshend, *When God Made Hell*, 35.
3 Donohoe, *With the Persian Expedition*, 24.
4 As a former soldier, I can personally sympathize. While stationed in southern Macedonia as a Canadian officer under NATO, I encountered entire fields covered so thick with flies that I could not see the actual ground. One particular forward operating base especially comes to mind, as a few of my soldiers were evacuated with fly-borne illnesses.
5 Donohoe, *With the Persian Expedition*, 21.
6 LAC, RG24, vol. 1840, file GAQ 10-28, "The Dunsterforce" (Baghdad Mission): Mesopotamian Expeditionary Force, 1918.
7 Savige, *Stalky's Forlorn Hope*, 30.
8 Campbell, Diary Entry, 3 March 1918.
9 Savige, *Stalky's Forlorn Hope*, 31.
10 Marshall, *Memories of Four Fronts*, 287; Moberly, *Campaign in Mesopotamia*, 118–19.
11 Warden, "Persian and Baku Operations," 7 March 1918.
12 Savige, *Stalky's Forlorn Hope*, 30.
13 Donohoe, *With the Persian Expedition*, 24.
14 Warden, Diary Entry, 5 March 1918.
15 LAC, RG24, vol. 1840, file GAQ 10-28, "The Dunsterforce" (Baghdad Mission): Mesopotamian Expeditionary Force, 1918; Donohoe, *With the Persian Expedition*, 37.

16 Campbell, Diary Entry, 24 March 1918; Warden, Diary Entry, 24 March 1918.
17 Rogan, *Fall of the Ottomans*, 273.
18 Warden, "Persian and Baku Operations," 51.
19 Savige, *Stalky's Forlorn Hope*, 33.
20 Warden, Diary Entry, 19 March 1918.
21 Warden, "Persian and Baku Operations," 57.
22 Donohoe, *With the Persian Expedition*, 62.
23 J.E. Tennant, *In the Clouds above Baghdad, Being the Records to an Air Commander* (London: C. Palmer, 1920), 255.
24 Occleshaw, *Dances in Deep Shadows*, 39, 144. The Military Intelligence Operations branch was dissolved in June as "the experiment of combining intelligence and operations work in one section was not a complete success." It was replaced by two distinct organizations – one for intelligence and another for operations.
25 Charles Marling, *West Meets East: An English Diplomat in the Ottoman Empire and Persia, 1890–1918: The Unfinished Autobiography of Sir Charles Marling*, ed. Keith M. Wilson (Istanbul: Isis, 2010).
26 Marshall, *Memories of Four Fronts*, 282–6.
27 NA, GB/NNAF/P127181, Papers and Correspondence of Lieutenant-Colonel Roger Lloyd Kennion Colonial Administrator; Roger L. Kennion, *Diversions of an Indian Political* (London: W. Blackwood, 1932).
28 McDowell, "Russian Revolution and Civil War in the Caucasus," 452–4.
29 Occleshaw, *Dances in Deep Shadows*, 46.
30 Ranald MacDonell, *And Nothing Long* (London: Constable, 1938), 187.
31 Ibid., 205.
32 Occleshaw, *Dances in Deep Shadows*, 227.
33 Buchan, *Greenmantle*, 12.
34 For a fascinating account, see Reginald Teague-Jones, *The Spy Who Disappeared: Diary of a Secret Mission to Russian Central Asia in 1918*, ed. Peter Hopkirk (London: Victor Gollancz, 1990).
35 IWM, 2347, 93/23/3,file CBS13/1, Private Papers of C.B. Stokes; Dunsterville, *Adventures of Dunsterforce*, 126.
36 See Donohoe, *With the Persian Expedition*.
37 See Rawlinson, *Adventures in the Near East*; Dunsterville, *Adventures of Dunsterforce*, 179.
38 Dunsterville, *Adventures of Dunsterforce*, 21.
39 Donohoe, *With the Persian Expedition*, 70.
40 Kazemzadeh, *Struggle for Transcaucasia*, 54–8, 82–94.
41 Trumpener, *Germany and the Ottoman Empire*, 167–71; Reynolds, *Shattering Empires*, 191–4.

42 W.E.D. Allen and Paul Muratoff, *Caucasian Battlefields: A History of the Wars on the Turco-Caucasian Border, 1828-1921* (Nashville: Battery, 1999), 458–9.

43 Fischer, *Germany's Aims in the First World War*, 552.

44 As the Russians abandoned the Caucasian front they left behind 3,000 artillery pieces, 3,000 machine guns, 100,00 small arms, 1 billion rounds of small-arms ammunition, 1 million artillery shells, rations to feed 100,000 men, 15,000 horses, and 100,000 pieces of military clothing and kit.

45 McDowell, "Russian Revolution and Civil War in the Caucasus," 455–6.

46 Sykes, *History of Persia*, 486–7.

47 French, *Strategy of the Lloyd George Coalition*, 243.

48 King, *Ghosts of Freedom*, 151.

49 Richard G. Hovannisian, *Armenia on the Road to Independence 1918* (Berkeley: University of California Press, 1967), 146–7.

50 David Lloyd George, *British War Aims* (New York: George D. Doran, 1918).

51 *British Documents on Foreign Affairs, Part II, Series H, The First World War, 1914-1918*, "Balfour to Marquis Imperiali," 30 October 1918, 4:75.

52 A.J. Plotke, *Imperial Spies Invade Russia: The British Intelligence Interventions, 1918* (London: Greenwood, 1993), 108.

53 NA, CAB/24/144, Eastern Report No. LI, 17 January 1918.

54 LAC, MG30, E192, Lt Col. J.W. Warden, "Notes Regarding Outline for a Narrative of Adventures." Warden notes diseases and illnesses that the soldiers of Dunsterforce contracted or encountered: "malaria, diphtheria, smallpox, dysentery, typhoid, sandfly fever, Egyptian anemia, cholera, bubonic plague, Baghdad boil, leprosy, typhus, blackwater fever, influenza, and many others."

55 Dunsterville, Diary Entry, 25 January 1918.

56 Ibid., 28 January 1918.

57 Dunsterville, *Adventures of Dunsterforce*, 17–18.

58 Savige, *Stalky's Forlorn Hope*, 47; Donohoe, *With the Persian Expedition*, 76–7.

59 Rawlinson, *Adventures in the Near East*, 53–4; Donohoe, *With the Persian Expedition*, 117–20.

60 Rawlinson, *Adventures in the Near East*, 55.

61 Dunsterville, *Adventures of Dunsterforce*, 57–8.

62 Ibid., 35–6.

63 Dunsterville, Diary, 17 February 1918.

64 NA, AIR 20/662: Dunsterville Correspondence, "Proceedings at Bolshevik Revolutionary Committee," 18 February 1918.

65 NA, CAB/24/43, Dunsterville to Robertson, 20 February 1918.

66 NA, AIR 20/662, Dunsterville Correspondence, February–March 1918; Moberly, *Campaign in Mesopotamia*, 4:107–11.

67 NA, AIR 20/662, Dunsterville Correspondence, February–March 1918; NA, CAB/24/144, Eastern Report No. LVII, 28 February 1918.
68 NA, AIR 20/662, Dunsterville Correspondence, Dunsterville to War Office and Marshall, 26, 28 February 1918.
69 NA, AIR 20/662, Dunsterville Correspondence, Communications between Dunsterville, Marshall, and War Office, March 1918.
70 Ibid.
71 Dunsterville, Diary Entries 19, 26 February, 13, 17 March 1918.
72 Plotke, *Imperial Spies Invade Russia*, 154.
73 Rawlinson, *Adventures in the Near East*, 57–8; Dunsterville, Diary Entry, 10 April 1918.

7 The Battle for Baku

1 Essad Bey, *Blood and Oil in the Orient* (New York: Simon and Schuster, 1932), 109–11.
2 Michael G. Smith, "Anatomy of a Rumour: Murder, Scandal, the Musavat Party and Narratives of the Russian Revolution in Baku, 1917–1920," *Journal of Contemporary History* 36, no. 2 (2001): 225.
3 Marshall, *Caucasus under Soviet Rule*, 88–9.
4 Imperial War Museum (IWM), 1845 92/21/1, Private Papers of William Henry Westwood Lacey, 1917–1919.
5 As usual, statistics for Muslim dead range from the Armenian estimation of 3,000 to the Muslim count of 13,000. Likely, the casualty figure most likely falls somewhere in the middle.
6 Bulent Gokay, "The Battle for Baku (May–September 1918): A Peculiar Episode in the History of the Caucasus," *Middle Eastern Studies* 34, no. 1 (1998): 32–3.
7 For an extremely tactical chronology of the Ottoman advance, see Allen and Muratoff, *Caucasian Battlefields*, 458–68.
8 Fischer, *Germany's Aims in the First World War*, 552–4.
9 Marshall, *Caucasus under Soviet Rule*, 89–90.
10 Hughes, *Allenby and British Strategy in the Middle East*, 50–2.
11 Townshend, *When God Made Hell*, 422.
12 Hughes, *Allenby and British Strategy in the Middle East*, 50–2.
13 Moberly, *Campaign in Mesopotamia*, 4:iii.
14 Hughes, *Allenby and British Strategy in the Middle East*, 50–1.
15 David Dutton, *The Politics of Diplomacy: Britain and France in the Balkans in the First World War* (London: IB Taurus, 1998), 13.
16 Fischer, *Germany's Aims in the First World War*, 553.

17 Hughes, *Allenby and British Strategy in the Middle East*, 52.
18 NA, CAB/24/44, Memorandum: Wilson to War Cabinet, 7 March 1918.
19 Ibid.
20 Kazemzadeh, *Struggle for Transcaucasia*, 115.
21 Zeman, *Germany and the Revolution in Russia*, 134–5.
22 Fischer, *Germany's Aims in the First World War*, 556.
23 Trumpener, *Germany and the Ottoman Empire*, 179.
24 Ibid., 180.
25 Kettle, *Road to Intervention*, 206.
26 Ibid., 205–6.
27 NA, WO95, 1530/4960, British Military Mission to the Caucasus Intelligence Reports, June–July 1918. German units deployed to the Caucasus eventually included 29th Bavarian Jager Regiment, 15th Bavarian Jager Regiment, 10th Sturm Battalion, II/65th Reserve Artillery Regiment, 28th Flieger Battalion (Aviation Detachment), one motorized machine gun section equipped with a variety of armored cars and trucks, elements of 7th Bavarian Cavalry Brigade (specifically the 7th Bavarian Chevauleger Regiment). *Thanks to Gregory Liedtke for supplying these statistics and order of battle.*
28 IWM, 4043, 84/48/1, Private Papers of Colonel Leslie R. Hulls, MC: "A Right and a Left during Two Wars."
29 Trumpener, *Germany and the Ottoman Empire*, 183–4.
30 Plotke, *Imperial Spies Invade Russia*, 155.
31 NA, WO95, 5043, British Military Mission to the Caucasus Intelligence Reports, June–July 1918.
32 W.M. Thomson, "Transcaucasia, 1918–1919," *Revolutionary Russia* 10, no. 1 (1997): 80.
33 Trumpener, *Germany and the Ottoman Empire*, 186–7.
34 Kazemzadeh, *Struggle for Transcaucasia*, 147.
35 Silverlight, *Victor's Dilemma*, 97; Arslanian, "British Wartime Pledges," 523.
36 Fisher, *Curzon and British Imperialism in the Middle East*, 162, 165.
37 Plotke, *Imperial Spies Invade Russia*, 163; Townshend, *When God Made Hell*, 422.
38 Dunsterville, Diary Entries 26, 28 May 1918.
39 Marshall, *Memories of Four Fronts*, 311–12.
40 NA, WO95, 5043, Correspondence: Dunsterville, Marshall, War Office, 27–9 June 1918.
41 IWM, 2347/93/23/3, file CBS 13/1, Papers of C.B. Stokes: Some Experiences in Persia, 1918.
42 Marshall, *Caucasus under Soviet Rule*, 94–5.

43 NA, WO95, 5043, Correspondence: Dunsterville, Marshall, War Office, 18–19 June 1918.
44 Reynolds, *Shattering Empires*, 209.
45 Kazemzadeh, *Struggle for Transcaucasia*, 135.
46 Hovannisian, *Armenia on the Road to Independence 1918*, 220–1; Kazemzadeh, *Struggle for Transcaucasia*, 134.
47 Gokay, "Battle for Baku," 40–1; Rawlinson, *Adventures in the Near East*, 69; Dunsterville, *Adventures of Dunsterforce*, 170.
48 Kazemzadeh, *Struggle for Transcaucasia*, 138.
49 Moberly, *Campaign in Mesopotamia*, 4:202.
50 Dunsterville, *Adventures of Dunsterforce*, 205–6.
51 IWM, 2347/93/23/3, file CBS 13/1, Papers of C.B. Stokes: Some Experiences in Persia, 1918.
52 Ibid.
53 Ibid.
54 Gokay, "Battle for Baku," 40–1.
55 Trumpener, *Germany and the Ottoman Empire*, 188.
56 Ludendorff, *Ludendorff's Own Story*, 322–6, 332.
57 LAC, RG9IIID, vol. 4809, file 188, Report: Cdn Corps Intelligence.
58 Lloyd George, *War Memoirs*, 2:1921.
59 Trumpener, *Germany and the Ottoman Empire*, 188–9.
60 NA, CAB/24/66, Foreign Office Political Intelligence Department, "Memorandum on Turco-German Relations over the Caucasus," 4 October 1918.
61 Dunsterville, *Adventures of Dunsterforce*, 219. Paul Kruger was the political leader and international face of the Boers during the Second Anglo-Boer War (1899–1902). "Uncle Paul," as he is affectionately known, was the first president of the South African Republic prior to its annexation by Britain after the 1902 Treaty of Vereeniging ended the war. He died in 1904 and is buried in Pretoria. The popular safari tourist destination Kruger National Park was named in his honour.
62 Warden, Diary Entry, 31 August 1918.
63 Rawlinson, *Adventures in the Near East*, 78–9.
64 Warden, Diary Entry, 1 August 1918.
65 Arslanian, "Dunsterville's Adventures," 211–12.
66 NA, WO95, 5043, Dunsterville Orders: 31 August, 5 September 1918.
67 Bey, *Blood and Oil in the Orient*, 260–5.
68 Warden, Diary Entry, 15 September 1918.
69 Teague-Jones, *Spy Who Disappeared*, 101.
70 IWM, 2347/93/23/3, file CBS 13/1, Papers of C.B. Stokes: Letter from Dunsterville, 20 October 1918.

71 McMeekin, *Berlin-Baghdad Express*, 315.

72 Trumpener, *Germany and the Ottoman Empire*, 196–8.

73 Townshend, *When God Made Hell*, 432–3.

74 Hopkirk, *On Secret Service East of Constantinople*, 378–80.

75 McMeekin, *Berlin-Baghdad Express*, 337.

76 Bey, *Blood and Oil in the Orient*, 269–70.

77 Kazemzadeh, *Struggle for Transcaucasia*, 166–8.

78 IWM, 17431, 10/3/1, The Private Papers of A.J. Foster: Diary Entry, Baku, 2 September 1919.

8 Peace and Petroleum

1 MacMillan, *Paris 1919*, xxv.

2 Strachan, *First World War*, 333.

3 James Barr, *A Line in the Sand: The Anglo-French Struggle for the Middle East, 1914–1948* (New York: W.W. Norton, 2011), 56–8.

4 French, *Strategy of the Lloyd George Coalition*, 262–3.

5 Barr, *Line in the Sand*, 58.

6 Fisher, *Curzon and British Imperialism in the Middle East*, 268–73.

7 Townshend, *When God Made Hell*, 463–4.

8 Jenkins, *Great and Holy War*, 352–9, 362–5.

9 Engdahl, *Century of War*, 83.

10 *British Documents on Foreign Affairs, Part II, Series B*, "Memorandum by Mr Balfour respecting Syria, Palestine, and Mesopotamia," 11 August 1919, 1:97–103.

11 MacMillan, *Paris 1919*, 382.

12 Ibid., 381–3.

13 Ford, *Eden to Armageddon*, 400.

14 *British Documents on Foreign Affairs, Part II, Series I*, "Memorandum by the British Delegation, Paris, on British Policy in the Middle East," 18 February 1919, 11:148–9.

15 Hahn, *Missions Accomplished?*, 16.

16 *British Documents on Foreign Affairs, Part II, Series B*, "Memorandum by Mr Balfour respecting Syria, Palestine, and Mesopotamia," 11 August 1919, 1:97–103.

17 MacMillan, *Paris 1919*, 395.

18 NA, CAB/24/59, Paper by Admiral Sir Edmund Slade on the Petroleum Situation in the British Empire, 30 July 1918; NA, CAB/24/110, Note on the Mesopotamia-Persia Situation by Sir Percy Cox, 30 July 1919.

19 NA, CAB/24/73, Petroleum Committee to War Cabinet, 8 January 1919.
20 NA, CAB/24/76, Memorandum for the War Cabinet: The Need for a Permanent Petroleum Department, 27 February 1919.
21 NA, CAB/24/93, War Cabinet Memorandum: Petroleum Committee, 24 November 1919.
22 B.S. McBeth, *British Oil Policy, 1919–1939* (London: Frank Cass, 1985), 32.
23 Adrian Gregory, *The Last Great War: British Society and the First World War* (Cambridge: Cambridge University Press, 2008), 295.
24 Aron, *Century of Total War*, 31.
25 *British Documents on Foreign Affairs, Part II, Series I*, "Memorandum by the British Delegation, Paris, on British Policy in the Middle East," 18 February 1919, 11:137.
26 S.L.A. Marshall, *World War I* (New York: Mariner Books, 2001), 468.
27 Michael B. Oren, *Power, Faith, and Fantasy: America in the Middle East, 1776 to the Present* (New York: W.W. Norton, 2008), 391.
28 *President Woodrow Wilson speaking on the League of Nations to a luncheon audience in Portland, OR.* 66th Cong., 1st sess. Senate Documents: Addresses of President Wilson (May–November 1919), vol. 11, *no. 120: 206.*
29 Reynolds, *Long Shadow*, 92.
30 Ibid., xvii, 37.
31 Ibid., 84.
32 Hahn, *Missions Accomplished?*, 12.
33 Fromkin, *Peace to End All Peace*, 533–4.
34 Donald Ewalt, "The Fight for Oil: Britain in Persia, 1919," *History Today* 31, no. 9 (1981): 3.
35 Ibid., 3–5.
36 Mohr, *Oil War*, 191.
37 NA, CAB/24/94, Report on the British Military Mission, South Russia, 8 October 1919.
38 *British Documents on Foreign Affairs, Part II, Series I*, "Memorandum by the British Delegation, Paris, on British Policy in the Middle East," 11:144.
39 MacMillan, *Paris 1919*, 443.
40 *British Documents on Foreign Affairs, Part II, Series A*, January 1917–December 1919, 1:49.
41 NA, CAB/23/14. Cabinet Minutes, 3 October 1918.
42 Sykes, "British Flag on the Caspian," 282–94; John Guard, "The Royal Navy in the Caspian Sea, 1918–1920," 6–8, World War I Document Archive. www.gwpda.org/naval/caspian.htm.
43 NA, CAB/23/21, Cabinet Minutes, 21 May 1920.
44 Arslanian, "Britain and the Transcaucasian Nationalities," 13.

45 NA, CAB/24/72, India Office to Cabinet and Eastern Committee, 17 December 1918.

46 Fisher, *Curzon and British Imperialism in the Middle East*, 279.

47 NA, CAB/24/72, Memorandum on the Caucasus, 20 December 1918.

48 NA, CAB/23/9, Minutes Imperial War Cabinet, 17 January 1919; NA, CAB/24/74, Petroleum Production in Russia, 25 January 1919.

49 NA, CAB/24/94, Petroleum Department Memorandum for Cabinet on Export of Oil from South Russia, 6 December 1919.

50 *British Documents on Foreign Affairs, Part II, Series A*, "Memorandum on a Possible Territorial Policy in the Caucasus Region," 7 November 1918, 1:46–7.

51 NA, CAB/24/72, War Cabinet Resolutions on the Caucasus and Armenia, 23 December 1918.

52 NA, CAB/24/72, War Cabinet Resolutions on the Caucasus and Armenia, 23 December 1918.

53 NA, CAB/23/42, Minutes Imperial War Cabinet, 23 December 1918.

54 MacMillan, *Paris 1919*, 379, 441.

55 Thomson, "Transcaucasia," 93.

56 NA CAB/24/86. Balfour to Lloyd George: Situation in the Caucasus, 9 August 1919.

57 *British Documents on Foreign Affairs, Part II, Series A*, "Stevens to Curzon," 2 June 1919, 1:192–4.

58 NA, CAB/23/12, Conclusions of War Cabinet Meeting, 2 September 1919.

59 NA, CAB/23/35, Conclusions of Cabinet Meeting, 16 January 1920.

60 Arslanian, "Britain and the Transcaucasian Nationalities," 10.

61 NA, CAB/23/35, Minutes of Cabinet Conference, 19 January 1920.

62 Marian Kent, ed., *The Great Powers and the End of the Ottoman Empire* (London: George Allen & Unwin, 1984), 191.

63 NA, CAB/24/86, Balfour to Lloyd George: Situation in the Caucasus, 9 August 1919.

64 MacMillan, *Paris 1919*, 443.

65 Venn, *Oil Diplomacy in the Twentieth Century*, 51–2.

66 Reynolds, *Long Shadow*, 203.

67 Fromkin, *Peace to End All Peace*, 565.

9 Oil and the New Great Game

1 Reynolds, *Long Shadow*, 3–4.

2 Fromkin, *Peace to End All Peace*, 456.

3 Zahra Abbassi, "Anglo-Iran 1919 Agreement," Iran Review, 23 July 2012. http://www.iranreview.org/content/Documents/Anglo-Iran-1919-Agreement.htm.

4 *British Documents on Foreign Affairs, Part II, Series B,* "Curzon to Davis," 11 September 1919, 16:57–59; Homa Katouzian, "The Campaign against the Anglo-Iranian Agreement of 1919," *British Journal of Middle Eastern Studies* 25, no. 1 (1998): 5–46.

5 Fromkin, *Peace to End All Peace,* 457.

6 NA, CAB/24/101, Memorandum: Oil Supplies, 18 March 1920.

7 *British Documents on Foreign Affairs, Part II, Series B,* "Grey to Curzon," 17 October 1919, 16: 69–70.

8 Delaisi, *Oil: Its Influence on Politics,* 39.

9 Fromkin, *Peace to End All Peace,* 458.

10 *British Documents on Foreign Affairs, Part II, Series A,* "GOC Mesopotamia to War Office," 23 May 1920, 3:188.

11 John M. Blair, *The Control of Oil* (New York: Pantheon, 1976), 49.

12 Over the course of their intervention in south Russia, the British supplied the White Russians, primarily Denikin's forces, with 1,200 artillery pieces, 6,100 machine guns, 200,000 small arms, 2 million artillery shells, 500 million rounds of small arms ammunition; 629 vehicles, 74 tanks, 6 armoured cars, 200 aircraft, twelve 500-bed hospitals, 25 complete field hospitals, as well as other stores and kit. Given the small size of his force, Denikin could never use all of this military hardware.

13 Marshall, *Caucasus under Soviet Rule,* 110–11.

14 De Waal, *Caucasus,* 67.

15 Yergin, *Quest,* 51.

16 Van der Leeuw, *Oil and Gas in the Caucasus & Caspian,* 97.

17 MacMillan, *Paris 1919,* 443.

18 *British Documents on Foreign Affairs, Part II, Series A,* "General Milne to War Office," 30 May 1920, 3:197–198.

19 Marshall, *Caucasus under Soviet Rule,* 106.

20 Briton Cooper Busch, *Mudros to Lausanne: Britain's Frontier in West Asia, 1918–1923* (New York: SUNY Press, 1976), 263–8.

21 King, *Ghosts of Freedom,* 171–3.

22 Barr, *Line in the Sand,* 143–4.

23 NA, CAB/24/94, Memorandum for War Cabinet from Petroleum Department: French Agreement, 6 December 1919.

24 Yergin, *Prize,* 179.

25 Hughes, *Allenby and British Strategy in the Middle East,* 121.

26 Ewalt, "Fight for Oil," 6.

27 Mohr, *Oil War*, 35–6. See Henry Bérenger, *Le Petrole et la France* (Paris: Ernest Flammarion, 1920).

28 DeNovo, *American Interests and Policies in the Middle East*, 170.

29 Robin M. Mills, *The Myth of the Oil Crisis: Overcoming the Challenges of Depletion, Geopolitics, and Global Warming* (London: Praeger, 2008), 107.

30 NA, CAB/24/94, Memorandum for War Cabinet from Petroleum Department: French Agreement, 6 December 1919.

31 McBeth, *British Oil Policy*, 60–1.

32 NA, CAB/24/108, Admiralty Memorandum: The Anglo-French Petroleum Agreement and Mesopotamia, 29 June 1920.

33 NA, CAB/24/94, Memorandum for War Cabinet from Petroleum Department: French Agreement, 6 December 1919; George E. Gruen, "The Oil Resources of Iraq: Their Role in the Policies of the Great Powers," in Simon and Tejirian, *Creation of Iraq*, 119–20.

34 Oren, *Power, Faith, and Fantasy*, 410.

35 *British Documents on Foreign Affairs*, Part II, Series B, "Curzon to Davis," 9 August 1920, 2:73–6.

36 McBeth, *British Oil Policy*, 62.

37 Delaisi, *Oil: Its Influence on Politics*, 21.

38 MacMillan, *Paris 1919*, 397–8.

39 Yergin, *Quest*, 230.

40 David Cuthell, "A Kemalist Gambit: A View of the Political Negotiations in the Determination of the Turkish-Iraqi Border," in Simon and Tajirian, *Creation of Iraq*, 86–7.

41 Reynolds, *Long Shadow*, 93.

42 Jenkins, *Great and Holy War*, 348–50.

43 Reynolds, *Long Shadow*, 93.

44 NA, WO 32/5227, "Reduction of Garrisons in Mesopotamia, 1919–1921," Memorandum 9 February 1920.

45 Rashid Khalidi, *Resurrecting Empire: Western Footprints and America's Perilous Path in the Middle East* (Boston: Beacon, 2004), 27.

46 Fisk, *The Great War for Civilization*, 177.

47 Hahn, *Missions Accomplished?*, 13.

48 Khalidi, *Resurrecting Empire*, 1.

49 Fisk, *Great War for Civilization*, 179.

50 Rutledge, *Addicted to Oil*, 25.

51 Maugeri, *The Age of Oil*, 28.

52 *British Documents on Foreign Affairs*, Part II, Series B, "Geddes to Curzon," 16 December 1920, 2:87.

53 *British Documents on Foreign Affairs, Part II, Series B,* "Norman to Curzon," 26 October 1920, 16:242.

54 *British Documents on Foreign Affairs, Part II, Series A,* "Curzon to Cox," 10 April 1920, 3:31–32.

55 Ewalt, "Fight for Oil: Britain in Persia," 7–8.

56 Engdahl, *Century of War,* 72.

57 Satia, *Spies in Arabia,* 299–300.

58 Sampson, *Seven Sisters,* 69.

59 Engdahl, *Century of War,* 81–2; Yergin, *Prize,* 194–8.

60 Sampson, *Seven Sisters,* 70–1.

61 Venn, *Oil Diplomacy in the Twentieth Century,* 74; Steve LeVine, *The Oil and the Glory: The Pursuit of Empire and Fortune on the Caspian Sea* (New York: Random House, 2007), x.

62 Marshall, *Caucasus under Soviet Rule,* 241.

63 For an excellent account, see Busch, *Mudros to Lausanne.*

64 NA, CAB/24/134, Report Cabinet: Iraq Oil, 13 March 1922.

65 Cuthell, "Kemalist Gambit," 89.

66 Gruen, "Oil Resources of Iraq," 121.

67 Barr, *Line in the Sand,* 145.

68 Fromkin, *Peace to End All Peace,* 536.

69 Maugeri, *Age of Oil,* 25.

70 NA, CAB/24/134, Report Cabinet: Iraq Oil, 13 March 1922.

71 Breakdown of percentages held in the Near East Development Corporation: Standard Oil NY, 25 per cent; Standard Oil NJ, 25 per cent; Atlantic Refining Company, 16.67 per cent; Gulf, 16.67 per cent; Pan American Petroleum & Transport Company, 16.67 per cent.

72 *British Documents on Foreign Affairs, Part II, Series B,* "Curzon to Davis," 28 July 1920, 2:72–73; Eleanor H. Tejirian, "The United States, the Ottoman Empire, and the Postwar Settlement," in Simon and Tejirian, *Creation of Iraq,* 158–9.

73 Yergin, *Prize,* 189.

74 Oren, *Power, Faith, and Fantasy,* 411.

75 Sampson, *Seven Sisters,* 58, 67.

76 Blair, *Control of Oil,* 34.

77 Ibid., 54–6.

78 Engdahl, *Century of War,* 91.

79 Ibid., 90–1.

80 Jones, *State and the Emergence of the British Oil Industry,* 239.

81 Sampson, *Seven Sisters,* 73–4.

82 He reigned from 1926 to 1941.

83 J.H. Bamberg, *The History of the British Petroleum Company* (Cambridge: Cambridge University Press, 1994), 2:46–57.

84 Doug Stokes and Sam Raphael, *Global Energy Security and American Hegemony* (Baltimore: Johns Hopkins University Press, 2010), 88.

85 Fisk, *Great War for Civilization*, 180–2.

86 Khalidi, *Resurrecting Empire*, 41. Legend has it that Saddam removed a bullet from his own leg with a razor blade.

87 Fisk, *Great War for Civilization*, 182.

88 See David Commins, *The Gulf States: A Modern History* (London: I.B. Tauris, 2012). These modern Arabian Gulf nations currently have well-equipped and modern military forces with weapons supplied/purchased from Western powers including the United States, Canada, Britain, and France.

89 Sampson, *Seven Sisters*, 76–89.

90 William Stivers, *Supremacy and Oil: Iraq, Turkey, and the Anglo-American World Order, 1918–1930* (Ithaca, NY: Cornell University Press, 1982), 29–31.

91 Galen Roger Perras, "Anglo-Canadian Imperial Relations: The Case of the Garrisoning of the Falkland Islands in 1942," *War & Society* 14, no. 1 (1996): 73–97.

92 Rutledge, *Addicted to Oil*, 84.

93 Jenkins, *Great and Holy War*, 346.

94 Oren, *Power, Faith, and Fantasy*, 460.

95 Marcel, *Oil Titans*, 21.

96 Rutledge, *Addicted to Oil*, 31.

97 Ford, *Eden to Armageddon*, 419; Jenkins, *Great and Holy War*, 356–7.

98 Fisk, *Great War for Civilization*, 22–36.

99 Ibid.

100 Paul Kennedy, *Preparing for the Twenty-First Century* (New York: HarperCollins, 1993), 208–11.

101 Ibid.

102 Jenkins, *Great and Holy War*, 334–42.

103 Yergin, *Prize*, 188–9.

104 Maugeri, *Age of Oil*, 30–2.

105 Venn, *Oil Diplomacy in the Twentieth Century*, 49–50, 76–8.

106 Catherine E. Jayne, *Oil, War, and Anglo-American Relations: American and British Reactions to Mexico's Expropriation of Foreign Oil Properties, 1937–1941* (London: Greenwood, 2001), 20, 78.

107 See ibid.

108 McBeth, *British Oil Policy*, 86–98; Venn, *Oil Diplomacy in the Twentieth Century*, 62–77.

109 Engdahl, *A Century of War*, 91.
110 Yergin, *Quest*, 47.
111 LeVine, *Oil and the Glory*, x–xi.
112 Ibid., xiii–xiv.
113 King, *Ghosts of Freedom*, 245.
114 Stokes and Raphael, *Global Energy Security and American Hegemony*, 116–18.
115 Rutledge, *Addicted to Oil*, 103.
116 Yergin, *Quest*, 62.
117 Rutledge, *Addicted to Oil*, 110–16.
118 Stokes and Raphael, *Global Energy Security and American Hegemony*, 123–5.
119 King, *Ghosts of Freedom*, 211.
120 Ibid., 218, 237–44.
121 Fisher, *Curzon and British Imperialism in the Middle East*, 164.
122 Yahia Said, "Greed and Grievance in Chechnya," in Kaldor, Karl, and Said, *Oil Wars*, 130–7.
123 King, *Ghosts of Freedom*, 237.
124 Mary Kaldor, "Oil and Conflict: The Case of Nagorno-Karabakh," in Kaldor, Karl, and Said, *Oil Wars*, 157–75.
125 King, *Ghosts of Freedom*, 15.

Conclusion

1 Stokes and Raphael, *Global Energy Security and American Hegemony*, 10–11, 17.
2 Kennedy, *Preparing for the Twenty-First Century*, 32–3.
3 Stokes and Raphael, *Global Energy Security and American Hegemony*, 42.
4 As of writing, Chevron is actively pursuing the acquisition of BP.
5 Scott Anderson, *Lawrence in Arabia: War, Deceit, Imperial Folly and the Making of the Modern Middle East* (New York: Doubleday, 2013), 493–4.
6 Yergin, *Prize*, 765.
7 The above paragraphs are paraphrased or quoted from Yergin, *Prize*, 763–9.
8 Ibid., 773.
9 May, *Hard Oiler!*, 11–12.

Epilogue

1 Brent Crude is one of two major global trading classifications of sweet light crude oil and serves as a benchmark for the worldwide price for purchases of oil. The other global oil pricing standard is the West Texas Intermediate (WTI), also known as Texas Light Sweet. While price per barrel between the

two markers is usual fairly even, recently, WTI ranges from $2.00 to $3.00 cheaper per barrel on international exchanges. For example, on 5 April 2016, Brent crude listed at $37.76 and WTI at $35.67. As of writing, the lowest closing price for Brent Crude was on 18 January 2016 at $27.67, and for WTI on 10 February 2016 at $26.14.

2 *Economist*, 6 December 2014, 7.

Bibliography

Archival, Library, and Manuscript Collections

Australian War Memorial, Canberra, Australia

AWM38 3DRL606/239/1. Official History, 1914–18 War: Records of C.E.W. Bean, official historian. Diaries and notebooks, 1917–18: Includes references to the 12th, 46th, 47th, and 58th Battalions, Dunsterforce, Polygon Wood, and Lagnicourt.
AWM38 3DRL606/259/1. Official History, 1914–18 War: Records of C.E.W. Bean, official historian. Diaries and notebooks, 1917–27: Covers Dunsterforce, units in Mesopotamia and AIF nurses in India and includes nominal rolls, diagrams, extracts from official records, and letters by E.K. Burke and Matron O. Davies.

Imperial War Museum, London, United Kingdom

1845 92/21/1. Private Papers of William H.W. Lacey.
2347 93/23/1–6. Private Papers of C.B. Stokes.
2914 94/46/1. Private Papers of H.B. Suttor.
4043 84/48/1 (P). Private Papers of L.R. Hulls.
9748 P157. Private Papers of A.A. Cullen.
11296 DS/MISC/34. Private Papers of W. Gout.
17431 10/3/1. Private Papers of A.J. Foster.

Leeds University Library, Leeds, United Kingdom

Liddle Collection, DU, vols. 1–4. Dunsterforce/Caspian Naval Force.

Library and Archives Canada, Ottawa

Record Group (RG)
R2614-0-2-E, MG30-E192, vol. 1, Lieutenant-Colonel John Weightman Warden Fonds.
RG9-III, vol. 3096, file 01-11-36. General Staff Headquarters, London: Reports on Dunsterforce.
RG24-C-6-e, vol. 1840, pt 1, file GAQ-10-28. Archangel, Dunster, Muman, Siberia, Palestine.
RG24-C-6-i, vol. 1872, pt 1, file SF-15-4. Scanlon's Files: The Dunsterforce/ Baghdad Mission: N.W. Persia to the Caspian Sea.
RG24, vol. 2944, pt 1, file CEF-US-75. Dunsterforce: Nominal Role.
RG150, vol. 608, file 1580. Bath War Hospital Admissions: Canadians Russia, 1 January 1918 to 31 December 1919.

Middle East Centre, St Antony's College, University of Oxford, Oxford

GB165-0023. Gertrude M.L. Bell.
GB165-0069. Major J.D. Crowdy.
GB165-0077. J.M. Dawkins.
GB165-0085. Lieutenant-Colonel Harold R.P. Dickson.
GB165-0105. Feisal Emir of Hijaz.
GB165-0113. Major-General William A.R. Fraser.
GB165-0133. John Almeric de Courcy Hamilton.
GB165-0207. Elizabeth Monroe.
GB165-0270. Benjamin W. Stainton.
GB165-0275. Sir Mark Sykes.
GB165-0291. U.S. Department of State.
GB165-0341. Sir Percy Z. Cox.

National Archives, Kew/London, United Kingdom

Air Ministry (AIR)
    20/660–62. Air Ministry and Ministry of Defence: Papers accumulated by the Air Historical Branch, 1918–20 on Operations in Persia, Mesopotamia, and Dunsterforce.
Cabinet Office (CAB)
    23/6–42. Documents, Orders, and Correspondence: South Russia, Central Asia, Persia, Mesopotamia, India, Egypt, Eastern Committee, Dunsterforce, January 1918 to September 1920.

24/4–144. Documents, Orders, and Correspondence: South Russia, Central Asia, Persia, Mesopotamia, India, Egypt, Eastern Committee, Dunsterforce, January 1918 to September 1920.

War Office (WO)

95/4960, vols. 1–8. First World War and Army of Occupation War Diaries, 1914–1923.

95/5042–4. Army of Occupation War Diaries Part VI: Mesopotamia, Iraq, Persia and Dunsterforce.

153/1032. War of 1914–1918: Maps and plans, Mesopotamia, Iraq, and North Persia.

157/854–6. War Office: Intelligence summaries First World War, Mesopotamia, Dunsterforce.

Royal Society for Asian Affairs, London, United Kingdom

RSAA/M/67. Dunsterforce Photograph Album, 1918–2003.

Private Collections

Diary and Photos of Sgt Crofford G. Campbell (CEF), January 1918 to January 1919. Courtesy of Jill Campbell.

Diary and Photos of Capt. Adam H. Gilmour (CEF), January 1918 to September 1919. Courtesy of Pam Hendy (Gilmour)

Letters and Photos of Sgt A.H. McGorm (AIF), January 1918 to October 1919. Courtesy of Debbie McGorm.

Other Sources

Abbassi, Zahra. "Anglo-Iran 1919 Agreement," Iran Review, 23 July 2012. http://www.iranreview.org/content/Documents/Anglo-Iran-1919-Agreement.htm.

Abrahamian, Ervand. *A History of Modern Iran*. Cambridge: Cambridge University Press, 2008.

Ahmed, Feroz. *Young Turks: The Committee of Union and Progress in Turkish Politics, 1908–1914*. London: Hurst, 2009.

Allen, W.E.D., and Paul Muratoff. *Caucasian Battlefields: A History of the Wars in the Turco-Caucasian Border 1828–1921*. Nashville: Battery, 1999.

Anderson, M.S. *The Eastern Question, 1917–1923*. London: Macmillan, 1966.

Anderson, Scott. *Lawrence in Arabia: War, Deceipt, Imperial Folly and the Making of the Modern Middle East*. New York: Doubleday, 2013.

Armstrong, Karen. *Fields of Blood: Religion and the History of Violence*. New York: Alfred A. Knopf, 2014.

Aron, Raymond. *The Century of Total War*. Boston: Beacon, 1955.

Arslanian, Artin H. "Britain and the Transcaucasian Nationalities during the Russian Civil War," *Kennan Institute for Advanced Russian Studies Occasional Paper*, Woodrow Wilson Center, 1980.

– "British Wartime Pledges, 1917–1918: The Armenian Case," *Journal of Contemporary History* 13, no. 3 (1978): 517–30.

– "Dunsterville's Adventures: A Reappraisal." *International Journal of Middle East Studies* 12, no. 2 (1980): 199–216.

Atabaki, Touraj, ed. *Iran and the First World War: Battleground of the Great Powers*. London: I.B. Tauris, 2006.

Austin, W.S. *The Official History of the New Zealand Rifle Brigade*. Wellington: L.T. Watkins, 1924.

Bailey, F.M. *Mission to Tashkent*. London: Cape, 1946.

Bamberg, J.H. *The History of the British Petroleum Company*. Vol. 2, *The Anglo-Iranian Years, 1928–1954*. Cambridge: Cambridge University Press, 1994.

Barker, A.J. *The First Iraq War, 1914–1918: Britain's Mesopotamian Campaign*. New York: Enigma Books, 2009.

Barr, James. *A Line in the Sand: The Anglo-French Struggle for the Middle East, 1914–1948*. New York: W.W. Norton, 2011.

Bean, C.E.W. *Official History of Australia in the War of 1914–1918*. Vol. 5, *The Australian Imperial Force in France, December 1917–May 1918*. Sydney: Angus and Robertson, 1937.

Bell, Christopher M. *Churchill and Sea Power*. Oxford: Oxford University Press, 2012.

Bérenger, Henry. *Le Pétrole et la France*. Paris: Ernest Flammarion, 1920.

Bey, Essad. *Blood and Oil in the Orient*. New York: Simon and Schuster, 1932.

Blacker, Latham V.S. *On a Secret Patrol in High Asia*. London: John Murray, 1922.

Blair, John M. *The Control of Oil*. New York: Pantheon Books, 1976.

Blinn, James W. *The Aardvark Is Ready for War: A Novel*. San Diego: San Diego State University Press, 1995.

Bloxham, Donald. *The Great Game of Genocide: Imperialism, Nationalism, and the Destruction of the Ottoman Armenians*. Oxford: Oxford University Press, 2005.

Bodger, Alan. "Russia and the End of the Ottoman Empire," in *The Great Powers and the End of the Ottoman Empire*, ed. Marian Kent, 76–110 (London: Allen & Unwin, 1984).

Bradley, John. *Allied Intervention in Russia*. New York: University Press of America, 1968.

Brennan, Patrick H. "Byng's and Currie's Commanders: A Still Untold Story of the Canadian Corps." *Canadian Military History* 11, no. 2 (2002): 5–16.

Brinkley, George A. *The Volunteer Army and Allied Intervention in South Russia, 1917–1921.* Notre Dame, IN: University of Notre Dame Press, 1966.

British Documents on Foreign Affairs: Reports and Papers from the Foreign Office, Confidential Print. New York: University Publications of America, 1982–1985.

Bryce, Viscount James. *The Treatment of the Armenians in the Ottoman Empire 1915–16: Documents Presented to Viscount Grey of Fallodon, Secretary of State for Foreign Affairs.* Edited by Arnold J. Toynbee. London: Joseph Causton and Sons, 1916.

Buchan, John. *Greenmantle.* New York: Penguin Classics Reprint, 2008.

Burke, Keast, ed. *With Horse and Morse in Mesopotamia: The Story of Anzacs in Asia.* Sydney: Arthur McQuitty, 1927.

Burne, A.H. *Mesopotamia: The Last Phase.* London: Gale & Polden, 1936.

Busch, Briton Cooper. *Britain and the Persian Gulf, 1894–1914.* Berkeley: University of California Press, 1967.

– *Mudros to Lausanne: Britain's Frontier in West Asia, 1918–1923.* Albany: State University of New York Press, 1976.

Butler, Daniel Allen. *Shadow of the Sultan's Realm: The Destruction of the Ottoman Empire and the Creation of the Modern Middle East.* Washington, DC: Potomac Books, 2011.

Candler, Edmund. *The Long Road to Baghdad.* 2 vols. Toronto: Cassel, 1919.

– *On the Edge of the World.* Toronto: Cassel, 1919.

Carew, Michael G. *The Impact of the First World War on U.S. Policy Makers: American Strategic and Foreign Policy Formulation, 1938–1942.* New York: Lexington, 2014.

Carmichael, Cathie. *Ethnic Cleansing in the Balkans: Nationalism and the Destruction of Tradition.* New York: Routledge, 2002.

Carter, Miranda. *George, Nicholas and Wilhelm: Three Royal Cousins and the Road to World War I.* New York: Vintage Books, 2011.

Churchill, Winston. *The World Crisis, 1911–1918.* New York: First Free Press, 2005.

Clark, Alan. *The Donkeys: A History of the British Expeditionary Force in 1915.* London: Hutchinson, 1961.

Clark, Christopher. *The Sleepwalkers: How Europe Went to War in 1914.* New York: HarperCollins, 2013.

Cohen, S.A. "The Genesis of the British Campaign in Mesopotamia, 1914." *Middle Eastern Studies* 12, no. 2 (1976): 119–32.

Commins, David. *The Gulf States: A Modern History.* New York: I.B. Tauris, 2012.

Comtois, Pierre. "Battle for Baku." *Military History* 22, no. 4 (2005): 54–60, 72.

Cook, Tim. *At the Sharp End: Canadians Fighting the Great War*. Vol. 1, *1914–1916*. Toronto: Penguin, 2007.

Cuthell, David. "A Kemalist Gambit: A View of the Political Negotiations in the Determination of the Turkish-Iraqi Border." In Simon and Tajirian, 86–7.

Dadrian, Vahakn N. *The History of the Armenian Genocide: Ethnic Conflict from the Balkans to Anatolia to the Caucasus*. Oxford: Berghahn Books, 2008.

Delaisi, Francis. *Oil: Its Influence on Politics*. London: George Allen and Unwin, 1920.

De la Tramerye, Pierre l'Espagnol. *The World-Struggle for Oil*. Translation by C. Leonard Leese. New York: Alfred A. Knopf, 1924.

Denny, Ludwell. *We Fight for Oil*. New York: Alfred A. Knopf, 1930.

DeNovo, John A. *American Interests and Policies in the Middle East, 1900–1939*. Minneapolis: University of Minnesota Press, 1963.

De Waal, Thomas, *The Caucasus: An Introduction*. Oxford: Oxford University Press, 2010.

Dobson, Alan P. *Anglo-American Relations in the Twentieth Century: Of Friendship, Conflict and the Rise and Decline of Superpowers*. New York: Routledge, 1995.

Donohoe, M.H. *With the Persian Expedition*. London: Edward Arnold, 1919.

Dreisziger, Nandor F., and Bela K. Kiraly, eds. *War and Society in East Central Europe*. Vol. 19, *East Central European Society in World War I*. New York: Columbia University Press, 1985.

Drummond, Ian M. *British Economic Policy and the Empire, 1919–1939*. London: George Allen and Unwin, 1972.

Dundar, Fuat. *Crime of Numbers: The Role of Statistics in the Armenian Question, 1878–1918*. New Brunswick, NJ: Transaction Publishers, 2010.

Dunsterville, Lionel C. *The Adventures of Dunsterforce*. London: Edward Arnold, 1920.

– "The Diaries of General Lionel Dunsterville, 1911–1922." World War I Document Archive. www.gwpda.org/Dunsterville/Dunsterville_main.html.

– "From Baghdad to the Caspian in 1918," *Geographical Journal* 57.3 (1921): 153–164.

– "Military Mission to North-West Persia, 1918," *Journal of the Central Asian Society* 8.2 (1921): 79–98.

– *More Yarns*. London: Jarrolds, 1931.

– "Six Months in North-West Persia," *Persia Magazine* 1.1 (1921).

– *Stalky's Reminiscences*. London: Jonathan Cape, 1928.

Dutton, David. *The Politics of Diplomacy: Britain and France in the Balkans in the First World War*. London: IB Taurus, 1998.

Eisenstadt, Michael, and Eric Mathewson. *U.S. Policy in Post-Saddam Iraq: Lessons from the British Experience.* Washington, DC: Washington Institute for Near East Policy, 2003.

Ellis, C.H. *The British "Intervention" in Transcaspia, 1918–1919.* Berkeley: University of California Press, 1963.

– "Colonel Ellis: At the Southern Outskirts of Russia." www.australiarussia. com/ellisENFIN.htm.

Engdahl, F. William. *A Century of War: Anglo-American Oil Politics and the New World Order.* Wiesbaden: edition.engdahl, 2011.

– *Myths, Lies and Oil Wars.* Wiesbaden: edition.engdahl, 2012.

– "Oil and the Origins of the 'War to Make the World Safe for Democracy.'" *Geopolitics-Geoeconomics* (2007). http://www.engdahl.oilgeopolitics.net/ print/Oil%20and%20the%20Origins%20of%20World%20War%20I.htm.

Erendil, Muzaffer. "The Ottoman Empire in World War I: The Home Front and Military Affairs." In *War and Society in East Central Europe*, ed. Bela K. Kiraly and Nandor F. Dreisziger, 369–80. New York: Columbia University Press, 1985.

Erickson, Edward J. *Ordered to Die: A History of the Ottoman Army in the First World War.* London: Greenwood, 2001.

Evans, R. *A Brief Outline of the Campaign in Mesopotamia, 1914–1918.* London: Sifton Praed, 1926.

Ewalt, Donald. "The Fight for Oil: Britain in Persia, 1919." *History Today* 31, no. 9 (1981): 10–11.

Ferguson, Niall. *Civilization: The West and the Rest.* New York: Allen Lane, 2011.

– *The Pity of War: Explaining World War I.* London: Penguin, 1998.

– *The War of the World.* New York: Allen Lane, 2006.

Ferrier, R.W. *The History of the British Petroleum Company.* Cambridge: Cambridge University Press, 1982.

Finkel, Caroline. *Osman's Dream: The History of the Ottoman Empire.* New York: Basic Books, 2007.

Fischer, Fritz. *Germany's Aims in the First World War.* New York: W.W. Norton, 1967.

Fischer, Louis. *Oil Imperialism: The International Struggle for Petroleum.* New York: International Publishers, 1926.

Fisher, John. *Curzon and British Imperialism in the Middle East, 1916–1919.* London: Frank Cass, 1999.

Fisk, Robert. *The Great War for Civilization: The Conquest of the Middle East.* New York: Harper, 2006.

Fong, Giordan. "Debate: The Movement of German Divisions to the Western Front, Winter 1917–1918." *War in History* 7, no. 2 (2000): 225–35.

Ford, Roger. *Eden to Armageddon: World War I in the Middle East.* London: Weidenfeld & Nicolson, 2009.

Frank, Alison Fleig. *Oil Empire: Visions of Prosperity in Austrian Galicia.* Cambridge, MA: Harvard University Press, 2005.

Freire, Bramcamp, Lord Lamington, and Valentine Chirol. "The Road from Baghdad to Baku: Discussion." *Geographical Journal* 53, no. 1 (1919): 16–19.

French, David. *British Economic and Strategic Planning 1905–1915.* London: George Allen & Unwin, 1982.

– *British Strategy & War Aims 1914–1916.* London: Allen & Unwin, 1986.

– *The Strategy of the Lloyd George Coalition 1916–1918.* Oxford: Clarendon, 1995.

Fromkin, David. *A Peace to End All Peace: The Fall of the Ottoman Empire and the Creation of the Modern Middle East.* New York: Henry Holt, 1989.

Fry, M.G. "Britain, the Allies, and the Problem of Russia, 1918–1919." *Canadian Journal of History* 2, no. 2 (1967): 62–84.

Gaunt, David. *Massacres, Resistance, Protectors: Muslim-Christian Relations in Eastern Anatolia during World War I.* Piscataway, NJ: Gorgias, 2006.

Glenny, Misha. *The Balkans: Nationalism, War and the Great Powers, 1804–1999.* London: Granta Books, 1999.

Gokay, Bulent. "The Battle for Baku (May–September 1918): A Peculiar Episode in the History of the Caucusus." *Middle Eastern Studies* 34, no. 1 (1998): 30–50.

Gregory, Adrian. *The Last Great War: British Society and the First World War.* Cambridge: Cambridge University Press, 2008.

Grey, Jeffrey. "A "Pathetic Sideshow': Australians and the Russian Intervention, 1918–1919." *Journal of the Australian War Memorial* 7 (1985):12–17.

Gruen, George E. "The Oil Resources of Iraq: Their Role in the Policies of the Great Powers." In Simon and Tejirian, 110–24.

Guard, John. "The Royal Navy in the Caspian Sea 1918–1920." World War I Document Archive. www.gwpda.org/naval/caspian.htm.

Gust, Wolfgang, and Sigrid, eds. "The Armenian Genocide 1915/16: Selected Documents from the Political Archives of the German Foreign Office." http://www.armenocide.net/armenocide/armgende.nsf/WebStart-En?OpenFrameset.

Hahn, Peter L. *Mission Accomplished?: The United States and Iraq since World War I.* Oxford: Oxford University Press, 2011.

Hanighen, Frank C. *The Secret War.* New York: John Day, 1934.

Hanioğlu, M. Şükrü. *Preparation for a Revolution: The Young Turks, 1902–1908.* Oxford: Oxford University Press, 2001.

Hanson, Neil. *Unknown Soldiers: The Story of the Missing of the First World War.* New York: Vintage, 2007.

Hardach, Gerd. *The First World War 1914–1918*. New York: Penguin Books, 1987.

Harington, Charles. *Plumer of Messines*. London: J. Murray, 1935.

Hart Liddell, B.H. *The Real War, 1914–1918*. Toronto: Little, Brown, 1930.

Hasanli, Jamil. *Khrushehev's Thaw and National Identity in Soviet Azerbaijan, 1954–1959*. New York: Lexington, 2014.

Hassmann, Heinrich, *Oil in the Soviet Union: History, Geography, Problems*. Princeton: Princeton University Press, 1953.

Hay, Angus. "Dunsterforce: The British in Northern Persia and Baku, 1918." *Asian Affairs* 34, no. 3 (2003): 387–91.

Haythornthwaite, Philip J. *The World War One Source Book*. London: Brockhampton, 1992.

Heller, Joseph. *British Policy towards the Ottoman Empire 1908–1914*. London: Frank Cass, 1983.

Herwig, Holger H. *The First World War: Germany and Austria-Hungary 1914–1918*. London: Arnold, 1997.

Historical Section (G.S.) Army Headquarters (Canada). *Report No. 84: Canadians in Mesopotamia, 1918–1919*. Ottawa: Queen's Printer, 1959.

Hopkirk, Peter. *The Great Game: On Secret Service in High Asia*. Oxford: Oxford University Press, 1990.

– *On the Secret Service East of Constantinople: The Plot to Bring Down the British Empire*. Oxford: Oxford University Press, 1994.

Hovannisian, Richard G. *Armenia on the Road to Independence, 1918*. Berkeley: University of California Press, 1967.

Howell, Georgina. *Gertrude Bell: Queen of the Desert, Shaper of Nations*. New York: Farrar, Straus, Giroux, 2006.

Hughes, Matthew. *Allenby and the British Strategy in the Middle East, 1917–1919*. London: Frank Cass, 1999.

Hughes, Thomas L. "The German Mission to Afghanistan, 1915–1916." *German Studies Review* 25, no. 3 (2002): 447–76.

Hussey, John. "Debate: The Movement of German Divisions to the Western Front, Winter 1917–1918." *War in History* 4, no. 2 (1997): 213–20.

Ironside, Edmund. *The Diaries of Major-General Sir Edmund Ironside, 1920–1922*. London: Leo Cooper, 1972.

Jack, Marian. "The Purchase of the British Government's Shares in the British Petroluem Company 1912–1914." *Past & Present* 39 (1968): 139–68.

Jablonsky, David. *Churchill, the Great Game and Total War*. London: Frank Cass, 1991.

Jayne, Catherine E. *Oil, War, and Anglo-American Relations: American and British Reactions to Mexico's Expropriation of Foreign Oil Properties, 1937–1941*. London: Greenwood, 2001.

Jenkins, Philip. *The Great and Holy War: How World War I Became a Religious Crusade*. New York: HarperCollins, 2014.

Jones, G. Gareth. "The British Government and the Oil Companies, 1912–1924: The Search for an Oil Policy." *Historical Journal* 20, no. 3 (1977): 647–72.

Jones, Geoffrey. *The State and the Emergence of the British Oil Industry*. London: Macmillan, 1981.

Judge, Cecil G. "With General Dunsterville in Persia and Transcaucasia." www.australiarussia.com/captain_judge.htm.

Kaldor, Mary. "Oil and Conflict: The Case of Nagorno-Karabakh." In Kaldor, Karl, and Said, *Oil Wars*, 157–82.

Kaldor, Mary, Terry Lynn Karl, and Yahia Said, eds. *Oil Wars*. Ann Arbor, MI: Pluto, 2007.

Karsh, Efraim and Inari Karsh. *Empires of the Sand: The Struggle for Mastery in the Middle East, 1789–1923*. Cambridge, MA: Harvard University Press, 1999.

Katouzian, Homa. "The Campaign against the Anglo-Iranian Agreement of 1919." *British Journal of Middle Eastern Studies* 25, no. 1 (1998): 5–46.

Kazemzadeh, Firuz. *The Struggle for Transcaucasia, 1917–1921*. Oxford: George Ronald, 1951.

Keegan, John. *The First World War*. Toronto: Vintage Canada, 2000.

Kennan, George, Douglas W. Johnson, and Warren B. Walsh. "May–June 1917: An Estimate of the Situation." *Russian Review* 27, no. 4 (1968): 468–70.

Kennedy, Paul. *Preparing for the Twenty-First Century*. New York: HarperCollins, 1993.

Kennion, Roger L. *Diversions of an Indian Political*. London: W. Blackwood, 1932.

Kent, Marian, ed. *The Great Powers and the End of the Ottoman Empire*. London: George Allen & Unwin, 1984.

– *Moguls and Mandarins: Oil, Imperialism and the Middle East in British Foreign Policy, 1900–1940*. London: Frank Cass, 1993.

– *Oil and Empire: British Policy and Mesopotamian Oil, 1900–1920*. London: Macmillan, 1976.

Kenez, Peter. *Civil War in South Russia, 1918*. Berkeley: University of California Press, 1971.

– *Civil War in South Russia, 1919–1920*. Berkeley: University of California Press, 1977.

– *A History of the Soviet Union from the Beginning to the End*. Cambridge: Cambridge University Press, 2006.

Kettle, Michael. *The Road to Intervention: March–November 1918*. London: Routledge, 1988.

Khalidi, Rashid. *Resurrecting Empire: Western Footprints and America's Perilous Path in the Middle East*. Boston: Beacon, 2004.

King, Charles. *The Ghosts of Freedom: A History of the Caucasus*. Oxford: Oxford University Press, 2008.

Kinross, Patrick Balfour. *The Ottoman Centuries: The Rise and Fall of the Turkish Empire*. New York: Harper, 1979.

Kinvig, Clifford. *Churchill's Crusade: The British Invasion of Russia, 1918–1920*. London: Hambledon Continuum, 2006.

Kipling, Rudyard. *Stalky & Co*. London: MacMillan, 1899.

Kleveman, Lutz. *The New Great Game: Blood and Oil in Central Asia*. New York: Atlantic Monthly, 2003.

Kolchak, Aleksandr V. *The Testimony of Kolchak and Other Siberian Materials*. Stanford: Stanford University Press, 1935.

Kopisto, Lauri. "The British Intervention in South Russia 1918–1920." PhD diss., University of Helsinki, April 2011.

Krammer, Arnold. "Fueling the Third Reich." *Technology & Culture* 19, no. 3 (1978): 394–422.

Lambert, Nicholas A. *Planning Armageddon: British Economic Warfare and the First World War*. Cambridge, MA: Harvard University Press, 2012.

Lawrence, T.E. *Seven Pillars of Wisdom*. Toronto: J. Cape, 1935.

LeVine, Steve. *The Oil and the Glory: The Pursuit of Empire and Fortune on the Caspian Sea*. New York: Random House, 2007.

Lincoln, W. Bruce. *Red Victory: A History of the Russian Civil War*. New York: Simon and Schuster, 1989.

Lloyd George, David. *British War Aims: Statement of 5 January 1918*. New York: George H. Doran, 1918.

– *War Memoirs of David Lloyd George*. 6 vols. London: Ivor Nicholson and Watson, 1933.

Louis, Wm Roger. *Great Britain and Germany's Lost Colonies, 1914–1919*. Oxford: Clarendon, 1967.

Luckett, Richard. *The White Generals: An Account of the White Movement and the Russian Civil War*. London: Longman Group, 1971.

Ludendorff, Erich von. *Ludendorff's Own Story*. New York: Harper, 1919.

MacDonell, Ranald. *And Nothing Long*. London: Constable, 1938.

MacLaren, Roy. *Canadians in Russia, 1918–1919*. Toronto: Maclean-Hunter, 1976.

MacMillan, Margaret. *Paris 1919*. New York: Random House, 2003.

– *The War That Ended Peace: The Road to 1914*. New York: Random House, 2013.

Madj, Mohammad Gholi. *The Great Famine and Genocide in Persia, 1917–1919*. Toronto: University Press of America, 2003.

Marcel, Valerie. *Oil Titans: National Oil Companies in the Middle East*. London: Chatham House, 2006.

Marling, Charles. *West Meets East: An English Diplomat in the Ottoman Empire and Persia, 1890–1918: The Unfinished Autobiography of Sir Charles Marling.* Edited by Keith M. Wilson. Istanbul: Isis, 2010.

Marriott, James, and Mika Minio-Paluello. *The Oil Road: Journeys from the Caspian Sea to the City of London.* London: Verso, 2012.

Marsh, F.G. "Experiences in the Caucasus and North Persia, 1914–1918." *Royal United Services Institution Journal* 70 (1925): 710–23.

Marshall, Alex. *The Caucasus under Soviet Rule.* New York: Routledge, 2010.

Marshall, S.L.A. *World War I.* New York: Mariner Books, 2001.

Marshall, William. *Memories of Four Fronts.* London: Ernest Benn, 1929.

Maugeri, Leonardo. *The Age of Oil: The Mythology, History, and Future of the World's Most Controversial Resource.* London: Praeger, 2006.

Mawdsley, Evan. *The Russian Civil War.* New York: Pegasus Books, 2007.

May, Gary. *Hard Oiler!: The Story of Canadians' Quest for Oil at Home and Abroad.* Toronto: Dundurn, 1998.

Maynard, Charles. *The Murmansk Adventure.* London: Hodder & Stoughton, 1969.

McBeth, B.S. *British Oil Policy, 1919–1939.* London: Frank Cass, 1985.

McCarthy, Justin. *Death and Exile: The Ethnic Cleansing of Ottoman Muslims, 1821–1922.* Princeton: Darwin, 1996.

McDowell, Robert H. "Russian Revolution and the Civil War in Caucasus." *Russian Review* 27, no. 4 (1968): 452–60.

McKale, Donald M. "Germany and the Arab Question before World War I." *Historian* 59, no. 2 (1997): 311–25.

– *War by Revolution: Germany and Great Britain in the Middle East in the Era of World War I.* Kent, OH: Kent State University Press, 1998.

McKay, John P. "Baku Oil and Transcaucasian Pipelines, 1883–1891: A Study in Tsarist Economic Policy." *Slavic Review* 43, no. 4 (1984): 604–23.

Mclean, David. "Finance and 'Informal Empire' before the First World War." *Economic History Review* 29, no. 2 (1976): 291–305.

McMeekin, Sean. *The Berlin-Baghdad Express: The Ottoman Empire and Germany's Bid for World Power, 1898–1918.* Toronto: Penguin Books, 2011.

Mejcher, Helmut. "British Middle East Policy 1917–1921: The Inter-Departmental Level." *Journal of Contemporary History* 8, no. 4 (1973): 81–101.

– "Oil and British Policy towards Mesopotamia, 1914–1918." *Middle Eastern Studies* 8, no. 3 (1972): 337–91.

Millman, Brock. "A Counsel of Despair: British Strategy and War Aims, 1917–18." *Journal of Contemporary History* 36, no. 2 (2001): 241–70.

– "The Problem with Generals: Military Observers and the Origins of the Intervention in Russia and Persia, 1917–1918." *Journal of Contemporary History* 33, no. 2 (1998): 291–320.

Mills, Robin M. *The Myth of the Oil Crisis: Overcoming the Challenges of Depletion, Geopolitics, and Global Warming.* London: Praeger, 2008.

Moberly, F.J. *The Campaign in Mesopotamia, 1914–1918.* Vol. 4. London: HMSO, 1927.

– *History of the Great War: Operations in Persia, 1914–1919.* London: HMSO, 1929.

– *Operations in Persia, 1914–1919.* London: Her Majesty's Stationery Office, 1929.

Mohr, Anton. *The Oil War.* New York: Harcourt Brace, 1926.

Mosley, Leonard. *Power Play: Oil in the Middle East.* New York: Random House, 1973.

Murgul, Yalcin. "Baku Expedition of 1917–1918: A Study of the Ottoman Policy towards the Caucasus." Master's thesis, Bilkent University, Ankara, September 2007.

Murray, W.W. "Canadians in Dunsterforce." *Canadian Defence Quarterly* (1931) 8, no. 2: 209–18; 8, no. 3: 377–86; 8, no. 4: 487–97; (1935): 12, no. 2: 211–13.

– "From Canada to the Caspian: Gentleman Adventurers of Dunsterforce." *Legionary* (1935–6).

Napier, G.S.F. "The Road from Baghdad to Baku." *Geographic Journal* 53, no. 1 (1919): 1–16.

Nash, Gerald D. *United States Oil Policy, 1890–1964.* Westport, CT: Greenwood, 1968.

Nicholson, G.W.L. *Canadian Expeditionary Force, 1914–1919: Official History of the Canadian Army in the First World War.* Ottawa: Queen's Printer, 1962.

Noel, E. "A Prisoner among the Jungali Bolsheviks." In *On the Run: Escaping Tales,* ed. H.C. Armstrong, 25–55. London: Rich & Cowan, 1934.

Norris, D. "Caspian Naval Expedition, 1918–1919." *Journal of the Central Asian Society* 10, no. 1 (1923): 216–40.

Nuriyev, Elkhan. *The South Caucasus at the Crossroads: Conflicts, Caspian Oil and Great Power Politics.* Berlin: Lit Verlag, 2007.

Occleshaw, Michael. *Dances in Deep Shadows: The Clandestine War in Russia, 1917–1920.* New York: Carroll & Graf, 2006.

Ordubadi, Mammad Said. *Years of Blood: A History of the Armenian-Muslim Clashes in the Caucasus, 1905–1906.* Reading, UK: Ithaca, 2011.

Oren, Michael B. *Power, Faith, and Fantasy: America in the Middle East, 1776 to the Present.* New York: W.W. Norton, 2008.

Overy, Richard. *Why the Allies Won.* New York: W.W. Norton, 1996.

Palmer, Alan. *The Gardens of Salonika: The Macedonian Campaign, 1915–1918.* London: Faber, 2011.

Pasdermadjian, Garegin. *Why Armenia Should Be Free: Armenia's Role in the Present War.* Boston: Hairenik, 1918.

Paul, Christopher, Clarke, Colin P., and Grill, Beth. *Victory Has a Thousand Fathers: Sources of Success in Counterinsurgency.* Santa Monica, CA: RAND, 2010.

Payne, David. "'Dunsterforce" on the Caucasian Front in the Great War." The Western Front Association. http://www.westernfrontassociation.com/the-great-war/great-war-on-land/general-interest/175-dunster-force. html#sthash.P3X8AIxj.dpbs.

Pearce, Brian. "Dunsterforce and the Defence of Baku, August–September 1918." *Revolutionary Russia* 10, no. 1 (1997): 55–71.

Pearton, Maurice. *Oil and the Romanian State.* Oxford: Clarendon, 1971.

Perras, Galen Roger. "Anglo-Canadian Imperial Relations: The Case of Garrisoning of the Falkland Islands in 1942." *War & Society* 14, no. 1 (1996): 73–97.

Perrett, Brian, and Anthony Lord. *The Czar's British Squadron.* London: William Kimber, 1981.

Persico, Joseph E. *11th Month, 11th Day, 11th Hour: Armistice Day, 1918, World War I and Its Violent Climax.* London: Hutchinson, 2004.

Platt, D.C.M. "Economic Factors in British Policy during the 'New Imperialism.'" *Past & Present* 39 (1968): 120–38.

Plotke, A.J. *Imperial Spies Invade Russia: The British Intelligence Interventions, 1918.* London: Greenwood, 1993.

Quataert, Donald. *The Ottoman Empire, 1700–1922.* Cambridge: Cambridge University Press, 2000.

Rawlinson, Alfred. *Adventures in the Near East, 1918–1922.* London: Andrew Melrose, 1923.

Remarque, Erich Maria. *All Quiet on the Western Front.* New York: Fawcett Crest, 1982.

Reynold, Nick. *Britain's Unfulfilled Mandate for Palestine.* New York: Lexington, 2014.

Reynolds, David. *The Long Shadow: The Legacies of the Great War in the Twentieth Century.* New York: W.W. Norton, 2014.

Reynolds, Michael A. *Shattering Empires: The Clash and Collapse of the Ottoman and Russian Empires, 1908–1918.* Cambridge: Cambridge University Press, 2011.

Rogan, Eugene. *The Fall of the Ottomans: The Great War in the Middle East.* New York: Basic Books, 2015.

Roosevelt, Kermit. *Arabs, Oil and History: The Story of the Middle East.* Port Washington: Kennikat, NY, 1947.

Rothwell, V.H. *British War Aims and Peace Diplomacy, 1914–1918.* Oxford: Clarendon, 1971.

– "Mesopotamia in British War Aims, 1914–1918." *Historical Journal* 13, no. 2 (1970): 273–94.

Rutledge, Ian. *Addicted to Oil: America's Relentless Drive for Energy Security.* New York: I.B. Tauris, 2005.

Said, Yahia. "Greed and Grievance in Chechnya," In Kaldor, Karl, and Said, *Oil Wars*, 130–56.

Sampson, Anthony. *The Seven Sisters: The Great Oil Companies and the World They Made.* London: Hodder and Stoughton, 1975.

Sareen, T.R. *British Intervention in Central Asia and Trans-Caucasia.* New Dehli: Anmol, 1989.

Sargent, Michael. *British Involvement in Transcaspia (1918–1919).* (London: Defence Academy of the United Kingdom, Conflict Studies Research Centre, 2004).

Satia, Priya. *Spies in Arabia: The Great War and the Cultural Foundations of Britain's Covert Empire in the Middle East.* Oxford: Oxford University Press, 2008.

Savige, S.G. *Stalky's Forlorn Hope.* Melbourne: Alexander McCubbin, 1919.

Schmidt, Donald E. *The Folly of War: American Foreign Policy, 1898–2005.* New York: Algora, 2005.

Seidt, Hans-Ulrich. "From Palestine to the Caucasus: Oskar Niedermayer and Germany's Middle Eastern Strategy in 1918." *German Studies Review* 24, no. 1 (2001): 1–18.

Seligmann, Matthew S., ed. *Naval Intelligence from Germany: The Report of the British Naval Attaches in Berlin, 1906–1914.* Burlington: Ashgate, 2007.

– *The Royal Navy and the German Threat, 1901–1914: Admiralty Plans to Protect British Trade in a War against Germany.* Oxford: Oxford University Press, 2012.

– *Spies in Uniform: British Military and Naval Intelligence on the Eve of the First World War.* Oxford: Oxford University Press, 2006.

Serle, R.P. "Byron, John Joseph (1863–1935)." *Australian Dictionary of Biography.* http://adb.anu.edu.au/biography/byron-john-joseph-5459.

Shields, Sarah. "Mosul Questions: Economy, Identity, and Annexation." In Simon and Tejirian, 50–60.

Silverlight, John. *The Victor's Dilemma: Allied Intervention in the Russian Civil War.* London: Barrie & Jenkins, 1970.

Simon, Reeva Spector, and Eleanor H. Tejirian, eds. *The Creation of Iraq, 1914–1921.* New York: Columbia University Press, 2004.

Sluglett, Peter. *Britain in Iraq, 1914–1932.* London: Ithaca, 1976.

Smedman, Lisa. "Dunsterforce." *Vancouver Courier,* 2006. http://conflicts.rem33.com/images/Azerbaijan/dunsterforce%20long.pdf

Smele, Jonathan D. *The Russian Revolution and Civil War, 1917–1921: An Annotated Bibliography*. London: Continuum International Publishing Group, 2003.

Smith, Michael G. "Anatomy of a Rumour: Murder Scandal, the Musavat Party and Narratives of the Russian Revolution in Baku, 1917–1920." *Journal of Contemporary History* 36, no. 2 (2001): 211–40.

Smith, Staniforth. *Australian Campaigns in the Great War*. Melbourne: Macmillan, 1919.

Soutar, Andrew. *With Ironside in North Russia*. London: Anchor, 1940.

Stewart, Alan. *Persian Expedition: The Australians in Dunsterforce, 1918*. Loftus, NSW: AMHP, 2006.

Stivers, William. *Supremacy and Oil: Iraq, Turkey, and the Anglo-American World Order. 1918–1930*. Ithaca: Cornell University Press, 1982.

Stokes, Doug, and Sam Raphael. *Global Energy Security and American Hegemony*. Baltimore, MD: Johns Hopkins University Press, 2010.

Strachan, Hew. *The First World War*. Vol. 1: *To Arms*. Oxford: Oxford University Press, 2001.

– *The First World War*. New York: Viking, 2003.

Sumida, Jon Tetsuro. *In Defence of Naval Supremacy: Finance, Technology and British Naval Policy, 1889–1914*. Boston: Unwin Hyman, 1989.

Suny, Ronald G. *The Baku Commune, 1917–1918: Class and Nationality in the Russian Revolution*. Princeton, NJ: Princeton University Press, 1972.

Swettenham, John. *Allied Intervention in Russia, 1918–1919: And the Part Played by Canada*. Toronto: Ryerson, 1967.

Sykes, Percy. "The British Flag on the Caspian: A Side-Show of the Great War." *Foreign Affairs* 2, no. 2 (1923): 282–94.

– *A History of Persia*. Vol. 2. London: MacMillan, 1921.

Sykes, Percy, Major Poole, and L.C. Dunsterville. "From Baghdad to the Caspian in 1918: Discussion." *Geographical Journal* 57, no. 3 (1921): 164–6.

"Sykes-Picot Agreement, 15 & 16 May, 1916." World War I Document Archive. http://www.gwpda.org/1916/sykespicot.html.

Tarbell, Ida Minerva. *The History of the Standard Oil Company*. New York: McClure, Phillips, 1904.

Teague-Jones, Reginald. *The Spy Who Disappeared: Diary of a Secret Mission to Russian Central Asia in 1918*. Edited by Peter Hopkirk. London: Victor Gollancz, 1990.

Tejirian, Eleanor H. "The United States, the Ottoman Empire, and the Postwar Settlement." In Simon and Tejirian, *Creation of Iraq*, 146–61.

Tennant, John E. *In the Clouds above Baghdad, Being the Records of an Air Commander*. London: C. Palmer, 1920.

Thomson, W.M. "Transcaucasia 1918–19." *Revolutionary Russia* 10, no. 1 (1997): 72–96.

Times. *The Times History of the War*. Vol. 12. London: Times, 1921.

Tolkien, J.R.R. *The Lord of the Rings*. New York: HarperCollins, 1995.

Tooze, J. Adam. *Statistics and the German State, 1900–1945*. Cambridge: Cambridge University Press, 2001.

Townsend, John. *Proconsul to the Middle East: Sir Percy Cox and the End of Empire*. London: I.B. Tauris, 2010.

Townshend, Charles. *When God Made Hell: The British Invasion of Mesopotamia and the Creation of Iraq, 1914–1921*. London: Faber and Faber, 2010.

Travers, Tim. "Debate: Reply to John Hussey: The Movement of German Divisions to the Western Front, Winter 1917–1918." *War in History* 5, no. 3 (1998): 367–70.

Trotsky, Leon. *The Trotsky Papers, 1917–1922*. Vol. 1. The Hague: Mouton, 1964.

Trumpener, Ulrich. *Germany and the Ottoman Empire 1914–1918*. Princeton: Princeton University Press, 1968.

– "Liman von Sanders and the German-Ottoman Alliance." *Journal of Contemporary History* 1, no. 4 (1966): 179–92.

Tuchman, Barbara W. *The Proud Tower: A Portrait of the World before the War 1890–1914*. New York: Macmillan, 1966.

Ullman, Richard H. *Anglo-Soviet Relations, 1917–1921*. 2 vols. New Jersey: Princeton University Press, 1961, 1968.

Ulrichsen, Kristian Coates. *The Logistics and Politics of the British Campaigns in the Middle East, 1914–22*. New York: Palgrave Macmillan, 2011.

Van Creveld, Martin. *The Transformation of War*. New York: Free Press, 1991.

Van der Leeuw, Charles. *Oil and Gas in the Caucasus & Caspian: A History*. New York: St Martin's, 2000.

Venn, Fiona. *Oil Diplomacy in the Twentieth Century*. New York: St Martin's, 1986.

– "Oleaginous Diplomacy: Oil, Anglo-American Relations and the Lausanne Conference, 1922–1923." *Diplomacy & Statecraft* 20 (2009): 414–33.

Von Ludendorff, Erich. *My War Memories, 1914–1918*. London: Hutchison, 1919.

Walvoord, John F., and John E. Walvoord. *Armageddon: Oil and the Middle East Crisis*. Grand Rapids, MI: Vondervan, 1974.

Weber, Frank G. *Eagles on the Crescent: Germany, Austria, and the Diplomacy of the Turkish Alliance 1914–1918*. Ithica, NY: Cornell University Press, 1970.

Wilson, H.W., and J.A. Hammerton, eds. *The Great War: The Standard History of the World-Wide Conflict*. Vol. 13. London: Amalgamated, 1919.

Winegard, Timothy C. "The Canadian Siberian Expeditionary Force, 1918–1919, and the Complications of Coalition Warfare." *Journal of Slavic Military Studies* 20, no. 2 (2007): 283–328.

– "Dunsterforce: A Case Study of Coalition Warfare in the Middle East, 1918–1919." *Canadian Army Journal* 8, no. 3 (2005): 93–109.

Winter, Denis. *Haig's Command: A Reassessment.* London: Penguin Books, 1999.

Woodward, David R. *Hell in the Holy Land: World War I in the Middle East.* Lexington: University of Kentucky Press, 2006.

Yergin, Daniel. *The Prize: The Epic Quest for Oil, Money and Power.* New York: Free Press, 2008.

– *The Quest: Energy, Security, and the Remaking of the Modern World.* New York: Penguin, 2011.

Young, Hubert. *The Independent Arab.* London: J. Murray, 1933.

Zeman, Z.A.B., ed. *Germany and the Revolution in Russia, 1915–1918: Documents from the Archives of the German Foreign Ministry.* London: Oxford University Press, 1958.

Zurcher, Erik J. *The Young Turk Legacy and Nation Building: From the Ottoman Empire to Ataturk's Turkey.* London: I.B. Taurus, 2010.

Index

Abadan, xiv, 53, 63–8, 149
Abdullah, Achmed, 267
Abkhazia, 14, 37, 179, 181, 188, 195, 199, 216, 276–8, 290–2
Achaemenid dynasty, 24
Achnacarry Agreement (1928), 258
Adana, 30, 83
Adbullah I, 251
Aden, Gulf of, 63, 145, 147
Adrianople, 27
Aegean Sea, 27, 30
Afghanistan, 10, 97–8, 128–30, 135, 139, 165–7, 192, 281, 329n43; American-led invasion (2001), 15, 143, 247, 265–6, 280, 285–6; Britain, 21–3, 32–4, 128, 216, 247; German mission (1915–16), 88–90, 133, 160; mujahedeen, 71, 217, 267, 277; Soviet War (1979–89), 71, 217, 265, 267, 273, 277
Aflaq, Michel, 125
Africa, 8–10, 13–15, 24, 41, 87, 128, 231, 266–7, 280, 285; colonization, 9, 21–2, 31–2, 135, 225
Agincourt (HMS), 45
Ahmadinejad, Mahmoud, 291

aircraft, 4–5, 13, 16–17, 115, 143, 175, 191–5, 201–2, 229, 239, 248, 266, 307n6, 342n12
Akbar, Ali, 154
Akkadians, 24
Albania, 27, 120
alcohol, 14, 79, 141, 145–6, 148, 163; fuel source, 102
Alexander the Great, xviii, 24, 114, 171
Alexandria, 1, 145–7
Algeria, 121, 216, 243, 284, 293
Allen, Herbert, 212
Allenby, Edmund, 75–6, 78, 86, 91, 142, 147, 174, 182, 210, 323n49
al-Qaeda, 8, 14, 25, 217, 248, 262, 267, 284
Alsace-Lorraine, 52, 217–18, 245
Amara, 65–6, 75, 156
Amiens, Battle of (1918), 200
Anglo-Afghan Wars, Second (1878–80), 23; Third (1919), 216, 247
Anglo-Boer Wars, First (1880–1), 132; Second (1899–1902), 132, 134, 136, 144, 156, 327n81, 338n61
Anglo-Persian Agreement (1919), 236–9

Anglo-Persian Oil Company
    (APOC), 18, 30, 50, 66, 95, 148–50,
    154–5, 243, 256–8, 272, 283; British
    government acquisition, xiv, 6,
    43–4, 58–63, 106; creation, 53–4,
    92, 314n2; oil fields, 63, 67, 238–9,
    259–63; protection, 33, 40, 61–2,
    65, 227
Anglo-Russian Entente (1907), 22,
    34, 54
Anglo-Swedish Oil Company, 95
Angola, 94, 293
Ankara, 29, 90, 123, 247
Antietam, Battle of (1862), 16
Antonius, George, 81
Arab Spring(s) (2010–), 216, 267,
    280, 285
Arambula, Jose Doroteo Arango, 269
Aramco, 18, 264, 284
Aras River, 32
Archangel, 72–3, 115, 231, 234, 319n13
Arctic, 14, 280, 288–9, 309n41
Ardahan, 26, 72, 98, 162, 179, 211
Argentina, 245, 271, 292
Armenia, xxii, 14, 37, 40, 55, 99,
    117–19, 127–8, 163–5, 174, 195–6,
    226, 228, 275, 279, 292; defence of
    Baku (1918), 133–4, 142, 158–61,
    164–6, 178–84, 193, 199–208,
    336n5; diaporas, 122; genocide,
    7, 120–6, 131, 254–5, 327nn3, 7,
    8; independence (1918), 55, 127,
    130, 162, 174, 185–8, 195, 216, 228,
    239, 241, 273; mandate, 225, 231–5;
    population, 27, 57, 122, 125, 151
Armistice, 11 November 1918, 5, 11,
    92, 198, 215, 220–1; of Mudanya
    (1922), 254; of Mudros (1918), 12,
    210–11, 228, 244; of Thessalonica
    (1918), 115

Armstrong, Karen, 8
Aron, Raymond, 61, 73, 223
Arras, Battle of (1917), 74, 320n22
Arslanian, Artin H., 12
artillery, 4–5, 39, 89, 98, 134–5, 161–3,
    174–5, 185, 192–3, 202, 228, 335n44,
    337n27, 342n12
Ashkhabad, 129
Asia Minor Agreement (1916). See
    Sykes-Picot Agreement
Asquith, Herbert, 82
Assad, Bashar al, 125
Assyrians, 24, 40, 133, 151, 165, 246,
    327n2; atrocities against, 117–18,
    120–1, 125
Astrakhan, 191, 196, 207
Atlantic Ocean, 62, 263, 282; Allied
    convoys, 5, 70, 183
Atlee, Clement, xiii
Australia, 53, 70, 94, 109, 141, 225,
    245, 263; in Dunsterforce, 119,
    137–40, 143–6, 158, 170
Australian Imperial Force (AIF), 75,
    84, 137; Australian Corps, 134, 137,
    200; Australian Light Horse, 147
Austria-Hungary, 6, 22–6, 33–4, 77–9,
    93–5, 121, 130, 182, 225, 276; oil, 52
automobiles, 5, 167, 171–5, 183, 196,
    201; statistics, 5, 108, 286, 308n6,
    337n27, 342n12
Azerbaijan, xxi, 14, 32, 37, 54, 120,
    134, 181, 188, 195, 199, 203, 207,
    210–12, 228, 241, 316n38, 327n3;
    independence (1918), 40, 55, 130,
    162, 174, 179, 185–7, 216, 231,
    239–40, 273; oil, 56–7, 212, 274–9,
    284; population, 164
Azeri-Armenian War (1905), 120,
    327n3
Aztec, 50

Babylon, 24, 50, 150, 156, 168; tower of, 7, 50, 147
Baghdad, xiv, 30, 43, 62, 65–6, 68, 86, 91, 101, 113, 128–9, 138, 142–3, 146, 149–51, 153–60, 166–77, 183, 190–1, 194–7, 203, 208, 246–50, 261: British capture (1917), 1, 14, 75, 77, 84–5, 96–7, 114, 142, 181, 220; American-led capture (2003), 1, 14
Bahrain, 262, 293
Bailey, Frederick M., 130, 161, 329n43
Bakr, Ahmed Hassan, 261
Baku, xv, 31, 40–1, 47, 50, 54–5, 68, 72, 81, 91–2, 94, 97, 100, 112, 117–18, 128, 130, 133, 138, 146, 159, 165, 185–8, 213, 215–16, 227–31, 239, 241, 250–4, 313n65; Battle of (1918), 193–210; ethnic atrocities, 55, 57–8, 120, 124, 130, 164, 174, 178–9, 207–8, 228–9, 230–2; oil installations, 7, 13, 23, 37, 55, 63, 66, 114, 126–7, 177, 183–4, 189–92, 208, 212, 252–3; oil production, 38, 55–8, 93, 120, 190, 253–4, 271, 274–6; Soviet committee, 114, 164, 172–3, 178–80, 186, 191–8
Balakian, Grigoris, 125–6
Balfour, Arthur, 42, 81, 106, 111–14, 158, 165, 228–37
Balfour, John, 270
Balfour Declaration (1917), 7, 81, 83–4, 86, 219, 242, 250
Balkans, 9, 14, 24, 26, 33, 75, 79, 126, 246, 272, 323n70
Balkan Wars, First (1912–13), 26–7, 79; Second (1913), 27, 79; 1990s, 14, 134, 246
Baltics, 71–3, 201, 319n11
Baluchistan, 129
Barrett, Arthur, 64

Barrow, Edmund, 150
Bartelott, Walter, 166
Basra, xiv, 30, 33, 62–4, 91, 99, 114, 117, 133, 138, 147, 175, 246; British capture (1914), 64–5, 150–1; description, 148–55
Batum, xxi, 26, 38, 40, 72, 97–8, 122, 146, 162, 179–81, 184, 215, 228, 231, 239, 241; port, 55, 179–80, 189–91, 201, 210–11, 228–9, 240
Bay of Pigs Invasion (1961), 118
Beaumont-Hamel, Battle of (1916), 69
Bedat, Leon, 144
Beirut, 210, 235
Belgium, 4–5, 52, 56, 74, 224–5, 257
Belgrade, 29
Benjamin, Samuel G.W., 23
Berenger, Henry, 92, 101–3, 222, 242
Berlin-Baghdad Railway, 11, 29, 30–1, 40–1, 72, 97, 112, 183, 222, 312n31
Bey, Djevdet, 123
Bey, Essad, 178, 207, 212
Bey, Halil, 27
Bible, 23, 50, 65, 76, 85, 117, 119, 146–7, 155–6, 166, 170–1, 235
Bicherakov, Lazar, xxi, 161, 168, 176, 191–4, 198, 205
Birdwood, William, 134, 137
Bismarck, Otto von, 22, 29–31
Bismarck Archipelago, 31
Black Sea, 12, 36–8, 73, 80–2, 99, 129, 165, 183–5, 230–2, 257, 278; ports, 36, 55, 186, 275, 277
Blair, Tony, 249–50, 292
Blinn, James W., 17
Bokhara, 40, 72, 97
Bolimow, Battle of (1915), 5
Bolivia, 271, 290

Bolsheviks, xxii, 13, 40, 68–73, 81, 97,
114, 118, 130, 142, 158–64, 171–4,
177–81, 186–201, 210–12, 226–9,
232–41, 253–4, 319n11, 320n15
Bonaparte, Napoleon, 1, 6, 31, 149,
190, 236
Borden, Robert, 134, 218, 234, 263,
330n66
Bosnia, 26, 120, 134, 246
Boxer Rebellion (1899–1901), 30, 144
Brazil, 15, 18, 271, 281–5, 289–93
Breslau, 36
Brett, Reginald (Viscount Esher), 48
Brezhnev, Leonid, 265
Britain, Admiralty, xiv, 83, 96–7, 100,
104, 106, 110–14, 127–9, 139, 142,
174–5, 183–4, 189–90, 211, 229,
233, 263; arms race, 42–7; Eastern
Committee, 106, 127–9, 134–5, 139,
158–9, 165, 215–16, 228; Foreign
Office, 29, 41, 50, 66, 92, 106, 184,
256, 270; Imperial War Cabinet,
xiv, 83, 96–7, 100, 104, 106, 110–14,
127–9, 139, 142, 174–5, 183–4,
189–90, 211, 229, 233, 263; India
Office, xiv, 43, 50, 63–5, 84, 92, 106,
129–31, 150, 190, 229; industry,
5–6, 16, 43–6, 73, 81–2, 92, 108–9;
mandates, 84–5, 125, 211, 215–26,
229; Military Intelligence, Section
6 (MI6), 253, 260; oil, 6–7, 9–15,
18, 30–1, 42–64, 66–8, 85, 91, 93–6,
100–17, 130–1, 142, 146, 154–5,
164–5, 177, 190–2, 200–1, 209,
211–75, 278, 280–1, 283–5, 295–306;
War Office, 34, 76, 84–6, 119–20,
126, 128–9, 132–4, 138–9, 142, 154,
157–62, 175–6, 187, 190–4, 197–201,
205, 208, 216, 231, 239–40, 252,
329n42, 330n66

British Expeditionary Force (BEF),
5, 39, 70, 75, 135, 323n49, 330n66;
Second Army, 5; Fourth Army,
161, 200, 319n13; Gurkhas, xii, 192;
Hampshire Regiment, 167–8, 176,
192; 14th Hussars, 176, 192–3
British Petroleum (BP), 6, 18, 95,
271–2, 275, 278, 282–4, 289, 291,
314n2
Brown, Jim, 67–8
Brusilov Offensive (1916), 93
Bryce, James, 121–2
Buchan, John, 10, 41–2, 100, 118, 160,
327n81
Budapest, 29
Buddhism, 37, 133
Bulgaria, 24, 26–7, 75–7, 114–15,
209–10
Burma, xiii, 52–3, 108, 132, 242
Burton, Richard, 150
Bush, George H.W., 292
Bush, George W., 14, 249–50, 265,
275, 284, 292
Byron, John J., 134–7, 154–5
Byzantine Empire, 24, 50

Cadman, John, 100, 241, 256–9
Cameroon, 31
Campbell, Crofford, 119, 143, 147,
151, 153
Canada, 21, 31–2, 56, 67, 70–1, 90,
94, 108, 218, 233–4, 239, 281,
293, 309n41, 331n79, 345n88; in
Dunsterforce, 119, 134–9, 143–6,
153–4, 158, 170, 194, 198, 331nn69,
75; oil, 50–2, 108–9, 245, 262–3,
272–3, 281, 288–90, 293; industry,
5, 82, 103, 109
Canadian Expeditionary Force
(CEF), 119, 143, 319n13, 330n66;

Canadian Corps, 74–5, 134–7, 200, 330n66; First Division, 5; First Overseas Canadian Pioneer Detail, 155, 323n50

Candler, Edmund, 40, 66–7

Caporetto, Battle of (1917), 70, 75, 140

Cardenas, Lazaro, 270

Casey, Roy, 145

Caspian Sea, 7, 32, 37–8, 40–1, 68, 86, 111–15, 128–30, 142, 146, 158, 166, 175, 180, 183, 191, 198, 202, 208; offshore oil, 272–7; ports on, 91, 97, 161, 171–2, 190, 197, 230–2, 239, 252

cavalry, 5, 22, 71, 129, 174–5, 193, 228, 323n49, 329n43, 337n27

Cecil, Robert, 106

Cento-Caspian Dictatorship, xxi, 197

Central Asian Railway, 129

Ceyhan, 275

Chanak Crisis (1922), 234, 254

Chavez, Hugo, 290–1

Chechen-Russian Wars (1994–6, 1999–), 231, 276–9

Chechnya, xxi, 14, 37, 179, 181, 188, 199, 216, 231, 277, 290

Cheney, Dick, 275

Chester, Colby, 256

Chevron, 18, 262, 264, 271–2, 275, 282–3, 291, 346n4

Childers, Erskine, 47, 315n13

Chile, 94, 271

China, 25, 30, 50, 132, 140, 147, 225, 309n41, 310n48, 323n70; oil, 15, 50, 274–6, 281, 284–5, 289–90, 293

China National Petroleum Company, 18, 284

Christie, Agatha, 29

Churchill, Winston, xiii–xiv, 13, 35, 72, 82, 96, 103, 182, 250, 313n61;

Gallipoli Campaign (1915–16), 63–4, 82–4, 314n5; oil, 6, 44–50, 58–63, 106, 239, 241, 248, 253, 256, 286

Cilicia, 83, 247

Circassians, 26, 120, 142, 242, 277

Clark, Christopher, 62

Clemenceau, Georges, 103, 224, 242; mandates, 217–24; Lloyd George, 214, 217–18, 220–1; Woodrow Wilson, 224; Paris Peace Conference, 219–24

coal, xiv, 4, 40, 81, 93, 217, 230, 277, 314n4; maritime fuel, 10, 43–9, 102–3, 106, 11

Cold War (1945–91), 9, 273

colonialism, 8, 11, 31–3, 80, 94, 135, 139, 145, 216, 225, 284; Britain, 29, 33, 58, 80, 225, 238; France, 5, 33, 225, 243; Germany, 21, 31–2, 225; United States, 223

Colorado, 226

Columbia, 271, 280

communism, 9, 275

Congo, 281

Conoco, 282

Conolly, Arthur, 22–3, 310n9

Constantine, 114

Constantinople (Istanbul), xxi, 19, 24–9, 32, 82–4, 88–9, 99–100, 122, 188, 210, 225; Haydarpasa Terminal, 29

Constantinople Agreement (1915), 82–4, 312n41

Coolidge, Calvin, 253, 256

copper, 45, 51, 57, 156, 230

Cossacks, 118, 161, 176, 191–3, 198, 239

Costa Rica, 271

cotton, 40, 57, 73, 133, 191, 221, 230, 313n65

Cox, Percy, 8, 65, 221, 236, 251,
    318n69
Creveld, Martin van, 6
Crewe-Milnes, Robert, 43
Crimean Peninsula, 26, 72, 181;
    Russian aggression (2014–),
    227–8
Crimean War (1853–6), 32, 156,
    312n33
Croatia, 134, 246
Ctesiphon, 156
Currie, Arthur, 134, 136–7
Curzon, George, 46, 84, 106–7, 127–8,
    156–8, 219–20, 247, 276; oil, 92,
    190, 215, 226–34, 236–41, 244,
    251–2; Persia, 23, 226–34, 236–41
Cyprus, 26
Cyrus the Great, 24, 156
Czechoslovakia, 225, 319n13

Dagestan, 32, 188, 198, 216, 231, 277,
    316n38
Dalmatian Coast, 218
Damascus, 19, 174, 210, 221
D'Arcy, William, 53–4, 92, 268
Dardanelles, 29, 63, 81–4, 99, 211,
    255, 312n41, 322n42
Darius III, xviii, 171
Davis, John W., 244, 251
de Bunsen Committee (1915), 84–5
Delaisi, Francis, 12, 246
Delphi, Oracle of, 50
Denikin, Anton, 198, 211, 216, 225–6,
    232–3, 239, 242n12
Denmark, 22, 95, 309n41
Derbend Gap, 38, 198
Deterding, Henry, 253–4, 258
Diaz, Porfirio, 268–9
Dickson, William E., 238
Diocletian, 114

disease, 4, 16–17, 85–7, 98, 117, 124,
    139, 149, 151, 156, 168, 182, 199,
    266, 282, 309n44, 335n54
Disraeli, Benjamin, 32, 62
Djavid, Mehmed, 27
Djemal, Ahmed, 27–8, 35, 211
Djibouti, 147
Dodecanese Islands, 26
Donnon, William W., 144
Donohoe, Martin H., 137, 145–8, 151,
    155–7, 160–2, 168, 170, 176
Drake, Edwin, 51
Dunsterforce, xv, 7, 16, 39, 72, 79–80,
    91, 117–18, 151–77, 190–210, 212,
    216, 228; creation, 134–43; defence
    of Baku, 186–210; humanitarian
    aid, 168–71, 209; mission, 7, 68,
    115, 126–30, 142, 146, 174–6, 190–1
Dunsterville, Lionel C., xv, 40,
    117–19, 129–30, 133–9, 142, 149–50,
    154, 157–61, 166–77, 190–210;
    career, 131–3, 205, 208–10; famed-
    youth, xv, 118, 132, 158, 209–10;
    relationship with General W.
    Marshall, 138–9, 158–9, 171, 175–7,
    192–5, 205, 208–9
Dutch Disease, 266, 282
Dutch East Indies, 61, 109, 245
Dyer, Reginald, 146

East Timor, 14
Eckardt, Heinrich von, 269–70
Ecuador, 271, 293
Eden, Anthony, xiii
Edward VII, 44, 58, 310n7
Effendi, Abdullah, 19
Egypt, 10–11, 24–6, 31–4, 41–2, 83,
    132, 140, 144, 212, 216–19, 231, 242,
    245, 310n13; Coptic Christians,
    125; Napoleon campaign

(1798–1801), 1, 31; Ottoman offensive (1915), 79–81, 99; Pyramids, 50, 147
Egyptian Expeditionary Force (EEF), 75–7, 85–6, 91, 142, 147, 174, 182, 210
El Alamein, Battle of (1942), 13
Engdahl, William, 11
Entente Cordiale, 33–4, 41, 70, 73, 79, 82, 114, 225
Enver, Ismail, 26–8, 79–81, 98–100, 122, 181, 188, 210–11, 325n32; alliance with Germany, 35–6, 98–9, 188, 201; pan-Turanian ideology, 11, 98–100, 181–2, 186–7
Enzeli, xxi, 91, 129, 159, 166–75, 190–8, 207–8, 239
Eritrea, 147
Erzincan, 99, 162, 179
Erzurum, 90, 99–100, 180, 275
Esso, 18, 272, 283
Estonia, 12, 72
ethnic cleansing, 117, 123, 134, 177, 179, 260, 279
Euphrates River, 9, 24, 30, 64, 86, 91, 113, 148, 150, 220–1, 235, 323n50
European Union (EU), 278, 281
Exxon, 17–18, 52, 264, 282–3
ExxonMobil, 18, 271, 275, 282–3, 291

Faisal I, 251, 260–1
Faisal II, 261
Faisal III, 261
Falkenhayn, Erich von, 90, 93, 182
Falklands War (1982), 292
Fall, Albert, 253
Fallujah, 66, 91
famine, 117; Persia, 85, 117–20, 166–70, 176, 209; Syria, 85
Fanshawe, Hew, 194–5

Fao, 64
Fashoda Crisis (1898), 33
Fiat Company, 5
Finland, 71, 309n41, 319nn11, 13
Fisher, Andrew, 141
Fisher, John, 44–50, 314n5
Fisk, Robert, 248
Fitzgerald, F. Scott, 15
Fleming, Ian, 29, 274
Ford, Henry, 55
Ford, Roger, 123
Ford Motor Company, 166, 169, 173, 192, 196
Foster, A.J., 212–13
France, 4–7, 12, 14–17, 22, 29, 31–5, 38, 46, 69–75, 80–4, 92–3, 133, 142–4, 186, 196, 202, 210, 222, 237, 248, 252–6, 281, 310n48, 319n13, 322n48, 345n88, 390n41; Comité Générale du Petrole, 92, 101; mandates, 8, 81–3, 113–14, 121, 165, 211, 214–25, 227–9, 232–7, 241, 247, 250–1; oil, 52–4, 56, 92, 101–4, 165, 215, 237, 241–5, 250, 256–8, 268, 274, 282–3, 289; Vichy, 261, 315n20
Franco-Prussian War (1870–1), 6, 22, 217–18, 312n33
French, David, 82
Fromkin, David, 30, 35, 226, 235, 237, 256, 325n30
Frontiers, Battles of the (1914), 15–16

Gabon, 266
Gaidar, Yegor, 73
Galicia, 52, 95, 109, 181, 245
Gallipoli Campaign (1915–16), 63, 74, 81–5, 99, 138, 147, 211, 226, 314n5, 315n23, 321n32, 322n43
Ganja, xxi, 188, 194

Gascoyne-Cecil, Robert (Lord
    Salisbury), 23–5, 106
gas warfare, 4–5, 248, 309n4
Gaugamela, Battle of (331 BCE), 171
Gazprom, 18, 284, 289
Geddes, Eric, 110–11
Gegechkori, Evgenii, 162
Genghis Khan, 24
Genoa Conference (1922), 254
genocide, 117, 130; Armenians, 7,
    120–6, 163, 207–8; Jews, 120
George V, 88, 310n7
Georgia, xxi, 14, 32, 36–40, 57, 120,
    127–8, 133–4, 174, 199, 240–1, 275,
    316n38; alliance with Germany
    (1918), 180–9, 195, 199, 201; army,
    142, 162, 165, 180–1, 189, 199–200;
    independence (1918), 55, 130, 162,
    179, 195, 201, 216, 228, 239, 273;
    Russian aggression (1991–2,
    2008–), 14, 273, 276, 278–9, 292
German Deutsche Bank, 58, 62, 242
German East Africa, 31, 135, 139,
    145, 212, 329n42
German South-West Africa, 31, 135
Germany, xiv–xv, 5, 8, 19, 22–3, 30–32,
    51, 63–73, 86, 102–4, 117–21, 130–5,
    141, 145–6, 159, 172, 186, 192–6,
    200–1, 217–18, 222–5, 234, 269, 281;
    Afrika Corps, 13, 261; alliance with
    Georgia (1918), 180–9, 195, 199,
    201; alliance with Ottoman Empire,
    27–9, 32–6, 64, 77–9, 81–3, 86–8, 90–
    1, 98–9, 117, 128, 162–3, 174, 177,
    180–9, 198–201; arms race, 10, 44–7,
    49, 60; Drang nach Osten, 8–11,
    20–2, 29, 38–42, 64, 72, 80, 87–90,
    96–7, 112, 188, 129–31, 135, 139–42,
    160, 165, 183–4, 200; oil, 12–13,
    29, 40–2, 49, 52, 56, 58, 61–3, 66–8,

73–5, 92–7, 108–9, 114–18, 128–30,
    146, 177, 180–3, 189–91, 201–3, 210,
    242, 245; Third Reich, xiii–xiv, 9, 13,
    15, 120, 222–3, 260–1, 270
Gettysburg, Battle of (1863), 16
Ghazi I, 260
Gibraltar, 62
Gilmore, Adam H., 144
Gladstone, William, 32
Goeben, 36
gold, 14, 54, 56–8, 73, 144, 242
Goldsmith, George M., 166, 172–3, 199
Gorbachev, Mikhail, 273
Gorlice-Tarnow Offensive (1915), 95
Great Depression, 286, 288
Great Game, 10–11, 22–7, 31–8, 58,
    89; new Great Game, 14, 17, 235,
    250, 263, 272–6, 284
Greco-Turkish War (1919–22), 17,
    214, 225–6, 244, 254–5
Greece, xxii, 26–7, 36–7, 50, 55, 75,
    150–1, 156, 165, 210, 225–6, 244,
    254–5, 327n8
Greenwood, Hamar, 222, 230, 242
Gregory, Adrian, 222
Grey, Edward, 33, 61–2, 83, 121, 237
Grosvenor, Hugh (Duke of
    Westminster), 135
Grozny, xxi, 13, 57–8, 189–90, 212,
    230, 239–40, 254, 276–7
Guatemala, 271
Guevara, Ernesto (Che), 216
Gulbenkian, Calouste, 257–8
Gulf Oil Company, 18, 259, 262, 264,
    269, 272, 282–3, 344n71
Gulf-plus pricing system, 258–9
Gulf War (1990–1), xiii, 14–15, 125,
    261–2, 265, 282, 292
Gulf War (2003–), xiii, 1, 14–15, 17,
    66, 248–9, 262, 286, 292

Habibullah, Emir, 88–91
Haifa, 84
Haig, Douglas, 70, 75
Haiti, 281
Hajibeyov, Uzeir, 56
Haldane, Aylmer, 249
Halim, Said, 27
Halliburton, 275
Hamadan, 131, 146, 159, 163, 166,
   168–71, 173, 175–6, 190, 195
Hamid II, Abdul, 19, 26, 29
Hamilton, Ian, 84, 315n23, 322n42
Hankey, Maurice, 100, 106, 111–15
Harcourt, Lewis Vernon, 6, 100–1
Harding, Warren, 253
Hardinge, Charles, 88, 106
Harington, Charles, 5
Harrison, Robert, 136, 143, 148
Hassan, Mohammed Abdullah, 247
Heller, Joseph, 17
Hentig, Werner Otto von, 88–90
Herat, 88, 129
Herodotus, 36
Hindenburg, Paul von, 96, 121, 186
Hitler, Adolf, 13, 120, 222, 261
Hittites, 24
Hooker, Joseph, 325n32
Hopkirk, Peter, 37, 133
Hormuz, Strait of, 9, 265
horse transport, xiv, 5, 99, 117, 153,
   163, 183, 193, 335n44
Hulls, Leslie R., 186–7
Hussein, Saddam, 14, 125, 248,
   261–2, 265, 345n86
Hussein, Sherif of Mecca, 7, 81–3, 85,
   249–51, 264, 321n33

Imperial Bank of Persia, 58, 155, 168
Imperial Oil Company, 263
Inca, 50, 310n13

India, 5, 10–15, 21–3, 26, 29–33,
   39–46, 50, 61, 64, 76, 80–91, 97–100,
   107–9, 111–12, 117–22, 128–35,
   139, 141–8, 160, 165, 194, 209, 212,
   215–22, 228, 230, 245–6, 281, 285,
   289, 309n41, 310n48,13; Northwest
   Frontier, 10, 40, 46, 88, 90, 97, 129,
   132–3, 229, 247; population, 42, 50
Indian Army of the British Raj, 97,
   132, 138, 141, 160, 247, 329n42;
   Indian Expeditionary Force D
   (IEF D), xiv, 64–5, 68, 156
Indian Mutiny (1857), 42
Indonesia, 290
industrial revolution, 4–5, 16, 43–6,
   50–1
influenza epidemic (1918), 4, 16–17,
   149, 335n54
Inter-Allied Petroleum Conference
   (1918), 92–3, 104
internal combustion engine, 14,
   48–9, 51, 316n30
Iran, xxi–xxii, 18, 37, 167, 248, 260–2,
   265, 279, 290, 293; ethnicities, 167,
   221, 261; oil, 18, 258, 260, 262, 271,
   283–6, 290–3; Islamic revolution
   (1979), 216, 260. See also Persia
Iran-Iraq War (1980–8), 261
Iraq, xiii, xxii, 14, 27, 125, 221, 225,
   246–8, 251, 255, 264; America-led
   invasion (2003), xiii, 1, 14, 17,
   66, 143, 248, 262, 265, 267, 280,
   285–6, 291; Ba'athist Party, 125,
   261; ethnicities, 125, 221, 246,
   251, 261, 267, 284; oil, 251, 255–7,
   260–2, 271, 286, 290, 293. See also
   Mesopotamia
Ireland, 135, 140, 145, 231, 315n13,
   331nn75, 79
iron, 40–1, 45, 57, 92, 217

Iron Curtain, 275
Iroquois, 50
Islam, 8–9, 11, 21–2, 29, 32, 41–2,
 56, 76, 79, 83–9, 124–7, 155, 165,
 169, 179, 186–9, 195, 199, 216–17,
 266–8; atrocities against, 26, 120–6,
 130, 134, 163–4, 178–9, 246, 255,
 336n5; caliphate, 8, 19, 25, 264–5,
 268; jihad, 8, 21, 29, 41, 64, 71,
 80–1, 88, 99, 118, 125, 160, 188–99,
 201, 217, 228, 247, 261–8, 277;
 Koran, 21; Mohammed, 21, 157;
 populations, 19, 21, 27, 37, 57, 98,
 130, 133, 164, 181; sectarian split,
 25, 311n16; sharia law, 216–17, 267;
 Shia, 25, 157, 216, 246, 251, 261,
 267, 291, 311n16; spread of, 24, 42,
 120, 150, 156–7, 311n16; Sunni, 25,
 134, 246, 251, 261–4, 267, 311n16;
 Wahhabism, 264–5, 291
Islamic State of Iraq and the Levant
 (ISIL), 14, 262, 267, 290–1
Israel, 18, 27, 84, 86, 147, 243, 284,
 310n48; creation of, 7, 86, 267. See
 also Balfour Declaration (1917)
Issus, Battle of (333 BCE), 171
Istanbul. See Constantinople
Italo-Turkish War (1911–12), 26, 79
Italy, 5, 15, 22, 26, 34, 47, 52, 70, 75,
 104, 140, 144, 186, 244–5, 255–8,
 271, 279, 281, 309n41, 312n44,
 319n13, 320n23, 328n8; mandates,
 7, 84, 114, 165, 218, 223–6, 232
Iwo Jima, Battle of (1945), 16,
 315n20
Izzet, Hasan, 98

Jackson, Henry, 101
Jangalis, 80, 91, 118, 163, 166, 171–3,
 191–7

Japan, xiii–iv, 13, 15, 33, 109, 145,
 218, 225, 246, 262, 266, 271, 274,
 281, 309n41, 319n13
Jellicoe, John, 103
Jenkins, Philip, 121, 264
Jerusalem, 19, 28, 75–8, 86, 156, 174,
 181, 217, 247
Jews, 55, 57, 76, 147, 151, 156, 202,
 246–7; diasporas, 86; population in
 Caucasus, 27, 37, 133; statehood, 7,
 9, 81, 86, 219–20; Torah, 156
Jordan, 27, 225, 235, 250–1, 264
Jutland, Battle of (1916), 103

Kabul, 88–90
Kaiserschlacht Offensive (1918), 71,
 183, 189, 200
Kaiser-Wilhelmsland, 31
Karbala, 66
Kars, 26, 72, 98, 162, 179–80, 187, 241
Karsh, Efraim, 123
Karun, 53, 66–8
Karzai, Hamid, 266
Kashgar, 129–30, 274, 329n43
Kasvin, 80, 145, 171, 176, 190–5
Kazakhstan, 37, 274–5, 284
Keegan, John, 27, 69, 320n22
Kemal, Mustafa (Ataturk), 226, 255,
 322n43
Kemp, Edward, 134
Kennan, George, 37
Kennedy, John F., 118
Kennedy, Paul, 266
Kennion, Roger L., 159
Kerensky, Alexander, 71
Kermanshah, 145–6, 159, 168, 190,
 195
Keystone XL pipeline, 281
Khalilzad, Zalmay, 265
Khanikin, 146, 167

Khomeini, Ruhollah, 216, 260
Khosrau I, 157
Khosrau II, 157
Killgil, Nuri, 129, 188, 199, 201, 207, 209–10
King, Charles, 241, 277
Kipling, Rudyard, xv, 23, 118, 132–3, 158, 209
Kirkuk, 190, 210, 257
Klare, Michael, 276
Kolchak, Alexandr, 72, 320n15
Konya, 29–30
Kosovo, 120; Battle of (1389), 24
Krasnovodsk, 129, 133, 161, 191, 207
Kress, Friedrich von Kressenstein, 181–2, 201, 210
Kruger, Paul, 202, 338n61
Kuchik Khan, 80, 91, 166, 168, 171, 192–3, 195, 216
Kurds, xxii, 151, 166–7, 172, 190, 220–1, 246–7, 327n8; atrocities against, 126, 163, 261; atrocities by, 118, 120–4; Kurdistan, 142, 220–1, 246; population, 27
Kursk, Battle of (1943), 13
Kut, Halil, 27, 188
Kut-al-Amara, Siege of (1915–16), 75, 156
Kuwait, 125, 147–8, 258–9, 261–2, 290, 293, Emir, 30, 64
Kuwait Petroleum Company, 262
Kyrgyzstan, 216

Lacey, William, 179
Laden, Osama bin, 265–8
Ladysmith, Siege of (1899–1900), 156
Lake Doiran, Battle of (1917), 75
Lake Superior, 37
Last Hundred Days, Battles of (1918), 6

Lawrence, Thomas Edward, 7, 11, 66, 86, 88, 90, 249–50, 285, 321n33
League of Nations, 7, 225, 248, 255; mandates, 7, 15, 225–7, 242
Lebanon, 27, 85, 125, 218, 225, 250, 261, 284
Leipzig, Battle of (1813), 6
Lenin, Vladimir, 58, 71, 97, 114, 162, 189, 194–6, 223, 239, 253–4, 273
Libya, 13, 26, 79, 216, 261, 280, 286, 288, 293
Littlewood, Joan, 39
Lloyd George, David, 76, 96–7, 100, 106, 111–16, 164, 189, 208, 250, 253, 313n61; intervention in Russia, 40–1, 73, 128; on Churchill, 47; on sideshows, 39, 77; Paris Peace Conference, 214–21, 224, 229–33, 241, 248
Long, Walter Hume, 100–2, 250
Loos, Battle of (1915), 133
Lossow, Otto von, 181
Ludendorff, Erich von, 12, 70, 93, 95, 97, 121, 179, 183–7, 189, 200–1, 210, 313n65
Luke, Harry, 56–7
Luther, Martin, 266–7

Macartney, George, 129–30, 161, 329n43
MacDonnell, Ranald, 159–60
Macdonogh, George, 106, 127, 158
Macedonia, 75, 120, 333n4
Machiavelli, Niccolo, 8, 83, 264
Mackensen, August von, 93–4
Maclaren, C.B., 159, 172
MacMillan, Margaret, 214, 219, 246
Mahan, Alfred Thayer, 10
Mahdist Rebellion (1881–98), 42
Maikop, 13, 57–8, 230, 239, 254, 309n32

Malaysia, 18, 245, 284
Malleson, Wilfrid, 129–30, 161, 228,
    329n42
Malmiss, 129, 228
Malta, 63, 132
manganese, 40, 57, 73, 184, 230,
    313n65
Marcel, Valerie, 7
Marling, Charles, 127, 159, 165, 171
Marmara, Sea of, 83, 156
Marsh, F.G., 77, 321n27
Marshall, William, 87, 91, 114, 138,
    141, 146, 163; Mosul, 12, 115, 190,
    210–11, 220; Dunsterforce, 138–9,
    153–4, 157–9, 168–9, 171–6, 190–5,
    197, 205, 208
Marx, Karl, 216, 253–4, 272–3
Masters, John, xiii, xv
Maude, Frederick, 1, 14, 75, 77, 85–7,
    156, 220
McDonald, Henry F., 143
McDowell, Robert H., 131, 159, 163,
    329n47
McKeller, Kenneth, 244
McMahon, Henry, 83–5
McMeekin, Sean, 126, 312n31, 325n30
McMunn, George, 150, 154
McWhirter, David, 140
Mediterranean Expeditionary Force
    (MEF), 84, 315n23
Mediterranean Sea, 10, 63, 82, 121,
    145, 241, 257, 332n97; ports, 42, 62,
    83, 86, 164, 221, 243, 275
Megiddo, Battle of (1918), 76, 210
Mehmed V, 26
Mehmed VI, 211
Meir, Golda, 243
Meshed, 129
Mesopotamia, xiv, xxii, 9, 14–15,
    24, 29, 39, 46, 58, 76, 80–3, 90, 96,

117, 121–3, 129, 133–5, 148, 150–2,
    155, 158, 160–5, 185, 189, 208, 212,
    216; British campaign, 9–10, 63–6,
    84–7, 91, 96–9, 128, 141–2, 146, 165,
    172–4, 181–3; mandate, 217–26,
    231, 236–7, 241–3, 246–7, 250–1;
    oil, 12, 19–20, 29–32, 50–4, 61–6,
    84, 96, 101–3, 109–13, 126, 230–3,
    241–4, 251–7; rebellion (1920), 216,
    231, 247–51. See also Iraq
Mesopotamian Expeditionary Force
    (MEF), 1, 84, 87, 91, 110, 134,
    138–9, 146, 157–9, 174–6
Messines, Battle of (1917), 5, 74
Mexican-American War (1846–8),
    270
Mexican Eagle Oil Company, 268–9
Mexico, 21, 144, 268, 281, 293; oil,
    108–9, 245, 268–72, 290
Millman, Brock, 11, 331n83
Milne, George, 232–3, 240
Milner, Alfred, 106
Minh, Ho Chi, 216
Moberly, Frederick J., 10
Mobil, 18, 52, 264, 272, 282–3
Molotov, Vyacheslav, 50
Moltke, Helmuth von (the Elder), 22
Mons, Battle of (1914), 5
Montagu, Edwin, 106
Montenegro, 26
Morgenthau, Henry, 121–2, 327n7
Moroccan Crises (1905–6, 1911), 33
Morocco, 5, 33, 216
Moscow, 190, 195, 199, 241, 275, 278
Mossadeq, Mohammed, 260
Mosul, 12, 19–20, 30–1, 43, 62, 66, 91,
    95, 101, 174, 180–1, 190, 210–11,
    246–9; dispute over, 101, 112–15,
    165, 211, 215–22, 226–7, 241–5, 255
Murmansk, 72–3, 115, 231, 319n13

Murray, Archibald, 85
Muslim Brotherhood, 125, 217

Nagorno-Karabakh War (1988–), 14,
276, 279
Najaf, 248
Nasiriya, 65–6
National Iranian Oil Company, 18,
284
naval blockade, 40–1, 73, 93, 95,
114–15, 182–3
Netherlands, 18, 52, 56, 95, 200, 225,
266, 309n41
Nevada (USS), 48, 315n20
Newcombe, Harold J., 194
Newfoundland, 50, 70, 84, 245, 263;
Regiment, 69
New Guinea, 31–2, 323n70
New Zealand, 70, 75, 84, 143, 158,
225, 234, 245, 263; Division, 137,
322n43; in Dunsterforce, 119, 134,
137, 331n75
Nicholas I, 10, 310n7
Nicholas II, 10, 73, 86, 100, 121,
310n7
Niedermayer, Oskar, 88–90
Nieto, Enrique Peña, 271
Nigeria, 14, 50, 266–7, 280, 285–6,
290–3; Boko Haram, 267
Nivelle Offensive (1917), 75, 320n22
Nixon, John, 65
Nobel brothers, 52, 55, 61, 252–3
Noel, Edward, 159–60
Norris, David T., 197, 229
North Atlantic Treaty Organization
(NATO), 14, 143, 275, 333n4
North Dakota, 281, 288
North Korea, 18, 310n48
North-Persian Force (Noperforce),
210, 212, 228–9, 232

Norton-Griffiths, John, 94–5, 245
Norway, 90, 140, 284, 289, 309n41
nuclear power, 17, 281
nuclear weapons, 17–18, 273, 291,
310n48
Nuremberg Laws (1935), 120

Obama, Barack, 281, 291–2
Odlum, Victor, 136
Oil Springs, 51–2
Okinawa, Battle of (1945), 16,
315n20
Oklahoma, 226
Oman, 257, 263, 293
Operation Sea Lion (1940), 50
Oppenheim, Max von, 8–9, 80
Organization of the Petroleum
Exporting Countries (OPEC), 18,
288, 293; oil crisis 1973, 18, 262,
264
Orlando, Vittorio, 218–19, 232
Osman I, 24, 35, 45
Ossetia, 37, 161, 188, 195, 199, 277,
292; North, 38, 278; Russian
aggression (1991–2, 2008–), 14,
179, 276–9; South, 14, 179, 276–8
Ottoman Empire, xiv–xv, xxii, 7–12,
19–21, 24–9, 31–42, 46, 54, 61–5,
72, 79–90, 96–100, 113–14, 120–6,
146, 156, 162–4, 174, 179–210, 214,
221, 225, 234, 246, 249, 254, 257,
264, 276; advance on Baku (1918),
180–210; Army of Islam, 188,
193–4, 199–201, 228; Committee of
Union and Progress (CUP), 26–7,
36; Pan-Turanianism, 11, 27, 36,
41, 87, 96–100, 127–30, 135, 162,
165, 180–2, 186–90, 211; the Porte,
26–7, 33, 325n30; Third Army, 80,
90, 98–9, 122, 179, 182, 199, 325n30;

Young Turks, 11, 26–7, 35–6, 412.
See also Turkey
Overy, Richard, 13

paganism, 25, 37, 133
Pahlevi, Reza (Khan), xxi, 259–60
Pak, Salman, 157
Pakistan, 133, 167, 247, 265, 310n48
Palestine, 7, 28–9, 54, 75–6, 81–6,
   90–1, 96, 99, 111, 129, 142, 144,
   162–5, 180–2, 185, 189, 208, 267,
   321n32,33, 323n50; Hamas, 125;
   mandate, 83–4, 215–20, 225, 242–3,
   250
Panama, 271
Pancho Villa, 144, 269
Paris Peace Conference (1919–20),
   4, 7–8, 11, 15–17, 71, 92, 113, 162,
   200, 213, 217–37, 241: mandates, 7,
   15, 213, 217–34, 241–3, 246–8, 251,
   255–7
Passchendaele, Battle of (1917), 5, 39,
   71, 75–6, 320n22
Pearson, Weetman, 268–9, 271
Pennsylvania, 51
Pershing, John, 269, 318n4
Persia, xiv–xv, xxi–xxii, 9–12, 15–17,
   21–5, 32–41, 50, 58, 80, 83–92, 106,
   117, 120–5, 127–32, 135, 139, 142,
   145–62, 165–77, 180–3, 188, 192,
   199, 202, 209–10, 216, 225–35, 265,
   267–72, 274, 318n69; mandate,
   236–9, 241–2, 251–3, 256–62; oil,
   23, 29–31, 45–6, 53–68, 92, 96, 104,
   108–12, 148–50, 154–5, 220, 226–7,
   236–9, 241–2, 244–6, 25–3, 256–62.
   See also Iran
Persian Gulf, xiv, 9–10, 29, 33, 46, 58,
   61–4, 86, 100, 147, 150, 242, 246,
   257, 262, 265–7, 274

Peru, 245, 271, 310n13
Petrobras Brazil, 18, 284
Petroleos Mexicanos (Pemex), 271
Petrolia, 52
Petronas Malaysia, 18, 284
Phillips Oil, 282
Picot, François Georges, 144, 215,
   321n33
Pike, Geoffrey D., 160, 165–6, 172
Plassey, Battle of (1757), 76
Ploieşti, 12, 52, 93–4
Plumer, Herbert, 5
Poland, 51, 225, 245, 309n41, 319n13
Polo, Marco, 54
Pope Leo XIII, 19
Port Said, 147
Portugal, 225
Poti, 185–6
Prinkipo Proposal (1918), 218
Prussia, 6, 22, 40–1, 245
Putin, Vladimir, 9, 273, 277, 290–4

Qassim, Abdul-Karim, 261
Qatar, 262, 284, 293
Quaiyara, 43, 95, 211
Quebec, 76, 140
Quebec City, Battle of (1759), 76
Queen Elizabeth (HMS), xiv, 48–9,
   315n23
Queen Victoria, 23, 88, 310n7
Qurna, 51, 65–6, 148, 150, 155
Qutb, Sayyid, 217

rationing, 97, 126–8, 138, 141–2, 158,
   183, 331n83
Rawlinson, Alfred, 23, 161, 170–1,
   176, 200, 202
Rawlinson, Henry Jr, 23, 161, 319n13
Rawlinson, Henry Sr, 23, 161
Reagan, Ronald, 273

Red Line Agreement (1928), xxv, 257–9, 268, 272
Red Sea, 63, 147, 257
Reformation (1517), 266
Remarque, Erich Maria, 69–70
Reshid, Mehmed, 122
Resht, 159, 171–2, 192–5
Rice, Condoleezza, 249
Roberts, Frederick, 135
Robertson, William, 97, 126–8, 138, 141–2, 158, 183, 331n83
Rockefeller, John D., 51–3
Romania, xxii, 24, 26–7; and Germany, 12, 75, 93–5, 245; enters war, 12, 75; oil, 12–13, 52–3, 61, 93–5, 108–9, 243–5, 271; surrender, 75
Romans, 24, 36, 50, 150, 156
Rommel, Erwin, 13, 93, 261
Roosevelt, Archibald, 253
Roosevelt, Franklin D., 182
Roosevelt, Kermit, 260
Roosevelt, Theodore, 224, 253, 260
Roskill, Stephen, 113
Rosneft, 284
Ross Rifle, 239
Rothschild family, 55, 58
Royal Air Force (RAF), 112, 158, 228–9, 239, 247–9
Royal Dutch Shell, 18, 49, 61–2, 95, 104, 109, 222, 230, 253, 256–9, 263, 269–75, 282–3, 291; and British Admiralty, 50, 56, 58–61
Royal Navy (RN), xiv, 6, 35, 40, 43–50, 58–63, 66, 73, 84, 93, 96, 99, 101–3, 106, 112, 115, 144–5, 191, 197, 229, 239, 247; Caspian Fleet, 190–1, 196–7, 205, 229, 239; dreadnoughts, xiv, 6, 35, 45, 48–9
Ruhr, 217
Rumaylah, 66

Rumsfeld, Donald, 1, 249
Russia, xv, xxi–xxii, 5, 7, 9, 11–14, 21–3, 26, 29–40, 44–5, 52, 54, 61, 68–75, 77–95, 97–104, 113, 118–34, 139, 142–7, 151, 155, 159, 191–7, 171–4, 178–83, 189–92, 195–7, 201–7, 218, 220, 224–5, 227–34, 238–41, 248, 252; Allied intervention (1919), 17, 72, 91, 115, 210, 229, 232–4, 342n12; Civil War (1917–22), 17, 55, 68, 72–3, 77, 117, 131, 159, 174, 178, 210, 214–16, 227, 233–4, 269, 327n81; oil, 18, 40–1, 47, 52, 55–8, 61–3, 66, 73, 80–2, 93, 104, 108–10, 115, 212, 245, 252–5, 258, 266, 269, 272–9, 281–6, 289–93; Red Army, 118, 131, 178, 193–6, 216, 225, 228, 231, 239, 241; revolution (1905), 57–8, 120, 178; revolution (1917), 9, 17, 22, 41, 54, 68, 71–2, 75, 77, 85, 87, 91–2, 97, 104, 131, 138, 142, 146, 159, 162, 165, 172, 223, 231, 239, 253–4, 312n41; White Army, 131, 198, 211, 216, 225, 232, 239, 319n13, 342n12. See also Soviet Union
Russo-Japanese War (1904–5), 33
Russo-Persian Treaty (1813), 22, 32, 55
Russo-Persian Wars (1804–13, 1826–8), 32
Russo-Turkish War (1877–8), 26, 29, 33, 35, 38, 72, 98, 100, 162, 185

Saarland, 218, 224, 245
Sadr, Maqtada, 248
Sahil, Battle of (1914), 64
Salonica, 26, 115, 209, 211, 229
Samoa, 31
Samuel, Marcus, 49
Sanders, Liman von, 80, 90, 98, 182, 321n32

San Francisco, 56, 90
San Remo Conference (1920), 244, 247, 256
Sarikamish, Battle of (1914–15), 80, 98–9, 122, 180, 211, 325n32
Sarkozy, Nicolas, 278
Sarnia, 52
Sassanids, 24, 157
Saud, Adbulaziz Ibn, 64, 262–5
Saud, Salman Abdulaziz Ibn, 291
Saudi Arabia, 34, 81, 83, 86, 121, 127, 148, 150, 164, 262, 265, 267; oil, 263–5, 273, 289–93
Saudi Aramco, 18, 264, 284
Savage Division, 118, 178, 188
Savige, Stanley G., 140, 143–5, 148, 151, 154, 156, 168
Sazonov, Sergey, 12, 35
Scotland, 102, 258, 331n75
Second World War (1939–45), 3, 12–15, 17, 50, 223, 254, 261, 272, 277
Serbia, 24, 26–7, 118, 134, 202, 246, 319n13
seven sisters, 18, 258, 282–4
Seven Years' War (1756–63), 76
sex, 124, 139, 145–6, 151, 156, 258
Shatt-al-Arab, 9, 53, 67
Shaumian, Stepan, 164, 172–3, 178, 181, 195–7
Shields, Sarah, 9
Shore, Offley, 127, 159–60
Siberia, 72–3, 140, 210, 232, 319n13, 320n15, 323n70
sideshow campaigns, 7, 68, 76–7, 91, 141–2, 210, 323n70
Sidqi, Bakr, 260
silver, 56–7
Sinclair, Harry, 253, 282
Slade, Edmond J.W., 106–13, 221, 295

Smith, Hermitage, 238
Smuts, Jan C., 106, 134, 144, 215–16
Smyrna (Izmir), 30
Sochi, 278
Social Darwinism, 25
Somalia, 14, 216, 247, 267; al-Shabaab, 267
Somme, Battle of the (1916), 3, 5–6, 15–16, 39, 69, 74, 93, 119
South Africa, 70, 106, 119, 202, 215, 225, 263, 338n61; in Dunsterforce, 132–5, 137–8, 143, 331n75
South Dakota, 281
South Korea, 309n41
South Persian Rifles, 80, 89, 146, 161, 228
South Sudan, 14, 280, 285–6
Soviet Union, xxii, 9, 13, 41, 172, 186, 196, 218, 238–41, 252–4, 260–1, 266, 279; Afghan War (1979–89), 71, 217, 265, 267, 273, 277; collapse (1991), 14, 18, 55, 73, 179, 272–4, 292; oil, 212, 239, 252–5, 258, 272–77. *See also* Russia
Spain, 71, 225, 309n41
Spanish-American War (1898), 144, 224
Stalin, Joseph, 13, 37, 57, 182, 195–6, 239, 254
Stalingrad, Battle of (1942–3), 13
Standard Oil, 18, 51–2, 56, 59, 96, 104, 226, 316n31, 316n32; of California, 18, 259, 262, 264, 269, 283; of Indiana, 272; of New Jersey, 18, 51, 104, 243, 252, 258, 263–4, 269–70, 272, 283, 344n71; of New York, 18, 51, 259, 269, 272, 283, 344n71; oil concessions, 52, 54, 243, 251–3, 256–7, 260–5, 269–72
steel, 40–1, 45, 51, 277, 320n18

Steel, Richard A., 142–3, 158
Stewart, Roy, 143
Stokes, Claude B., 160, 192–3, 197–8, 209, 241
Strachan, Hew, xv, 34, 37, 214, 325n30
Sturdza, Dimitrie, 52
submarine warfare, 48, 145, 183, 239; Allied losses to, 5, 70, 102–4, 332n97
Sudan, 5, 14, 26, 33, 42, 132, 280, 285–6, 290
Suez Canal, 39, 46, 62, 86, 146, 148, 219–20, 257; Crisis (1956), 14; Ottoman Offensive (1915), 80–1, 99
Suleiman the Magnificent, 24, 120
Sumerians, 24
Sumida, Jon, 103
Sweden, 71, 95, 145, 263, 281, 309n41, 319n11, 327n8
Switzerland, 52, 71, 253–4, 266
Sykes, Mark, 14, 114, 127, 215, 321n33
Sykes, Percy, 65, 80, 90, 115, 117, 146, 161, 163
Sykes-Picot Agreement (1916), 7, 12, 14, 81, 83–4, 114, 127, 165, 215–17, 220, 225
Syria, 18, 27–9, 31, 81, 85–6, 123, 125, 164–5, 180, 182, 186, 246–8; Alawites, 125; Civil War (2011–), 18, 125, 249, 267, 278, 284–5, 291; mandate, 83, 218–22, 225–6, 228, 241–3, 247–8, 250–1; oil, 54, 241–3

Tabatabai, Seyid Zia, 252
Tabriz, 163, 171, 175–6, 188, 190, 325n30
Taghiyev, Zeynalabdin, 56–7, 179
Tajikistan, 216

Talaat, Mehmed, 26–7, 35, 122–3, 211
Taliban, 217, 247, 265, 267
Tamerlane, 24, 268
tank warfare, 4–6, 13, 16, 308n6, 342n12
Teagle, Walter, 258
Teague-Jones, Reginald, 160, 209, 334n34
Teapot Dome scandal (1922), 253–4
Tehcir Law (1915), 123
Tehran, 90, 127, 159–60, 171, 194, 236
Tehran Conference (1943), 14, 182
Tennant, John, 158
terrorism, 14, 25, 262, 267, 277–8, 284–6, 290; 9/11, 278, 284, 286; Beslan School crisis (2004), 278; Boston Marathon bombings (2013), 278
Texaco, 18, 259, 262–4, 269, 272, 282–3
Texas, 27, 226, 274, 288, 346n1
Thomson, William, 209–10, 212, 229, 232
Thrace, 27, 83, 211, 247
Tibet, 23, 33
Tiflis, xxi, 38, 40, 55–7, 127, 129, 133, 138, 159, 162, 166–7, 171–5, 184–9, 191, 198, 209, 211, 215, 228–9, 240–1, 275
Tigris River, 9–10, 24, 30, 43, 64–5, 68, 86, 91, 113–15, 148–9, 155–6, 220, 235, 323n50
Tikrit, 66, 210
Togoland, 31
Tolkien, J.R.R., 3
Total, 257, 282, 289
Townshend, Charles, 75, 156
Toynbee, Arnold J., 121, 218
Transcaucasian Railway, 38–40, 55, 87, 129, 161, 180, 184–6, 188, 194, 199–200, 210, 215, 228–31, 239–40

Trans-Caucasian Republic, xxii,
   128–30, 162, 166, 173, 179–80, 184–5
Treaty of Berlin (1885), 31; (1899), 31
Treaty of Brest-Litovsk (1918), 41,
   71–2, 86, 128–30, 162, 178–9, 182,
   188, 201
Treaty of Darin (1915), 264
Treaty of Defensive Alliance
   (1812), 32
Treaty of Guadeloupe-Hidalgo
   (1848), 270
Treaty of Kars (1922), 241
Treaty of Sevres (1920), 244, 247,
   254–5
Treaty of Versailles (1919), 9, 213–14,
   218, 222–5, 234–5, 245, 256
Treaty of Westphalia (1648), 236
Trebizond, 99, 180
Trinidad and Tobago, 245, 271, 314n1
Trotsky, Leon, 71–2, 275
Trucial States, 262–3
Tsingtaò, 30–1
Tulfa, Khairallah, 261
Turkey, 27, 125, 221, 226, 235, 241,
   244, 246–7, 254–5, 275, 279, 322n43.
   See also Ottoman Empire
Turkish National Bank, 58, 62
Turkish Petroleum Company (TPC),
   58–61, 242, 251, 256–7, 268
Turkmenistan, 23, 37, 98, 111, 129–30,
   190, 211, 216, 265
Turner, Richard, 143, 332n90

U-boats. See submarine warfare
Ukraine, 40–1, 71–3, 115, 130,
   181, 184, 186, 286, 292; Russian
   aggression (2014–), 14, 273, 277,
   292
United Arab Emirates (UAE), 262,
   290, 293

United Services College, 118, 132
United States of America, 7–10,
   12–16, 21–4, 31–2, 37, 58, 71, 86,
   113, 117, 121–2, 126, 131, 143, 151,
   156, 168–9, 218, 247–8, 263; Central
   Intelligence Agency (CIA), 260–1,
   274; Civil War (1861–5), 6, 16,
   309n44, 325n32; entry war (1917),
   9, 70, 85–6, 96, 104, 165; industry,
   5, 14, 23–2, 82, 85, 103–4, 108, 223,
   236; mandates, 217–29, 232–7, 244,
   248, 250, 255–7; Monroe Doctrine
   (1823), 23, 31, 269; oil, xiii, 12, 14,
   17–18, 47–56, 95, 102–4, 108–11,
   190, 215, 226–30, 235–8, 241–6,
   251–65, 267–86, 289–94; open door
   policy, 236, 252, 256–8; *Sherman
   Antitrust Act* (1890), 51
Urumia, 76

Van, 99, 122–3, 180, 185
Vardar River, 75
Vehib, Mehmed, 179, 182, 187–8
Venezuela, 18, 61, 245, 268, 271–2,
   280, 284, 286, 290–1, 293
Venn, Fiona, 235
Verdun, Battle of (1916), 5, 39, 69, 74,
   90, 93, 103
Victorian era, 4, 25
Vienna, 29, 88; Battle of (1683), 24–5
Vietnam War (1956–75), 16
Vimy Ridge, Battle of (1917), 74, 138
Vladivostok, 72–3, 115, 231, 234,
   319n13
Vorontsovka, Battle of (1918), 188

Wales, xiv, 43
Wallace, Hugh C., 244
Wannsee Protocol (1942), 120
war brides, 144, 241

Warden, John W., 136, 144–8, 154, 156–8, 175, 202–3, 208–9
War of 1812, (1812–15), 224
war on terror, 14, 25, 262, 267, 277–8, 284, 286, 290; 9/11, 278, 284, 286
Washington DC, 102, 251–2, 265, 274, 281
Wassmuss, Wilhelm, 66, 88
Watson, David, 136
Waziristan, 132, 247
Wemyss, Rosslyn, 112, 230
wheat, 12, 40, 45, 57, 73, 75, 81–2, 93, 115, 191, 221, 291
Wheatcroft, Geoffrey, 9
Whitehall, 6, 111, 132, 229
Wilhelm II, 8, 19, 22, 31, 33, 35, 40–2, 52, 60, 71, 80, 88, 90, 94, 112, 184, 200, 261; conversion to Islam, 21–2, 29; Ottoman Empire tour (1898), 19–21, 29, 41, 76; personality, 19–22, 29–30, 41, 310n7
Wilson, Arnold, 14
Wilson, Edith, 236
Wilson, Henry, 97, 104–6, 158, 183, 190–1, 205, 231–3, 247
Wilson, Woodrow, 15, 103–4, 109, 113, 218–19, 238, 243, 252, 269;

Fourteen Points, 221–4; Paris Peace Conference, 218–19, 221–7, 230–2, 236–7
Wyoming, 226, 253, 281

Yazdi, Abdul-Karim, 248
Yeltsin, Boris, 73
Yemen, 14, 147, 263, 284, 290
Yergin, Daniel, 246, 274, 284
Yildirim Army (Heeresgruppe F), 90, 181
Yorktown, Battle of (1781), 156
Young, Hubert, 43, 95, 314n1
Ypres, 39, 75; Second Battle of (1915), 5, 136, 332n90; Third Battle of (1917). *See* Passchendaele
Yudenich, Nikolai, 86, 97, 123
Yugoslavia, 134, 225; Yugoslav Wars, *see* Balkan Wars

Zagros Mountains, 167
Zedong, Mao, 216, 224
Zimmerman, Arthur, 269
Zimmerman Telegram (1917), 269–70
Zionism, 7, 219
Zoroastrianism, 36, 54
Zululand, 144